The Official America Online Internet Guide

WINDOWS EDITION

The Official
America Online
Internet Guide

WINDOWS EDITION

David Peal

Osborne **McGraw-Hill**

Berkeley   New York   St. Louis   San Francisco
Auckland   Bogotá   Hamburg   London   Madrid
Mexico City   Milan   Montreal   New Delhi   Panama City
Paris   São Paulo   Singapore   Sydney
Tokyo   Toronto

Osborne **McGraw-Hill**
2600 Tenth Street
Berkeley, California 94710
U.S.A.

For information on translations or book distributors outside the U.S.A., or to arrange bulk purchase discounts for sales promotions, premiums, or fundraisers, please contact Osborne/**McGraw-Hill** at the above address

The Official America Online Internet Guide, Windows Edition

Screenshot Credits:

Page 320: Text and artwork copyright 1996 by YAHOO! All rights reserved. YAHOO! and the YAHOO! logo are trademarks of YAHOO!, Inc.

Pages 335, 337, and 389: Reprinted with permission from CNET: The Computer Network, copyright 1996

Page 305: Reproduced with the permission of Digital Equipment Corporation. AltaVista and the AltaVista logo and the Digital logo are trademarks of Digitial Equipment Corporation.

Page 311: Reprinted by permission. Infoseek, Ultrasmark, Ultraseek, iSeek, Quickseek, Imageseek, Ultrashop, "proof of intelligent life on the net," and the Infoseek logos are trademarks of Infoseek Corporation which may be registered in certain jurisdictions. Other trademarks shown are trademarks of their respective owners. Copyright © 1995 - 1997 Infoseek Corporation. All rights reserved.

Page 475: © 1996 Nando.net

Page 436: © 1997 Exploratorium; used by permission.

Page 442: Credit for buttons on Carnegie Library site: Mark Friedman & Associates

1234567890 DOC 9987

ISBN 0-07-882370-6

Publisher Brandon A. Nordin	**Copy Editor** Sally Engelfried
Editor-in-Chief Scott Rogers	**Proofreader** Pat Mannion
Acquisitions Editors Megg Bonar	**Indexer** Valerie Robbins
Project Editor Claire Splan	**Computer Designers** Jani P. Beckwith, Peter F. Hancik
Associate Project Editor Cynthia Douglas	**Illustrator** Leslee Bassin
Editorial Assistant Gordon Hurd	**Series Design** Roberta Steele
Technical Editors Jenn Thompson, America Online Shawn LoCascio	**Cover Design** Arlette Crosland
	Cover Illustration/Design Doug Keeffe Graphic Design

For Carol, Ella, and Gabriel

About the Author

David Peal is the author of *Access the Internet*, co-author of the 1997 Small Business Resource Guide to the Web, and former Editorial Manager of the Internet Connection at America Online. At AOL he helped create the AnswerMan, NetGirl, InBusiness, and NetHelp forums, and was responsible for the content of the award-winning CD, AOL's Internet Adventure.

1 America Online: Your Gateway to the Internet 1

2 Navigating From America Online to Get to the Internet . . . 33

3 Communicating with E-mail 61

4 Discovering Internet Mailing Lists 103

5 Discovering Newsgroups 135

6 Exploring the Web with America Online 171

7 Publishing on the Web with Personal Publisher 225

8 Downloading Software from AOL and the Internet 261

9 Finding What *You* Want on the Internet 297

10 Beyond AOL: Exploring Internet Applications 339

11 The AOL 300 Directory 379

A Your AOL Connection 497

B Indispensable Terms 515

Index 541

CONTENTS AT A GLANCE

Acknowledgments xv

Introduction xvii

1 America Online: Your Gateway to the Internet 1

The Indispensable Internet 3

How America Online Differs from Ordinary
    Internet Service Providers 11

What Kind Of Beast Is the Internet? 23

All Sorts of Computers Communicate on the
    Internet 24

Different Programs to Do Different Things 26

The Internet as a Social Network 27

From Here… 32

2 Navigating From America Online to Get to the Internet 33

Getting Online 34

Signing Off 37

Using Windows 39

Ordering from Menus 44

The AOL Tool Bar 50

The World of AOL Forums 53

Where on AOL Is the Internet? 56

Doing Several Things at Once on AOL 59

Using AOL with Other Windows Applications 60

From Here.... 60

3 Communicating with E-mail 61

It's All in the Message 63

What Is an E-mail Address? 63

Composing and Sending an E-mail Message 65

Keeping an Address Book on America Online 72

Adding Pizzazz to Your AOL Mail 75

Working with Files: Getting and Sending
    Attachments 78

You've Got Mail! Reading Your Mail 81

Using Mail Controls to Filter Incoming Mail 86

Managing Your Messages 88

CONTENTS

Saving and Printing Messages 92

Putting Your Best Foot Forward 96

From Here… 101

4 Discovering Internet Mailing Lists **103**

Mailing List ABCs 104

Discussion Lists and Distribution Lists
(Newsletters) 106

Moderated Lists and Unmoderated Lists 106

Finding a Mailing List for You 108

Subscribing to a Mailing List 110

Mailing List Netiquette 113

Managing Your Mail 115

Good and Great: A List Sampler 118

Beyond AOL: Net Newsletters 122

Reference: Joining and Using Listserv, Listproc,
and Majordomo Mailing Lists 124

From Here… 134

5 Discovering Newsgroups **135**

How Newsgroups and Mailing Lists Are
Different 137

How Newsgroups Are Organized 138

Newsgroups and Parental Controls 142

Finding Newsgroups 144

Keeping Track of Newsgroups 147

Scanning Newsgroup Articles for the Good
Ones 154

Articles and Their Particles 156

Responding to an Article 159

Reading and Posting Offline 162

Don't Be a Jerk! 164

Getting Files from Newsgroups Is a Breeze 165

Essential Reading: FAQs 167

Saving and Printing Messages 169

From Here… 169

6 **Exploring the Web with America Online** **171**

Terms That Changed the World: URL and HTML 175

A Page and Its Elements 177

Your Dashboard: A Closer Look at Your
Browser 186

Getting from A to B: How to Visit a Web Site
Using AOL's Browser 198

Managing Your Web Session 204

The 15-Second Web Search 207

Sights, Sounds, Moving Pictures: Working with
Multimedia Files 208

Your All-Purpose Browser 216

Saving Web Pages 219

When Things Don't Work 221

From Here… 223

7 **Publishing on the Web with Personal Publisher** **225**

Three Ways to Make a Web Page 227

Publishing and Maintaining Your Web Pages in
My Place 228

Using Personal Publisher 234

Editing Your Personal Page 246

Next Step: Refining Your Page 249

Telling the World About Your Site 255

Sharing Your Page with Other AOL Members 256

Notable AOL Home Pages 257

From Here… 259

8 **Downloading Software from AOL and the Internet** **261**

Understanding Files and File Types 262

Finding FTP Files 268

Using FTP the AOL Way 274

Navigating FTP with Your Browser 282

Using the Files You Download: Graphics,
Sounds, and Beyond 284

Downloading Files from America Online 289

Where to Find the Great Files on AOL 291

From Here… 295

9 **Finding What *You* Want on the Internet** **297**

What's on the Internet and What's Not? 298

Finding Information on the World Wide Web 300

Search Arsenal: The Best Search Tools 304

Finding People with Information: Mailing Lists
and Newsgroups 321

Searching Newsgroups with Other Search Tools 326

Finding People One at a Time 327

Searching the Megasites: Finding Specialized
Information 332

Pulling It All Together 334

From Here… 338

10 **Beyond AOL: Exploring Internet Applications** **339**

All You Need to Know About Winsock 340

Netscape Navigator 343

Virtual Places 353

Chatting on the Internet with mIRC 362

Telnet 372

11 **The AOL 300 Directory** **379**

How Channels Use Internet Resources 380

What's Missing? 382

How Do I Use the AOL 300? 383

Feedback 383

AOL Members' Choice 383

Computers & Software 389

Digital City 394

Entertainment 400

Games 406

Health & Fitness 412

The Hub 416

International 422

Internet Connection 427

Kids Only 434

Learning & Culture 440

Life, Styles & Interests 445

MusicSpace 452

Newsstand 457

Personal Finance 462

Reference 468

Sports 473

Style 480

Today's News 485

Travel 490

A **Your AOL Connection** **497**

What You Need 499

Signing On 504

Using AOL with a Network or Internet Service
    Provider 506

Modifying Your Settings 510

Upgrading AOL 511

Major Upgrades (with a New Version Number) 512

Minor Upgrades (Same Version Number, New
    Tool) 512

B Indispensable Terms 515

Index **541**

America Online made this book possible in many ways, and I'm especially thankful to John Dyn, Brad Schepp, and Judy Karpinski for supporting this project. My former colleagues in the Internet Connection kept me in the loop after I left to write the book. Jenn Thompson, in particular, read the manuscript beginning to end, and offered countless suggestions for improving it. John Ayers and Nicole Flanagan kept me apprised of Internet goings-on at AOL.

David O'Donnell (AOL's Postmaster), Bob Hirsh (AOL's FTP Administrator), and Lindlee Jenner (Newsgroups Development Project Manager) read specific chapters and offered many recommendations. Beth Wiley read the introductory chapters and the glossary and found some glaring oversights, which I hope I've remedied. For helping me anticipate the next generation of AOL's Windows software, thanks to Adam Bartlett, Tim Barwick, Dominic Stirpe, Reggie Fairchild, and Travis Good.

For doing much hard work on Chapter 11, I'd like to thank Mariva Hannah Aviram and Charlie Armstrong. Few people know AOL as well as Charlie, who for years has been the omnicompetent coordinator of the Internet Connection's cyberjockeys.

Dave Moon and Rob Stoiber, members of the WebDiner staff (keyword: Web Diner), gave me advice for topics to cover and pages to describe in Chapter 7. Thanks also to Tim McCanna, who leads the WebDiner forum.

Osborne/McGraw-Hill's civility made the publishing process a genuine pleasure. The people there who made the book happen are Brandon Nordin, publisher, and Scott Rogers, editor-in-chief, who supported the project from the outset and stuck with it. Polly Fusco, too, helped get the project off the ground. Special thanks to Megg Bonar, my editor, confidante, and advocate. Her assistant, Gordon Hurd, ably coordinated a complicated project. For his technical editing and sharp eye, thanks to Shawn LoCascio. The following people did an amazing job making the physical book despite a painfully compressed production schedule: Claire Splan, project editor; Sally Engelfried, copyeditor; Roberta Steele, Jani Beckwith, Lance Ravella, and Peter Hancik, designers; and Pat Mannion, proofreader.

Kevin Savetz, AOL's AnswerMan and coauthor of the Macintosh edition of this book, offered advice at many points and provided indispensable last-minute help getting Chapter 11 in shape. Jean Armour Polly was always there with support, commiseration, and sage advice. Thanks to her I think I finally understand domain names.

ACKNOWLEDGMENTS

Juliet Amann, nanny supreme, kept the kids happily distracted during the last five or so months of nonstop work. My wife, Carol, sustained my spirits through what seemed like five years of work. With Gabriel and Ella, she again put everything in perspective, which is why the book is dedicated to them.

America Online has created the biggest and easiest-to-use online service in the world. America Online has also done more than any organization on the globe to bring easy Internet access to millions of people.

If it's so easy, why do you need this book?

For one thing, there's just so much of the Internet: some 60 million people taking part in 60,000 mailing lists and 20,000 newsgroups, and producing 100 million World Wide Web pages—or is it 150 million, as I recently read? *Where do you start?* This book provides both the orientation and the starting points you need.

For another thing, *how* do you start? There are many ways of getting information and meeting people on the Internet—the Web, mailing lists, and newsgroups, to mention just the major Internet services. What's more, AOL's Internet tools for have gotten very powerful in a very short period. The Web "browser" in particular is a major application in itself. How do you learn to use all this stuff? How do you find out what's *worth* learning for a particular purpose? This book provides all the "how-to" you need, in one place. Its goal is to help you make the Net an integral and fun part of your life.

America Online: A Different Kind of ISP

Many Internet Service Providers (ISPs) give you some software and a phone number and drop you onto the Net without a life preserver. With most ISPs, you get a dialtone. With AOL, you get a community.

You get a *very big* community, at that—eight million people and counting, including a rapidly growing overseas contingent. You also get many ways to interact with people for both private exchanges (electronic mail and Instant Messages) and small-group conversations (chat rooms and Virtual Places). On AOL you even get a customizable Buddy List. I couldn't have written this book without e-mail, IMs, my Buddy List, and, of course, my AOL buddies.

On AOL you get a community and communications tools. You also get hundreds of places to meet and hang out with others, including Internet-related forums such as AnswerMan and NetGuide, where you can learn about the Internet directly from other members and from experienced Internauts. No other ISP or service offers all this.

When you're on AOL, you're not on the Internet. But with easy-to-use forums *about* the Internet and easy-to-use communications tools such as e-mail, you are more than half-way there, and Internet services and resources are always at your fingertips. Think of AOL as a comfortable electronic community from which the Net is a click away.

"Click away" is not an exaggeration. If you're a sports fan, in the Sports channel you'll get great AOL forums plus links to Internet resources like ESPNet and SportsZone. In the MusicSpace channel, you'll find Rolling Stone on AOL *plus* Internet resources like the Internet Underground Music Archive and Virtual Library's Classical Music directory. And in the Computers & Software channel, you get access to 100,000 files and file utilities *on* AOL, plus you can click to the Web sites of all of the major and most of the minor hardware and software vendors.

AOL's goal is to make Internet access seamless and almost secondary. The premise is that what you want to do and who you want to meet are more important than *where* content is available or *how* it's accessed. So thoroughly is the Internet integrated into AOL that it can be hard to *find* the Internet on AOL. It's certainly not clustered in one place. Think of this book as that "one place."

What Version of AOL Does this Book Cover?

This book is for people using either AOL 3.0 for Windows 95 or AOL 3.0 for Windows. Which do you have? See "AOL 3.0: Two Versions" in Appendix A. Throughout this book you'll see figures and illustrations showing the Windows 95 display, and I did in fact primarily use the Windows 95 version to write the book. However, AOL 3.0 Windows 95 differs in only small ways from the non-Windows 95 version.

Where the two versions *do* differ in important ways, I have more to say about the non-Windows 95 version of the software. Chapter 6 in particular explains the differences between the different browsers included in the two versions. The Windows 95 version includes the feature-rich Microsoft Internet Explorer browser.

Whichever version you have, you'll find all you need in this book. A Macintosh edition of this book will be available shortly as well.

Who this Book Was Written For

If you're new to both AOL and the Internet, this book is definitely for you, beginning with Chapter 1. This book is also for seasoned AOL members who are just getting their bearings on the Internet. If you have experience using the Internet on another ISP, you'll want to use this book to find out how to use the Internet services and resources available on AOL and where to find them. Finally, if you're a developer, this book can help you better understand the AOL member experience, which separates AOL from an ordinary ISP.

What You'll Find Inside

The book has eleven chapters, each organized more or less logically, but the book is meant to be used as a reference. Read what you need.

Chapters 1 through 10 provide all the orientation and how-to information you need to use the Internet on AOL. After introducing the Internet (Chapter 1) and America Online (Chapter 2), each of the next six chapters looks at the major Internet services.

Note   *In this book I've used the word* service *to refer to a type of networked application delivered over the Internet, such as electronic mail, file transfers (FTP), and World Wide Web. A* tool *is the AOL software, such as the browser, that lets you use a service.* Resources *draw you to the Internet in the first place—they're the Web sites, mailing lists, file archives, "Gopher" sites, and newsgroups with the specific information, expertise, or community you're looking for. The first ten chapters are about tools and services; Chapter 11 is about resources.*

In Chapters 3, 4 and 5, you'll learn about AOL's tools for communicating with people on the Internet (mail, mailing lists, newsgroups). Then, in Chapters 6, 7 and 8, you'll find out how to use AOL's "information" tools for browsing the Web, publishing on the Web, and downloading files. Chapter 9 shows you how to do effective searches on the Internet, whether you're seeking an e-mail address, a newsgroup posting, or a Web page. Chapter 10 shows you how to go beyond AOL's built-in Internet tools using "Winsock": how to get and use great software like Netscape Navigator and Virtual Places, and how to find and take part in Internet communities such as Virtual Places, Internet Relay Chat, and Muds.

Chapter 11 is a directory of some 300 Internet resources—Web sites and newsgroups, arranged by AOL channel, from Computers & Software to Travel. Most of these sites are actually integrated in the various channels. Others are sites I really like and think you may want to know about.

Appendix A is a primer about your basic AOL connection: What you need *before* you install the AOL software, how to sign onto the service, and where to get help.

Appendix B is a glossary, if you're ever in the dark about some term you see in the book. And if it's not in the glossary, I recommend several additional glossaries.

Elements

Throughout this book you'll find lots of Tips—shortcuts and easy ways of doing things. You'll also find Notes and Warnings to keep you aware of what's *really* going on and to prevent you from driving into potholes. Text boxes provide Deep Thoughts, amusing diversions, and everything in between. Wherever appropriate, I'll flag what's unique to AOL with an "Only on AOL" icon.

What Do You Think?

This book will succeed only if it helps you get more out of your Internet experience on AOL. I can improve the book only if you let me know what's not correct, what's missing, and what you'd like to see more of (or less of). Occasional praise is fine, too. Any and all suggestions for improvements are welcome, and I'm especially interested in knowing how the Internet has become indispensable in *your* life. Please send your suggestions or share your experience in an e-mail message to screen name **inetbook97**. If you've never sent a message, please read Chapter 3! Thank you!

Chapter 1

America Online: Your Gateway to the Internet

To newcomers, the Internet can seem difficult, even scary. But folks with even a little experience on the Net have a different story to tell. They experience the Internet not as a network of cables and computers but as a community—actually, a collection of many thousands of small communities. On the Internet, as in any community, it's the people who count. Here you will find people from all over the country and the world who share your hobbies, passions, and preoccupations.

The Internet, or *Net*, is also a staggeringly large source of information, but, unlike other information resources, anyone can access the Internet, and anyone can *contribute* to it.

On America Online it's easy to do both. On your travels you will find that the communities and information resources of AOL and the Net complement each other. What you don't find on one, you're likely to find on the other. And when you have questions about finding information or locating people on the Internet, AOL can help in many ways, as you'll see later in this chapter.

The Internet is an immense enterprise, whether it's measured in the amount of content or the number of people or in the rate of growth of both. America Online makes the Net a manageable and seamless extension of the AOL community. AOL's full-powered Internet software lets you communicate with millions on the Internet. AOL also provides the behind-the-scenes technologies to give you the most reliable and enjoyable experience on the Internet. Finally, AOL, with its large and helpful community, never leaves you alone on the Net. Think of AOL as your home and safe haven on the Internet.

If you want to learn to navigate the Net's rich resources and take part in the creation of new electronic communities, this book is for you! Read it to find out how America Online can make your Internet experience as fun, useful, and easy as possible. This chapter gives you an overview of:

- How the Internet can be indispensable in your daily life

- How America Online differs from other Internet Service Providers

- How the Internet got to be what it is today

This is a "big picture" chapter. You'll find sections later in the book with all the ground-level explanation and step-by-step procedures you need. Appendix B has a glossary of essential terms.

THE INDISPENSABLE INTERNET

I can still recall the excitement of discovering, in early 1994, the "first elementary school with a site on the World Wide Web": Mr. Marshall's fifth grade class in Grand River, Michigan. Recently, I needed the phone numbers and an orientation schedule for my kids' new schools—public elementary schools in Maryland. I didn't think twice about how to get the information; I used America Online to go onto the World Wide Web, the graphical part of the Internet. Within minutes I found just what I needed (Figure 1-1 shows a Web site you can use to access school sites around the world). Even better, I saved the cost of a phone call and avoided the bother of getting put on hold or playing phone tag.

FIGURE 1-1   I found home pages for my kids' Maryland elementary schools using this site

What follows are some other examples of some indispensable Web sites. There's a lot more to the Internet than the Web, but chances are that you'll be spending a good deal of your time on the Internet using great (and fun) sites like these (see "The Web: Just a Part of the Net").

Planning a Vacation?

Last year, while planning a family vacation on the Delaware beach, I used the World Wide Web to find a place to stay. I also located a list of restaurants and found a site called **The Weather Channel**, shown in Figure 1-2, which provides current weather reports and forecasts for any location in the U.S. (Note how the entire AOL "interface" is available to you when you browse the Web. Chapter 2 shows how to get around on both AOL and the Net.) Another service, **City Net**, can help you plan a trip to just about anywhere. If you need maps, resources on the Internet such as **MapQuest** can provide street maps for any address in the U.S. And you can "zoom out" from any street address to see a larger region so you can plan your car trip.

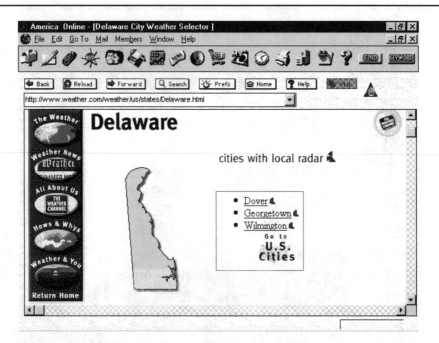

FIGURE 1-2 The Weather Channel can help you plan that weekend outing, no matter where you live

Note   *Internet addresses for all three of these great trip-planning resources (Weather Channel, MapQuest, and City Net) are listed in Table 1.1, along with other essential resources. Chapter 9 introduces a series of other sites for finding local addresses, street maps, ZIP codes, and other community information.*

Site	Address (URL)
Amazon.com (bookstore)	http://www.amazon.com/
Bartlett's Quotations	http://www.cc.columbia.edu/acis/bartleby/bartlett/
Career.com	http://www.career.com/
CDNow (compact disc store)	http://www.cdnow.com/
City Net	http://www.city.net/
Clnet (computer information)	http://www.cnet.com/
Disability information	http://www.webable.com/websites.html
Excite (to find anything)	keyword: Excite
Fedex (to track packages)	http://www.fedex.com/
HomeArts Recipe Finder	http://homearts.com/waisform/recipe.htm
Internal Revenue Service	http://www.irs.ustreas.gov/prod/
Internet Shopping Mall	http://www.internet-mall.com/
MapQuest (to get a map of any place in the U.S.)	http://www.mapquest.com/
ParentSoup	http://www.parentsoup.com/
Salon	http://www.salon1999.com/
Shakespeare	http://the-tech.mit.edu/Shakespeare/works.html
Switchboard (to find anyone)	keyword: Switchboard
Virtual Hospital	http://vh.radiology.uiowa.edu/
Weather Channel	http://www.weather.com/
Web66 (a registry of schools with Web sites)	http://web66.coled.umn.edu/schools.html

TABLE 1-1   Twenty essential internet resources

See Chapter 6 for everything you need to know about the Web and Internet addresses, or URLs. See Chapter 11 for 300 more great Internet resources.

The Web: Just a Part of the Net

The Internet used to be a place where all you could do was read. It was inhabited primarily by academics, scientists, and researchers. Things have changed. Think of the World Wide Web as the *graphical* part of the Internet, with more and more sites featuring video, animation, and other multimedia features. (You can read more about the Web in Chapter 6.) The Web consists of perhaps 100 million *pages* with words and pictures (and more) *linked* together in a way that makes it easy to find related information. You'll learn how to make your own using AOL's Personal Publisher service in Chapter 7.

Changing Jobs?

Chances are good that your dream company has a Web site. If not, you can still make an informed career choice using one of the many Web sites, such as **Career.com,** designed for people who are changing jobs. You can also apply for some jobs electronically by sending your resume in an electronic mail (*e-mail*) message. In Chapter 3 you can read all about getting and sending e-mail to people on the Internet.

Too Busy to Shop?

More than a dozen stores, such as **CDNow**, offer electronic storefronts, each offering over 100,000 CDs for sale. You can search for specific CDs, do some comparison shopping, hear sample sound clips, and even purchase CDs. You can't buy a car online yet, but you'll find information about auto insurance as well as details on every make of car on the road. What else can you buy online? Books, chocolate, wine, software, hardware, stocks, you name it. Check out the **Internet Shopping Mall**, an Internet institution that lists more than 7,500 electronic stores.

Need Medical Information?

Whether someone in your family has a particularly nasty cold or you want to reduce the risks of a heart attack, you'll find information and knowledgeable people on the Net, as well as sources of online solace and support. I have helped family members find excellent sources of information about Alzheimer's disease and autism on the Net. The **Virtual Hospital** Web site (at the University of Iowa), shown in Figure 1-3, offers a huge amount of information for both patients and clinicians. You'll find some excellent health-related sites in the "Health & Fitness" section in Chapter 11.

No Time to Read the Newspaper?

Hundreds of magazines and newspapers are now available on the Internet, including some that are available *only* on the Net. Computers, music, politics—whatever your interest, it's there. **C|net**, for example, is a superb information resource for the computer and communications industries. Electronic magazines that exist only on the Web, such as **Salon** and **Urban Desires**, feature some of the best new writing around (Figure 1-4). For daily news of the old-fashioned kind, **U.S. Newspapers on the Net** links you to hundreds of newspapers available in whole or part on the Internet. C|net, Salon, and Urban Desires are all available as *keywords* on America

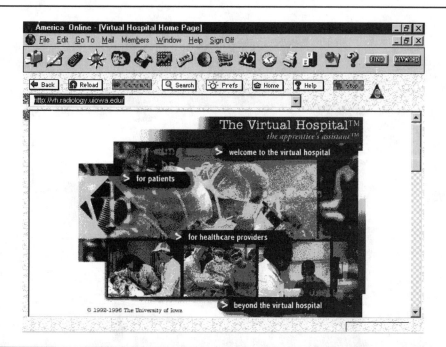

FIGURE 1-3   The Virtual Hospital, a world of information for patients and healthcare professionals alike

Keywords

If you're already comfortable getting around AOL, you can use keywords to get anywhere on AOL or the Net. In this book, *keyword: Such-and-such* is shorthand for the following:

1. From the Go To menu, select Keyword to bring up the Keyword window.

2. Type in *Such-and-such* (or **Hecklers** or **Netgirl** or **Nethelp** or **Netguide** or **Answerman** or **Internet** or whatever!) and click Go.

The next chapter has the nitty-gritty details about keywords and navigating AOL.

FIGURE 1-4 Salon. It's difficult to *buy* a magazine this good. On the Internet, it's free!

Online; see the previous section "Keywords." For other newspapers on the Net, see "Today's News" in Chapter 11.

Looking for Just the Right Word?

If you ever need an apt quote, don't reach for a reference book. Instead, visit the **Bartlett's Quotations** site on the Web, a searchable list of thousands of notable quotations. Writers and speakers in need of a **Shakespeare** quote in particular will love MIT's searchable archive of the great writer's entire corpus (see Figure 1-5). And if you ever need to find the meaning of TLA, you will probably benefit from one of the Internet's acronym-unscramblers (type in *TLA* and it spits out *Three-Letter Acronym*!). One great acronym dictionary, with 15,000 searchable entries, is discussed in the "Reference" section of Chapter 11. Search and you shall also find thesauruses, dictionaries, and other reference works.

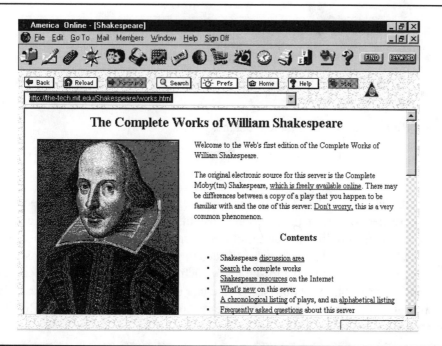

FIGURE 1-5   For pithy and wise words, turn to Shakespeare

> ## AOL's Channels
>
> AOL is organized in *channels*, which you can choose from the Channel menu (see Figure 2-6). Think of a channel as a big community, sometimes with millions of people, whose members have a strong interest and considerable expertise in some general subject such as sports, style, or the day's news. An AOL channel is a much bigger thing than a TV channel. For one thing, it's interactive, which means you help shape the content. If you're new to AOL, choose a channel and settle in! The next chapter takes a closer look at AOL's channels, and Chapter 11 brings you hundreds of Web sites arranged by channel.

Need Help Managing Your Finances?

AOL's Personal Finance channel provides just about everything you need to make an informed investment decision. With this channel's services you can do the following:

- Compare related stocks and funds

- Find summaries of analysts' recommendations

- Get the latest on-target observations of the Motley Fools, AOL's resident financial wizards

- Retrieve up-to-the-moment business news

- Scour Morningstar's reviews of mutual funds or Hoover's Business Resources

On AOL, you can also access the Internet to visit hundreds of personal finance–related Web sites for additional insights. At the **American Express** Web site, for example, you'll find a series of online calculators you can use to figure out how much you're worth, how much you need to save in order to retire in reasonable comfort, how much you have to salt away each year to send a kid to college, and other indispensable information (see "Personal Finance" in Chapter 11). To calculate the penalty of your prosperity, visit the all-too-informative **Internal Revenue Service** Web site.

1

It's Not *All* Serious!

Most of it's not, in fact. The Internet's roots reached deep into the world of academic research in the 1970s and 1980s, but even then there were games, jokes, and other stuff that wasn't serious. I find myself laughing out loud at the parodies in **the Onion** (**http://www.theonion.com/**), the Web version of a brilliant student newspaper at the University of Wisconsin. On AOL itself, you'll find lots to laugh at in forums such as Hecklers Online (keyword: Hecklers) or Comedy Pub (keyword: Comedy).

HOW AMERICA ONLINE DIFFERS FROM ORDINARY INTERNET SERVICE PROVIDERS

New people are continually joining the Internet community, adding their pages and postings to what is already an ocean of information. If you have plain Internet access from an Internet Service Provider (*ISP*), the Net can seem like some strange city in a foreign country whose language is incomprehensible. In contrast, on AOL you'll get the pleasures of big-city life while avoiding the big-city frustrations of growth, congestion, and the anxieties of feeling lonely and getting lost. On AOL you'll find out what it means to experience the Internet as a community.

Any Internet service provider can give you some software and hook you up to the Net, but you'll find that accessing the Internet through AOL adds layer upon layer of value to the plain Internet connection you can get anywhere else. On AOL you get:

- Community—the tools for communicating with people you know, such as message boards, chat, e-mail, and Instant Messages, and a congenial environment to make new friends

- Context—the integration of the best Internet resources into AOL's forums and channels, simplifying navigation and providing a clear framework for what you do on the Internet

- Value—the best of the Net and the unique AOL experience in a single affordable package

- Speed—the AOL software, servers, network, and compression technologies

- Safety—the tools to keep your kids out of trouble as well as the technologies to buy something securely on the Web

- Openness—the access to just about all Internet software and the ability to go anywhere and do anything on the Internet

- Help—assistance that is available any time, in any way that works for you.

I'm on AOL. Am I on the Internet?

On America Online you are always one mouse click away from the Internet.

America Online is a commercial online service that runs on hundreds of powerful computers in Virginia. AOL provides information from a wide variety of sources (such as magazines and news services) in a wide variety of formats (such as forums and software libraries). More and more of the content is original (AOL produces it). For many people, the best content comes from members themselves, who can express themselves and communicate with each other by e-mail, on message boards, and in chat rooms. Much of what you may like best about AOL—the chat rooms, the Instant Messages, the online versions of magazines such as *NetGuide* and *Newsweek*—is *not* available to people who aren't members.

While AOL is centralized, the Internet is decentralized. No one owns it. No one guarantees the content or is accountable for the quality of the service. It can be difficult to navigate, mostly because there's so much of it.

From AOL, at no additional cost and with no special software, you have full access to the Internet. The result? AOL provides the benefits of both a comfortable environment that's easy to use and the access you want to dynamic, globe-spanning Internet content that's growing by the hour. This access to the Internet is built right into your AOL software.

Still don't know where you are? Here are some ways to tell if you're on the Internet:

- You're using AOL's World Wide Web "browser" (shown in Figures 1-1 through 1-5) to visit a site such as **http://www.whitehouse.gov**.

- You're sending e-mail to, or receiving e-mail from, someone whose address includes an "at" sign (@) and an "address," such as **president@whitehouse.gov**.

- You're reading a newsgroup such as **rec.autos.antique**.

Community

What really sets AOL apart from the myriad Internet Service Providers is community. With eight million members and counting, AOL offers many opportunities for you to meet like-minded people. This also means that on AOL you can always find answers to your questions about the Internet. This is especially important because people on the Internet don't always like to answer newcomers' questions over and over again. You can also find friends on AOL with whom you can swap Internet discoveries.

Community comes in many forms on AOL:

- Communities based on live communication (chat rooms and Instant Messages)

- Communities based on communication that's delayed, such as electronic mail, mailing lists, and message boards

- Cool new communities that combine Web browsing with live chatting

Chat

Chat lets you communicate live with a group of people. You type your comments, press ENTER, and everyone sees your words. Chat is one of those things you'll find only on AOL. Yes, the Internet does have something called IRC (Internet Relay Chat), which you can read about in Chapter 10, but an AOL chat room is like a local deli, soda fountain, or tavern: you'll usually know who you can find there, and you'll likely talk the same "language." (With the creation of AOL's International channel, however, the language may not be English!) You'll find a list of hundreds of chat rooms in the People Connection channel.

Tip   *AOL's Buddy Lists let you know which of your AOL friends are online at the same time you're online. From the Buddy List window, you can send an Instant Message to a friend who's online, or you can invite a group of friends into a private chat room. More information about this feature is available from the AOL Members menu; choose Buddy Lists. If you're unfamiliar with using menus—or haven't installed AOL yet!—Chapter 2 provides all you need to know.*

Instant Messages

Instant Messages allow you to have an electronic "conversation" with other members who are online at the same time. To send an Instant Message, go to the Members menu and select Send an Instant Message. Enter your friend's screen name, type a message and click Send. (AOLers call instant messages *IMs*, and to send someone such a message is to "IM" them.)

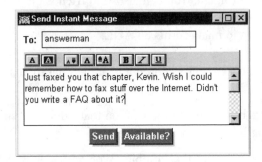

Note   *This book does not cover in detail AOL-only features such as chat rooms, Instant Messages, and message boards. I strongly recommend that you get a copy of Tom Lichty's* Official America Online Tour Guide *for a complete discussion of all the features unique to AOL. Another excellent title is* America Online for Busy People, *by David Einstein (Osborne/McGraw-Hill, 1996). Both books are available in the AOL Marketplace.*

Electronic Mail

Electronic Mail or *e-mail* (or sometimes just *mail*), is hardly unique to AOL, but AOL does offer a uniquely simple-to-use e-mail program. With e-mail you can send letters ("messages") to anyone on AOL or the Internet. Unlike chat and Instant Messages, e-mail does not take place "live." Your mail will arrive in minutes (seconds if your recipient is an AOL member), but the recipient of your missive might be on vacation in Fiji and won't get around to answering you for a couple of weeks. Messages can be composed and refined while you are offline, you can keep a copy of every message you send and receive, and, with messages to AOL members, you can actually change your mind and unsend it if it hasn't been read yet. AOL makes it easy not only to exchange messages with individuals on the Internet but also to exchange files with them and to communicate with *groups* on the Net by e-mail. Chapters 3 and 4 cover mail and mailing lists.

Electronic Newsletters

Electronic newsletters are fairly new in the AOL community, but the technology on which they are based—the mailing list—has been around a long time on the Net. Chapter 4 is devoted to mailing lists. You'll find newsletters for many of your favorite channels and forums, such as: AOL Tip of the Day; AnswerMan; IC-Hilites (Internet Connection); Chatters (People Connection); AOL Live, with schedules of live chat events on AOL; NetGirl, NetGuide, NetNoir, and many more! Newsletters go out to subscribers once a week or so with information about forum or channel events, as well as special tips and member contributions. On AOL you can subscribe to dozens of mailing lists simply by clicking the appropriate button. Just use keyword: Mail to go to the Mail Center and get information about Online Newsletters.

Road Trips and Virtual Places

Chat's fine if you want to talk *about* the Internet or if you need help using an Internet tool. But AOL now lets you chat with others while you're all visiting a Web site. There are two ways in which AOL makes the Web interactive: Road Trips and Virtual Places. Both give you an experience that's like going to the movies but being allowed to talk—and even heckle.

Road Trips are for members only. In a special window (shown in Figure 1-6) a Web site is displayed in the top *pane*, or part of the window, while a chat pane at the bottom of the screen allows you to share your thoughts about the sites with other members. You can either take a Road Trip created by another member (schedules are posted at keyword: Road trips) or create your own trip.

Virtual Places takes the idea of chatting on the Web a step further using technology from an Israeli company called Ubique, which AOL acquired in 1995. Figure 1-7 shows what you see when you use Virtual Places, which is available to both members and non-members. Participants can choose little pictures (called *avatars*) to represent themselves on the Web site—animals or cartoon characters that suit their persona. You can expect some amazing enhancements to Virtual Places in the future. Real-time interaction on the Web is where the Internet is headed, and this particular future is available now on AOL. You'll find out more about Virtual Places in Chapter 10.

Context

Unlike what you find on AOL, the information on the Internet follows no standards. That doesn't mean that the Persian cat Web site you just discovered is not reliable; it's just that no one guarantees that it's reliable or accurate or that it's particularly

FIGURE 1-6   With Road Trips you can visit Web sites with a group—and it's OK to chat or heckle

useful for your purposes. If you're changing jobs, writing a paper, researching your competition, or moving to a new city, you don't want to take chances on old or incorrect information.

Here's where AOL offers more value than the garden-variety ISP. AOL gives you clear guideposts as you start your Internet explorations. You'll find the best Internet sites integrated into channels, you'll find the best non-Internet resources, and you'll find lots of opportunities to interact with members via message boards, chat rooms, and e-mail, so you can get help and exchange discoveries about shared interests. All this content—Net sites, AOL resources, and community features—is organized into some 1,500 forums such as AnswerMan, NetGuide, Motley Fools, Hecklers Online, and NetGirl (you can read more about forums in Chapter 2). An AOL forum can provide essential context and vastly simplify your search for people and information on the Internet.

Web page viewed by a group

Avatars representing each person in the group

List of people watching and taking part

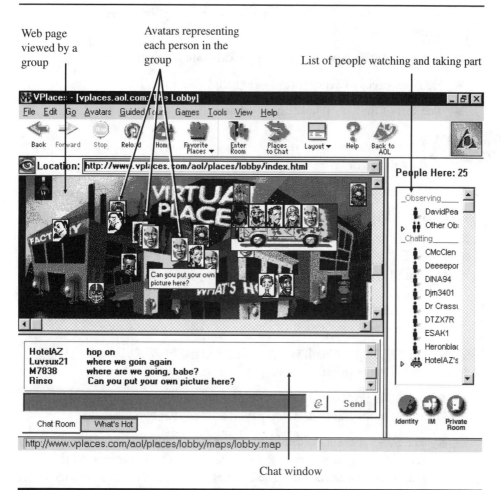

Chat window

FIGURE 1-7 Virtual Places lets you assume a new identity and broaden your social network—to the entire Internet

Value

For one reasonable monthly fee you get unlimited access to the entire Internet in addition to all the bounties of AOL's exclusive content and community (see "AOL's Billing Plans"). Other providers offer flat-rate pricing, too, but only on AOL do you get:

- Human contact and the comforts of community

- Exclusive content that provides essential context to the Internet's tools and information resources

- An open platform that puts the whole Internet at your fingertips but keeps it manageable

- Controls that help parents keep their kids safe in cyberspace

- Help resources in every forum—human, fax, e-mail, BBS, and phone

- The sort of fun you'll never have on an ISP!

 For all those questions about how much it all costs, complete information is available at keyword: Billing.

AOL's Billing Plans

In 1996, AOL began offering several price plans to fit a variety of needs:

- The $19.95 per month standard plan provides unlimited use of AOL, including access to the Internet. Fondly known as "all you can eat," this plan is available at an even lower rate if you pay ahead of time (see the next two items).

- For $17.95 per month you get unlimited use of AOL, including access to the Internet, if you pay in advance for one year.

- For $14.95 per month you get unlimited use of AOL, including access to the Internet, if you pay in advance for two years.

- The $9.95 per month, "bring your own access" plan provides unlimited access to thousands of unique AOL features, including access to the Internet, if you already have an Internet connection or access through a network on your job or at school. See the section "Using AOL with a Network or Internet Service Provider" in Appendix A.

- The $4.95 per month light-usage plan provides three hours of AOL, including the Internet, with additional time priced at just $2.50 per hour. Members with this plan are notified via a small window when they go back and forth between AOL and Internet content (which traditionally incurs an hourly cost), and "free" areas such as keyword: Help (which traditionally does not incur a cost).

Keyword: Billing has the details about the billing plans, plan switching, your account, your bill, and other good stuff.

Speed

AOL provides *faster* Internet access than any Internet Service Provider on the market. Independent lab results, from tests of seven configurations of browsers and networks attempting to access 15 popular Web sites, show that AOL's Web access is faster overall than other leading Internet services. Speed is especially important on the World Wide Web, which works by sending words and graphics to your computer; large sites in high demand can be s-l-o-w. Chapter 6 gives you tips for making your Internet connection even faster.

AOL's latest World Wide Web software was built by Microsoft and customized for the AOL service. AOL also has the tremendous resources and technical expertise to run a huge collection of finely tuned Internet computers, or *servers*. Most ISPs these days offer very good browsers, such as Microsoft's Internet Explorer and Netscape's Navigator, but if the computers and Internet connections of these ISPs are working slowly or not at all, even the best software doesn't do you any good. AOL offers great software *and* the blazing connections required to make the Internet work for you. Both the "client" software (on your computer) and the "server" software (on AOL's computers) use a technology called *caching*—a way of storing frequently used data to significantly speed up your access to the World Wide Web.

Here's another reason AOL is so fast: It owns one of the fastest networks in the communications industry, AOLnet, based on the ANS network, which America Online purchased in 1995. (In the late 1980s ANS formed the backbone of the network that predated today's Internet.) AOLnet allows you to connect to AOL (and the Net) using any modem up to 28.8 kbps. Research on faster access, including cable modems, is underway.

Finally, AOL has helped to develop a special *compression* technology created by the Johnson-Grace Company, another company AOL recently acquired. This technology reduces the size of the computer files you get over the World Wide Web and AOL, allowing for faster transmission and better image quality.

Safety

Every community has its darker side and shadier characters, so America Online gives parents the tools and the flexibility to assert some control over what their kids see and do on the Internet. What is "unsafe" is a matter of perspective and of personal taste, of course, so AOL's policy is not to censor but to give parents the tools to make such restrictions as they see fit.

AOL gives parents powerful controls to limit kids' access to this material. It makes these controls available in the Parental Controls area, available from the

Members menu, as shown in Figure 1-8. One of the choices available allows parents to restrict a child to the Kids Only channel, where it's not possible to freely browse the Web.

With these tools parents can impose one or several (or all) of the following controls:

- Keep kids out of chat rooms and prevent them from receiving Instant Messages.

- Restrict receipt of e-mail—either all e-mail or e-mail from specific e-mail addresses. See Chapter 3 for more information about mail controls.

- Block kids' access to specific newsgroups (or all newsgroups) and prevent them from downloading files from newsgroups. Chapter 5 has the details.

- Restrict kids to the Kids Only channel, where kids' content is concentrated and where the Web-browsing opportunities are limited (see Chapter 6).

- Limit kids to sites approved for children, or a somewhat broader collection of sites approved for teens (see Chapter 6).

Openness

AOL is open in two important ways.

- AOL's Internet access is open in that it is not censored. You can use AOL's built-in software to access any Web site, any mailing list, any newsgroup (with the exception of a very small number of patently illegal ones), and any other site whose address you know. *AOL doesn't censor sites in any way*, but instead gives parents the power to control what their kids do and see on the Net, as spelled out in the "Safety" section.

- AOL's Internet access is also open in that it gives you the choice of using other Internet software with your AOL software. AOL's built-in Internet tools are easy to use and will probably do anything you want them to do. But if you have a yen to use a different World Wide Web browser (such as Netscape Navigator) or a tool that has no built-in counterpart (such as a Telnet or Internet Relay Chat program), you can do it with AOL for Windows. A little file called Winsock gives you this flexibility, as you'll find out in Chapter 10.

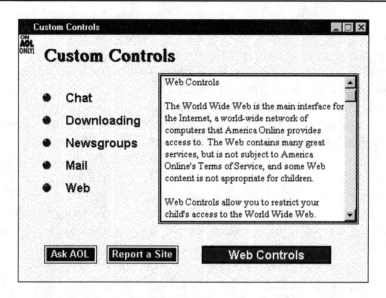

FIGURE 1-8   America Online provides parents with the ability to limit what their kids can see and do on the Net

Lots of Ways to Get Help

Most Internet Service Providers turn the Internet into one of those holiday toys that "require instruction": you've got to find software, figure out how to use it, stumble around searching for things to do with the software, and waste time on hold trying to get phone help during business hours. Want to find out who else is having the same problem? Good luck.

AOL provides all the Internet Help resources you're likely to want. The following Help resources are always at your disposal when you're using America Online.

Great Customer Service

At any time while you're on the service, keyword: Help takes you to a huge range of online and offline customer service resources, whether you need help connecting to AOL, using AOL, or finding your way on the Net. You'll find live, interactive help, voluminous help text, information about AOL's fax and BBS-based help, and lots of phone numbers to call any time of the day or night. For technical assistance with AOL for Windows, you can always call 1-888-265-8006, and at the end of Appendix A you'll find a list of other phone numbers you can use to get help.

Safe Transactions

There's another sense in which AOL provides for your safety. Your commercial transactions on the service have always been transmitted over AOL's private network with a very high degree of security, so you can shop on AOL knowing that your financial transactions are confidential.

You can save time and money by taking advantage of the buying opportunities at the AOL Store in the Marketplace channel and throughout the other channels. On the Internet as well, you can now buy directly from many sites. CDs, chocolates, books—everything can be safely bought today, thanks to the security features and "encryption" standards supported by the latest AOL Web browser, a specially customized version of Microsoft's Internet Explorer browser that's brimming with security features. Industry experts foresee a huge expansion in "electronic commerce" in the years leading up to the turn of the twenty-first century. Chapter 6 has more information about buying stuff on the Web.

Net.help and AnswerMan

For those Internet questions, you'll find help in two closely related forums: Net.help (keyword: Nethelp) and AnswerMan (keyword: Answerman). Figure 1-9 shows what you'll find in the AnswerMan forum. This book (and its Mac edition) were written by two of the people who created these areas. If you like the books, you'll love the forums!

Mail Center

At keyword: E-mail you'll find e-mail tutorials, tips, and general information for making e-mail an indispensable part of your life. At keyword: Mailing lists you'll get the lowdown on lists, plus an AOL-only directory of several thousand of the best mailing lists. Better yet, when you're using the Compose Mail window (see Chapter 3), just click Help for assistance with any feature.

Browser and WWW Help

Whenever you're using the AOL browser, just click the Help button for complete help with its functions. At AOL's Web site (keyword: WWW, or just click the Globe icon on the tool bar), click the Help button for pointers to the general best Help resources on AOL.

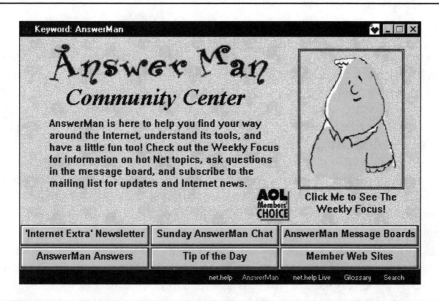

FIGURE 1-9 Help is always a click away on AOL. For all Internet Help, go to keyword: Answerman

WHAT KIND OF BEAST IS THE INTERNET?

I've gotten this far without defining the Internet—that's because I'm wary of the common but too simplistic definition of the Internet as a "network of networks." For one thing, the Internet was never intended by some "inventor" to be the globe-spanning, dynamic thing it is today. For another, once you get the hang of the Internet, you will probably experience it as a community, not as as a network of computers and cables. So defining the Internet as a network doesn't really say much about the Internet experience. Understanding three simple facts about the Internet can make for a better experience of the Net community:

- All sorts of computers communicate on the Internet.

- Using the Internet requires different programs to do different things.

- To people who use it, the Internet is not a physical network but a social one.

AOL's Stake in the Net

Across the service, you'll discover that AOL either owns key Internet technologies or has a strategic alliance with the companies that create these technologies. Some of these technologies are available to members for free or at reduced rates, such as PrimeHost (keyword: Primehost), a commercial "hosting" service for businesses and organizations that want someone else to host and maintain their Web sites.

In 1994–95, AOL acquired a series of companies or Internet content, including Navisoft, Booklink, WAIS Inc., ANS, Johnson-Grace, GNN, and Ubique. Many of these companies' products and services, such as Johnson-Grace's compression technology, have been thoroughly integrated into AOL.

Since then, AOL has shifted its strategy from buying cutting-edge companies to making alliances with the companies that lead the Internet industry. America Online's past acquisitions and current alliances with the most important players in the Internet industry—Netscape and Microsoft—ensure that AOL members will always have access to the best technologies in the marketplace. When you use Virtual Places, for instance, you're benefiting from the alliance with Microsoft, the acquisition of Ubique, and the network capacity of AOLnet. Currently, AOL is working with Bolt Beranek Newman, the consulting company that helped create the Internet some 25 years ago, to improve the performance of AOLnet.

All Sorts of Computers Communicate on the Internet

When you talk on the telephone, you set up what's called a *dedicated connection* between your phone and the phone you're calling. When you send someone electronic mail, the connection is *not* dedicated. Instead, the message is broken up into *packets*—little pieces of data, all the same size, with information about their sequence, origin, and destination. The packets are sent separately to their destination using the best available path and crossing many separate and autonomously run networks in the process. Packets from the same message might find different routes to their destination, where they're put back together again, as shown in Figure 1-10. Since packets contain information about the whole file and the correct sequence of packets, any errors in reassembling some information cause packets to be re-sent.

What It All Means

In Appendix B you will find a list of essential Internet terms, with short definitions. When you're online, the AnswerMan Glossary (keyword: AM Glossary) has a longer list of Internet terms. Who *is* AnswerMan? Kevin Savetz, author of the Mac edition of this book.

What goes for a simple e-mail message also applies to more complex things like the World Wide Web. When you visit a Web site, the various files making up the page are separately sent to you and are turned into tiny data packets at the source computer and reassembled at your computer.

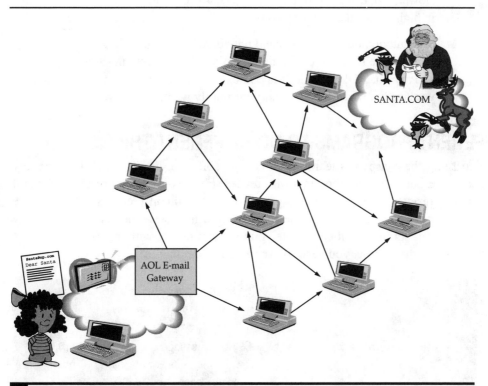

FIGURE 1-10   Packet switching at work. How that message gets to Santa

Here's the important point: *Any* computer—whether it's based on Windows or the Mac or on bigger systems such as Unix or even a mainframe—can take part in this exchange of packets if it has some software conforming to an Internet standard called TCP/IP, which does the work of making packets, correcting errors, and reassembling files. (See Appendix B for fuller definitions.)

TCP/IP also allows two-way communication. That's what the word "interactive" really means: on the Internet you produce information as well as consume it. On AOL you can produce a Web site, an e-mail message, a newsgroup article, or an FTP file, and you'll find all the Internet applications that allow you to share information with other people everywhere.

What does this all mean for you as an AOL member?

■ Packets move at different speeds, over congested networks, and through sluggish servers, which can account for why a Web site visit can be slower than using a forum on AOL. That's the value of AOL's investment in high-performance technology.

■ The autonomous computers and networks hooked up to this global network are the source of content that's wildly diverse in subject, quality, and appeal. AOL provides the context, parental controls, and search tools you need to find what you and your family want.

DIFFERENT PROGRAMS TO DO DIFFERENT THINGS

Learning the Net means learning to use Net software, which is like learning any software but with two important differences. First, you must learn to use several smaller programs—not one big program—to do several different tasks. Second, the tasks don't take place on a single PC, but on a network. The tasks are not only networked, but most of them enable you to communicate with others.

To use the Internet you need to use several programs:

An e-mail reader	To send and receive e-mail messages with other individuals on AOL and the Internet. See Chapter 3.
A newsgroup reader	To post messages on any of tens of thousands of international "bulletin boards," each devoted to a specific subject; anyone interested in the subject can read your messages. See Chapter 5.

| A World Wide Web "browser" | To browse multimedia creations of words, pictures, and sounds. See Chapter 6. |
| An FTP (file transfer protocol) "client" | To retrieve software, images, sounds, programs, and other kinds of files from distant Internet computers, and to make these files available to others everywhere. See Chapter 8. |

Each of these programs is built into your AOL software. One of them, the World Wide Web browser, is becoming a truly comprehensive application—it's the tool that gives you access to all other tools. On AOL you can use your Web browser to visit FTP sites, to send an e-mail message, and to call up AOL's newsgroup reader. Soon, you may be using the browser to search your hard disk!

For now and the near future, however, effective use of e-mail, newsgroups, and FTP requires use of the specific software "clients" built into the AOL software. The browser's great, but it's best suited to browsing the Web.

THE INTERNET AS A SOCIAL NETWORK

America Online differs from other online services in many ways. Most important, AOL is a community. Everyone doesn't know everyone else, but AOL members do have plenty of ways—from IMs to e-mail—to get to know other members safely and reliably. They also have countless places, from chat rooms to forums, to meet people and make friends.

AOL's access to the Internet, unmatched by other online services, puts members in touch with a much larger community as well, a community with its own history, culture, and ways of governing itself. In fact, the Internet community is big enough to be considered a sort of country. Before setting off to explore this new country, it's a good idea to understand something about the sort of place you're about to visit.

A Little History

The Net is the unintended result of many separate dreams and real-world developments. Nobody invented it. First, there were dreamers—early visionaries like Vannevar Bush (in the 1940s), J.C.R. Licklider (in the 1960s), Ted Nelson (since the 1960s), and Tim Berners-Lee (since the late 1980s). Licklider dreamed of a future in which interconnected computing machines would take over people's routine tasks and allow them to spend more time at creative and productive tasks. As a director in the government's Agency for Advanced Research Projects (ARPA) in the early 1960s, Licklider had direct influence on the people who built government networks in the 1960s.

Bush, Nelson, and Berners-Lee were pioneers of a different sort. They imagined new ways of linking related knowledge in a universally available format, laying the groundwork for what is now known as *hypertext* (see Chapter 6). Their work continues to inspire the creators of today's World Wide Web.

Packets and Protocols

In the 1960s, for less-than-visionary reasons, the U.S. Department of Defense wanted to create a network that could operate in the event of war despite possible outages of part of the network. The solution first proposed by Paul Baran at the Rand Institute in California was a packet network, as described earlier in "All Sorts of Computers Communicate on the Internet." Working independently of Baran was Donald Davies, an English engineer who devised a packet-based network that formed the basis of a flexible public network. His motives were anything but military.

Larry Roberts, a computer wizard who came to Washington in 1966 to direct ARPA's networking projects, was influenced by the ideas of pioneers like Davies and Baran and by the sheer technical challenge of enabling different computers to exchange data. In 1969, with ARPA's support, the consulting firm of Beranek, Bolt and Newman in Cambridge, Massachusetts successfully built a packet network, linking four universities on the West Coast, which formed the ARPAnet. New universities were attached to the ARPAnet one at a time in the early 1970s.

One challenge with ARPAnet was that computers could only be added one at a time, through the creation of custom software and hardware *interfaces*—special computers that handled the routing of data between computers. Another challenge was to interconnect different kinds of packet networks, including radio and satellite networks. The big breakthrough in Internet history came in the early 1980s with the development of TCP/IP by Vinton Cerf and several graduate students at UCLA. Cerf is sometimes called the father of the Internet, but he is only the most prominent of a collective effort that involved hundreds of people, some of them visionaries and some not, some envisioning the whole and some focusing on specific parts of the whole.

Birth of the Present

In the 1980s, American research scientists wanted a way to more effectively share information, and they began to demand the same sort of access to networks that, at that time, only computer scientists had. In 1985, the National Science Foundation gave them that access by linking supercomputers at six major American universities, forming the NSFnet, ARPAnet's successor. Each of the nodes became the center of a regional network accessible to all universities, schools, and libraries in the region.

What really fueled the growth of the Net from about 1992 onward was the World Wide Web, an easy-to-use way to access global network resources, which you can read about in Chapter 6. In 1995, the government ended its support of the NSFnet and turned the Internet over to the companies and other organizations that now manage the Internet's rapid expansion.

How Many People Are on the Internet?

In late 1996, approximately 35 million adults *in the United States* were using the Internet, about a quarter of the U.S. adult population and an increase of more than 100% from a year earlier, according to Lou Harris & Associates. (Source: Cyberatlas, **http://www.cyberatlas.com**.)

In January 1997, approximately 57 million people *in the world* used the "consumer Internet" (defined as "users of computers that can *access* information by interactive TCP/IP services such as WWW or FTP"), according to John Quarterman, President of Matrix Information and Directory Services (MIDS) in Austin, Texas. Adding the people in the world who have access only to e-mail makes for a total of some 71 million people. Quarterman also predicts there will be approximately 700 million people using the "consumer Internet" in January 2000, saying "There is to reason to believe that the current rate of Internet growth cannot be sustained for three more years." MIDS's Web site has authoritative information about the size, growth, and definition of the Internet (**http://www.mids.org**).

A Global Community

Chances are very good that most of what you do on the Internet will involve American Internet users and American Internet content. Two thirds of all *hosts* (computers directly on the Internet) are American. However, more than 170 countries have access to the Internet, and on the Internet the information about the rest of the world is overwhelming in scope and quality. Whether you're planning a trip to Fiji, writing a paper about ancient Mesopotomia, studying English gardens, learning about the teas of Sri Lanka, dreaming of a golf trip to Scotland, or trying to find a pen pal in Italy—the Internet can make your job easier, faster, less costly, and more fun.

How to Behave Like a Native

Through e-mail, mailing lists, newsgroups, and Internet Relay Chat, the Internet gives you many ways of communicating with other people around the world. Like any community, the Net has its own guidelines (or *netiquette*), which can be boiled down to two precepts:

- Respect the people who might be reading anything you write and make available on the Net, because you can never predict in whose hands (or mailbox) something will wind up. No one can read your mind or see your body language on the Net, so what you write in jest may be taken seriously. Also, be aware that what you send to one person or place can be forwarded to thousands of people or places.

- Respect the physical Internet itself by not wasting *bandwidth* and storage space with unsolicited or inappropriate messages, especially commercial postings to uncommercial places.

What happens when you break the "laws" of netiquette? Minor infringements can get you *flamed*—verbally abused in mailing lists and newsgroups. It's not a particularly pleasant experience. Major infringements can get your membership revoked on AOL. In between, you may discover the existence of various blacklists that limit access to some Internet services.

Note   *America Online does not limit members' access to the Internet, but it does expect them to comply with its Rules of the Road guidelines while they're using all Internet services. All networks expect their users to comply with rules when they use the network to explore the world; AOL is no different. You'll find more details about these rules later in this book, but all you need to know is available at keyword: Rules of the road.*

Do unto others, and do unto the network. That pretty much sums up netiquette. Chapters 4 and 5 give more details about proper behavior on mailing lists and newsgroups, the two places where netiquette really matters.

How the Net Community Governs Itself

Netiquette goes a long way to explaining how the Internet citizenry control their own destiny. It's the Net's common law. The closest the Net comes to formal government is the Internet Society, an international organization made up of companies, individuals, and government agencies that work to guarantee the well-being of the Internet as a physical network.

Based in Reston, Virginia, a couple of miles from America Online's new headquarters in Dulles, the Internet Society helps set the standards with which tens of thousands of autonomous networks comply, making the Net possible. It does its work through annual meetings, regular publications, and subgroups such as the Internet Engineering Task Force and the Internet Architecture Standards Board. Neither elected by the Internet community nor appointed by the world's "real" governments, the Internet Society nonetheless effectively plans the standards required for the Internet's future growth. More and more, companies such as Microsoft, Netscape, and AOL itself are exerting influence on the standards-making process, especially the part of the process that relates to the World Wide Web.

Doing Business in the Net Community

The Internet was built with public money, and "acceptable use policies" kept businesses and all for-profit activity *off* the NSFnet at first. Since 1991, however, business has assumed more and more financial and technological responsibilities for maintaining publicly accessible networks.

What do businesses do on the Internet? Many people and companies see the Internet as a way to make money, and when they don't immediately succeed at this, they label the Internet a failure. This is nonsense. Smart businesses know that, for now, the Net's a great way of cutting costs in every aspect of a business: doing competitive research, learning about markets, recruiting employees, doing targeted interactive marketing, selling products, and providing customer support. As security technologies mature, the Net *will* become a place to make money, creating a better experience for consumers as well as companies small and large. AOL's InBusiness forum, led by Dr. Jill Ellsworth, is devoted to the wise business use of the Internet (keyword: Inbusiness).

The Internet has a reputation for being "anti-business." True, there are pockets of hostility to business on the Internet, and there are places where commercial postings are inappropriate. Plus, many small businesses new to the Net are insensitive to the finer points of netiquette. But if government made the early Net possible, it's business that's keeping it going today.

FROM HERE...

This chapter conveys the benefits of the Internet, the benefits of using the Net on AOL, and the *reality* of the Internet on AOL. In the next chapter you learn how to sign onto and get around AOL, and you'll find out exactly *where* the Internet is on AOL.

Chapter 2

Navigating From America Online to Get to the Internet

As your home on the Net, America Online offers many opportunities to learn about the Internet, get help, and share your Internet experiences with other AOL members. AOL also offers hundreds of links to the best World Wide Web sites and other resources on the Net, and it gives you the freedom to go anywhere you want. This chapter starts with the basics:

- Signing on

- Working with windows, menus, and tool bars

- Finding and navigating AOL forums

- Finding out exactly how to get to the Internet on AOL—the menus, channels, forums, and buttons that take you there

If you're new to AOL, Windows, and computers, you'll want to read or skim this entire chapter. If you're already familiar with AOL you're probably also comfortable using Windows, so you can skip the early sections and jump straight to *"Where* on AOL is the Internet?"

 This chapter assumes you have installed the AOL software. Appendix A walks you through the process if you haven't yet done so.

GETTING ONLINE

With mouse in hand, you're ready to sign onto AOL. *Signing on*, *connecting*, *logging on*—it's all the same: connecting with AOL in order to read and take part in AOL forums and to use the Internet. To connect with AOL, start your computer (first making sure no one is using the phone and that the modem is on), and follow these steps:

1. With your mouse, double-click the AOL icon if it's in a Windows 3.1 program window or on the Windows 95 desktop; if the icon is on your Windows 95 Start menu, a single click will do. The AOL program may take a moment or two to display or "load"—it's a big program. When it does display, the Welcome window appears:

2. Type your password in the Enter Password box.

3. Click the Sign On button. AOL now looks for the modem, dials the local phone number you chose during installation (covered in Appendix A), establishes connection with the AOL network, and verifies your password. You're ready to navigate the Internet!

When you successfully sign onto AOL, you'll see two screens: the Channels menu shown in Figure 2-1 and the Welcome screen shown in Figure 2-2. You're online, and you're almost on the Net! (See "Where Am I—Online, Offline, On the Net?")

Where Am I—Online, Offline, On the Net?

You're online from the time you sign onto AOL to the time you sign off. The rest of the time you're…offline. Unlike other providers, AOL gives you many ways to automate routine online tasks, so you can go online only when you have to (or want to). You can do many of your everyday tasks, such as composing e-mail and taking part in newsgroups, while you're offline. The AOL feature that makes this possible, FlashSessions, is discussed in Chapter 4.

You can visit the Internet while you're signed onto AOL. You don't have to sign off AOL and then sign on somewhere else or use any special software. The

Internet is not "parallel" to AOL but a seamless extension of the AOL experience. You don't have to pay anything extra to use anything on the Internet, unless, of course, you purchase something over the Internet or use one of the very few for-fee subscription services available over the Internet.

Later in this chapter you'll find a directory of the places on AOL from which you can start your explorations of the Internet ("*Where* on AOL is the Internet?").

The Channels menu shown in Figure 2-1 gives you direct access to AOL's *channels*. They're called channels because AOL programs and distributes content, just like the studios and networks of the TV world do. But AOL's channels differ from TV channels in that they are *interactive*. They give you many opportunities to take polls, offer your opinions, share your experiences, and meet other members. Each channel is devoted to a broad subject of interest to members, such as entertainment, personal finance, or sports. You'll find access to Internet content throughout AOL's channels in the form of links to great Internet Web sites and newsgroups. (See "The World of AOL Forums.")

FIGURE 2-1   The Channels menu lets you access the subjects of most interest to you

The Welcome Screen, shown in Figure 2-2, gives you access to AOL's most popular features, such as e-mail, People Connection, and the Internet, as well as to any new features or live events that are currently going on. You can close the Channels window, but the Welcome window always stays open. After all, you're always welcome on AOL! (If you're unsure how to open and close windows, read "Using Windows.")

SIGNING OFF

AOL gives you several ways to sign off. Which way you use depends on how you like to do things—with the mouse, from menus, or with the keyboard. These options differ primarily in whether they leave the AOL program open (displayed on your computer monitor) after you sign off. You might want to keep the AOL program open if you'll be signing on again with the same screen name, or with a different screen name or *location* (see Appendix A on locations).

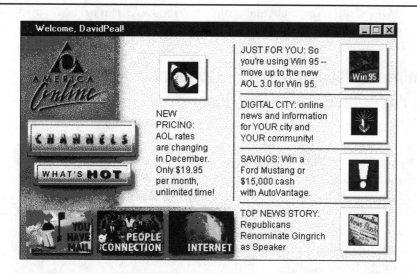

FIGURE 2-2   The Welcome Screen takes you to AOL events going on right now, as well as to e-mail, the Internet, and People Connection

To sign off AOL but leave the AOL program open:

■ Move your mouse cursor to the Go To menu at the top of your screen and click and release your mouse. Then slide the mouse cursor to Sign Off and click again.

■ AOL also has a menu called Sign Off that's available only when you're online. Click this menu and select the single item, Sign Off.

To sign off AOL and close the AOL program, use any of these standard Windows techniques for closing a program:

■ Press ALT-F4 (on your keyboard, hold down the ALT key. Keeping that key pressed, press F4).

■ In Windows 95, click once in the little box with an X in the far upper-right of the main AOL window.

■ Double-click in the Control box in the upper-left corner of the window. In Windows 95 this usually looks like the icon of the program (in this case, AOL's distinctive triangular icon). In Windows 3.1, it's a box with a minus sign through it.

Signing Off from a Network Connection (TCP/IP or an Internet Service Provider)

A new billing plan allows you to access AOL using your local network at work or another Internet Service Provider (ISP). See the "Using AOL with a Network or Internet Service Provider" section of Appendix A for more information. The benefits of this plan are the lower cost and the ready access to AOL via less congested networks. Signing off can be tricky, though. Using any of the methods above to sign off AOL will *not* log you off this other connection. So, if you're signing off AOL, make sure you also log off your other connection to avoid running up your phone bill—unless, of course, you want to continue using your ISP or network account after signing off AOL.

Tip   *If you use AOL with a network or ISP and you want to sign off AOL, logging off the* other *connection is a good way to pull the plug on both AOL and the network connection by which you access AOL.*

USING WINDOWS

A window is the box that displays words or pictures. Windows have their own controls, so you can move them, close them, and change their size. Figure 2-3 shows AOL's New Mail window within the larger AOL window. All windows appear in this larger window when you're using AOL.

Window Controls

The windows you use on AOL have the following elements:

- Title bar

- Scroll bar

- Controls for adjusting a window's size

FIGURE 2-3 The New Mail window keeps track of the electronic mail messages you receive. It appears within the larger AOL window that always stays on your desktop (Windows 95)

Title Bar

Every window has a title bar—the thin line of text at the very top that displays a particular window's name. Figure 2-3 shows a window with New Mail in its title bar. When you are browsing the World Wide Web and don't know where you are, the title bar will usually give you the site's plain-English name (unless it's French or some other language!).

You use a title bar to move, or *drag*, a window. Just click on the title bar, keep the mouse button pressed, move the mouse to drag the window to where you want it, and release the mouse to *drop* the window in its new position.

 Sometimes you'll see a little heart off to the right side of the title bar. Click the heart to save the window in your Favorite Places folder, a list of your favorite sites on both AOL and the Internet. Chapter 6 has more to say about this essential AOL feature.

Scroll Bar

A scroll bar lets you see a document that's too long to fit in a single window. Web sites usually require *vertical* scrolling (see Figure 2-3). From time to time you will see a window so wide that it requires a *horizontal* scroll bar as well; this will appear along the bottom of a window.

You use scroll bars to move by clicking the little square scroll box and dragging it up or down (or right and left). Or, click with your mouse above or below the little box to move up and down half a screen at a time (on a horizontal scroll bar, click to the right or left of the square). Or, click on the arrow at either end of the scroll bar to move a little bit at a time for each click. You'll come to rely on scroll bars when you read long e-mail messages, access newsgroup postings, or navigate very long Web pages.

Minimizing, Maximizing, and Resizing Windows

Windows can be adjusted in size so you can easily manage several windows open at the same time. With a single click you can change a window's size in the following ways:

- *Maximizing* a window makes it as big as possible, so that no other windows can be seen within the larger AOL window.

- *Minimizing* a window removes it from view but keeps it readily available from the AOL Window menu.

- *Restoring* a window makes it possible to see several open windows at the same time.

Note   *In Windows 95 you'll see your window controls in the upper right-hand corner of every window (see Figure 2-3). The function of the middle box changes depending on context. When a window is maximized, the middle control box lets you restore it (keep it visible but make it smaller). When a window is neither maximized nor minimized, the middle control lets you maximize it. Windows 3.1 has controls for minimizing and maximizing but not for closing. Many AOL windows cannot be maximized, but instead assume a fixed shape; if that's the case, the maximize button may be gray and unclickable. Finally, in both Windows 95 and Windows 3.1, there is the control box in the upper-left corner of the window. Clicking this once brings up a menu with options to minimize, maximize, move, close, or restore, although you won't always be able to use each of these options. Double-clicking in this box closes the window.*

In both Windows 3.1 and Windows 95, you *resize* a standard window by slowly passing your mouse over the window's outside border until the mouse cursor (the arrow) turns into a double arrow. Now click and drag the border to resize the window as you please.

Note   *Many AOL windows cannot be resized, but instead have a fixed rectangular shape. That's because they make heavy use of graphics and are designed to present the most information in the smallest (and fastest downloading) window.*

On AOL, almost everything you do causes a new window to open. To keep your screen from getting cluttered, it's a good idea to close windows you are not using. You can close any open window by double-clicking in the control box in the upper left-hand corner. In Windows 95, you can also close a window by clicking the box with the X in the upper right-hand corner. No matter what version of Windows you use, you can close *all* windows by going to the Window menu and selecting Close All.

There are windows and there are windows. AOL itself is an "application window" and is always available when you're using AOL (though it can be restored and minimized too!). Things you do within AOL, like sending e-mail and browsing the Web, each take place within their own "document window." Sometimes the elements of open windows can get in each other's way. Scroll bars, for example, can get confusing, because it's not always obvious whether a scroll bar belongs to a document window or an application window. Maximizing the document window and the AOL application window can make it easier to tell what part of a window belongs to which particular open window. Maximizing also lets you see an entire scroll bar (with a window not maximized, the bottom part of the scroll bar—the little arrow—is often not visible). When you maximize in version 3.0 of AOL for Windows, the little Favorite Places heart is no longer visible and Add Favorite Places becomes available from the Window menu.

Inside a Window

Within a window you will find the following elements. They give you a graphical way of finding what you're looking for or doing what you want to do.

Listboxes

In an AOL forum, listboxes contain everything from text articles to links to Internet sites. If the list is too long to fit in the little box, a vertical scroll bar lets you quickly move up and down. (On AOL, if a list is too wide, a horizontal scroll bar *won't* appear!) To open (or go to) an item on the list, double-click it (clicking once merely selects it). Here's the listbox from AOL's Personal Publisher service, which is what you use to create your own Web pages.

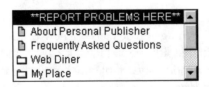

Drop-Down Lists

Drop-down lists do the work of a listbox but take up less space. The most common drop-down list you will encounter while using the Internet on AOL is the Address field at the top of the World Wide Web browser (which you can read all about in Chapter 6). You click the downward-pointing arrow with the mouse to see it:

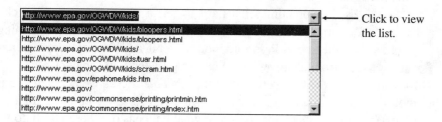

Click to view the list.

Interactive Elements

Windows has several ways of letting you make a choice or specify a preference.

With a *radio button* you make a single, exclusive choice from a set of options. Simply click with your mouse inside the circle of your choice. Clicking inside another circle selects that button and automatically deselects your first choice.

File release timeframe: Select only one
○ All Dates   ○ Past Month   ⊙ Past Week

Check boxes let you choose as many things as you want; click inside any of the boxes as you want (or don't click on any boxes).

☐ Applications   ☐ Games   ☐ OS/2
☐ Development   ☐ Graphics & Animation   ☐ Telecommunications
☐ DOS   ☐ Hardware   ☑ Windows
☐ Education   ☑ Music & Sound

A *text box* lets you make a free-form choice by typing some text and providing some information: your address, your name, what you like about a site, what you're searching for, or whatever.

3. Enter a Search Definition: Narrow search by typing in key words.

midi   **SEARCH**

A clickable *button* performs some action; it takes you to a new place in a new window. In the Welcome screen, for example (Figure 2-2), buttons can fetch your electronic mail and spirit you to live events currently underway on AOL.

Sometimes it's hard to tell a button from a nonclickable graphic. How do you know for sure whether something is clickable? Pass your mouse over it, and if the mouse pointer turns from an arrow into a pointing finger, you can click.

More and more on AOL, you'll encounter *bubble text* as well. When you pass your mouse cursor over a button, it turns from an arrow into a pointing finger, and a small text bubble comes up that tells you what happens or where you'll go when you click on the button.

ORDERING FROM MENUS

A menu gives you a set of related choices. The Mail menu, for example, lets you send a message, see the messages you've sent and received, get information about using e-mail on AOL, edit your Address Book, and more.

Take a moment to explore each of AOL's menus that are lined up horizontally at the top of your window:

To open a menu so you can see your choices, just move your mouse over the menu and click. To make a selection, move the mouse arrow down the menu to the menu selection you want and click once to make your selection. If you don't find what you are looking for, just move the mouse cursor off the menu to close it.

Note   *Rather use your keyboard? Pressing* ALT *and the underlined letter in the menu name (*ALT-F *for the File menu, for example) is another way of opening a menu.*

Internet: On Today's Menu

AOL doesn't offer an Internet menu, but it does integrate Internet services into other menus wherever it makes sense. You'll find essential Net or Net-related tools and features in the following places.

2

Keyboard Alternatives

For some menu items, a keyboard alternative is available. This means that you can go directly to the item using the keyboard instead of selecting from the menu. For example, in the Mail menu, to the right of Compose Mail you'll see CTRL-M. This means that from *anywhere on AOL*, you can compose an e-mail message by holding down the control (CTRL) key and pressing the letter M. Keyboard alternatives are a shortcut to menu items you use all the time.

Here are some useful keyboard alternatives:

- To compose an e-mail message: CTRL-M

- To open a file: CTRL-O

- To open the Keyword window: CTRL-K

- To print something that's displayed: CTRL-P

- To read your e-mail: CTRL-R

- To save a file: CTRL-S

Keyword Window (Go To Menu)

The Keyword Window gives you access to every feature *about* the Internet, as explained in "Your Key(word) to the Internet." Some of the most important keywords for using the Internet are listed in Table 2-1. To enter a keyword, you bring up the Keyword window by either selecting it from the Go To menu or pressing CTRL-K:

Keyword

Keyword

To quickly access an area, type its keyword below and click Go. To locate areas that match your topic of interest, type words that describe what you are looking for and click Search.

Enter word(s): | excite

[Go]   [Search]   [?]

To use the Keyword window, simply type in the keyword (such as one of the keywords listed in Table 2-1), and click Go. If you're not sure of a keyword, type in the subject (such as Internet) and click Search to bring up a list of related AOL areas. Double-click any item to go to an area.

Your Key(word) to the Internet

The easiest way to navigate AOL and the Internet is by using *keywords* (Table 2-1). Think of a keyword as a shortcut. Every AOL forum and many Web destinations have keywords assigned to them—the keyword for the NetGuide forum is **Netguide**, for example.

Here's how to use keywords: First, bring up the Keyword window from the Go To menu, then enter a keyword, and press Go. If you know a URL, or Internet address, such as **http://www.aol.com**, you can enter it in the Keyword field, press Go, and you'll go directly to the Web site. Chapter 6 plumbs the mysteries of URLs.

The most popular Web sites have plain-English keywords, instead of URLs, for example: **Excite**, **Switchboard**, **PathFinder**, and **Disney.com**. A list of such keywords is available at keyword: Web keywords. Keywords can make it easy to get where you going, whether it's on the Net or on AOL. Some of these Web keywords (such as **Excite**) take you directly to the Web, others (such as **Disney**) to an intermediate screen that gives you a set of links to places on both AOL and the Internet.

Note   *Keywords are not case sensitive:* ftp, FTP, *and* Ftp *all take you to AOL's File Transfer Protocol area. This book will uppercase the first letter of keywords, but you don't have to follow that practice.*

2

Keyword	Takes You To
Access	Information about global and domestic AOL access, including a list of numbers
Answerman	AnswerMan forum, with Kevin Savetz, co-author of the Macintosh edition of this book, can answer all your Internet questions and offers a chat room, newsletter, message boards, and more
Billing	Explanation of everything related to your bill, with forms for changing your billing information
Excite	Search the Web and newsgroups (see Chapters 6 and 9)
FTP	Access to thousands of FTP sites (where you can download files) (see Chapter 8)
Gopher	An older Internet service, Gopher still offers many treasures, nicely packaged by AOL for easy access
Http	A Web site whose URL, or Internet address, you know. For instance, type **http://fool.web.aol.com** to go to the Motley Fools Web site
Internet applications	Half a dozen of the coolest "Winsock" applications you can run with AOL (see Chapter 10)
Keyword	A master list of keywords, including Internet-related keywords
Mailing list	A selective, annotated mailing list directory designed for AOL members (see Chapter 4)
Member services	Comprehensive AOL help
Modem	All things modem-related, including configuring, connecting, troubleshooting
Netguide	AOL's edition of *NetGuide* magazine, with an abundance of tips, columns, and interactive features
Nethelp	Comprehensive Internet help, a part of the AnswerMan forum
Net highlights	The best of AOL's Internet services, forums, and links

TABLE 2-1   25 essential keywords for using the Internet on America Online

Keyword	Takes You To
Newsgroups	A starting point for exploring 20,000-plus public discussion groups, or newsgroups (see Chapter 5)
PP2	Instructions and tips on how to make your own Web page using Personal Publisher (see Chapter 7)
Quickstart	Tips for new users of AOL and the Net (also Keyword: LearnAOL and Keyword: Discover)
Screen name	Add a screen name or change your existing name
Software	More than 100,000 files to download, including dozens of Internet utilities and thousands of files also available via FTP
Telnet	Telnet Center. Telnet software and tips for accessing remote computers (see Chapter 10)
Web	AOL's Web site
Web keyword	A list of the many dozens of Web sites that can be accessed directly by keyword
Web Diner	Friendly help and useful tools if you're building your own Web page
WWW (same as keyword: Web)	AOL's Web site

TABLE 2-1   25 essential keywords for using the Internet on America Online (*continued*)

Favorite Places (Go To Menu)

Gives you a way to keep track of your favorite newsgroups, Web sites, AOL forums, and even your most important e-mail messages. You can go directly to your Favorite Places folder from the Go To menu. Or, on the tool bar, you can click on the folder with the heart in it. Chapter 6 has the lowdown on Favorite Places.

The Mail Center (Mail Menu)

Takes you to tons of useful information about electronic mail (e-mail), including links to related resources and a long list of electronic newsletters you can receive via e-mail for free. From the Mail menu you can also send a message (by selecting Compose Mail) or get your e-mail (by selecting Read Mail). Both features are available from the tool bar as well. From the same menu, you can also see lists of messages you have opened (Check Mail You've Read) and messages you have sent (Check Mail You've Sent). Chapter 3 is devoted to e-mail.

Preferences (Members Menu)

Takes you to a window that lets you adjust many aspects of your Internet experience, from specifying your home page on the World Wide Web to controlling the colors of links you see on the browser; from how you reply to your e-mail messages to whether you save them on your hard disk (see the "On Your Own Terms: Setting Preferences for AOL and Windows"). Preferences are also available from the tool bar, by clicking the MyAOL button.

On Your Own Terms: Setting Preferences for AOL and Windows

America Online offers members many ways to customize the way the service looks and works. You'll find a broad range of choices—*preferences*—and clear online instructions for specifying what you like.

Some of these preferences—called *Parental Controls*—are available only to the master account holder (the person who registered the account) and can be used to set limits on the sorts of things children can do on AOL and the Internet. Parental Controls are all available at keyword: Parental Controls are discussed in Chapters 3, 5, and 6.

Other preferences, which can be used by any screen name within a master account, can be accessed from the Members menu. To do this, select Preferences, then click the appropriate button to adjust your preferences on, for example, AOL's Web browser (click WWW), e-mail services (click Mail), or file downloading on the service (click Download). The browser preferences can be set within the browser, too, by clicking the Prefs button.

 Throughout this book, specific preferences are mentioned as they're relevant to the use of specific Internet services, such as e-mail, newsgroups, and the World Wide Web.

Some aspects of the way your display looks and system works cannot be set within AOL. Using your Windows 3.1 or Windows 95 control panels, some of the things you can adjust are:

- The sounds associated with particular "events" such as signing on (through the Sounds control panel); if you don't like sounds, just turn them off!

- The "palette" used to define the colors of every window element (through the Display control panel)

- The responsiveness of your keyboard and the shapes assumed by your mouse cursor (through the Keyboard and Mouse control panels)

In Windows 95, control panels are available from the Start menu (select Settings, then Control Panels), in Windows 3.1 from the Program Manager. *Windows 95 for Busy People, Second Edition,* by Ron Mansfield (Osborne/ McGraw-Hill, 1997) provides all the help you need in all Windows matters.

Parental Control (Members Menu)

Allows parents to restrict the activities of their children while they're on the Internet with separate and easy-to-use controls for e-mail, newsgroups, and the Web. Chapters 3, 5, and 6 have the details.

The Help Menu

For general AOL help, including using windows, connecting, troubleshooting, and billing. This valuable comprehensive help resource is available even when you're not signed on.

THE AOL TOOL BAR

The AOL *tool bar* is the row of *icons,* or small clickable buttons, that you see at the top of your AOL window, just below the menu bar. The tool bar icons are listed in Table 2-2. Tools vary in purpose: some of these tools let you do something (like the Printer icon, which lets you print). Others take you to a place, such as your Favorite

Places folder. Menu commands will do the same things and take you to the same places, but they're tucked away and less intuitive.

 The tool bar's Online clock is primarily for the benefit of members on the light-usage plan (see "AOL's Billing Plans" in Chapter 1).

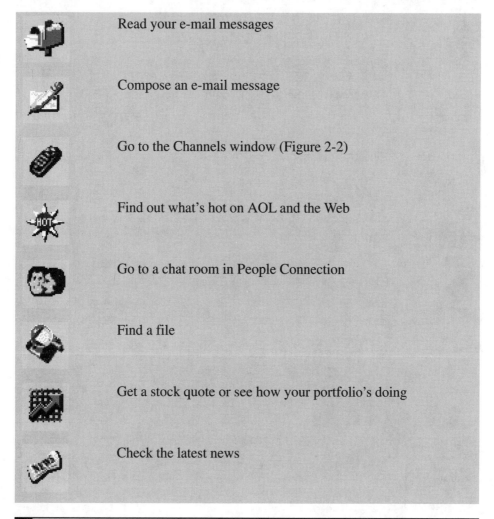

	Read your e-mail messages
	Compose an e-mail message
	Go to the Channels window (Figure 2-2)
	Find out what's hot on AOL and the Web
	Go to a chat room in People Connection
	Find a file
	Get a stock quote or see how your portfolio's doing
	Check the latest news

TABLE 2-2   The tool bar gives you quick access to the most commonly used AOL and Internet features

	Jump directly to the World Wide Web
	Buy something in AOL's Marketplace
	Set your preferences
	Watch the online clock if you don't have unlimited usage
	Print something that's displayed
	Look for something in your Personal Filing Cabinet
	Visit a Favorite Place
	Get help
	Find an AOL area
	Go to the Keyword window

TABLE 2-2 The tool bar gives you quick access to the most commonly used AOL and Internet features (*continued*)

THE WORLD OF AOL FORUMS

On the Internet they're called *sites,* on AOL they're called *areas* or *forums.* In either case, think of them as places to go—the reason you go online in the first place. In both sites and forums, you'll find a lot of variations in the ways you get around. Figure 2-4 shows NetGuide, one of the best new AOL forums and one of the most useful if you need general help getting around the Internet.

Elements of an AOL Forum

Forums draw people who share a specific interest—health, investing, relationships, parenting, humor, you name it. In a forum you'll find gobs of information about a specific subject gathered up in one place for easy access. Forums take you to the best Internet sites, too, so you don't have to go searching for them on your own.

Some forums have leaders; others don't. The most important part of any forum is the people who frequent it. There are many ways forums can support their communities. Some have dedicated chat rooms. Others have regular "events" in which the forum leader or a guest chats with members about a specific topic. In many, you'll find automated e-mail, which makes it easy to ask the forum leader a question or to subscribe to an e-mail newsletter. Others take polls and share the results with members. And most forums have message boards, so members can communicate directly with each other.

A forum makes information available through *buttons, images, listboxes,* and more, which often let you go directly to related sites on either the Internet or AOL. Sometimes you'll find listboxes with files to download, and you'll often find text to read—*lots* of text to read. More and more sites are providing an index and search feature to make it easier to get around.

Finding Forums on AOL

AOL offers you more than 1,500 forums to choose from, with subjects ranging from woodworking to relationships, from Mars to alternative medicine. How do you find forums of likely interest to you? You can either search for something specific or browse to see what's available.

To *search* for a specific area of interest on AOL, click the Find button on the tool bar to bring up the Find window (shown in Figure 2-5). Then type in any word describing what you're looking for in the text box and click Search.

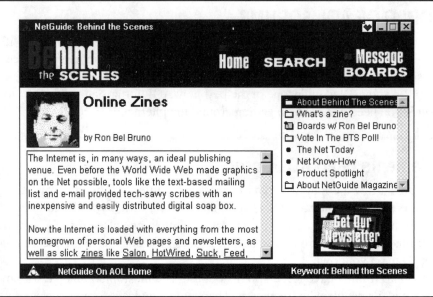

FIGURE 2-4 Informative text, links to the Web, message boards, a newsletter—NetGuide has it all

Enter text here to do a search

Click a tab to browse for a forum, find a person, or take part in a live event

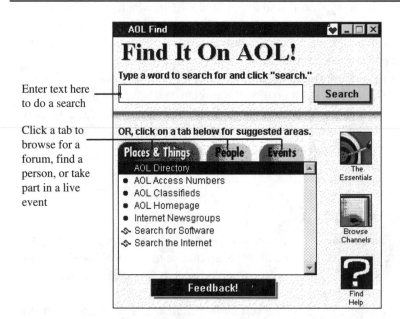

FIGURE 2-5 The Find window lets you search for a specific area or browse through all of AOL's offerings

You *browse* for content and community by clicking one of the following three tabs:

- **Places & Things**   A channel-by-channel listing of AOL forums

- **People**   A set of directories where you can search for someone's e-mail or real-world address

- **Events**   A current schedule of AOL's live events, where you can interact with members and celebrities

Tip   *Whenever you find a place you like, make sure to note its keyword, so you can return there directly in the future. Even better, click on the little heart in the forum's title bar to store it in your Favorite Places folder, so your favorite places are also a click (or double-click) away (see Chapter 6 for more about Favorite Places).*

Another way to find forums that match your interests is to use keyword: Quick Start. Click Match Your Interests to bring up a list of topics, such as "Computers and Internet" and "Reference and Research." Click any topic to find a handful of the best, exclusively AOL resources on that topic (see Figure 2-6).

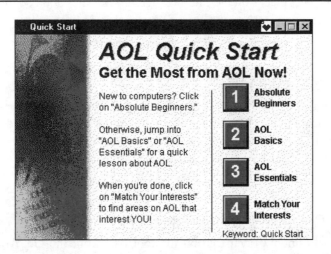

FIGURE 2-6   If you're new, Quick Start helps you find your way around AOL and identify forums that match your interests

WHERE ON AOL IS THE INTERNET?

On AOL you're a click away from the Internet. You can get to the Net from the tool bar, from menus, and throughout AOL's channels and forums. Figure 2-7 shows the most visible points of access to the Internet from AOL, but in time you'll blaze your own paths to the Net. The best Net services and resources on AOL are available in Net Highlights (see "Net Highlights or, What Happened to the Internet Connection?").

Net Highlights or, What Happened to the Internet Connection?

Until recently, AOL made its Internet services and most of its links to Internet sites available in a single place, the Internet Connection. Nowadays, since all channels give you access to Internet sites and since the browser has become familiar to more and more AOL members, the need for an Internet channel has decreased. It's more fun to go directly to the Internet than to read about it!

When you click Internet Connection on the Channel menu (Figure 2-1) or Internet on the Welcome screen (Figure 2-2), you go to a new area called Net Highlights (keyword: Net highlights). This area gives you one-stop access to the core Internet services available to you on AOL, including newsgroups, the World Wide Web, and file transfers (FTP). With each service you also get direct links to the best places on the Internet—great Web sites and cool newsgroups, for example.

Where Is AOL's Web Site?

From the main AOL window, click the little globe on the AOL tool bar to go directly to the America Online Web site, shown in Figure 2-8. Keyword: WWW and keyword: Web do the same thing. In Chapter 6 you'll find out more about this site and learn how to adjust your Web preferences so that a different Web page comes up when you click the globe or use those keywords.

How Do I Get to a Web Page Other Than AOL's?

The Keyword window (available on the tool bar, from the Go To menu, or by pressing CTRL-K) lets you go directly to any Web site whose address you know. Just enter the full address (for example, **http://www.netscape.com**). If you have a

Send an email message anywhere in the world

Explore the Web

Visit any Internet site or newsgroup whose address you know

Read your AOL and Internet email

Net Highlights: the best of the Net on AOL

FIGURE 2-7 The Internet is everywhere when you're on AOL. Here are some menus, icons, and keywords to start your exploration

browser open, enter the URL or Web address in the box at the top of the browser and press ENTER. See "Your Key(word) to the Internet."

Where Do I Go to Create My Own Web Page?

At keyword: Personal Publisher (or simply PP2) you will find everything you need to create your own "personal page" on the World Wide Web. Making your own page is a breeze on AOL, as you'll see in Chapter 7.

Where Do I Go to Send or Receive E-mail?

Let your mom or your accountant or your elected representative hear from you! E-mail is always a click away on AOL because you can read your mail and send a message from the tool bar. (Figure 2-3 shows the New Mail window, where you read your e-mail). Chapters 3 and 4 provide all you need to know to become a Great Communicator.

FIGURE 2-8   The America Online World Wide Web site is one of the most frequented on the Internet—and one of the best places to start exploring the Net

Where Do I Go to Take Part in a Global Bulletin Board (Newsgroup)?

Newsgroups are like bulletin boards devoted to topics ranging from scuba diving to vegetarian cooking. You can read postings from the more than 20,000 newsgroups carried by AOL, or you can write newsgroup postings for millions of people to see. Keyword: Newsgroups takes you to the Newsgroups window. In Chapter 5 you'll get the complete scoop on newsgroups.

Where Do I Go to Get Internet Software?

You don't have to go onto the Internet to get the best Internet software. AOL's software library at keyword: Software has a huge archive for you to choose from—and the programs are virus-free! If you need additional files or want to download files from the Internet, you can use FTP, the Net's File Transfer Protocol, which is always available at keyword: FTP. Chapter 8 provides everything you need to know about getting files from either AOL or the Internet.

DOING SEVERAL THINGS AT ONCE ON AOL

The Internet is made up of lots of different types of information which you can access with different types of programs (an e-mail reader, Web browser, and newsgroup reader, for example). You can easily use several Internet programs at the same time while also taking part in exclusive AOL activities such as chatting, sending Instant Messages, and exploring forums. You can open one window to read your e-mail, another to browse the Web, and yet another to make a confession to NetGirl or do stock research.

Of course, with two hands and limited time, you can really only *do* one thing at a time, but, with several windows open at the same time, you can easily transfer data between windows. You can, for instance, copy a URL (Internet address) from the browser or a newsgroup article into an e-mail message and send it to someone else. In Chapter 3 you'll learn to *hyperlink* the address so that another AOL member can go directly to the Web site by clicking the hyperlink in your e-mail message.

How do you do this? First use the mouse to select what you want to copy. Then press CTRL-C (C is short for copy). Then switch to the window into which you want to "paste" the text and press CTRL-V to paste it (put it somewhere else).

How do you switch between open windows? Pressing CTRL-F6 allows you to view open windows one at a time (called *cycling* through them). You can also find the names of open windows listed at the bottom of the Window menu. Select a window listed in this menu to bring that window to the top of your display. Or, clicking any part of a window brings that window to the top of the pile of open windows.

Tip   *Is your monitor too small? Here's a neat trick I learned from the AOL Tips mailing list to actually increase the amount of* horizontal *space you have on your screen. With several windows open, grab a window and drag it to the left or right (you* grab *a window by clicking its title bar, and, with the mouse button pressed, moving the window). Simply move the window as far to the left or right as you can, and then let go of the mouse button. When you do, you'll see a horizontal scroll bar appear at the* bottom *of your AOL screen. Grab the small box in the scroll bar and move it to the left or right to bring the window you just moved into full view. Now grab the little scroll box again and move it back in the other direction. This brings you back to where you started. You can get AOL Tips free by going to the Go To menu, and selecting Keyword. In the Keyword window type* **Toptips** *in the text box. Then press Go. You can sign up for the mailing list just by clicking a button!*

USING AOL WITH OTHER WINDOWS APPLICATIONS

Working with multiple applications is like working with many windows within a single program. To copy and paste information between programs, use the CTRL-C and CTRL-V keystrokes.

Why would you want to do this? For one thing, anything you *download* (copy to your computer) will likely require another program to use: a word-processing document will require a program such as Word, for example, and a spreadsheet will require a program such as Excel.

FROM HERE....

The road from here can go any direction you want. Personally, I think it's best to get familiar with all of AOL's Internet capabilities, even if (for example) you're most interested in e-mail and the Web. It's worth having a sense of what's possible if only because on AOL so *much* is possible.

The next three chapters of this book are devoted to human communications on the Internet: mail and mailing lists in Chapters 3 and 4 and newsgroups in Chapter 5.

Chapter 3

Communicating
with E-mail

For millions of people, in every country, *electronic mail*, or *e-mail*, or just *mail*, has become a necessity as routine and universal as the telephone and toothbrush. This chapter provides the essential information you need to use e-mail to communicate with people on AOL and the Internet. It covers:

- Addresses and the elements of a message

- Sending and receiving messages

- Sending *effective* messages

- Managing your incoming and outgoing mail

- Sending and receiving files attached to messages

The next chapter is all about the Internet's thousands of e-mail-based communities, also known as mailing lists.

Where Is E-mail on AOL?

On AOL you have a choice of ways of writing and reading e-mail messages:

- You can write e-mail by clicking the Compose icon (showing a pencil) on the tool bar, by selecting Send Mail from the Mail menu, or by using the keyboard shortcut CTRL-M.

- You can read your new e-mail from the Welcome screen by clicking the big You Have Mail button, clicking the New Mail icon (showing a mailbox) on the tool bar, or selecting Read Mail from the Mail menu.

The Mail Center, available from the Mail menu, is loaded with advice, tips, and troubleshooting hints.

IT'S ALL IN THE MESSAGE

Think of an e-mail message in terms of the letters you get via the U.S. Postal Service. Both have a sender and a recipient, and both contain a *message* that one person wants to share with another.

However, e-mail differs in many ways from paper mail, and the differences are what make e-mail a better medium in some ways:

- The same e-mail message can go, at no extra cost, to many people at the same time.

- E-mail messages allow for a subject line that states, in the sender's words, what the e-mail message is about, such as "Urgent request" or "History of lemurs." The subject line is a courtesy to the person receiving the message. When you receive e-mail on AOL, the Subject line can help you figure out which messages to read first. Subject lines can also help you keep track of old messages.

 AOL requires you to supply a subject, or short description of the content, in all the messages you send.

- E-mail messages can have useful files attached to them—anything from a Word document or an electronic newsletter to a MIDI sound file. It's easier to get files via e-mail than via FTP or the Web (discussed in Chapters 6 and 8), and there's no extra charge.

WHAT IS AN E-MAIL ADDRESS?

How does your message get to someone else's computer? That's the purpose of the e-mail address you include when you send the message. Your e-mail address is typical of any Internet address. It has two simple parts, the user name and the domain name, separated by the "at" sign (@). Think of the *user name* as a person and the *domain name* as the computer attached to the Internet through which the person gets access.

What Is Your Internet E-Mail Address?

Anyone sending you an e-mail message over the Internet must know your e-mail address. There is a very simple formula for figuring out your e-mail address on the Internet. Just take your screen name and add an "at" sign (@) and **aol.com**. If your screen name is SteveCase, anyone with Internet access, anywhere in the world, can send a message to you by addressing it to **stevecase@aol.com**. It doesn't matter whether you use uppercase or lowercase letters, although lowercase is the norm.

Don't know your screen name or the screen name you're currently using? Just check out the title bar of the Welcome screen (Figure 2-2 in Chapter 2 shows mine).

Who You Are on the Internet: User Name

A *user name* on the Internet is the same thing as a *screen name* on AOL: it's the bit of text that identifies individual people on a specific network. On AOL, for example, other members can get mail to you just by using your screen name.

Usually, user names and screen names clearly refer to an actual person or are chosen so that they can be easily remembered. On the Net, it's common to use some combination of first and last names to create a user name. On AOL, there is a stronger tendency to choose personas and amusing names.

Tip *If you're going to get and receive much Internet mail, you might want to create a special screen name that clearly reflects who you are, especially if you plan to take an active part in mailing lists (Chapter 4). On the Internet you'll find AOL-style nicknames on IRC and MUDs, discussed in Chapter 10.*

Where You Are on the Internet: Domain Name

People use *domain names* to identify and communicate with computers connected to the Internet. Every domain name is unique. A domain name has two or more parts, proceeding from specific to general and separated by periods, pronounced "dots" when spoken. Your domain name, **aol.com**, is pronounced "a-o-l dot c-o-m."

The last part of a domain name (*gov*, for example) is considered the "top-level domain," the most general part. Domains outside the U.S. *usually* have two-character top-level domains: *fi* for Finland, *dk* for Denmark, *ca* for Canada, *uk* for the United Kingdom, and so on. In the U.S., top-level domains *usually* have one of the three-letter names shown in Table 3-1:

Domain	Example	Description
com	**aol.com**	commercial domains (a huge group and the fastest-growing category)
edu	**rtfm.mit.edu**	non-profit educational institutions
net	**commerce.net**	a large group, usually networks
mil	**dscc.dla.mil**	domains operated by a branch of the U.S. armed services
gov	**helix.nih.gov**	non-military domains owned and operated by the U.S. government
org	**eff.org**	non-profit organizations

TABLE 3-1 Top-level three-letter domains

The system works well but isn't always predictable. Many American schools, for example, belong to the Departments of Education of their states and not to an *edu* domain. My kids' schools have the domain name of **mcps.k12.md.us** (Montgomery County Public Schools, grades K through 12, in the state of Maryland, USA). In using a two-letter top-level domain, this particular domain name is consistent with the international practice of using two-letter country codes to indicate a country. Some foreign domain names have top-level names that indicate both domain type *and* country. In the United Kingdom, for example, university (*ac*ademic) domain names sometimes end in **ac.uk** and commercial domain names in **co.uk**. In the near future the system is likely to be dramatically expanded through the creation of new top-level domains, some with more than three letters. A few of the new domains under consideration are *store*, *info*, and *inc*.

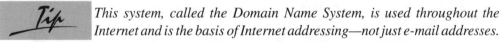

This system, called the Domain Name System, is used throughout the Internet and is the basis of Internet addressing—not just e-mail addresses. Chapter 6 goes into Internet addresses, commonly known as URLs.

COMPOSING AND SENDING AN E-MAIL MESSAGE

To compose a new message from scratch, click the Compose icon on your tool bar:

Every message you compose on AOL uses the window you see in Figure 3-1. It doesn't matter whether you're composing a brand-new message or replying to or forwarding a message you've received from someone else. In each case, you use the same window.

With AOL's mail program you must provide the following three pieces of information every time you start writing a new message:

■   The **recipient's e-mail address** goes in the To field. If the recipient is on AOL, all you have to do is fill in the screen name; you can omit **@aol.com**. Recipients on the Net require full e-mail addresses—user names plus host names.

FIGURE 3-1   Compose your messages here, whether they're going to AOL or the Internet. Don't forget to fill in the To and Subject boxes!

Note *E-mail addresses must be exact, in contrast to paper mail. While the U.S. Post Office might be able to figure out the sender's intentions if the recipient's address is hard to read or partially incorrect, the mail computers on the Internet need to have everything exactly right. The importance of addresses isn't unique to AOL; it's the way network computers work. Just like regular letters, messages that can't be delivered over the Internet come back—they bounce—and they'll be returned to you with a cryptic message. On AOL you'll know right away if you attempt to send a message to an AOL screen name that doesn't exist. However, if you misspell an Internet address, your message will be sent and then bounced as undeliverable, because AOL cannot check the accuracy of Internet e-mail addresses you put in the To or CC field. Double-check your Internet addresses before clicking Send!*

- The message's **subject**, in the Subject line, which gives your recipient some idea of what the message is about.

- The **message** itself, in the big box with the scroll bar. A message can be a word or several pages; an entire book could be written about how to write messages. "Putting Your Best Foot Forward," at the end of this chapter, has tips for writing messages that get attention.

If you leave out any one of these pieces of information, you won't be able to send the message. Instead, you'll get an AOL error message and be asked to supply the missing information.

Tip *You can compose e-mail when you're offline. Just run the AOL software, and, without signing on, click the Compose Mail icon on the tool bar. When you're ready to send the message, sign on (the message will still be there) and click Send.*

Sending E-Mail to More Than One Recipient

When you're sending mail to more than one person, separate their addresses by commas. It doesn't matter whether they're on AOL or not on AOL; you put their addresses in any order, separated by commas. If you find yourself sending messages to the same group of people over and over, you can use AOL's Address Book to create a special distribution list, so that you can send one message automatically to everyone on the list (see "Keeping an Address Book on America Online," later in this chapter).

Differences Between AOL Mail and Internet Mail

In principle, sending e-mail over the Internet seems just like sending it to someone on AOL, but in practice there are some important differences:

- **Address.** On AOL the person to whom you send messages can be addressed by screen name alone. On the Net you must know the domain name as well. This is standard practice, by the way. If you omit the domain name, the Net's mail protocol assumes you're sending the mail to someone on the same domain as you. So if you leave off the domain in that message to **kevin@northcoast.com**, the kevin whose domain is **@aol.com** will get your message. This is one error that AOL is not going to catch!

- **File size.** You cannot send or receive file attachments greater than about 2 Mb over the Internet. On AOL-to-AOL mail, however, the limit is higher—about 16 Mb. See "Working with Files: Getting and Sending Attachments."

- **Ability to unsend.** Once a message has left AOL and gone on to someone on the Internet, AOL knows nothing of its whereabouts. Thus, you can't change your mind and unsend it, as you can with a message sent over AOL to someone on AOL.

- **Availability of status.** Likewise, the status of a message sent over the Internet is not available. See "If You Change Your Mind: Unsending a Message," later in this chapter.

CCing and BCCing

You'll often want others to be apprised of messages you send. For example, in a company setting, you may want to notify your boss if you're sending a message to her boss or someone outside the department. With AOL you can send a *carbon copy* (also known as a *courtesy copy*) to people who should know of your message but aren't its main recipients.

There's often a subtle calculation involved in choosing the persons to CC. If you've prepared a long report for someone and are sending it as an attached file, CCing your boss can make your boss the true recipient. There can be a downside, too. If the message turns into a thread—a series of replies and counter-replies—anyone initially CCed may want to take part.

Finding Mail Help on AOL

ONLY ON AOL

Several areas on AOL provide online help and information as you use e-mail. The Mail Center, available from the Mail menu, offers a tutorial, FAQs (compilations of frequently asked questions), links to e-mail resources, and message boards. The focus of the Mail Center is on e-mail sent from one member to another. (By the way, if you've been on AOL for awhile, you'll know that the Mail Center used to be called the Post Office.)

The E-mail Gateway (keyword: Mail gateway) is a good compact overview of AOL's Internet e-mail capabilities. An even more comprehensive overview of AOL's Internet mail capabilities is now available in the Net.help area (keyword: Nethelp).

Tip　　*If a message to many direct (To) and indirect (CC) recipients turns into a two-way discussion or becomes personal in any way, it's a good idea to prune the list of participants. This way you can turn a potential free-for-all into a true tête-à-tête. To do this, edit the To and CC fields when you make replies (covered later in this chapter).*

To CC someone, just put their addresses in the CC: field. For multiple people being CCed, separate their names by commas. These recipients can be on AOL or the Internet and in any order—although alphabetizing long lists can keep feathers from getting ruffled if certain people don't like to be listed last.

A BCC, short for *blind carbon copy*, is an even subtler and riskier proposition. Unlike a regular CC, BCCs, as the name suggests, are carbon copies that the direct (To) recipients won't be aware of.

There's a downside here, too. Imagine that you *receive* a BCC but neglect to notice that the sender wanted to keep the BCC secret from the direct recipients. Suppose you decide to reply to the message and you send your reply to the original sender and all the direct recipients. The "To" recipient(s) may be offended by this botched attempt at secrecy.

An occasion where BCCs do make sense is when you don't want a long list of recipients of the same message to know of each other's existence (or e-mail address).

Say you want to send a joke out to both coworkers and family or friends, and you don't want the coworkers to see the addresses of your family or friends, and vice versa.

To send a BCC:

- In the CC field, place any recipients' addresses *in parentheses*. For multiple BCC recipients, separate the addresses-in-parentheses by commas. You can BCC people on AOL and the Net, in any order. In the CC field, you can use both BCCs and CCs.

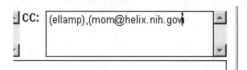

Sending Your Message

With the address(es) typed in, write a short and punchy Subject line to characterize the content of your message. Now type your message in the big box, as shown in Figure 3-1.

Once you've composed a message, you send it on its way by clicking Send. Clicking Send Later places your message in a *queue* to be sent either during a FlashSession (discussed in the next chapter) or when you're ready to sign off AOL. (The message is available by selecting Read Outgoing Flashmail from the Mail menu.) After you click Send, the message closes automatically, and a little window comes up confirming that the message was sent. Click OK.

AOL gives you the choice of *not* closing the message you just sent (See "Mail Preferences.") Why? It's a good way to double-check your message. If you change your mind about sending the message, AOL gives you a way to *unsend* messages sent to other people on AOL. Keeping a message open is also an alternative to using blind carbon copies (BCCs). For example, after you've sent a message to the direct recipient, you can change the To: and CC: addresses to another address. It's an easy way of sending multiple copies of the same e-mail without rewriting it.

Another reason to keep a message open after you've sent it is to save it—an alternative to using your Personal Filing Cabinet (see the "Saving and Printing Messages" section on that feature). With the message displayed, go to the File menu and select Save As, then provide a filename and directory.

Cancelling a Message

If you decide not to send a message and you've got Windows 95, just click the little X in the upper right-hand corner. In Windows 3.1, double-click in the control box in the upper left-hand corner. If you've entered any of the three required pieces of information—the To field, the Subject field, and the message itself—you'll be asked whether you want to save the message. Click Yes if you do, then navigate to a directory (folder) where you want to save your message and give it a name. With the message saved, you can later edit it with a word processor or AOL's built-in text editor. You bring up the text editor by simply going to AOL's File menu and choosing Open, then hunting for that message.

Mail Preferences

America Online lets you define several aspects of the way you use e-mail—for example, you can confirm that messages have been sent and you can store your messages in your Personal Filing Cabinet. Some of these aspects will matter to you more than others. Specific preferences are discussed throughout this chapter.

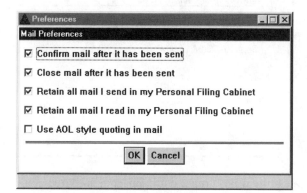

To bring up this window, click the MyAOL button in the tool bar, click first on Preferences, then on Mail Preferences, and, finally, on Set Up Now. Check or uncheck a preference by clicking inside the little box. Click OK when you're done.

If You Change Your Mind: Unsending a Message

I unsend messages for many reasons: I reread my message and find I've been intemperate, or that I've made a typo, or that, for some reason, the file I wanted to attach didn't get attached.

 You can unsend messages to other AOL members but not to people on the Internet.

To reread a message you've sent, go to the Mail menu and select Check Mail You've Sent. In the Outgoing Mail window, double-click the message. The last message sent will be at the top of the list.

To unsend the message:

1. Select the message from the Outgoing Mail window, and click the Status button. If the message has been read, the screen name of the recipient will appear alongside the time the message was opened.

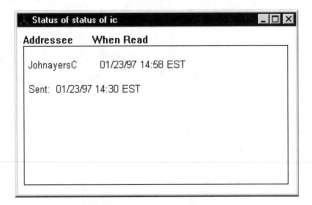

2. If the message wasn't read, click Unsend, and then confirm that you don't want to keep a copy of the message. If the message went to more than one recipient, and if any one of them has read the message, you can't unsend it to the others. If a message goes out to a couple of people and if one of those people is on the Internet, it can't be unsent either.

KEEPING AN ADDRESS BOOK ON AMERICA ONLINE

AOL's Address Book makes it easier for you to keep track of those complex Internet addresses. It can help you create miniature mailing lists, too, so you can routinely send a message to the same group of people. The Address Book can keep your Net mail from bouncing and vastly simplify your communication with the small groups you're routinely in touch with, especially if group members have messy numerical MCI or CompuServe addresses.

Tip *You can edit your Address Book while offline, which is useful if you compose offline messages or if you don't want to sign on just to add someone's address.*

To add an entry to your Address Book:

1. Bring up the Address Book by selecting Edit Address Book from the Mail window.

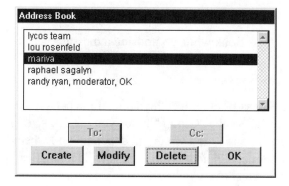

2. Click the Create button. The Address Group window comes up.

The window has two boxes for entering text. In the Group Name box, type in the names you want to see in the Address Book—the personal name or nickname you associate with the e-mail address or the group name, if you're creating a *list* of addresses to communicate with at the same time.

Note *The term* Group Name *is confusing, since you can use the Address Book to keep track of individual addresses as well as group names. Group Name is like a nickname—it's the way you think of the person or people to whom you regularly send messages.*

In the Screen Names box, you enter the e-mail address(es) of the person or group you put in Group Name. Separate multiple names by commas, just as in the To and CC fields of the Compose Mail window.

3. Click OK.

To use your Address Book while composing a message:

1. Click Address Book.

2. From the Address Book, select the name of the person to whom you want to send a message—the "Group Name" you used in setting up the entry. Click the To button or the CC button, depending on whether the person is a direct or indirect recipient. The address will automatically be plugged into the field you chose. Click OK.

3. Type and send your message!

Note *Using the Address Book is like having your own personal mailing list software. Although less powerful than a mailing list, the Address Book automates the task of sending one message to many people, and it's easy to maintain. Dramatic changes are planned in the near future for AOL's Address Book that will make it even easier and more flexible. Mailing lists are covered in depth in the next chapter.*

Finding an Address

The million-dollar question is, "How do you find someone's Internet e-mail address?" A few years ago, the answer was highly involved, requiring a raft of complex programs such as **whois** and **netfind** and other tools devised in the days when Internet users were likely to be researchers or network adminstrators. Today it's a lot easier to find an e-mail address. On AOL, start with the Member Directory (available from the Members menu); on the Internet, start with BigFoot, which is available over the World Wide Web (**http://www.bigfoot.com**). This and other Web services are discussed in Chapter 9.

ADDING PIZZAZZ TO YOUR AOL MAIL

E-mail is ugly! Black letters against a white background, just like a typewriter. With version 3.0, AOL gives you the ability to make your messages more visually pleasing. However, this neat new feature is available only for your messages to other AOL members, so your creations won't be appreciated on the Internet.

In your member-to-member messages you can now take your text and add flair, color, and outrageous effects:

- Text color

- Background color

- Font

- Text size

- Style (bold, italic, underlining)

- Alignment (to align a message with the left, right, or both margins, or to center it)

Applying these features couldn't be easier. In the Compose Mail window, type a message. Use your mouse to select some text. Now click each of the little buttons to see what it does (Figure 3-2). Figure 3-3 shows a formatted message.

Formatting gives you some powerful new ways to emphasize words: italics for important words, large bold text for headers, and colors for attention-getting backgrounds, for example. Like all such effects, these mail enhancements can also be distracting, so, unless you're writing ransom notes, only use them when they reinforce your point.

Tip　*In your mail to AOL members, you can even add bullets, those dots you use in a word processor to list things. Here's how: with the cursor at the beginning of a line, hold down the* ALT *key and, keeping it pressed down, type 249 on your numeric keypad, then release the* ALT *key. But don't put symbols in your non-AOL mail. They won't make it through AOL's e-mail gateway to the Internet.*

Adding Clickable Hyperlinks to Your AOL Mail

Another hot new feature added with Version 3.0 is embedded *hyperlinks*. A hyperlink (or just *link*) is a special kind of text that, when you click it, takes you to a Web site

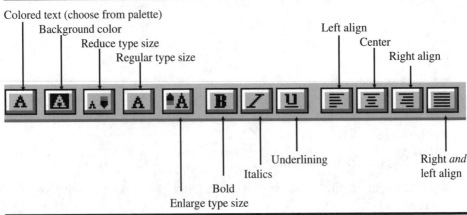

FIGURE 3-2　Formatting your e-mail message is now easy on AOL

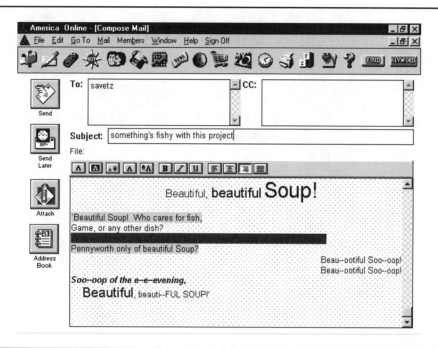

FIGURE 3-3   An awful-looking e-mail message. See if you can do better

or AOL area (jump ahead to Chapter 6 to find out more about linking). Like formatting, hyperlinks are available only in messages sent to other AOL members. They will *usually* be "stripped out" of messages to people who aren't on AOL.

There are two ways to add hyperlinks:

■ *If you know the Internet address (or URL).* Select some text in a message you're writing in the Compose Mail window. Ideally, the text should concretely describe the site—it's what gives the recipient the *incentive* to click. Click the right mouse button and select Create Hyperlink. In the Edit Hyperlink window, type in a Web address (which usually begins **http://**). Click OK, finish the message, and send it. Chapter 6 discusses URLs in detail.

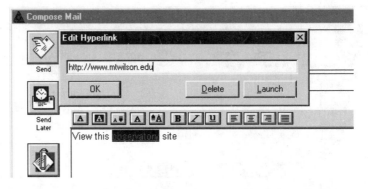

- *If the site you want to link to is in your Favorite Places folder.* If you want to send a link to an AOL forum, use this method. Select some text in your message. Open your Favorite Places folder and position it so you can see it and the selected text at the same time. Now click and drag the item from Favorite Places onto the selected text of your e-mail message. Double-click the Favorite Places item to make sure it's the one you want. Then finish the message, and send it. You can add hyperlinks even when you're offline this way.

This is what the recipient of the message sees. Clicking the underlined text takes your friend to one of your favorite places on AOL or the Internet:

View this <u>observatory</u> site

WORKING WITH FILES: GETTING AND SENDING ATTACHMENTS

Files are everywhere when you use a PC. You use files when you create documents with your word processor or spreadsheet, when you install AOL, and when you make a Web page. Early in the history of the Internet, it was discovered that files could be attached to e-mail messages and could thus be exchanged almost as easily as simple messages (that was before they invented FTP, the standard way of transferring files, discussed in Chapter 8). On AOL, it's easy to attach files to messages you send. Likewise, you can receive files if they've been attached to messages sent to you. The next section is about attaching files; see also "Retrieving a File from a Message" a little later in this chapter.

Note *As a rule of thumb, you can both send and receive over the Internet any file that's less than 2 Mb. Ordinary word processing documents are rarely greater than 50K (1/40th of 2 Mb). A more realistic limit is 1 Mb, according to David O'Donnell, AOL's Postmaster. Don't know how big your file is? Using Windows 3.1's File Manager or Windows 95's Explorer, navigate to the folder (directory) where the file you want to send is located and look in the Size column.*

Attaching a File to a Message

AOL makes it easy to attach any file you want to a message as long as you know its filename and location. I use this feature daily for sending screen captures (such as the figures used in this book), contracts, chapters, drafts, outlines, and other word-processed documents (files) relating to the writing process. On AOL, you can send files both to other members and over the Net; with multiple To's and CCs you can simultaneously send the *same* attachment to several people on AOL and the Net.

There's one hitch, but it's a small one. AOL's e-mail program adheres to a standard called "MIME," the Multipurpose Internet Mail Extension, which was designed to simplify the transfer of files through the gateways that separate different e-mail systems. To send someone a file attachment over the Internet, your recipient must also be using an e-mail program that supports MIME. Basically, MIME works by converting your *binary* document (a formatted word-processed file, say) into a *text* document, and then telling the recipient's e-mail program how to handle the attached file. Sometimes a MIME document is received as gibberish and has to be *decoded*, but there is plenty of software on AOL that will do this.

To attach a file to your e-mail:

1. With the Compose Mail window open, type in the recipient's address, the subject, and the message, then click the Attach button. The Attach File window comes up.

2. Navigate to the place on your hard disk where the file is located, then double-click the file. The filename appears in small letters under the Subject line.

3. Click Send. The File Transfer box, with its *thermometer* (blue bar), now pops up to tell you that your file is being sent; it measures the percentage of the file that's been uploaded from your PC to AOL's server and tells you the amount of time left before the file will be completely uploaded. A little window tells you when your file has been sent. Click OK.

Note   *The AOL for Windows software does not yet let you attach multiple files (and automatically "stuff" them into a single file), unlike the AOL for Mac software. Look for this feature in the near future.*

If you change your mind before sending a file as an attachment, just click the Detach button. After you've sent a file, you can check whether the message was read but not whether the file was downloaded and used. To check the message status, from the Mail menu select Check Mail You Have Sent, select the message, and click Status.

Tip   *You cannot send a file that is in use by some other program, such as a spreadsheet that's still open in Excel. Some programs, such as Microsoft's Word, don't "let go" of files even after you've closed the document. If a file is either in use by another program or still in its grip (as in the annoying case of Word), it will appear that your file is attached to your message, but it won't be sent. You'll have to close the application (Word, in this case), and then send the file again. To avoid embarrassment, you should probably unsend the file-less message.*

Sending Spam

The Internet term for unsolicited mail is *spam*. Sending spam on the Internet is a taboo, but not because Internet denizens have delicate feelings. Rather, spam wastes space on people's hard disks, wastes network bandwidth, and wastes the time of many, perhaps thousands of people. For most people, it's a nuisance, and for some it's an invasion of privacy.

Sending spam from AOL is a bad idea. Here's the official word from AOL's Community Action Team (CAT):

"If you send unsolicited commercial e-mail messages to individuals on AOL or on the Internet, you run the same risk as in posting such messages to mailing lists. You may receive a TOS warning, and repeated violations may lead to the termination of your AOL account."

See "Avoiding Spam" a little later in this chapter for tips on avoiding junk e-mail.

YOU'VE GOT MAIL! READING YOUR MAIL

You've got mail! If your PC is equipped for sound, you may have heard a male voice say this to you when you signed onto AOL. Reading your mail is easy on AOL. Just click the big You Have Mail button on the Welcome screen. You can read your mail at any point during an AOL session by clicking the Mailbox icon on your main tool bar at the top of the screen.

The New Mail window, or New mailbox, now comes up. This is the most important mailbox (see Figure 3-4) of three mailboxes. (You've already seen the Outgoing mailbox, where you check the status of mail you've sent. The final mailbox is for Old mail, messages you have read but are not "kept as new.") Each mailbox looks the same but has different mail-processing buttons at the bottom of its window. All the mailboxes are discussed further in "Managing Your Mailboxes," later in this chapter.

With the New mailbox open, what do you read first? I get a lot of mail and usually start by scanning the subjects and senders. I read personal messages first. Then I

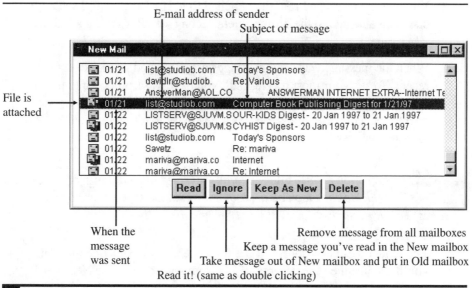

FIGURE 3-4   New mail arrives throughout the day and night on the Internet

read mailing lists; they're not personal, but deal with subjects I care about and contain messages from people whose opinions I want to know. Junk mail usually stands out because of the unknown sender and cheesy subject line:

> MAKE MONEY EVEN FASTER!

Such mail I'm likely to delete instantly, although AOL has a new and useful way to deal with such stuff automatically (see the "Avoiding Spam" box) so it won't even get to your mailbox.

> *Tip* *On AOL, you can use FlashSessions to do most of your mail-reading offline. The technique is especially useful if you have a high volume of mail or subscribe to many mailing lists. You can read about FlashSessions in Chapter 4.*

Each line of your mailbox is devoted to a single message and has four pieces of information (Figure 3-4):

- Whether the message has a file attached to it. If it does, you'll see a little disk icon attached to the ordinary letter icon (see "Retrieving a File from a Message").

- When the message was sent, messages are displayed from oldest to most recent. To see your most recent mail, you have to scroll down to the end of the list. The date and time a message was sent automatically appears next to the letter icon and serves as a postmark to tell you when the message was sent.

> *Note* *Messages you receive* after *opening the New Mail window won't show up. Click the Mailbox icon on the tool bar again to see whether you have new messages. The newest messages will be at the end of the list.*

- The sender's e-mail address. If the message is from someone on AOL, you'll see just the screen name. If it's from someone on the Net, you'll see the domain name as well. If it's from a mailing list, you'll see the name of the software that sent the message (LISTSERV, for example). Chapter 4 delves further into the mysteries of mailing lists.

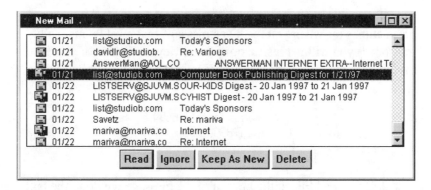

- The message's Subject line, exactly as the sender typed it. If the Subject doesn't fit in the space allotted, it will be cut off.

To open a message, just double-click on it or select the message and click Read.

Tip *If you get a message that you don't want to respond to right away or that you want to keep for future reference, close it, select it in New Mail, then click Keep as New. This will keep the message in New Mail.*

Retrieving a File from a Message

You can always tell if someone's sent you a file as an attachment to their message. Ordinarily, a new message sent to you has this little icon in its header:

If there's an attachment, you'll see:

To retrieve a file:

1. To open a message in New Mail window, double-click it. Just under the headers, you will see the name and size of the file, plus the estimated time

it will take for you to retrieve the file given the speed of your modem. Sometimes (as when you receive a message that must be manually decoded) you will get instructions for retrieving the file or you'll be referred to the Mail Center for more information.

| File: computer.txt (46594 bytes)
| DL Time (28800 bps): < 1 minute

2. Click Download File at the bottom of the message window (the button appears when there's something to download). Click Download Later if you want to download the file later (during a FlashSession) or just before signing off. The file will be in your Download Manager (available from the File menu).

3. In AOL's Download Manager window, confirm the filename (change it, if you want) and navigate to a directory on your hard disk where you want to store it. (The default—AOL's first choice—is to download the file using its original name and to drop it into the Download subdirectory of the current AOL directory.) Click OK to confirm either the default or the directory of your choice. If a file of the same name already exists, you'll be asked to confirm that you want to get this file and overwrite (delete) the existing one. (This happens all the time with mailing list digests because they usually have the same name. It's unlikely you'll want to save the existing file in this case, but if you do, rename the one you're downloading, and then click OK.) The File Transfer box (just like the one you see when you attach and send a file) tracks the download and tells you when it's done.

Note *AOL's Download Manager, available from the File menu even when you're offline, is a wonderful tool for keeping track of files you download, whether you get them from an FTP site, a newsgroup, an e-mail message, or an AOL software library. It conveniently lets you download files in batches, and it helps you keep track of the names of downloaded files and the directories in which you placed them. See Chapter 8 for more information about AOL's Download Manager.*

To make use of the file you've downloaded, you'll need a program to view it, play it, run it—in other words, to let it do whatever it does. In some cases, AOL gives

Managing Your Mailboxes

On AOL every screen name gets three mailboxes on one of AOL's "host" computers. Because we're talking about *AOL's* computers here, you cannot keep unlimited amounts of mail, but AOL is generous in its limits:

- **New** mailbox—messages you haven't yet read or that you have read and decided to keep as new

- **Old** mailbox—messages you've read in the past three to five days and haven't kept as new

- **Outgoing** mailbox—messages you've sent in the past month (27 days, actually).

If you want to save all your messages, you can do so on *your* computer using one of the techniques described in "Saving and Printing Messages" at the end of this chapter.

Here's how AOL handles your mail from the three mailboxes. Every message you *send* goes into your Outgoing mailbox (from the Mail menu, choose Check Mail You've Sent). This mailbox can hold up to 550 messages, and the oldest messages will get bumped by new ones when you reach this magic number. Also, no outgoing message is available after about a month, no matter how many messages are in the mailbox.

Your Old mailbox holds messages that you've read *but not kept as New*. Your Old mailbox holds only about four days' worth of e-mail, so it's only useful if you've accidentally neglected to keep-as-new a message you recently read. To see your Old mailbox, go to the Mail menu and select Check Mail You've Read.

Every message you receive goes into your New mailbox (what you get when you click the big You Have Mail button), which can also hold 550 messages. The 550 figure includes the small number of messages in your Old mailbox.

Sound complicated? Just remember to prune your New mailbox, deleting messages so it never gets full, as explained in the "Managing Your Messages" section. Keep-as-new your most important recent messages. And actively use your Personal Filing Cabinets, so you can keep the mail you've read and sent on your computer, as explained later in "Use Your Personal Filing Cabinets to Save Your Messages."

you the tools you need. In other cases, you'll need a special application that could be anything from an MPEG viewer for a video file or a word processor for a **.doc** file. If you've downloaded a program, you will probably want to run the file from Windows's File menu (Windows 3.1) or taskbar (Windows 95). Chapter 8 gives you lots of advice for using files of different formats.

Some files you download will not be usable with any program you have on your computer because they are either encoded (scrambled, to facilitate transfer as text) or compressed (reduced, for quicker download). The message with the attached file will indicate what kind of file is attached—a MIME file (.MME), UUencoded file (.UUE), or compressed (.ZIP) file, for example. In any of these cases, you'll need a special program to decode or decompress the file and make it useful. At keyword: File Search, you can search AOL's great download libraries for a program to help you with this. Do a search, using the type of file type as a keyword. Now, download the program, run it, and follow the instructions (on the screen or in the Help menu) for converting files.

 Three programs I like for decoding or decompressing attached files are **Stuffit**, *a Macintosh program now available for Windows (useful for unzipping certain files),* **WinZip** *(for creating zipped files as well as unzipping them); and* **ZRFW**, *which can decode UUE and MME files. All are available, free, on AOL at keyword: File Search.*

Replying to and Forwarding a Message with an Attachment

If someone sends you an attachment and you reply to it, the attachment won't be included with the reply. If someone sends you an attachment and you forward it to someone else, the attachment *will* be included. You aren't given the option of detaching the file when you forward a message.

USING MAIL CONTROLS TO FILTER INCOMING MAIL

 If you're a parent, you may wish to restrict e-mail access for children who have screen names on your master account (the account you registered with). There are strangers on the Internet, just as there are in the real world. If you don't want your children "talking to strangers," you may well want to take advantage of these controls. Here's how:

1. Go to keyword: Parental to go to the Parental Controls area. Click on Custom Controls. In the Custom Controls window, click Mail, then Mail Controls. Finally, select the screen name(s) for which you want to limit incoming mail. The E-mail Parental Controls window, shown in Figure 3-5, comes up.

2. Make *one* of the following choices:

   ■ Allow all mail to the screen name

   ■ Block all mail to the screen name

   ■ Allow e-mail to and from specific people (you must list their addresses at the right side of the screen)

   ■ Block e-mail to and from specific people (you must list their addresses at the right side of the screen)

FIGURE 3-5   Decide exactly what kind of e-mail you want a minor to send and receive

If you allow receipt of *any* mail, you can then choose to block all file attachments. If you choose to add or block *specific* e-mail addresses, you must enter the prohibited or allowed addresses one at a time in the Add address field (clicking the "Add address" button after each entry). To remove addresses from the list, just select and click Remove. Click OK when you're done.

 One of the purposes of blocking attachments is to block the exchange of possibly offensive materials.

 ## Avoiding Spam

Junk e-mail—unsolicited commercial mail—is an unpleasant by-product of the commercialization of the Internet. It is usually sent out of ignorance of how the Internet works. As people learn about you or see your screen name on AOL (especially in chat rooms and message boards), you may find yourself the recipient of such unwelcome mail.

AOL offers a unique, free service called Preferred Mail™ (keyword: Preferred mail), which filters out all mail addressed to you from mail addresses known to send unsolicited commercial messages on the Internet. These are the messages that show up from unknown senders with Subject lines that are meant to entice and with messages that usually try to separate you from your money. If you don't mind getting such messages, just click in the "I want mass e-mail solicitations from all these sites!" box.

To receive e-mail from a specific domain on the "blocked list," you can unblock the domain for any screen name at keyword: Mail Controls (Figure 3-5). First, make sure "Allow all mail" is selected on the left. Then, in the E-mail Address list, type in the addresses from which you'd like to receive mail and press ENTER.

MANAGING YOUR MESSAGES

Every message you get can be handled in several ways. You can:

■ Read it and respond (reply) to it

■ Read it and forward it to someone else

■ Keep it as new

- Delete it

- Ignore it

Tip   *If you receive more than one e-mail message at a time, you can move to the next message simply by clicking the Next button at the bottom of the screen. To read the previous message, click Prev.*

3

Return Mail: Replying

The easiest way to *send* a message is to reply to a message someone has already sent you. What makes it so easy? When you reply to a message, some or all of the message itself, as well as the address and subject, automatically become part of your new message. All you have to do is write your own message. Usually, you'll want to *quote* the part of the original message to which you want to respond in order to frame and focus your response. If your message elicits a reply, you may be quoted in turn.

Let's say you receive a message, and want to send a message to the person who sent you the message:

1. Use your mouse to select the part of the message to which you want to respond. Select the entire message if there are numerous points you want to reply to. (This is the text that will appear quoted and will be set off by special characters in the recipient's e-mail.) Click either Reply or Reply to All. Replying to All sends your reply to all the recipients of the message, including all the people CCed. If they were CCed on the original message, they'll be CCed on your reply.

2. You'll see a Compose Mail window, with the Subject line in the title bar, preceded by the word *Re* and a colon. Edit the To and CC fields by adding and dropping names (either AOL screen names or Net addresses), remembering to separate multiple addresses by commas.

3. If you want, select the bit of text that forms the first line:

   In a message dated 97-01-21 16:39:21 EST, you write:

   and type in a personal greeting, such as:

   David, in your message you wrote (and I quote):

4. Now type in your actual reply—your comments replying to the original message.

5. When you're done, click Send or Send Later.

Replies are tracked in your Outgoing mailbox, just like any message you send. As with a message you originate from scratch, a reply can be unsent, and you can keep track of its status (whether it's been read). See "If You Change Your Mind: Unsending a Message," earlier in this chapter.

On AOL you have a choice in the way you "quote" in your replies. You can place "AOL-style" quote marks at the beginning and end of the quoted passage (<<...>>), or you can place "Internet-style" quotes at the beginning of each quoted line. In the latter, each line begins with the greater-than sign (>). I strongly prefer the Internet style because it makes clear what is being quoted and makes it possible to reply to several different parts of the original message. The downside is that it looks ugly and there's a possibility for weird formatting when the recipient opens the message. To set your preferences, click MyAOL on the main toolbar, click Set Preferences, select Mail, and click in the appropriate radio button (AOL-style or Internet-style).

Sharing a Message: Forwarding

Forwarding a message means sending it to someone who wasn't a direct (To) or indirect (CC) recipient. As with a reply, you can choose to forward an entire message or a part of it.

To forward a message:

1. With the message-to-be-forwarded displayed, select the exact part of the message to be forwarded and click Forward. Selecting nothing will cause the entire message to be forwarded. A Compose Mail window comes up, with either part of the message quoted or nothing, which is what you see when the whole message is being forwarded.

2. Enter the address(es) of the recipient(s) in the To field, and, if you want, include additional recipients in the CC field.

3. Edit the Subject line if you wish. It will automatically read *Fwd:* plus the Subject line of the forwarded message.

4. Type any comments of your own into the message box; they'll precede the message you're forwarding. Click Send.

Tip *If you use AOL in any kind of a company or organization, forwarding can be a more effective way of taking part in a group exchange than replying. Why? Because forwarding retains the entire message as-is, without the intrusive quote marks that are used in replies. Plus, it preserves the entire thread of the message. For example, if you send a message requesting information to someone who can't help you, but that person then forwards it to another person who forwards it to yet another person, the ultimate recipient will have a complete record of the exchange. The end recipient will know who wanted the information and why, as well as who has already been approached. You're likely to get better and faster information than you would if you pursued it by phone and wound up playing phone tag with several people.*

Keeping as New

When you read a message and then close it and return to the New Mail window, a check appears through it.

☑ 01/21

This tells AOL to remove the message from New Mail when you close New Mail. Next time you open New Mail, the message won't appear, but it will be available for a few days in Old Mail. To keep a message in New Mail, you must select the message and click Keep as New.

Why would you keep a message "new"? It's a good way to keep your most recent mail in one place, especially the personal messages. Why wouldn't you do this? Because it slows down the window's display when you open it, and it is redundant if you're using your Personal Filing Cabinet. The wisely moderate solution is to keep your most important recent messages in your New Mail window and to get into the habit of using your Personal Filing Cabinet (which are always available offline), as explained in the next section.

What if you've read a message and banished it to your Old mailbox (closed the New mailbox after you read it without keeping-as-new)? You can bring it back to your New mailbox by selecting the message from the Old mailbox and clicking Keep as New. It shows up again in the New mailbox next time you open it. See "Managing Your Mailboxes" for an overview of how the different mailboxes work.

Deleting and Ignoring Messages

Of course, you don't have to read, reply to, and forward messages. You can also delete them—even without reading them. Actively deleting messages from your New Mail window is a good idea, because on AOL you can keep only 550 messages in your New and Old mailboxes. While deleting messages makes room for new messages, it doesn't necessarily mean you have to throw away copies of old messages. The next section, "Saving and Printing Messages," offers several techniques for saving messages.

To delete a message that's in your New Mail window, just select the message and click Delete. To delete a bunch of messages that are located right next to each other, hold down the SHIFT key, click on all the messages you want to get rid of, and then click Delete. To delete messages scattered throughout your New mailbox, hold down the CTRL key, click on each message you want to delete, and then click Delete.

If there's a message or messages you don't want to read (a mailing-list thread you aren't following, for example), select the message(s) and click Ignore. Notice the check mark through the message's icon on the far left. This tells AOL that you have either read or acknowledged a message and don't want to retain it as new. Messages you want to Ignore and that you never open won't ever appear in your Personal Filing Cabinet.

SAVING AND PRINTING MESSAGES

AOL gives you several ways of saving copies of individual e-mail messages that you send and receive. In any organization, you may want to keep a record of all messages for legal and archival purposes. Any particularly important individual messages (to bosses or buddies, for example) are worth archiving as well. In general, saving a message can also save you time and trouble.

Any open message can be easily saved on your hard disk as a "text file." With the message displayed, go to the File menu and select Save As. Then give the file a name and find a directory to save it in. You can later read the message by selecting Open from the File menu and navigating to the place where you've stored the message file.

Tip   *Saving a message as a separate text file is the safest way to keep a copy of your message. You can even copy it to a 3 1/2-inch disk for safekeeping. You can't use a word processor to individually access messages kept in your Favorite Places folder or Personal Filing Cabinet, but can access saved messages in this way.*

Use Your Personal Filing Cabinet to Save Your Messages

On AOL, you get three mailboxes for every screen name and up to five screen names for every account! Because AOL deletes old mail to make room for new mail when your new mailbox is full, it is a good idea to use your Personal Filing Cabinet (Figure 3-6) to keep a copy of *every* message you send and receive on your hard disk—not on AOL's computer.

3

1. To store mail in your Personal Filing Cabinet, go to keyword: Preferences, click on Preferences, click on Mail Setup, and click Set Up Now.

2. Make sure there's a check in the boxes by either or both of the two options: "Retain all mail I send in my Personal Filing Cabinet" and "Retain all mail I read in my Personal Filing Cabinet." Click OK.

FIGURE 3-6   Use your Personal Filing Cabinet to keep a copy of all the mail you send and receive

Now messages will automatically be kept on your hard disk and will be available to you when you click the Personal Filing Cabinet icon on the AOL tool bar.

How do you find a message saved in your Personal Filing Cabinet? Clicking the Search button at the bottom of the PFC window gives you a choice of searching messages by their headers or by their *content*—words used in the actual body of old messages you've sent and received. Since you're more likely to know what a message was about than you are to know its exact header, searching by key word can help you quickly zero in on specific messages.

To find a message by what's in its header, click Search. In the Type of Search section of the Search box, click Title Only. Now type your keywords into the Find What box, and click Find Next. Keep clicking until you find what you're looking for. To find a message by what's in the body of the message, click Full Text in the Type of Search field, then proceed as above.

> *Tip* *Messages kept in your Personal Filing Cabinet and Favorite Places folder are available to you even when you're offline. That means you can search, read, and print old messages without having to sign on first.*

Since your Personal Filing Cabinet is created on your hard disk, you should manage it to keep it from getting too big. For one thing, a big Personal Filing Cabinet can take awhile to open and especially close; it can also slow the AOL program overall. To set your Filing Cabinet preferences:

1. Click on the MyAOL icon of your tool bar.

2. Click on Preferences, Filing Cabinet Setup, and Setup Now.

3. Use the Preferences box to indicate how much of your computer to devote to your Personal Filing Cabinet, whether you want to be notified of the deletion of filing cabinet items when the amount of allocated space is reached, and whether you want to be notified when the total amount of disk space reaches a certain percentage of your hard disk space. When you're running out of disk space, you may want to reduce the size of your Personal Filing Cabinets.

Favorite Places

Your Favorite Places folder gives you a way to save individual messages. Like just about any window you see on AOL, e-mail message windows have a little heart on the title bar in the upper right-hand corner. To transfer a message from a mailbox to your Favorite Places folder, click the heart. The message will be moved to the Favorite Places folder.

To read a message saved in this way:

1. Open the Favorite Places folder by clicking the Favorite Places folder on the tool bar:

2. Double-click the message to read it. Note that the standard "Prev" and "Next" buttons don't appear on Favorite-Place e-mail messages. Instead, all you see is a Delete button, which you can click to remove the message from Favorite Places.

Why would you save a message in Favorite Places? In general, it's a way of saving particularly important messages. For example, I use Favorite Places to save the Welcome messages of the mailing lists to which I belong, and I use it to save project-related messages. You can also customize Favorite Places by adding folders for certain kinds of messages. While writing this book, I kept a Favorite Places folder for every chapter, with mail related to specific chapters stored in the appropriate folders.

Tip   *If you're a heavy e-mail user, use both Personal Filing Cabinet (to keep track of everything) and Favorite Places (to keep track of e-mail messages you may want to use for a specific purpose in the future).*

Printing Messages

The reasons for printing messages are pretty straight-forward: to keep a record of a message in your real filing cabinet, to edit it, to read it at your leisure, and so on.

1. Make sure you have a printer attached to your computer, and make sure it works and is turned on. This book can't help you with printer problems, but AOL's Computing channel has special forums devoted to companies that make printers, such as Hewlett-Packard (keyword: Company Connection).

2. Retrieve the message to print so that it's displayed. It may be in a mailbox, your Favorite Places folder, or your Personal Filing Cabinet. Or it may even be saved as a text file.

3. Click the Printer icon on the AOL tool bar just to the left of the Personal Filing Cabinet icon (or simply press CTRL-P):

PUTTING YOUR BEST FOOT FORWARD

Think of an e-mail message in the same way you think of a phone call. In both, you're communicating from a distance. There are plenty of differences between e-mail and a phone call, of course. In e-mail, you can't hear the timbre of someone's voice, and you can't interrupt someone, as you can when they're talking. And e-mail's "asynchronous": you can take as long as you want to respond, since you're not communicating in "real time." Here are some suggestions for communicating as effectively as possible using e-mail.

Cries and Whispers—Don't Do Either in E-mail

A way of showing you really want to get attention is by *shouting*—putting letters in ALL CAPITAL LETTERS. Business spammers, the people who send out unsolicited make-money-fast mail to thousands of people, use the technique all the time. But the attention you get is sure to be negative.

```
GREETINGS FRIEND. HAVE YOU BEEN DREAMING OF BECOMING YOUR OWN
BOSS? DO YOU WANT TO MAKE THOUSANDS OF DOLLARS A WEEK WITHOUT
RISK? WELL...
```

The best way to emphasize individual words in messages you send to someone on AOL is to use italics, as explained in "Adding Pizzazz to Your AOL Mail." To emphasize words in messages sent over the Net, I like to use asterisks on either side of the word (to get some *attention*). Other people use underscores to get _attention_. But, ultimately, the best way to get attention on both AOL and the Net is to write concisely, clearly, and respectfully. Sounds dull, but it's true.

Whispering means using all small letters and no punctuation, and it can be contagious. It looks cool, at first, kind of like an ee cummings poem:

```
hi guys what do you think of that new design have a look at
the comps on the wall and let me know what you think come to
our team meeting today with ideas...
```

Whispering is pleasanter than shouting, but whispered messages can be even harder to read and *parse* (figure out) than shouted messages. Avoiding punctuation can make a message subject to misinterpretation. The alternative? Use well-chosen words and take the time to think through what you want to say.

Take a Deep Breath Before Clicking Send

The powerful features and flexible controls you enjoy on America Online don't always extend to the Internet, which is, after, highly decentralized. In the case of e-mail, for instance, you can't unsend a message after it's been sent. That's just another reason to avoid sending any message you might later regret. It's easy to misunderstand a message you receive because there's no body language to clarify the context, and messages are often hastily typed and sent. Be sure to double-check messages you write so that any emotional freight is clearly marked as such and not subject to misinterpretation. In other words, if you are angry when you write something, count to ten and reread what you've written.

Personalize Your Message

Brevity may be a virtuous way to conserve bandwidth in e-mail, but excessive brevity can sound clipped—insultingly to-the-point and impersonal. Unless this is the message you want to project, it's often a good idea to personalize your messages. Begin with the recipient's name on a separate line, for example. And in replies, make sure to type over the bit that begins

In a message dated 96-10-15 04:53:40 EDT, you write:

Don't be averse to saying "you" in the body of the message. As in any discussion, if you disagree strongly about something, try to find something positive in your opponent's position or some point of agreement, and phrase your criticisms constructively. In e-mail it is simply too easy to take polar positions on issues that are less than profound. Keeping things personal can defuse an e-mail fight (also known as *flame*). Finally, I like to end messages with a "thanks" and my real name. On mailing lists in particular, nothing is more annoying than not knowing the real person behind a strong opinion.

Quote Aptly

You'll save a recipient's time (multiplied by the number of recipients) if you quote very sparingly in your replies. You do this by selecting the most pertinent word or words in the original message before clicking Reply or Reply to All. Keep your reply to the point and, in general, devote one idea to one message.

Sometimes It's Faster in Person

Not everyone communicates effectively in writing. Some people don't like to write at all or don't answer their mail in a timely manner. If your message matters and your recipient may not be a writer or an e-mailer, talk to the person…in person. If you're messaging many people who work in the same place, the overhead of everyone reading and responding to your message may be greater than the trouble it takes to walk door to door to get a response. A face to face (*F2F*) conversation receives many more replies, counter-replies, and nuances in a minute than an e-mail exchange can in an hour. And it's a good chance to schmooze.

Keep Track of Your Messages

With the volume of e-mail many people receive every day, it is nearly impossible to predict which messages will really matter. Print messages from your boss, your mother, or anyone who matters in your life. And save everything in your Personal Filing Cabinet. Having an e-mail audit trail can save your skin.

Delete Messages Before AOL Deletes Them for You

Because of the limits on the number of pieces of mail you can hold in your various AOL mailboxes (New, Old, and Outgoing), and because of the volume of e-mail you're likely to receive, especially if you join mailing lists, keep your New mailbox as lean as possible. If you have a total of 550 pieces of mail in your New mailbox, mail sent to you will not be deliverable, and AOL members will get a nice message to this effect; your friends on the Net will get a less-nice message. If you're using your Personal Filing Cabinet, there's no reason to hold any nonessential messages in your New mailbox.

Signal Your Feelings

Words on paper can't convey intention and emotion the way a raised eyebrow or wrinkled nose can. Many *emoticons*—ways of expressing emotion through typewriter characters—were invented in newsgroups. This whole subject will be more fully covered in Chapter 5. For now, it's enough to recommend that you tell people when you're kidding as well as when you're angry. At keyword: Shorthand you'll find a long list of abbreviations to help you signal your feelings (for example, ROFL means "rolling on the floor laughing"). Since many people don't know what these things mean, it can be best to use Smileys. Everyone's familiar with a Smiley face :-) If you're not, turn your head to the left to get the effect.

Rewrite Again and Again, Offline If Necessary

The single most frequent reason why I unsend a message is that I discover a mistake in it. Rereading your messages before sending them can spare you both the negative consequences of an intemperate remark and the flush of embarrassment if you've made a particularly silly error in spelling. The more important the message, the greater the consequences of sending it off prematurely. For my most serious (dullest) messages, I usually draft the message in a word processor, save it as text, spell check it, copy it from the word processor, and paste it into the Compose Mail window. (Make sure you've saved the message as pure text to avoid having weird characters appear in place of your word processor's curly quotes and other nontext characters. Weird characters don't make such a hot impression either.) A final thing to remember: if a single recipient of your message is on the Net (i.e., does not have an AOL screen name), you will not be able to unsend the message.

Another way to avoid sending an embarrassing message is to take advantage of another America Online feature: AOL won't let you send a message until the To, Subject, and Message areas are all filled in. I use this feature by not filling in the Subject or To box until I am done writing a message.

Respond to as Much Mail as You Can

As troublesome as it seems to reply to an e-mail message, it is a lot easier than sitting down to write a response, attaching a stamp to an envelope, and mailing it; it's cheaper than the phone; and it's faster than doing it face to face. Everyone gets a lot of mail today, but communication works only if it's two-way. Not answering mail, especially if it's from someone you know and a reply has been requested, may seem rude. It weakens a fabulous communications medium. You don't, of course, have to answer obnoxious unsolicited mail. (Though the temptation to send an obnoxious reply is great, it almost certainly won't be read and does add to bandwidth clutter.) On the other hand, mailing lists (Chapter 4), for all their interactive potential, are pretty passive experiences—only take part if you have something to say.

What's the Point of Your Message?

To make everyone's life easier, it's a good idea to put one idea, or point, in each message (and never send a message without a point). The way to tell whether you have one point in your message is if you can express that point concisely in the Subject line. The reason to avoid multiple points is that they can't easily be replied to, short of quoting the entire message. It's especially maddening if there are multiple recipients, since they will each have varying degrees of interest in the various themes of your message, and the replies may turn into a messy thread. If more than one recipient is involved, the resulting threads can get all tangled up.

Make It Easy on Your Reader

Here are some mechanical devices for making it easier for your reader to read your message. Add a blank line between paragraphs; the white space gives people a chance to breathe. If you want to include items in a list form, keep each item short and make sure it has the same structure as the others. Usually, I use asterisks (*) for unnumbered lists (things whose order has no necessary sequence) and numbers (1,2,3…) for numbered lists (things whose order matters, as in a recipe or any procedure).

FROM HERE...

AOL's e-mail gives you power, flexibility, and ease of use without the bother of having to install and configure complex software. Features like the Personal Filing Cabinet, Favorite Places folder, Address Book, FlashSessions, and the informative Mail Center add more value to the mix. The next two chapters look at mailing lists and newsgroups, two different tools that allow you to engage in regular communication with groups of people about a topic of shared interest.

3

Chapter 4

Discovering Internet
Mailing Lists

Welcome to mailing lists—e-mail on steroids. A mailing list, or *list*, lets people anywhere in the world easily share their thoughts with each other about a common interest. The principle is simple. Think of a mailing list as a fancy version of your AOL Address Book. Using the Address Book, you can send the same message to many people at the same time by making a single name stand for several individual e-mail addresses. Send an e-mail message to the group address, and the message automatically goes into each person's private mailbox.

Mailing lists all work a little differently, but the principle is the same. You don't need to understand the workings of the list-management software that makes them possible in order to benefit from the communities that result. Currently there are more than 60,000 mailing lists—triple the number of newsgroups, which are covered in the next chapter.

This chapter does the following:

■ Introduces the key distinctions between lists (discussion lists vs. newsletters; moderated vs. unmoderated lists)

■ Shows you how to find lists of likely interest to you

■ Provides instructions for joining any list

■ Gives advice for taking part in lists and managing your list mail

■ Highlights some of the best lists available to AOL members

MAILING LIST ABCS

Lists vary in a couple of ways. Some support active discussion, while others are one-way newsletters. Some are moderated, but most are not. And lists are administered by different kinds of list software that have different commands for doing basic things like subscribing and unsubscribing. These mechanical nuances are spelled out in the "Reference" section at the end of this chapter.

4

What You Really Need to Know About Mailing Lists

Behind the minor mechanical variations from list to list, you'll find the same vibrant, self-regulating microcommunities of interest and passion. Lists are probably the best way to meet other people on the Internet, to get current information about any topic of personal or professional interest, and to keep up with new Internet resources about any topic. Lists are where "community" happens on the Internet.

Here's another thing to remember about mailing lists: all you need in order to use them is e-mail; the fancy list software that does all the work is located on some Internet computer that you don't need to worry about. You communicate with people on the list and with the list software itself by e-mail.

To join any list, you must pretty much follow the same three simple steps:

1. *Find a list to join.* Whatever your interest, you'll learn to uncover good mailing lists in "Finding a Mailing List for You." A selection of lists is provided in "Good and Great: A List Sampler," which includes many easy-to-get electronic newsletters created especially for AOL members.

2. *Subscribe to the list.* "Subscribing" means sending a simple e-mail message to the list's administrative e-mail address, as explained in "Subscribing to a Mailing List." Subscribing to a list isn't like subscribing to a magazine—it doesn't cost anything, for one thing. To subscribe and *unsubscribe* (as it's called on mailing lists), you send a message to software, not a person, which handles these tasks. Once you're subscribed, there are usually all sorts of options at your disposal, such as receiving all the lists' messages in a single e-mail *digest.* The software handles these options too. For more details about the mechanics of joining and customizing lists, see the "Reference" section at the end of this chapter.

Tip   *Whenever you learn about a list, make sure to get the information spelled out in the "What You Need to Subscribe" box later in this chapter.*

3. *Take part in the list.* Taking part means actually sending messages to the *people* on the list. Tips for making your messages to others as effective as possible are provided in "Mailing List Netiquette." To avoid getting swamped by e-mail, have a look at the guidelines for "Managing Your Mail" later in this chapter.

Discussion Lists and Distribution Lists (Newsletters)

Some mailing lists let everyone on the list talk to everyone else. I belong to a great list called **our-kids**, for example, which is a small community consisting of about 500 parents of kids with developmental disabilities. Parents share their problems, offer suggestions, give support, and generally prove themselves to be good listeners. This kind of *discussion* list is genuinely interactive. There are other lists for parents with "spirited" kids, asthmatic kids, deaf kids, and kids of every other variety. You'll find thousands of other discussion lists devoted to topics such as body piercing, violin playing, Japanese animation, and Internet advertising.

The other type of mailing lists goes into your mailbox but doesn't let you take part. These *distribution* lists are really electronic newsletters, like the one shown in Figure 4-1. They can tie a community together by providing everyone with the same information at the same time. The difference with electronic newsletters is that you usually do not know who else is subscribing and what they think of the topics discussed in the newsletter. These electronic creations cost nothing to print, very little to distribute, and don't add to the world's garbage.

AOL's channels and many individual AOL forums make active use of the Internet's list software to distribute forum and channel newsletters. You can read about some of them later in this chapter ("Good and Great: A List Sampler").

MODERATED LISTS AND UNMODERATED LISTS

For the most part, only people who are serious about a list's topic will take the trouble to subscribe to it (although it's not much trouble once you get the hang of it). In practice, some lists have an additional level of control to make sure the people on the list are serious about a topic or stay *on topic*. This second level of control takes the form of a person, or *list moderator* or *editor*.

A list moderator, if there is one, must personally approve every new subscriber and can personally approve every message sent from one member to the whole list. This screening of people and messages can keep a list on topic, but it violates some

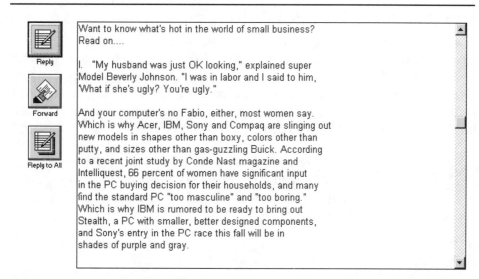

Reply

Forward

Reply to All

Want to know what's hot in the world of small business? Read on....

I. "My husband was just OK looking," explained super Model Beverly Johnson. "I was in labor and I said to him, 'What if she's ugly? You're ugly."

And your computer's no Fabio, either, most women say. Which is why Acer, IBM, Sony and Compaq are slinging out new models in shapes other than boxy, colors other than putty, and sizes other than gas-guzzling Buick. According to a recent joint study by Conde Nast magazine and Intelliquest, 66 percent of women have significant input in the PC buying decision for their households, and many find the standard PC "too masculine" and "too boring." Which is why IBM is rumored to be ready to bring out Stealth, a PC with smaller, better designed components, and Sony's entry in the PC race this fall will be in shades of purple and gray.

FIGURE 4-1   Excerpt from the Your Business newsletter, created by AOL's Your Business channel and available at keyword: Mail Center

people's sense of free speech. It's also a lot of unpaid work for the moderator, so really active moderation is not common.

However, moderated lists can be more informative and can prevent Internet rituals such as flaming (trashing) from getting out of hand. A moderator can be especially welcome in large groups and groups devoted to contentious topics. But there are some moderators who define the list's topic more narrowly than some subscribers are comfortable with—and from such tensions new lists are born.

A list I belong to for computer book authors is moderated, and the moderator does step in from time to time to end "off-topic" threads or patently commercial messages. The effect is not chilling, but then again I have never been the one to overstep the list's bounds. Mostly, lists moderate themselves collectively, with subscribers sharing a purpose and gently (or sometimes not so gently) reinforcing it, especially among newcomers.

How do you tell whether a list is moderated? One way is to read about the list before joining it, using one of the resources described in the next section.

FINDING A MAILING LIST FOR YOU

If you're looking for a mailing list to join, here are two places to start. First, America Online's Internet Mailing List Directory (keyword: Mailing Lists) brings together several thousand lists that AOL members belong to. A handy subject directory (Figure 4-2) makes it easy for you to find a list of interest to you, and you can find useful guidelines for taking part in lists and interacting with people on lists (also have a look at "Mailing List Netiquette," later in this chapter).

Note   *On the Net you'll often find half a dozen ways to do the same thing. Searching for mailing lists is no exception. Several other ways of tracking down mailing lists of likely interest to you are available at keyword: Nethelp (click QuickSearch, then select Mailing Lists).*

← Back	🔁 Reload	Forward	🔍 Search	Prefs	🏠 Home	❓ Help	Stop

http://www.idot.aol.com/mld/production/mld-master-index.html

Animals and Pets	Education - General	Medical Disabilities
The Arts	Gay, Lesbian, Bisexual, and Transgender Interests	Music
Automobiles / Cars	Genealogy	Politics
Britain and the UK	Germany	Psychology and Psychiatry
Business, Commerce, and Industry	Health and Medicine	Eastern Europe and the Former Soviet Union
Canada		
History	Religion and Mythology	
Computers - Macintosh	Humor	Science Interests

FIGURE 4-2   Browse AOL's Internet Mailing List Directory by subject to find a mailing list you're interested in

The AOL directory is small (relative to the number of lists on the Internet), but it does offer complete information for each list, including the purpose of the list, how to subscribe and unsubscribe, and where to find related information about the list's mission.

If AOL's directory doesn't have what you're seeking, try Liszt on the World Wide Web. Keyword: Liszt takes you there directly. This gigantic searchable database provides information about more than 60,000 mailing lists (Figure 4-3)! It doesn't offer the same level of detail for each list as AOL's mailing list directory, and it's difficult to browse, but it's fairly complete and, more important, it's searchable.

Like AOL's mailing list directory, Liszt gives you useful information about specific lists and an overview of other people's favorite lists. You can also subscribe directly. Chapter 9 introduces you to Liszt in detail.

"Good and Great: A List Sampler," later in this chapter, provides subscription information for some lists you might want to join.

FIGURE 4-3   Liszt has become the preeminent Internet tool for finding and joining Internet mailing lists

SUBSCRIBING TO A MAILING LIST

Lists vary in some fundamental ways, as described in the previous sections. Some are fully interactive discussion lists, while others are for distribution only (newsletters). Some are moderated, but most are pretty much self-regulating. These factors can shape your experience of belonging to a list.

There's another way in which lists differ: they are administered by different kinds of software, which you use to subscribe to (join) and unsubscribe from (leave) lists. The oldest and most widely used list software is *LISTSERV*, invented by Eric Thomas in 1986. *LISTSERV* is the actual name of the software to which you send e-mail whenever you join or leave a LISTSERV-based list. LISTSERV is widely used because it can support very big lists (such as Clnet's Dispatch) and because it offers a ton of options. LISTSERV was recently acquired by L-Soft Inc., in Washington, D.C., which is actively developing the package and extending it to several computer operating systems. It's the software of choice at America Online, so it's a good idea to learn how it works (see "LISTSERV: Joining, Leaving, and Customizing").

Note   *A product called Unix Listserv (only the L is capitalized) is used to run some lists. It is not the same as the LISTSERV product in use at AOL and other sites. This chapter capitalizes LISTSERV to make the distinction from the Unix product. Traditionally, you'll see LISTSERV lists and their associated commands in capital letters, but you can use lowercase.*

Listproc is a piece of software modeled after LISTSERV and customized to run on Unix computers. Its commands are broadly similar to LISTSERV's. The third big name in mailing-list software is *Majordomo*, invented by Brent Chapman. Majordomo is a free package meant for smaller systems than LISTSERV, and it isn't generally used to support large lists with many subscribers.

You'll also find smaller packages such as Smartlist, Mailbase, Mailserv, and a host of improvised *reflectors,* which are simple distribution lists with primitive features that merely redistribute a message to several individuals when it was originally sent to a specific address.

Note   *At the end of this chapter, in "Reference," you'll get the specifics of how you join and use these mailing lists.*

What You Need to Subscribe

For every mailing list, you'll need three pieces of information to subscribe:

1. The list name (for example, there is **Roots-l**, the list name for the Genealogy Discussion List). Sending a message to the list causes your message to be sent to all the individuals who have subscribed to the list. Many list names end in hyphen *l* (*-l*), for *list*. Note: that's the letter *l,* not the number one (*1*).

2 The administrative address, that is, the e-mail address to which you send your subscription and unsubscription requests (in the example of the Genealogy Discussion List, it is **roots-l-request@ rootsweb.com**). Some administrative addresses indicate the type of list software (*listserv, majorodomo, listproc*), while others take the list name and tack on *-request*. Traditionally, the "-request" lists are maintained by a person who individually approves all new subscriptions.

3. The list address, that is, the e-mail address to which you send messages to the group when you want to take part. Generally, the list address consists of the list name, the @ sign, and the domain name. For example: **roots-l@rootsweb.com**. Note that the domain name (the bit after the @ sign) is usually the same for the administrative and the list address (e.g., **rootsweb.com**).

Popular Mailing List Commands

The many types of list software vary in the commands they make available, but they all offer commands for joining and leaving (subscribing and unsubscribing), and they all offer the important option of receiving a digest. The slight variations between names can be confusing, but Table 4-1 can help you keep the major commands straight.

	LISTSERV	**Listproc**	**Majordomo**
To subscribe	**subscribe** *listname* *[your full name]* or **sub** *listname* *[your full name]*	**subscribe** *listname* *your name* or **join** *listname* *your name*	**subscribe** *listname* [*your.address*] Note: *your.address* is the e-mail address at which you want to receive the list, if different from the address you're subscribing from—useful if you're using AOL's "bring your own access" service.
To get a digest	**set** *listname* **digest**	**set** *listname* **mail digest**	**subscribe** *listname*-**digest** Note: The list owner can choose not to set up a list as a digest. To get a digest (if there is one), you must first subscribe to the regular list. When requesting the digest, you should also send a message (it can be in the same e-mail message) simultaneously *unsubscribing* from the regular list (see below)
To unsubscribe	**signoff** *listname*	**unsubscribe** *listname* or **signoff** *listname*	**unsubscribe** *listname* [*your.address*] Note: Use *your.adddress* if you receive the list at a different address from the one you used to send the unsubscribe message.

TABLE 4-1   Popular mailing list commands

> *Note*   *In this chapter, whenever text is just bold, that's exactly what you type in the Compose Mail window:* **listserv.nodak.edu** *(for example). Whenever text is bold and italics—***domain.name*** (for example)—you must type something, but what you type will depend on the name of the list, its address, domain name, or your address. Any text in square brackets—[ ]— is optional.*

What do you do with these commands in Table 4-1? In the Compose Mail window, the administrative address goes in the To field, the Subject field is blank, and the actual command goes in the message box. Note that AOL requires an entry in the Subject field; you can put anything in that field (a period, for example) and the list software will just ignore it. Just click Send when everything's in order. See the example a little later in "Subscribing to a LISTSERV List."

Tip   *You can place several commands in one message,* **help** *and* **subscribe listname***, for example. Just make sure they're on separate lines. Some commands are contingent on others, however, so you'll have to send separate messages. For example, you can't get a LISTSERV digest without first subscribing to the list. Finally, don't worry about case. Mailing list purists (like AOL's David O'Donnell) capitalize everything associated with LISTSERV, from list names to command names, but in fact, the software will accept lowercase.*

4

Every List Has Two Addresses

Never, ever send your administrative e-mail—messages about joining, leaving, or customizing—to the people on the list itself. They're not interested in your efforts to join the list or to leave it, and they may give you a hard time about it. Administrative e-mail goes to **listserv@***domain.name*... or **majordomo@-***domain.name*... or *listname***-l@domain.name**. Real e-mail (to the other people who subscribe to the list) goes to *listname***@domain.name**.

MAILING LIST NETIQUETTE

Chapter 3 modestly offered some general guidelines for communicating effectively by e-mail ("Putting Your Best Foot Forward"). All of those guidelines—quote aptly, stick to one subject, respect the other guy, signal your feelings, etc.—apply to mailing lists as well, because the communications problems are just the same. In addition, mailing lists have their own sets of guidelines that mostly have to do with the mechanics of lists. Sending a message to a list is a shade more anonymous than sending a message to an individual, and the netiquette requires that much more sensitivity since you'll be communicating with people you may not know personally. Here are some things to keep in mind:

■   Don't send a message to the members of a list when it should be sent to the list-management software.

- Joining a list is not like visiting a Web site or browsing a newsgroup. Make sure the list's for you before joining it.

- Read the list for several weeks before posting. *Lurking* (just reading the messages) is the way to take the pulse of an e-mail microcommunity and decide whether it's for you.

- Keep your messages to lists on topic. Messages go into the mailboxes of all subscribers, and subscribers will not appreciate junk mail.

- Remember that list owners control their lists. America Online has no control over lists or list owners. Obscenities that might not faze one moderator might be cause for a TOS violation on AOL (see keyword: TOS). That's why AOL offers the Mail Controls described in the last chapter.

- Save the Welcome message you automatically receive when you subscribe to a list. It contains useful information about how best to use the list, how to unsubscribe, and so on.

Tip   *On some lists, you'll regularly (usually monthly) receive a FAQ—a list of frequently asked questions about the list. This FAQ will include an overview of the list's scope as well as instructions about customizing your subscription and leaving the list. Save the FAQ with the Welcome message. Sometimes the FAQ will include the same information as the Welcome message but will be more up to date.*

- If you are going to be away from your computer for some time, either leave any lists to which you subscribe or (if it's a LISTSERV list) use the LISTSERV NOMAIL feature (see Table 4-2) to temporarily suspend your subscription.

- Do not send a commercial solicitation to any mailing list. The only time it's okay to send a commercial solicitation is when buying or selling has been explicitly approved by the list's leader or in the list's charter or FAQ (Frequently Asked Questions) document.

- If you are going to delete a screen name that is subscribed to one or more lists, or if you will be closing your AOL account, please be kind to everyone and unsubscribe from any list(s) you are on. Steps for unsubscribing can be found in the list's Welcome message.

- Respect people on the list. People from different cultures and persuasions might not understand or appreciate jokes and irony. When personal comments are appropriate, send them to an individual, not the list.

- Take personal responsibility for what you write. A strong opinion will probably be taken more seriously if it's associated with a real name than if it's associated with an AOL screen name that doesn't reveal a real first or last name. However, while it is a good idea on Internet mailing lists to let people know your true identity, it's *not* a good idea to provide contact information such as address and phone number.

MANAGING YOUR MAIL

A single discussion list can fill up your mailbox in a few days. If that happens, messages will start bouncing—getting returned to the list. In this case, list owners are within their rights to remove you from a list. Moreover, unless you have infinite time at your disposal and a list is of grave professional importance to you, you won't want to read every message that every subscriber sends. Even the best lists have their share of off-topic messages, usually known as *noise*.

Here are some tips for keeping up with the traffic and avoiding a full mailbox:

- If a mailing list offers a digest, get it. LISTSERV-type lists offer digests as a rule, as do some of the newer software packages. Majordomo offers digests too, but instead of first subscribing to a list and then *setting* it to digest mode, you subscribe to a separate list called (for example) **majordomo-users-digest**. Listproc is like LISTSERV in that you first subscribe to the list, then set it: **set anthro-lib mail digest**, for example. Note the addition of the word *mail* to the Listproc command. When in doubt, inquire with the list's owner, as described in "Finding Out Who Owns A List" at the end of this chapter.

- If you subscribe to several mailing lists, consider creating a screen name for each list or group of related lists. For every AOL account, you can have five screen names, and each can keep up to 550 pieces of mail in the New and Old mailboxes combined. (To create additional screen names for use with your account, go to keyword: Names, and follow the simple onscreen instructions.) If you follow this advice, *do not delete screen names without first unsubscribing from any mailing lists to which the screen name belonged.*

- Use a FlashSession to download unread e-mail and send outgoing e-mail. See "Taming E-Mail with FlashSessions" for the how-to.

- If your mailing list is also carried as a Usenet newsgroup, you should consider quitting the mailing list and participating in the newsgroup. Information on how to do so will be given in AOL's Internet Mailing List Directory entry for that list (available at keyword: Mailing Lists under the Browse the Database button), on the list's Welcome message, or possibly in both places. The *bit.listserv.* * newsgroups *mirror* more than 300 Internet mailing lists and are available at keyword: Newsgroups. Chapter 5 is all about newsgroups.

 The word mirror, *on the Internet, refers to a site or service that carries an exact copy of another site or service in order to improve service, relieve network pressure, or make a popular service more widely available. The best FTP and Web sites have FTP and Web mirrors, and AOL features a set of FTP mirrors for members' favorite sites.*

- The archives for some lists are available on the World Wide Web. They lack the interactive quality of mail-based lists but are a useful way of accessing old information. A very useful set of computer-related list archives can be found at **http://alt.venus.co.uk/hypermail/**. Inquire with a list's owner to find out whether the list has a Web archive. Otherwise, you may have to learn a list's *index* commands by sending the **help** command to any list's administrative address.

Taming E-Mail with FlashSessions

Here's another feature that sets AOL apart. Using FlashSessions, you can retrieve your new unread mail automatically, either at a specified time every day or on demand when you're online. With this feature, AOL automatically performs a series of tasks you request, and, if you want, signs off automatically afterward. Messages downloaded in a FlashSession are stored for you in your Personal Filing Cabinet, where you can read them offline, without incurring the cost of being online or the bother of tying up the phone line. Your outgoing mail (messages you send to mailing lists) can also be sent during a FlashSession. Incoming and outgoing mail messages transferred during a FlashSession are also available from the Mail menu on the main AOL menu bar.

Setting up FlashSessions requires two basic steps:

1. Indicate *what* you want to do during the FlashSession: From the Mail menu, select Set up FlashSession. From the FlashSession window shown in Figure 4-4, specify whether you want your automatic session to handle your incoming mail, your outgoing mail, the files attached to incoming messages, your file downloads, or your incoming and outgoing newsgroup messages. Click Walk Me Through to learn about the subtleties of each of the options. Click Schedule FlashSession Now to schedule your automatic sessions.

2. Many people run FlashSessions on demand. If you want to run a FlashSession at a fixed time each day, indicate *when* you want AOL to sign on automatically for you and carry out the activities you requested in Step 1. First, make sure there's a check mark in the Enable Scheduler check box; click in the box if there's not. A FlashSession won't run unless the box is checked. Then, specify some combination of time, interval, and day of the week. Figure 4-5 shows a session scheduled for every hour, Monday to Friday, at around 9 A.M. Click OK when you're done.

FIGURE 4-4   FlashSessions let you automatically send and retrieve batches of e-mail—a good way of taking part in high-volume lists lists

Schedule Flashsessions

☑ **Enable Scheduler**

Starting time: [8] ⊟ : [41 ▼]

☐ Sunday
☑ Monday
☑ Tuesday   **How often:**
☑ Wednesday   [Once each day ▼]
☑ Thursday
☐ Friday   [OK] [Cancel]
☑ Friday
☐ Saturday

FIGURE 4-5   Setting up the times when you want the automatic sessions
to occur

Note   *If you are* offline *when you start a FlashSession, there must be at least
one name and password specified (using Select Names), and the session
will run for those screen names. If you are online, you needn't specify any screen
name, and it doesn't matter which ones you do specify; your FlashSession is only
going to download messages for the screen name with which you signed on.*

GOOD AND GREAT: A LIST SAMPLER

Once you have a taste of how easy it is to subscribe to a mailing list, it's tempting
to start subscribing right away. Where to start? If you are searching for a list devoted
to a particular subject, start with the "Finding a Mailing List for You" section. If
you'd just like to browse and try out some of the best mailing lists, have a look at
the following lists. These are general interest electronic newsletters, not highly
focused discussion lists. Distribution lists, by their nature, have a clear voice (they
come from a single person) but aren't interactive. They can be a superb way to stay
informed about a subject.

Tip   *In the Mail Center, available from the Mail menu, you can find a long list of online newsletters, created by AOL partners, forum leaders, and channels. The following AOL lists should all be available to you on that list. You can subscribe to most of them by clicking a button.*

AOL's Mailing Lists

Mailing lists support thousands of communities on the Internet—but the mechanics of joining and customizing them can seem a bit unfriendly, with all those inflexible computer commands! America Online has recently begun to integrate LISTSERV-based mailing lists throughout its channels. Figure 4-6 shows the AOL Marketplace's newsletter. To join and leave an AOL-sponsored mailing list you will probably never have to send messages with arcane commands. For the most part, AOL forums and channels use distribution lists (one-way electronic newsletters).

Reply

Forward

Reply to All

1-800 FLOWERS: WORKERS UNITE
Hectic workdays and demanding bosses gain special meaning after reading a "Dilbert" cartoon. Remind yourself (or overworked colleagues) of the lunacy of it all with a "Dilbert" gift basket from 1-800 Flowers. "Dilbert" doodads come, appropriately, with a cactus.

Enter the "Dilbert" contest for the chance to win a basket or a limited-edition lithograph. It's not lunch, but it is free.
[Keyword: Flowers>Contests & Promotions>Welcome DILBERT!]

AT ONCE SOFTWARE: ELIMINATING THE MAILMAN
Immediately load your computer with software from the atOnce Software Download Store. Click the download button, atOnce verifies your credit card number and, whoosh!, you're beating your machine at Championship Pool or Gin Rummy.

Join Club atOnce to get free and discounted software, special promotions and notification of atOnce contests. Click on "Customer Service" to sign up. It's free. [Keyword: atOnce]

GODIVA: IT MELTS IN YOUR MIND
Devour every last bonbon described in Godiva's Complete Chocolate Guide. Fabiola, Lion of Belgium, Praline Almond, Chocolate Mousse: The names alone make us melt. Its

---

FIGURE 4-6   Attention shoppers! The AOL Marketplace newsletter, with deals of the week highlighted and linked to the AOL Store

Top Tips

At keyword: Top Tips, you can sign up for several newsletters that will deliver a tip a day, or every few days, to your mailbox. Tips for beginners (such as how to forward your e-mail) are at your fingertips, as are more advanced tips (such as how to increase your horizontal screen "real estate"). For Internet tips, start with the AnswerMan Internet Extra.

AnswerMan Internet Extra

This weekly newsletter serves AOL members who enjoy the AnswerMan forum, the fun, interactive half of the Internet help forum on AOL (keyword: Nethelp). The newsletter is written by Kevin Savetz, forum leader and co-author of the Mac edition of this book. Each newsletter contains Internet tips and resources and usually focuses on a specific topic each week, such as FTP or Music. You can subscribe at keyword: AnswerMan. From the main AnswerMan screen, click on the Internet Extra Newsletter button. You can also see the current issue and read past issues there.

Tip   *All of AOL's mailing lists use LISTSERV software, and all are run at* **listserv.aol.com** *(which you can abbreviate as* **list***). To unsubscribe to any of them, just send an e-mail message to* **listserv@listserv.aol.com** *or just* **listserv@list***, with anything in the Subject line, and put the following in the body of the message:* **signoff** **listname***, substituting* **AnswerMan***,* **NetGirl***,* **InBusiness***, or whatever for* **listname***. Instructions for unsubscribing are provided at the end of every AOL newsletter.*

NetGirl Newsletter

The NetGirl forum, devoted to the newfangled world of online relationships, is one of AOL's most popular. The weekly newsletter brings romance-starved AOL members selected questions and answers about cyber-relationships, together with information about upcoming NetGirl events, new Web sites, questions and answers, and the like. You can subscribe to the newsletter at keyword: NetGirl; click Newsletter on the navigational bar at the bottom of the screen. You can also unsubscribe here, read the current edition online, and read earlier editions.

Most AOL mailing lists are weekly; they won't clutter up your mailbox. All include information for unsubscribing. On some you'll find AOL-only features such as text that's been enriched with color, formatting, and even hyperlinks (Figure 4-6).

Parental Controls on Mailing Lists and AOL's Policy

If you're a parent who has taught your children to be wary of strangers, you may be concerned about the strangers they can encounter on mailing lists or anywhere on the Internet. There's no better way to meet new people—strangers—on the Net than on mailing lists, so you might want to take a moment to read AOL's policy about allowing kids access to mailing lists:

"Internet mailing lists are not monitored, censored, or otherwise filtered by America Online, and America Online is not responsible for any content distributed via a mailing list. It is important for parents and guardians of minors to be aware of this fact and exercise discretion when evaluating how their children participate in mailing lists.

"The Internet is similar to real life in the sense that it is possible to electronically meet people and interact with them. Minors should be cautioned to never give out personal information, such as complete real name, telephone numbers, or addresses, to any strangers. If your child receives unsolicited or objectionable Internet e-mail, you should forward a complete copy of the e-mail to AOL screen name Postmaster and explain that it was unsolicited. You should send objectionable or unsolicited mail received from America Online members to AOL screen name *TOSEmail1* or *TOSEmail2*. In general, you should apply common-sense guidelines from the non-electronic world to your child's online sessions…. If you have specific questions about Internet mailing lists, you can send e-mail to AOL screen name ListMaster."

To provide even better protection, AOL has recently introduced Mail Controls, which enable parents to restrict the mail received by their kids. See Chapter 3 for more information.

Your Business Newsletter

This weekly newsletter for small businesses is created by Your Business (keyword: Your Business), AOL's small business resource center. A sample is shown earlier in this chapter, in Figure 4-1. In addition to schedules and promotions of the channel's chat sessions and other events, the newsletter contains guest columns and information from AOL partners such as *Business Week, Inc.* and *Home Office Computing*. Automatic subscription is available at keyword: Your Business.

BEYOND AOL: NET NEWSLETTERS

The following small sampling of what the Internet has to offer shows the kind of information you can have for free on the Internet. These newsletters can be a great way to stay informed about the things you're interested in. I'm leaving out of the picture the many excellent interactive mailings I've belonged to over the years, such as com-priv (devoted to issues surrounding the commercialization of the Internet), the Children with Special Health Care Needs list, Community Memory (devoted to the history of cyberspace), and Netscribes (for people who write about the Internet). Using Liszt and the AOL Internet Mailing List Directory, you can identify lists that address your specific personal and professional interests. For a profile of a classic Internet discussion list, BELIEFS-L, see "A Community of Believers."

A Community of Believers

BELIEF-L
Subscribe To: listserv@list
Subject line: *anything*
Body: subscribe belief-l *your name*

David O'Donnell, AOL's Postmaster, is the owner of this lively mailing list, hosted on AOL's mailing list computer. The list focuses on discussions of personal ideologies. Subscribers debate everything from religious, ethical, and moral issues to political upheaval in Bosnia, along with more whimsical subjects. Belief-L has developed quite a special community over the years, so it's important to carefully read the FAQ and Welcome message. You should also check out the Belief-L Web Site at **http://www.idot.aol.com/atropos/elf-bile/** before jumping into the fray. Beware: Belief-L is a *high* volume list, sometimes exceeding 150 messages a day, so be prepared to spend a lot of time trying to keep up.

Tour Bus

Subscribe To: listserv@listserv.aol.com [or **listserv@list**, if you're subscribing from AOL]
Subject line: *anything*
Body: subscribe tourbus

Bob Rankin and Patrick Douglas Crispen write this very popular newsletter (hosted at AOL), which each week focuses on new or must-see Internet resources. These Internet old-timers have much experience helping newcomers make the most of the Net. Two things to note about this newsletter: because so many people subscribe, this newsletter accepts advertising (the more "eyeballs" a newsletter has, the keener sponsors' interest); don't be surprised or shocked to see ads in this and other newsletters. Also, this newsletter is available, as are more and more newsletters, on the Web (**http://www.worldvillage.com/tourbus.htm**).

Scout Report

Subscribe To: listserv@lists.internic.net
Subject line: *anything*
Body: subscribe scout-report

This weekly newsletter containing serious new Internet resources is written by Susan Calcari and supported by InterNIC, an important Internet institution that keeps American universities informed about the Internet. With all the emphasis on "hot" and "cool" sites elsewhere, the Scout Report is committed to discovering and sharing useful and informative sites. The Scout Report is also available on the World Wide Web (**http://www.cs.wisc.edu/scout/report/**). The newsletter itself is available in either ASCII (plain text) or HTML, for reading in a World Wide Web browser (see "Using a Mailing List in HTML Format"). When you use the browser to open the Scout Report in HTML format, text is both formatted (bold, etc.) and linked to actual Web sites. The Scout Report is also available via Gopher and FTP.

Yahoo!'s Picks of the Week

OK, you *are* interested in hot and cool sites. The folks at Yahoo have created a very big directory of Web sites, and they add to this list daily (Chapter 9 has more to say about Yahoo). Each week they post their favorite-site picks at their Web site. You can find out their favorites by e-mail, too, by simply visiting **http://www.yahoo.com/picks/** and (at the bottom of the page) typing in your e-mail address and clicking a button. You unsubscribe by sending a message to **yahoo-picks-request@yahoo.com**, with anything in the Subject line and **unsubscribe** *your.e-mail.address*.

Using a Mailing List in HTML Format

Some Web-related mailing lists, like NetSurf Digest and Scout Report, give you the option of receiving a list as simple text (which you read as a plain message) or as HTML (which you read using a browser such as AOL's). Using the HTML format lets you link directly to Internet resources. If you get such a mailing list, here's how to use an HTML message to browse the Internet:

1. Display the message as you would any message.

2. Save the message as a file on your hard disk: from the File menu, select Save. Give the file a name *that includes **htm** as the extension*, such as **netsurf1.htm**. On DOS and Windows, "HTML" files are shortened to "HTM" files to fit the three-letter restriction on file extensions. (If the file arrives as an attachment because it is over 28K, you can download it and save it as an *htm* file.)

3. From the File menu, select Open. Navigate to the directory where you saved the file, and select it. Because the file has *htm* as its extension, the browser automatically opens, with the page displayed, including formatting and clickable links.

REFERENCE: JOINING AND USING LISTSERV, LISTPROC, AND MAJORDOMO MAILING LISTS

Mailing lists are adminstered by different kinds of software. You communicate with this software by e-mail, sending messages and receiving replies. You'll find great lists of both kinds—discussion lists and distribution lists (newsletter)—on all the major types of mailing-list software. People often use what's convenient or available to them at their organizations, not always what's best for a specific task. The slight variations in software commands and capabilities is a small price for the incredible community experience available on mailing lists. *Just remember that it's not important to understand exactly what ACK and Repro mean, as long as you know what they can do for you and how you can use them to make the most of your mailing list experience.*

LISTSERV: Joining, Leaving, and Customizing

LISTSERV bristles with features. The majority of these features are not used by most people, but they can add substantially to the power and usefulness of the program.

If you are interested in subscribing to a particular LISTSERV-type mailing list and know the administrative address, you can usually get information about the list (what it's about and who it's for) by sending a message to **listserv@*domain.name***, putting anything in the Subject line, and typing **info *listname*** in the body of the message. To get information about the famous Tourbus mailing list, for example, send a message to **listserv@listserv.aol.com** (or just **listserv@list**), put a period or anything you please in the Subject line, and write **info tourbus** in the body. Then click Send.

Subscribing to a LISTSERV List

When you subscribe to a LISTSERV list, you're talking (by e-mail, that is) to a piece of software called *LISTSERV*—its e-mail name is **listserv**. All your *administrative* dealings with the list go to the administrative address (**listserv@*domain***), not the actual list address (**listname@*domain***). LISTSERV administrative addresses look like this:

```
listserv@peach.ease.lsoft.com
listserv@listserv.aol.com
```

To subscribe to a LISTSERV list, follow these general steps. (Figure 4-7 shows a sample subscription message.)

1. Open the Compose Mail window (choose Compose Mail from the Mail menu). Type **listserv@*domain.name*** in the To field (for example, **listserv@peach.ease.lsoft.com**), leave the CC field blank, and type anything in the Subject field. LISTSERV ignores the Subject line, but AOL requires it. A period in the Subject line will do.

2. Put the following in the body of the message:

```
subscribe listname [your real name]
```

Whether you include your real name (separated by spaces) is optional. If the list supports a command that lets people view a listing of subscribers, your name will appear on the listing.

3. Click Send.

> *Tip* *When you use AOL's Internet Mailing List Directory or one of the Net's directories, such as Liszt (keyword: Liszt), you'll find all the information you need to join, leave, and customize individual mailing lists. Always follow those instructions, because they apply to individual lists.*

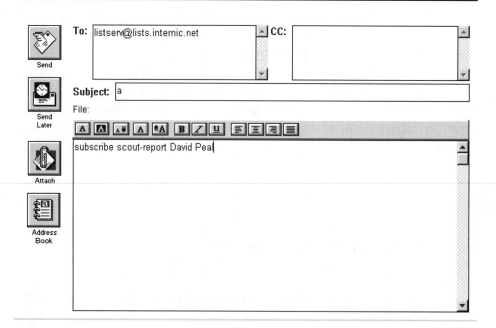

FIGURE 4-7 What a subscription message looks like. Note the *a* in the Subject line. AOL requires that you put something there—any character will do

If the address seems generic, it is; one piece of LISTSERV software can be used to administer any number of mailing lists at a specific domain. There are dozens of mailing lists at **listserv.aol.com**, for example.

Remember that it's a piece of software that's reading your message, not a person. Any human message such as:

```
hi, please sign me up for the kennel management list. thanks,
wendell poodle
```

will be read as if it were a computer command, and returned to you via another e-mail message, because the words you've typed, beginning with the "hi," are not recognized commands.

Tip   *You can use the special abbreviation* **list** *in place of* **listserv.aol.com** *when sending mail to AOL's LISTSERV computer.*

Unless you've made a typo, you'll usually get a response by return mail saying that you have been added to the membership list. For larger LISTSERV lists, you may be asked to reply within 24 or 48 hours to the confirmation and say *ok* or something similar in your message (see Figure 4-8).

Once you are added, you usually receive a message welcoming you to the list (see Figure 4-9 for an example). Some Welcome messages provide an overview of the scope of the list's topic, and some lists provide a monthly FAQ to answer administrative and substantive questions. You may also receive a message called "Output of your job," which summarizes the computer time used to process your request. You can delete this message.

Tip   *The easiest way to save a Welcome message is in your Favorite Places folder. To create a special folder there for your Welcome messages, open Favorite Places, click Add Folder, and name the new folder* Mailing lists. *With a new Welcome message open, just click the little heart on the title bar. The message will be removed from your New mailbox and dropped automatically into your Favorite Places folder. Open Favorite Places and drag the new Welcome message to the* Mailing list *folder.*

Reply

Forward

Reply to All

Date: 96-11-25 21:54:29 EST
From: LISTSERV@lists.internic.net (L-Soft list server at InterNIC Registration Services (1.8b))
To: DavidPeal@AOL.COM (David Peal)

Your command:

SUBSCRIBE SCOUT-REPORT David Peal

has been received. You must now reply to this message (as explained below) to complete your subscription. The purpose of this confirmation procedure is to check that the address LISTSERV is about to add to the list for your subscription is reachable. This is a typical procedure for high-volume lists and all new subscribers are subjected to it - you are not being singled out. Every effort has been made to make this verification as simple and painless as possible. Thanks in advance for your cooperation.

With most mail programs, you can confirm the command by simply using the "reply" function, without including the original text, and typing "ok" (without the quotes) as the text of your message. Just "ok" - do not retype

FIGURE 4-8   LISTSERV sometimes wants to verify your interest in the list before signing you up

Reply

Forward

Reply to All

Your subscription to the SCOUT-REPORT list (The Scout Report) has been accepted.

Please save this message for future reference, especially if you are not familiar with LISTSERV. This might look like a waste of disk space now, but in 6 months you will be glad you saved this information when you realize that you cannot remember what are the lists you are subscribed to, or what is the command to leave the list to avoid filling up your mailbox while you are on vacations. In fact, you should create a new mail folder for subscription confirmation messages like this one, and for the "welcome messages" from the list owners that you will occasionally receive after subscribing to a new list.

The scout-report and scout-report-html lists are moderated lists, used only for distribution of the Scout Report once a week. Submissions to the Scout Report can be sent to scout@internic.net

You may leave the list at any time by sending a "SIGNOFF SCOUT-REPORT" command to LISTSERV@LISTS.INTERNIC.NET. You can also tell LISTSERV how you want it to confirm the receipt of messages you send to the list. If

FIGURE 4-9   A typical Welcome message that you will receive when you join a list. Keep this message for future reference

Customizing Your LISTSERV Experience

For many, the most useful way to customize a LISTSERV list is to get a *digest*. The automatic availability of a digest mode is a great advantage of LISTSERV. A digest is a single message you receive in which all the day's messages are compiled. The benefits? If you belong to more than one high-volume list, your mailbox will soon be overrun with messages, but a digest packages the day's traffic in one tidy little (or not so little) message. Having the day's messages in a single message makes it easy to skim the list and follow *threads*—discussions about the same topic. Usually, each digest is preceded by a numbered list of the day's topics, so you can jump to messages of likely interest, especially if the digest is so big that it arrives as an attached file that you must read in a word processor.

 To get a digest, you must first subscribe. Once you've requested the digest, the individual messages will stop coming to your mailbox.

The downside? Digests usually exceed the size limit AOL sets on messages, so they're automatically turned into attachments that you must download. Since every day's digest (attachment) will probably have the same file name, you'll have to rename each attached digest if you want to save it and not overwrite it with the next day's digest. Also, it's a bit more difficult to respond to messages if you're reading a message within a word processor!

To get the daily digest of a list to which you are subscribed, send a message to **listserv@*domain.name***, put anything in the Subject line, and put the following in the body of the message:

```
set listname digest
```

Other LISTSERV commands let you turn off digest mode, retrieve files (archived messages, usually), and get help. These options for customizing LISTSERV are outlined in Table 4-2.

Leaving a LISTSERV Mailing List

To leave any LISTSERV mailing list, send a message to **listserv@*domain.name***, putting a period or something else in the Subject Line and writing the following message in the body:

```
signoff listname
```

To...	Send this message to listserv@*domain.name*
Get help	**help**
Subscribe to list	**subscribe** *listname [your name]*
Unsubscribe to list	**signoff** *listname*
Get a copy of messages you send to the list (as a record and to verify that the list is distributing messages appropriately)	**set** *listname* **repro**
Don't get a copy of your messages	**set** *listname* **norepro**
Temporarily "turn off" the list (when you go on a vacation, for example)	**set** *listname* **nomail**
Turn a list back on—after you get back from vacation	**set** *listname* **mail**
Get the list in digest form	**set** *listname* **digest**
Return to regular form (lots of mail)	**set** *listname* **nodigest**
Get a brief acknowledgement of messages you send the list	**set** *listname* **ack norepro**
Turn off acknowledgement	**set** *listname* **noack norepro**
Get a list of files associated with the list (usually archived messages)	**index** *listname*
Get a complete, long list of all the things you can do with LISTSERV	**info refcard**

TABLE 4-2   A few ways of customizing a LISTSERV-type mailing list

That's it. You don't have to provide your name or any other information. Unless there's a typo, you will be unsubscribed and your unsubscription attempt will be confirmed.

Tip   *LISTSERV automatically makes a note of the e-mail address when you ask to subscribe to (join) a list. Make sure to leave the list using the same address! Using different accounts, different service providers, or different screen names can confuse LISTSERV.*

Basics of Listproc Lists

Listproc, a popular variant of LISTSERV, is another program used to administer many mailing lists. In other words, to join, customize, and leave a Listproc list, you must send messages to the Listproc software (not to the people on the list). The basic Listproc commands are summarized in Table 4-3. Sometimes the Listproc administrative address is *listserv* or *listserver*, which can be confusing, since the commands for LISTSERV and Listproc differ in slight ways.

Basics of Majordomo Lists

If you're familiar with other types of list software, Majordomo won't present any shocking departures from your experience. Majordomo is a popular type of list software for smaller lists. To join, customize, and leave a Majordomo list, you send messages to the Majordomo software. Table 4-4 summarizes the stuff you can do with Majordomo. As with Lisproc, Majordomo's options are limited relative to the myriad LISTSERV options. Note that the digest is a separate mailing list, not a version of the regular mailing list, so to request the digest you must first subscribe to the regular list, then request listname-digest, and then unsubscribe from the regular list.

To...	Send this message to listproc@*domain.name*
Join	**subscribe** *listname your real name* **join** *listname your real name*
Leave	**unsubscribe** *listname* **signoff** *listname*
Get digest	**set** *listname* **mail digest**
Get a list of people on the list	**review** *listname*
Get help	**help**

TABLE 4-3 The most important Listproc commands

To...	Send this message to majordomo@*domain.name*
Join	**subscribe** *listname* [*your e-mail address*]
Leave	**unsubscribe** *listname* [*your e-mail address*]
Get digest	**subscribe** *listname*-**digest** **unsubscribe** *listname*
Find out what files are available for the list	**index** *listname*
Get files related to the list	**get** *listname filename*
Find out who's on the list	**who** *listname*
Get the Welcome message again	**intro** *listname*
Get help	**help**

TABLE 4-4   The most important Majordomo commands

Tip   *Once you've taken part in (or at least subscribed to) a mailing list for a long time, it is quite easy to forget what kind of list it is (LISTSERV, Listproc, etc.), and it is also easy to forget to keep your Welcome messages. If you study the* **headers** *of your messages, you will find lots of useful information about the list's address, the owner's address, the type of list software being used, and even information about how to unsubscribe. If you receive a digest, the header will tell you the e-mail address of the original sender and of the list itself, so you can reply to an individual or to the group, as appropriate.*

Finding Out Who "Owns" a List

Every mailing list has at least one "owner"—the person who sets up the software and makes sure that it's working, that messages don't bounce, and that patently inappropriate messages don't find their way onto the list. It's useful to know this person's e-mail address, just in case you have problems *using* the list—posting messages or accessing archives, for example. Such "administrative" problems should be shared with the list's owner and *not* with all the actual subscribers. Before asking the owner a question, it's wise to consult the Help file available for every kind of major list software.

How do you find out who owns a list? When you first subscribe to a list, chances are good that you will receive a Welcome message. This message will often include the name of the list owner and his or her e-mail address. In general, it's always a good idea to read and save this message. AOL's LISTSERV software has the address **listserv@listserv.aol.com** (or just **listserv@list**), and you can write that address for "automated" help (put anything in the Subject line and the word "help" in the message body, then click Send).

Here is advice from AOL's Postmaster General, David O'Donnell, about finding out who owns a list if it's not obvious from the Welcome message:

"First, determine the type of software that's administering the list by sending the Help command to the software administering the list. For example, send a message to **listserv@listserv.aol.com** with anything in the Subject line (the software ignores the Subject line, but the AOL mail program requires it!) and **Help** as the body of the text. In the reply, there may be a line in the headers that indicates what particular server software is being used—LISTSERV, Listproc, Majordomo, and so on."

- For a LISTSERV list, you can contact the list owner by writing to *listname*-**request@***domain.name*. For example, the owner of **belief-l@listserv.aol**.com can be reached at **belief-l-request@ listserv.aol.com**.

- For a Majordomo list, you can typically contact the list owner by writing to *listname*-**approval**, although a number of sites are now adopting *owner-listname* or *listname-owner*. For example, to contact the list owner of **2020WORLD@seatimes.com**, you could write to **2020world-approval@seatimes.com** or perhaps **owner-202world@seatimes.com** if the former didn't work.

- As a last resort, you can attempt to write to the *Hostmaster* at the site where the list is hosted. The Hostmaster (if one exists) may choose to forward the message to the list owner, provide you with an address, or ignore the request. If there isn't a Hostmaster, you may attempt to contact the site's *Postmaster*, who may take any one of those steps. If you choose to write to either of these accounts, provide the details of how you've already tried to contact the list owner and a brief description of why you are doing so; it may just make the difference between being ignored and getting a response, especially at larger sites.

FROM HERE...

Without special software beyond your e-mail program, mailing lists let you join any of tens of thousands of communities and receive information about anything you're likely to be interested in. Mail on every subject, from like-minded people located anywhere in the U.S. and the world, comes reliably, securely, and in great volume to your mailbox. Join a mailing list today!

The next chapter introduces newsgroups, which are more public, less cozy places than mailing lists. While mailing lists can be private, newsgroups can be noisy and raucous. Mailing lists and newsgroups are at the heart of the traditional community experience on the Internet.

Chapter 5

Discovering
Newsgroups

If you wanted to tell your neighbors about your garage sale, you might put a notice in the local newspaper or attach a sign to the phone poles in your neighborhood. If you wanted to announce something to attendees at a large conference, maybe you would thumbtack a scrap of paper on a bulletin board designated for the purpose. And if you were selling something at work, you'd probably post a notice where everyone would see it—on the bathroom doors, the bulletin boards, the candy machines. On the Internet, you can reach a public audience by using newsgroups, collectively known as *Usenet News* or just *News*.

News is like a big bulletin board insofar as it's (1) public, (2) usually not controlled by anyone, and (3) a little wild at times. Instead of a single bulletin board serving a single public, however, News consists of thousands of *newsgroups*, organized by subject and serving thousands of small communities—groups of people with the same belief, passion, or interest. It's a big world with many passions, so whether you have a taste for Indonesian music, a particular TV show, or a certain Mexican fast-food chain, you're likely to find a newsgroup devoted to it. The newsgroup communities can become tightly knit social groups with their own cultures and traditions. The AOL feature that's most similar to newsgroups is the message board, where members can ask questions, provide help, and just mingle.

Newsgroups were invented in 1979 by several graduate students at the University of North Carolina as a way of sending and receiving messages between their university and Duke. Using the same technology, a network of discussion groups, or newsgroups, grew very rapidly in the 1980s. This collection of newsgroups came to be called *Usenet*. You can think of Usenet as the universe of newsgroups, not as a real physical network. The "real" network is made up of Network News Transport Protocol (NNTP) servers. AOL's News servers receive some 20,000 newsgroups and send AOL members' postings around the world.

With so many newsgroups, it's hard to know where to start. America Online can make it easy. This chapter tells you all you need to know about the workings of newsgroups as a global system for sharing information among millions of people. Among other things, you'll discover ways of :

- Finding newsgroups of interest to you

- Keeping track of your favorite newsgroups

- Taking part in newsgroups

- Saving and printing postings

First, let's get a better idea of what newsgroups are by looking at how they're different from mailing lists and how they're organized.

HOW NEWSGROUPS AND MAILING LISTS ARE DIFFERENT

Mailing lists and newsgroups are often lumped together as "discussion groups." It is true that they both involve groups of people discussing topics of shared interest; sometimes, mailing lists even find their way onto Usenet and become available as newsgroups (see "Mailing Lists That Masquerade as Newsgroups"). And they're both great ways to meet people who share an interest. I have a friend who met her husband on a newsgroup.

Mailing lists and newsgroups are different animals, however, and it's good to keep the differences in mind, especially if you'll be using both. For one thing, mailing lists aren't really public; they're semiprivate. You must take the time to subscribe to them. Newsgroups, on the other hand, can be read by anyone. No subscription is necessary.

Note   *AOL allows you to keep a list called Read My Newsgroups, which makes it easy for you to access the newsgroups you like best and to keep track of the articles you've read in those newsgroups. You do not formally "subscribe" to newsgroups the way you do with mailing lists.*

Because newsgroups are public and because they are rarely moderated, no one guarantees that they are kept civil or even that they remain on topic. Larger and more popular newsgroups can get wild, but smaller newsgroups on more focused topics can be every bit as informative and intimate as a mailing list.

The beauty of newsgroups is the absolutely uniform way you use them. While mailing lists require that you learn to subscribe and unsubscribe in a slightly different way for each type of mailing list, on Usenet you access **alt.gothic.fashion** in just the same way as you access **sci.chem.analytical**. America Online makes it easy to browse newsgroups too. There is no good way to browse mailing lists.

A final difference is that newsgroup articles can contain attached files (actually, they're inserted). While mailing lists are used primarily to send text, newsgroups can contain both text and files, including software, sounds, and images. All these files are available to anyone with full access to newsgroups, and America Online's unique FileGrabber service makes it painless to retrieve them.

Mailing Lists That Masquerade as Newsgroups

Several hundred mailing lists are also available as newsgroups, simplifying access and reducing the volume of incoming mail for those who take part. Unlike mailing list messages, newsgroup postings, or *articles*, have to be retrieved—but only when you want, on the specific subjects you want. The **bit** hierarchy (see the next section, "How Newsgroups Are Organized" for more information on hierarchies) contains hundreds of mailing lists in newsgroup form.

A list of mailing lists available over Usenet is also available via FTP at **ftp://rtfm.mit.edu/pub/usenet-by-hierarchy/news/groups/Mailing_Lists _Available_in_Usenet**. (Chapter 8 covers FTP, which you use to send long documents and other files over the Internet.) All lists available as newsgroups accept articles from both Usenet and mailing lists.

HOW NEWSGROUPS ARE ORGANIZED

There are more than 20,000 or so newsgroups available to you via AOL's News servers, which form a big link in the network of worldwide News servers that exchange postings with each other. Here are five newsgroups you might find some evening on America Online:

- **alt.animation.warner-brothers**
- **alt.fishing**
- **misc.taxes**
- **rec.autos.antique**
- **sci.diseases.med.cancer**

At first glance, these newsgroup names look like the addresses you see in e-mail articles (like **answerman@aol.com**) and on Web pages (like **http://www.aol.com**).

Actually, newsgroups are organized and named in a way that's unique to Usenet (see "Which Is It? Internet Address or Newsgroup Address?").

Which Is It: Internet Address or Newsgroup Address?

Unsure whether you're looking at an Internet address or a Usenet newsgroup address? Both kinds of addresses consist of elements separated by a period (pronounced "dot," when spoken). But here's how they differ:

- In an Internet address, or URL (uniform resources locator), the most general element (*com, edu, gov,* etc.) is the *last* part: http://www.aol.**com**, for example. See Chapter 3 on domain names and Chapter 6 on URLs.

- In a newsgroup address, the most general element (*sci, comp, news, alt,* etc.) is the *first* part: **biz**.jobs.offered, for example.

There's another difference: Internet addresses identify actual computers or banks of computers, together with the networks to which they belong. That's why URLs begin with *protocols,* such as *http://* and *ftp://* and *news:*, which govern how physical machines "talk" to each other. Newsgroup names, by contrast, are abstractions used to classify and keep track of people's postings.

Newsgroups are organized in big categories called *hierarchies*. There are two big types of hierarchies on Usenet: *standard* and *alternative*. Each contains subhierarchies, abbreviated in such a way as to indicate their subject matter. At the lowest level are thousands of individual newsgroups. In the standard hierarchies, for example, you'll find the **misc** subhierarchy, which has *miscellaneous* personal-finance and family-oriented newsgroups such as **misc.taxes**. The **misc.taxes.moderated** newsgroup is even more focused, thanks to the presence of a human moderator who keeps conversations on topic and who shares expertise.

Tip   *Newsgroups are the best place to learn about newsgroups, and the most useful hierarchy for beginners is* **news** (*devoted to* newsgroups, *not the evening news*). *The* **news.newusers.questions** *and* **news.answers** *newsgroups, in particular, have a wealth of information if you're just starting out.*

A Matter for the Name Police

On the Internet, newsgroup messages—the documents written by individuals—are called *articles* or *postings*. On AOL they're usually called *messages*, even though e-mail messages and News messages are different.

On the Internet, people refer to clusters of articles devoted to the same topic as *threads*; on AOL, threads are called *subjects*.

And while Internet folks are used to speaking of *hierarchies* and *subhierarchies* of newsgroups, on AOL you'll usually see *categories* and *topics*.

The Standard Hierarchies

Newsgroups were originally organized into the standard—sometimes called the Big Seven or "traditional"—hierarchies listed in Table 5-1. Think of a hierarchy as a sort of bucket in which newsgroups about a certain large theme are stored. Newsgroups in the **sci** hierarchy all have to do with science, and serious, academic science at that. Newsgroups in the standard hierarchies have general circulation via News servers around the world. These newsgroups are created according to a strict protocol (see the "Creating a Newsgroup" box) and tend to be a bit more serious than the alternative hierarchies. The need for a new newsgroup must be established and

Standard Hierarchies	Subject Matter
comp	Computers, networks, hardware, operating systems, multimedia, and the Internet
misc	Taxes, family, kids, investing, education—family matters
news	Usenet news-related topics (*not* the evening news)
rec	Sports, movies, the arts, entertainment, and the like
sci	Serious science—archaeology, biology, chemistry, physics, etc.
soc	Social issues, foreign cultures
talk	Controversial issues—gun control, abortion, etc.

TABLE 5-1   The standard, or traditional, newsgroup hierarchies

accepted by other members of the community, then voted upon. On America Online, you can reliably expect to be able to find all of the standard newsgroups.

Creating a Newsgroup

If you want to create a standard newsgroup, check out "Guidelines for Usenet Group Creation," which is regularly posted to the **news.answers** newsgroup. If you want to create an alternative newsgroup, there's a document for you called "So You Want to Create an Alt Newsgroup," which is regularly posted to the same newsgroup. You can get a sense of the two cultures of the alternative and standard hierarchies by skimming these documents. "Guidelines…" has rigorous protocol that must be followed. In the instructions for creating alt newsgroups, you will read: "Votes? Did someone say vote? Let me repeat. There are _no votes_ in alt. Period." Voting or no voting, both types of hierarchy are deeply democratic in process—no individual or organization controls them.

The Alternative Hierarchies

Alternative hierarchies consist of newsgroups that are relatively easy to form. These hierarchies are growing faster and contain more newsgroups than the standard hierarchies. Sometimes alternative newsgroups pop up before a need for them has been established and then fade away before a community has been able to form.

Because of their low volume and the sometimes limited audience, not all alternative newsgroups are carried by the entire network of News computers. Some alternative newsgroups, however, are devoted to exactly the sort of topics you find in the standard hierarchy, nicely complementing the standard newsgroups. Many alternative newsgroups were, in fact, created to accommodate the volume of a popular standard newsgroup or to handle a fundamental disagreement or because they weren't approved by the Usenet community.

AOL makes an effort to carry a full "feed" of alternative newsgroups, that is, they try to carry all the newsgroups and all their postings. One result of this openness is that some newsgroups are available via AOL that have no articles in them; these newsgroups are "extinct." You can post to them, but it's unlikely anyone will respond. AOL can't do anything about extinct groups. Another result of the vast scope of the newsgroups carried by AOL is that some alternative newsgroups may be highly objectionable to some AOL members, especially parents.

NEWSGROUPS AND PARENTAL CONTROLS

America Online does not censor what you see within a newsgroup. It blocks only those few newsgroups that plainly break U.S. law (because they're used as distribution sites for pirated software, for example). Some newsgroups are thus available on AOL that may contain offensive content.

AOL offers parents several sets of controls to make it more difficult for kids to use objectionable newsgroups. First, AOL makes it difficult to browse any newsgroup that's likely to be objectionable. For more about browsing, see the "Keeping Track of Newsgroups" section.

Parental Controls offer a more powerful second line of defense. For any screen name under a master account, parents can restrict or prevent access as follows:

1. From the Newsgroup window (keyword: Parental), click Parental Controls.

2. Specify a screen name for which to set controls, and click OK. The Blocking Criteria screen comes up (Figure 5-1).

3. Set controls as appropriate, placing a check in one or more of the check boxes for the following options:

Block Expert Add	Prevents a child (if the child has her own screen name) from accessing a newsgroup available on AOL using Expert Add but not listed using the Add Newsgroup feature. Both features are discussed later in this chapter.
Block All Newsgroups	Prevents a child from using *all* newsgroups.
Block Binary Downloads	Prevents a child from downloading possibly objectionable pictures. A binary download may be an image file, included with a newsgroup article.
Use Full Newsgroup List	*Doesn't* restrict newsgroup access, unless you single out specific newsgroups for exclusion (see Step 4).

4. In the first big text fields at the bottom of the Blocking Criteria window, indicate which parts of newsgroup names, if any, you wish to block (*sex* or *binaries*, for example). In the second big text box, indicate which specific newsgroups you do not wish the screen name to use.

5. Click OK to confirm your choices.

The Regional Newsgroups

Regional newsgroups are a type of alternative newsgroup. They're easy to form, but instead of being focused on some subject, they're focused on a geographical area (a city, university, or region). For that area, newsgroups can be devoted to all subjects. Like other alternative newsgroups, the regional newsgroups are not universally carried by the globe's News computers. These alternative newsgroups reside primarily on News servers in the region to which they are devoted.

FIGURE 5-1   Parental Controls are used to restrict access to all newsgroups, certain newsgroups, and downloads

Because America Online is available throughout the U.S. and, increasingly, throughout the world, AOL's News feed includes regional hierarchies ranging from **bermuda.*** and **boulder.*** to **utah.*** and **utexas.***.

> *Note* An asterisk (*), as in bermuda.*, refers to the entire family of newsgroups in a hierarchy, such as **bermuda.jobs.offered**, **bermuda.general**, **bermuda.politics**, and **bermuda.sports**.

More Alternative Hierarchies

Many alternative newsgroups focus on topics of somewhat limited interest but are every bit as serious as the standard newsgroups. At keyword: Newsgroups, click Add Newsgroups to get a list of dozens of alternative hierarchies carried by America Online. Here are a few alternative hierarchies devoted to specific topics or professions.

bionet	For biologists
biz	The proper place to sell and buy commercial products and services
hepnet	For physicists
k12	For teachers in grades kindergarten through twelfth grade

> *Note* AOL does not carry the well-known hierarchy called **Clarinet**, whose newsgroups consist of edited newsfeeds from the commercial wire services. Instead (and better), AOL offers the newsfeeds available in the News channel; the cool news "ticker tape," also in the News channel; and the custom "clipping service," delivered right to your mailbox, available at keyword: News Profile. On the Web, you will find numerous news sources that now compete effectively with the Clarinet service. See the "Today's News" section of Chapter 11.

FINDING NEWSGROUPS

Where do you start? How do you find newsgroups you'll want to read? The standard approach is to either search, if you know just what you're looking for, or browse, if you want to see what's available. If you already have the name of a newsgroup you want to read, you can use the Expert Add feature, as explained in the "Keeping Track of Newsgroups" section.

Searching for Specific Newsgroups

If you're looking for a newsgroup about a specific subject, follow these steps:

1. Go to keyword: Newsgroups. This brings up the main Newsgroups window, shown in Figure 5-2.

2. Click Search All Newsgroups to go to the Search Newsgroup Titles window.

3. Type in a simple but specific search phrase such as *cooking*. Click Search.

4. If your search had results, they'll appear in the Search Results window. Select any newsgroup you want to read and click Add, to add it to Read My Newsgroups. To read the newsgroup, close the window, then click Read My Newsgroups on the main Newsgroups window.

Read your favorite newsgroups

Select newsgroups to be downloaded and read offline

Browse newsgroups

Restrict access for certain screen names

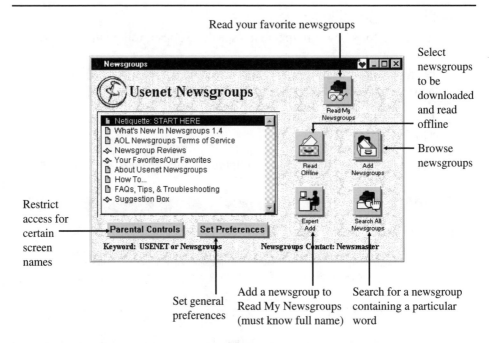

Set general preferences

Add a newsgroup to Read My Newsgroups (must know full name)

Search for a newsgroup containing a particular word

FIGURE 5-2   The main Newsgroup window on AOL

Searching Newsgroups

You can "search newsgroups" in three ways.

First, you can *search for a specific newsgroup*. The easiest way to do this is by using the Search All Newsgroups feature, available from the main Newsgroups window (Figure 5-3). Second, with a newsgroup displayed, you can *search for an article about a specific subject*. (See the "Searching a Long List for Something Specific" box.) Finally, you can *search the body of articles for specific words*.

The first two types of search are easy with AOL. The last kind of search is covered in Chapter 9, which introduces easy-to-use search tools such as DejaNews, Excite, and Infoseek.

Browsing for Newsgroups

You can also *browse* for newsgroups that interest you.

1. From the main Newsgroup window shown in Figure 5-2, click Add Newsgroups.

Add
Newsgroups

2. A list of categories comes up—all the standard and alternative hierarchies. Select a category by double-clicking. The Topics window comes up (Figure 5-3). For each topic, or subhierarchy, you'll see how many newsgroups are associated with it. If there's only one newsgroup, the topic is itself a newsgroup. Double-click to see the associated newsgroup(s). You'll know you're at the bottom of the hierarchy when the window's title bar (at the top) changes from *Topic* to *Newsgroup*.

3. In the Newsgroups window, shown in Figure 5-4, double-click the newsgroup name to go directly to it and start reading (but not posting).

Newsgroup Scoop

The World Wide Web is all the rage, but how do you find out about other Internet resources, such as newsgroups? *Harley Hahn's Internet and Web Yellow Pages* (Osborne/McGraw-Hill, 1997) is an excellent place to start if you're looking for groovy newsgroups.

You can find out about great newsgroups on AOL as well. Each week, in the Newsgroup Scoop (keyword: Scoop), you can read the reviews of three newsgroups recommended by other members. Each newsgroup is rated for its content, traffic, "heat" index, and camp value. A full review gives you a good idea what you're in for if you decide to take part in the newsgroup. If a newsgroup name (such as **rec.arts.anime**) is unfamiliar to you, the introductions provide valuable context. Past weeks' sites are conveniently organized into categories such as Culture, Diversions, Intelligentsia, and Science. Message boards give you the chance to talk about the reviewed

---

KEEPING TRACK OF NEWSGROUPS

With so many newsgroups to read, how do you keep track of the ones you like? America Online lets you do just that in its Read My Newsgroups list. When you

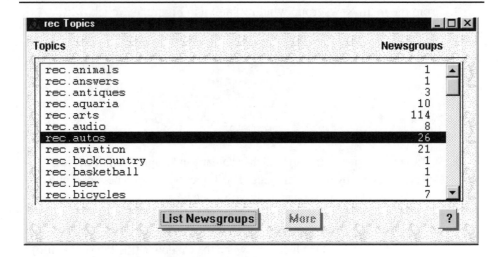

FIGURE 5-3   A list of recreational topics

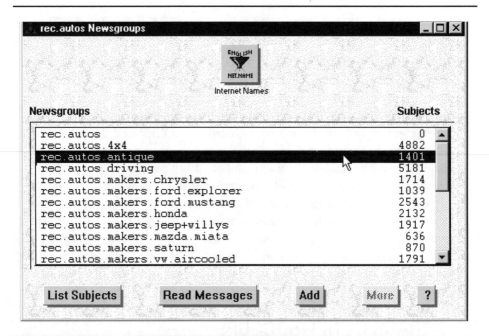

FIGURE 5-4   Use the Add Newsgroups window to "drill down" to the
rec.autos.antique newsgroup; double-click to browse

register as an AOL member, you will find several newsgroups included in this list. You can add and remove newsgroups to and from this list as you please, making it easy to return and read your favorites on a regular basis.

Adding newsgroups to Read My Newsgroups doesn't really "subscribe" you in any formal way; you can read newsgroups without subscribing, and there are times when you want to do just that (see "Just Passing Through: Browsing Newsgroups").

The Read My Newsgroups list has three benefits for you:

- It's a convenient way of quickly getting to the newsgroups you like.

- It's a way of keeping track of articles you have read *within* a newsgroup.

- You can read offline only those newsgroups included in Read My Newsgroups.

 There's another good way of keeping track of your favorite newsgroups—see the "Favorite Place It" text box.

Just Passing Through: Browsing Newsgroups

If you're just browsing, you may *not* want to keep track of all the newsgroups you stumble across. If you're looking for a newsgroup with a particular focus, you won't, for instance, want to keep track of every newsgroup you read on your path to the right one. An easy way to browse is by using Add Newsgroups, as described in "Finding Newsgroups." Or, use keywords. When you browse newsgroups, you read them but can't take part in them (Figure 5-5).

Keywording to a Newsgroup

If you know a specific newsgroup's name—from the newspaper, a book, a friend, or a search of newsgroups, as explained in the previous section—you can go *directly* to the newsgroup using the Keyword window. This is a great, direct way to read newsgroups, but it doesn't give you the option of saving a newsgroup in Read My Newsgroups.

1. From the GoTo menu, select Keyword.

2. In the Keyword window, type in **news** and a colon (**:**) and the name of the newsgroup. For example:
   news:comp.internet.net-happenings.

FIGURE 5-5 When you're browsing, you can only *read* newsgroup postings

Staying a While: Adding to "Read My Newsgroups"

The main reason for keeping track of newsgroups you like is pretty obvious—it makes it easier to return in the future, even when you're offline. If you *don't* know the exact newsgroup name you want to add, start by clicking Add Newsgroup. Burrow down through the hierarchy to the particular newsgroup, and click Add, as described above. If you *do* know the name, you use AOL's Expert Add feature:

1. Go to the main Newsgroup window, and click Expert Add to bring up the Expert Add window.

2. Type the newsgroup's name, and click the Add button. (The field is called "Internet" name, but in fact you're using the "Usenet" name.) Your choice will be confirmed; click OK.

3. Close the Expert Add window.

4. To go to the newsgroup you've just added, click on Read My Newsgroups (Figure 5-6).

5. To open any newsgroup you've ever added, double-click to bring up the screen shown in Figure 5-7. To delete any newsgroups, select them and click Remove.

> *From time to time, you'll get an Invalid Group article when you attempt to read a particular newsgroup using Expert Add. You've either incorrectly entered the newsgroup's name, or the newsgroup is not carried by America Online. Double-check the name, and re-enter it. If you're having persistent problems and you feel the newsgroup should be carried, send e-mail to screen name* **newsmaster**.

5

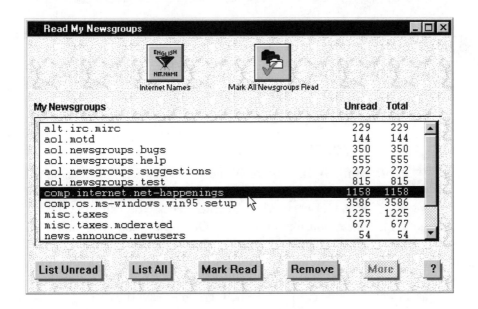

FIGURE 5-6   Read My Newsgroups keeps track of newsgroups you want to revisit. AOL automatically includes several general-interest newsgroups in this list

FIGURE 5-7 When you open a newgroup from Read My Newsgroups you can take part instead of just browsing

Favorite Place It!

Using AOL 3.0 for Windows software, you can add a newsgroup to your Favorite Places folder (available from the AOL tool bar). With Favorite Places, you can store links to every kind of content you like to use on AOL and the Internet—individual e-mail articles, AOL forums, Web pages, and newsgroups. Here's how: With the main window of a newsgroup displayed (you'll see a list of Subjects and Number of articles per subject, as shown in Figure 5-2), there's a heart in the title bar. Just click the heart to add the newsgroup to Favorite Places.

To access the newsgroup, open the Favorite Places folder and double-click the entry for the newsgroup:

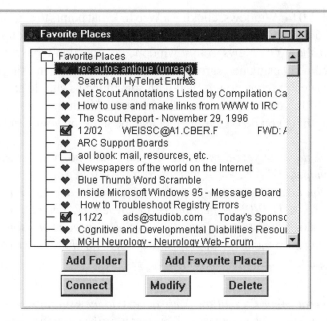

With Favorite Places, you can create a folder for newsgroup, AOL, and Web content—all related to the same subject, for example.

What's the difference between Read My Newsgroups and Favorite Places? Read My Newsgroups consists only of newsgroups, while Favorite Places can be just about any kind of resource. Favorite Places is available offline as well: while offline, open Favorite Places, double-click a newsgroup, and you'll sign onto AOL and open that newsgroup. Finally, with Favorite Places you can keep track of individual articles, although, unlike e-mail messages, the articles won't be available once AOL has archived them (removed them from the list of current articles for a newsgroup), which happens after about two weeks.

Using the Browser to Go to a Newsgroup

Every newsgroup has a URL, or Internet address (see Chapter 6 on URLs). This means that a World Wide Web page can have a link pointing to a newsgroup; click on the link and you go directly to the newsgroup.

Note   *A newsgroup's URL is simple. It consists of* **news:** *plus the newsgroup name, without any spaces and also without slashes (//). You are using URLs when you use the Keyword window to go directly to a newsgroup, as in* **news:comp.internet.net-happenings**.

With AOL 3.0 for Windows, clicking a Web link that points to a newsgroup takes you directly to the newsgroup. When you click a link to a newsgroup in this way, you bring up the AOL Newsgroups window, so you don't have to master an additional method of using newsgroups. On the other hand, when using newsgroups in this way you can't return to the Web with something as simple as a click on the Back button. Still, you do get a taste of a future in which the browser will be the center of everything you do on the Internet and, perhaps, on your computer as well.

Note — *AOL does not yet allow members to use third-party newsreaders such as Trumpet, WinVN, or Agent over its Winsock, but you can use such programs if you take advantage of the "bring your own access" billing plan and access AOL over a TCP/IP connection, as described in Appendix A. If you use a third-party Newsreader over your other connection, you won't be using AOL's News servers, and you must make the appropriate settings for that reader (NNTP server, signature, organizational information, etc.).*

Tip — *Several Web sites allow Web access to newsgroups. One particular favorite of AOL members is Zippo, at **http://www.zippo.com/**. In Chapter 9, you can read about several search services on the Web (notably Excite and DejaNews) that give you access to specific newsgroups and individual posting through the browser. Zippo (an AOL Members Choice site) also provides lists of favorite newsgroups.*

SCANNING NEWSGROUP ARTICLES FOR THE GOOD ONES

Figure 5-7 shows a listing of articles in the **comp.internet.net-happening** newsgroup. Whenever the More button is active (can be clicked), then not all articles are listed; keep clicking More until they're all there. On AOL you can control this listing in a couple of ways:

- Marking articles read or unread
- Ranking articles earliest to most recent or vice versa

Searching a Long List for Something Specific

With newsgroup articles displayed, you can search for articles of special interest by searching for a specific word in their headers.

1. From AOL's Edit menu, select Search in Top Window.

2. In the little window, type in the words of interest, and click Search.

You can use this trick to search your e-mail mailboxes and Personal Filing Cabinet as well.

Read, Unread—What's the Difference?

Figure 5-6 displays articles you have not yet read. This is just like your New mailbox when you're using e-mail, which displays only new messages. However, unlike your New mailbox, you can't tell whether a newsgroup article has been read or not merely by looking at it.

When you read an article, it's automatically defined as *read*, and it won't display next time you open the newsgroup. You can also deliberately define ("mark") one or more articles as *read*. Why would you do this? Some newsgroups have a good deal of *noise*—off-topic, obnoxious, useless, argumentative, and offensive postings, for example. Marking such postings *read* can get them out of the way and help you focus on the articles you're really interested in. Or, if you've just returned from vacation and don't have the time to plow through thousands of articles, just mark them all *read* and close the window.

Why mark articles *unread*? So you can take the time to draft a well-thought-out response to the group (after reading subsequent articles on the same subject). Marking an article unread also lets you download it for offline reading (only unread articles can be downloaded).

With AOL, you can mark articles as *read* or *unread* one at a time, or a bunch at a time. To do so, select the article(s) and click the appropriate button. You can mark all of them read by clicking the Mark All Read button.

Listing Articles First to Last, or Last to First

AOL also gives you the choice of listing articles from most recent to least recent, or vice versa. Here's how:

■ From the main Newsgroup window, click Set Preferences, and click the appropriate button indicating whether you wish to see old or new articles first.

Following a newsgroup in chronological order (with the oldest articles posted first) gives you a sense of how discussions evolve and interrelate. Following in reverse order (from now to then) brings you up to date more quickly; most people are interested in the most recent articles, even though they may lack the context of the previous several weeks' articles. First-to-last (to see what's new) or last-to-first (to see how a thread evolves)—it's your choice.

ARTICLES AND THEIR PARTICLES

Newsgroup articles all contain *headers* and *bodies*. They can contain *files* and *signatures*. Figure 5-8 shows you what you see when you pull up a newsgroup on AOL.

Each line is either a single article or a *thread*. A thread, as the name implies, is a group of articles with the same subject line and, in principle, the same subject. It can consist of two articles or a hundred articles. When you're viewing one article in a thread, you can go to other adjacent articles in the thread by clicking the Previous and Next buttons. If you want to focus on a specific thread while reading a newsgroup, select it and click List to bring up a little window showing the individual postings in the thread, including their authors and the times they were posted.

Let's look at a single article (Figure 5-9). The *header* contains a little information about who sent the article (not shown here) and what the article is about (cars, in this case). Like an e-mail message, it can also provide a time and date. The subject line is uniquely important in newsgroups because it provides the "hook" used to catch the attention of people you don't know. When an article's Subject line is preceded by "re:" the article is a *reply* to another article, and the two form a part of

FIGURE 5-8 A list of articles and threads. If the Number on the right is greater than 1, there's a *thread* available—more than one article on the same subject

a thread. Some newsgroup programs offers a range of other optional headers, including e-mail addresses to use for responding. Here's what a full header can look like:

```
Path:
newsbf05.news.aol.com!newstf01.news.aol.com!audrey01.news.aol.com!not-for-mail
From: lindad72@aol.com
Newsgroups: rec.autos.antique
Subject: Buick 340 V8 crank in 215 block?
Date: 28 Nov 1996 04:42:30 GMT
Organization: AOL http://www.aol.com
Lines: 6
Message-ID: <19961128044400.XAA13056@ladder01.news.aol.com>
NNTP-Posting-Host: ladder01.news.aol.com
X-Admin: news@aol.com
```

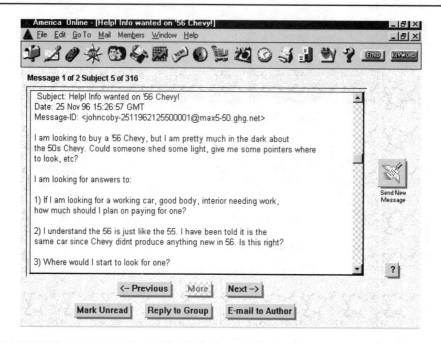

FIGURE 5-9 A newsgroup article, posted to **rec.autos.antique**. The head reads "message 1 of 2," so there's a reply to this article

Tip With AOL you can choose whether to have headers appear at the beginning of articles or at the end. Placing them at the end makes it easier to get to the article but harder to see essential information such as the sender's name. To place headers at the end of messages, click Set Preferences from the Newsgroups window, click the Headers at Bottom button, and click OK.

The *body* of the article is its content. If an article is part of a thread, content from earlier articles will probably be quoted, with each quoted line preceded by a particular character or "spaced in" from the left (Figure 5-10).

Note With newsgroups, as with e-mail, you can quote an article—select only the pertinent parts of the original in order to frame your response when you reply to it. Just use a little program called QCLIP, available in the Software Center at keyword: FileSearch. This is not an AOL utility but was designed to work with the AOL for Windows software.

FIGURE 5-10   Part of the body of a reply to the article shown in Figure 5-9.
An original article and a reply to the article form the start of
a thread

Messages can contain *files*—anything from image and sound files to Windows
utilities. Using other Internet providers, it can be a time-consuming and technical
matter to download, convert, and use files. Using AOL's unique FileGrabber feature,
however, you can extract a file with a point and a click of your mouse, as you'll see
in "Getting Files from Newsgroups is a Breeze."

A final and optional element of an article is the *signature*. If you choose to use
it, this bit of text that identifies you will be automatically added to the end of your
postings. If you want to create a signature file, see the "Who You Are: Adding a
Signature" section for instructions.

RESPONDING TO AN ARTICLE

So, you've read an article. Now what? With an article open (as in Figure 5-9), there
are a couple of things you can do:

- Read it and move on. The article will automatically be marked *read* and won't be displayed next time you visit the newsgroup. If you want the article to be displayed next time you visit the newsgroup, click the Mark Unread button. If the article you've just read is part of a thread, clicking the Previous and Next buttons takes you to the neighboring articles in the thread. If you're at the beginning or end of a thread, Previous and Next take you to the previous and next threads, respectively.

- Respond to the article by sending a reply to the newsgroup. AOL does not let you respond to other newsgroups at the same time (this is called cross-posting). You can respond only to the newsgroup you are reading.

Note   *With newsgroups, your postings go from News server to News server, so it can take a while for your posting to become available to all of the ten million-plus people in the world with News access. Because of the volume of postings worldwide, most News servers get rid of (expire) postings after a couple of days or weeks.*

- Respond only to the author, using e-mail, instead of responding to the entire newsgroup. Click E-mail to Author.

Tip   *Responding to the author is appropriate for personal, heated, and off-topic responses to an author's posting to the newsgroup. It's the right choice if what you have to say would not be of likely interest to the group at large.*

- Start an entirely new thread, or at least send an article to the newsgroup on a new topic, by clicking Send New Message (read "Threads of Your Own: Starting a New Subject").

Who You Are: Adding a Signature

If you plan on sending articles to a newsgroup, it's a good idea to add a signature. A *signature* is a bit of text that will be automatically added to every posting you make to any newsgroup. It's a way of tacking on a joke, a motto, or some contact information. You can also advertise a Web site or feature information that promotes your business. You can even add elaborate ASCII (text) drawings of dragons, cows, and other pictures, though some people on the Internet object to signatures longer than four lines as a waste of shared computer resources.

To add a signature:

1. From the main Newsgroups window, click Set Preferences (note that this is different from the Preferences button on the window you use to read an individual newsgroup).

2. In the Signature box at the bottom of the window, type in the text you want to use (see Figure 5-11). Click OK.

Tip *Before you share your signature with the world, you might want to post a test article to one of the newsgroups devoted exclusively to this purpose, such as **alt.test** or **misc.test**.*

Threads of Your Own: Starting a New Subject

If you don't want to respond to another person's posting but do have something to say, start your own thread! From the newsgroup window, click the Send New Message button to send an article.

FIGURE 5-11   Supply a signature to *automatically* add a personalized message on every article you post to any newsgroup

The Post New Message window asks you for only two things: a Subject line and a Message, and lets you make the choice of whether to include a signature file as well (see the "Who You Are: Adding a Signature" section). When you've polished your article, click Send. Your article will join a global flow of information that reaches every continent and is accessible by millions of people. The window appears very similar if you are replying to an article, except the Subject line is filled in ("re: such and such"), and you have the choice of sending the post to the author of the original post, by e-mail.

READING AND POSTING OFFLINE

FlashSessions is an AOL feature that lets you take care of some Net chores even when you are not logged on. For communication such as e-mail and newsgroups, where people aren't communicating in *real time* (at the same time), working offline makes perfect sense.

With a FlashSession, your computer signs on automatically at times you specify, performs a task such as reading newsgroup articles, then logs off again. You can download all your newsgroup postings at regular intervals, then browse them in leisure.

To read your newsgroups offline with FlashSessions:

1. In the Newsgroups window, click Read Offline to bring up the Choose Newsgroups window (Figure 5-12).

2. The Subscribed Newsgroups list shows the newsgroups you've put in the Read My Newsgroup list—*these are the only newsgroups you can read offline.* The Newsgroups to Read Offline list shows the newsgroups you want to read offline. Highlight the newsgroup you want to read offline in the Subscribed Newsgroups list and click the Add > button. You can quickly select all newsgroups in your personal list by clicking the Add All >> button. Any newsgroups you select are moved to the Newsgroups to Read Offline list. To remove a newsgroup from offline status, select its name in the Newsgroups to Read Offline list and click the < Remove button. Click << Remove All if you don't want to read any newsgroups offline. *You must click OK to save any changes you have made.* If you don't want to save your changes, click the Cancel button. Exit the newsgroups area.

FIGURE 5-12   Add newsgroups from your Subscribed Newsgroups list to a
FlashSession for offline reading

Now, set up a FlashSession:

1. From the Mail menu, select Set up FlashSession. The window shown in
   Figure 4-5 comes up. The last two check boxes listed allow you to
   "retrieve unread" and "send outgoing" newsgroup postings.

2. Place checks in one box or both.

Tip   *If you use "Copy author of original article by e-mail" when replying to
an article and then do an offline session, you must also check the Send
Outgoing Mail box in order to send your e-mail response(s).*

3. To participate in a newsgroup while offline, you need to activate a FlashSession. You have a choice. From the Mail menu, select Activate Session Now. AOL immediately downloads or uploads articles for you. To schedule regular sessions, click Schedule FlashSession, indicate your time preferences, and click OK. Your computer must be on during the times you have indicated.

Tip *You may need to run several FlashSessions to retrieve all your new articles. An easy way to do this is to run your FlashSession with the "Sign off when finished" box unchecked. Then you can run several in a row.*

4. Your selected newsgroups are downloaded into your Personal Filing Cabinet. To read them, click the Personal Filing Cabinet icon on the tool bar. Double-click on the Newsgroups folder. To read newsgroup articles, double-click on any article.

Because all of the items in the Personal Filing Cabinet are stored on your computer, it is a good idea to delete folders and articles that you've read and don't want to keep.

DON'T BE A JERK!

In your private e-mail, netiquette is important because it's easy to be misunderstood. E-mail is so ubiquitous that good netiquette can make a big difference in how you get along with others. On mailing lists, netiquette becomes more important because you're dealing with people you probably don't know—people who won't extend to you the benefit of the doubt. But in newsgroups, netiquette is even *more* important, because you are communicating with people you definitely don't know—unlike mailing lists, no one really knows who reads newsgroups. Your words can get you in trouble in countless ways. They can make the wrong impression or rub people the wrong way. Newsgroups themselves can be damaged by careless language, if quarrelsome behavior and flaming distract from their purpose.

What follows are some guidelines, distilled from Chuq Rosbach's classic "Primer on How to Work With the Usenet Community." If you're serious about newsgroups, read this document from beginning to end; it's regularly posted to the **news.answers** newsgroup.

- Lurk before you leap.

- Respect your reader.

- Respect people who *might* be your readers.

- Be brief.

- Write carefully.

- Use clear and descriptive subject lines.

- Post to the correct newsgroup.

- Avoid sarcasm and irony.

- When responding, summarize.

- Do not use a newsgroup as an advertising medium.

- Don't post the same message repeatedly.

GETTING FILES FROM NEWSGROUPS IS A BREEZE

 Newsgroups are a source of more than text articles. They are also a source of files such as software, images, and sounds. You can use the Search All Newsgroups button on the main Newsgroups window to find such newsgroups.

In e-mail, you can get files *attached* to articles. With newsgroups, files are *inserted* inside articles. How? They are "encoded" using a technique called UUE (UNIX to UNIX Encoding). Encoding articles is a way of taking *binary* files (programs or the documents used by programs) and turning them into text files. To the eye, these files look like gibberish, but, rest assured, they're meant to be understood by computers, not people:

```
begin 644 Dannyboy.mid
M351H9`````8`0`("A-5')K````0@#_?PH``%LC`0`%`@L``/\M#"'41A;FY Y
M($$)O>0#__5`5@@`,````#__$0$0#($)9`:\0#@!::``@:\_`U_$`$$T)`'0`$$8`$$U4
M<FL```1\V/\###49L=49L;F=.`0'P`$$W`P/H$$/$$%OL2%p#=#D___#`3/A#c`=#`$HHXxx
M2```2F$l2@`U3&&!I-$P``$IA/$$H`l$$$QAl$$ly`ll`lx&l/yl$`l$$]Alolil`l$$QAl$$il`
M`$IAl$$H`l$$AAl$@`l$$$l5A@l31%`l`!(83Q(`!,83Q,`l!-83Q-`l!/88$$T3P`
M46$$\40`l3V$$\l3P`l3&$\l3`l`2&$\l2`l`l3&$\l3`l`2F&"+$$H`l$$=Al$$<`l$$AA
```

The great virtue of these files is that they can be transmitted the same way simple text is transmitted. The resulting text files can be very long, so files encoded as text are often automatically broken up (by the encoding programs) into several files. In the olden days, decoding UUE files took work, luck, and time: you'd consolidate many files into one file, then run that one file through a special *de*coding utility. The result: the same file (an image, a sound, a program, whatever), but on someone else's computer.

AOL's FileGrabber tool makes it easy to extract and use files that have been UUEncoded. Here's an article in a newsgroup that contains a file, or part of a file (in this case a tuneful MIDI file with an electronic version of "Moon River"):

1. Click Download File.

2. Indicate where to put the file on your hard disk and click OK. Make sure to download your files to a safe place, not in the AOL Download directory, which might be deleted if you make a major upgrade of your AOL software. A progress bar tracks the download, letting you know approximately how long the download will take. If the file is spread out over a couple of articles, FileGrabber automatically finds all the articles and puts them together before downloading and decoding.

If you're downloading an image file (GIF, PCX, JPG format), you will see the file after it's been entirely downloaded. If it's a sound file (WAV, MIDI format), AOL displays or plays the file automatically. Chapter 8 goes into file types, with tips for handling types of downloaded files that aren't automatically played or displayed.

When Files Aren't Immediately Usable

FileGrabber is a neat feature when it works, and it usually does. If you've ever decoded a UUEncoded file, you will be instantly impressed by FileGrabber's power and ease of use. But sometimes, FileGrabber is unable to handle the files inserted into newsgroup articles for the following reasons:

- Some files you extract from newsgroups will be compressed for quicker downloading, or "zipped" up to make it possible to retrieve several files at the same time. You'll need special software for decompressing or unzipping these files. WinZip, from AOL's software libraries (keyword: FileSearch), can help you with most files. (See Chapter 8.)

- Some files won't be usable because they are spread out over several articles and at least one article is missing. There is nothing you can do about this except to send e-mail to the poster of the file and request a reposting.

- Some files are in an unusual format or are "MIME-encoded," and can't be handled by FileGrabber. You may have better luck decoding the file manually using software available in AOL's software libraries. The article itself will usually indicate the format clearly at the top. At keyword: FileSearch, do a search for that format to retrieve software for *handling* the format. Double-click a likely-seeming program and read the accompanying information file. Download and install the software as instructed in the information file.

Sending Files in Newsgroups

AOL makes it very easy to retrieve files from articles, but you'll need extra software to post files to newsgroups, because you'll need to convert a binary file into a text file—you may also need to split the text file into several smaller files. At keyword: FileSearch, you can search for programs that UUEncode. Follow the instructions of any of these programs for converting binary files. Once a file has been converted, it's a simple matter to paste the article(s) into the Post New Message window and to post it to the appropriate newsgroup.

ESSENTIAL READING: FAQS

Many claims are made about the Internet as a source of information about everything under the sun. Much of this vaunted treasure, especially on the Web, is neither systematic nor reliable. In newsgroups, however, information has been systematically collected and, more important, *cooperatively* reviewed and refined, sometimes over many years. The result is a large collection of Frequently Asked Question documents, or FAQs. These FAQs address questions about either individual newsgroups or the topics to which the newsgroups are devoted. Sometimes they look at both.

What's special about FAQs is that they are written and commented on by many members of a newsgroup's community. Over time, they become widely accepted as authoritative within the community and genuinely useful beyond it. In theory, everybody can recommend changes to the FAQs' maintainer, who is as a rule prominently identified in the FAQ.

Note *The assumption behind FAQs is that it's a waste of people's time and network bandwidth for old-timers to repeatedly answer beginners' routine questions. So, the idea that the Net has lots of people ready and eager to answer your questions is not always true. If you need human help, the best place to start is on AOL in a forum such as AnswerMan or NetGuide.*

Some FAQs make for good reads and serve as useful introductions to difficult topics. Some provide great sources for self-instruction if you want to learn more about anything Internet-related, for example, MIME, graphics formats such as JPG, access forms such as ISDN, and Usenet itself. Look for FAQs on non-technical subjects such as dogs, puzzles, specific disabilities, running, medicine, model rockets, and on and on.

FAQs are routinely published in the newsgroups they grow out of, as well as in the **news.answers** newsgroup. The FAQ archives of **news.answers** are available in a famous collection called **rtfm.mit.edu**, an FTP site. (Think of an FTP site as a big public hard disk on someone else's computer—a collection of files contained in folders contained in more folders. Chapter 8 goes into more detail about FTP.) Several Web sites carry this FAQ archive as well, including:

```
http://www.cis.ohio-state.edu/hypertext/faq/usenet/
http://www.uni-passau.de/archive/faq/news.answers/
```

The good news for AOL members is that the FAQ archive is easily available on AOL as well. Here's how to access it:

1. Use keyword: FTP to go to AOL's FTP area. Once there, click the Go To FTP button.

2. From the listbox of FTP sites, double-click on **rtfm.mit.edu:/pub**. Information about the site comes up. Click OK.

3. Navigate the site by double-clicking the **usenet-by-hierarchy** folder, then the **news** folder, and finally the **news.answers** folder—the archives of the **news.answers** newsgroup.

4. Browse the list for topics of interest. Note that topics are alphabetically arranged, and that topics with capital letters precede topics with small letters.

SAVING AND PRINTING MESSAGES

Newsgroups, especially FAQs, are extraordinary repositories of information and knowledge. Saving and printing them is a way of extending their value by making them easily available when you're not online. As always on the Internet, do not incorporate any content from FAQs in your own writing without explicit mention of the source and without permission from the writer of the original material.

To save an article:

1. Display the article and then, from the Edit menu, select Save.

2. Give the file a name and move it into the appropriate folder, then click OK.

To print an article, display the article and click the Printer icon on the tool bar.

FROM HERE...

Community is what draws people to the global Internet. Traditionally, community on the Internet can be found in newsgroups and mailing lists, the 100,000 or so discussion groups in which you are likely to learn something new and meet other people with similar interests. On AOL, you have no effective limits on your access to these small but planet-circling communities.

The next chapters focus on *information* on the Internet. The World Wide Web, the driving force in today's Internet, is the focus of the next two chapters.

Chapter **6**

Exploring the Web
with America Online

If it's human, it's on the World Wide Web. People use the Web to advertise their products, market their services, celebrate their ideas, amuse their friends, *make* friends, vent their frustrations, campaign for President, publish their magazines without cutting down trees or paying postage, and teach children how to discern stars and dissect frogs. The Web has been called a publishing revolution comparable to the invention of movable type. Maybe it is, maybe it's not, but it *has* produced approximately 100 million globally distributed pages of information, on every subject, in an amazingly short period of time. The entire experience of exploring the Web and creating Web pages is available to you through America Online.

What *is* the Web?

In its origins, the Web was just a way of getting at information available through *other* Internet services; it was a common interface to newsgroups, Telnet, and FTP. The physicists and computer scientists who launched the WWW Project in 1989 shared the vision of *hypertext*: linking related information located on networks anywhere in the world into a seamless and easy-to-navigate web of information.

What happened next made the Web the white-hot center of the Internet. Thanks to the fundamental simplicity of the hypertext language, called HTML (for Hypertext Markup Language), the Web quickly evolved into a way for people, and not only scientists, to both access and *publish* information, thereby creating even more sources of information.

Then came a major change in the software you use to navigate the Web—*browsers*. The first browsers were meant for reading text. In 1993, a browser called Mosaic, with a "graphical" interface, displayed images as well as text and allowed users to get around by the click of a mouse. In 1994, Mosaic went commercial and was refined and marketed by a new company called Netscape Communications Corp. In a brilliant marketing ploy, Netscape distributed *free* Macintosh, Windows, and Unix versions of their browser to almost anyone who wanted the software.

In 1995, software giant Microsoft got into the act with a competing browser called Internet Explorer, also free. With free software such as Netscape and Internet Explorer, and with an exploding universe of information to browse, the Web went mainstream in 1995. The Microsoft browser is now integrated into the AOL software, and a customized version of Netscape is available as well, at keyword: Netscape.

Where Is the Web on AOL?

Eager to get started? You can get the hang of the Web yourself by just playing around. For all the fine points, you can use this chapter as a reference. The Web's always a click away when you're on AOL:

- From the main AOL window, click the Globe on the toolbar to go to the AOL Web site.

- In the Keyword window, type in the entire Web address, or URL. See "Where Is That Page? URLs?" Try it now if you want, using any of the hundreds of URLs provided in Chapter 11. Or, just go to keyword: Web or keyword: WWW, a quick way to get to the AOL Web site.

- Whenever you see one of the following icons in an AOL channel, double-click it to go directly to a Web site:

Whenever you see underlined text in a different color, you can click on it to link to related information. For more information on getting to specific places on the Web, see "Getting From A to B: How to Visit A Web Site Using AOL's Browser."

America Online gives you everything you need to enjoy the World Wide Web's multimedia feast of sounds, pictures, and animations. This chapter provides everything you need to get started. You'll learn how to:

- Use the AOL browser

- Get from place to place on the Web

- Search for information on the Web

- Enjoy multimedia files with helper applications and "plug ins"

- Use the browser to access other Internet services—Gopher, FTP, e-mail, Telnet, and newsgroups

- Get out of jams

Note   *AOL 3.0 for Windows comes in two versions, and each version has a different integrated browser. This chapter focuses* primarily *on the Windows 95 version of the AOL browser, which includes version 3 of Microsoft's Internet Explorer. The other browser was made by an AOL company called BookLink. The primary differences between the two browsers lie in the preferences they offer and the way they handle multimedia. These differences are spelled out in the appropriate sections of this chapter.*

How It Works

A *page* is the unit of the Web. When you access the Web on America Online, you are requesting a single page of information. Your request goes to one of AOL's big computers, or *servers*, which opens up a connection over a very fast communications line to the computer (also called a server) where the page is located. AOL then requests a copy of the page. When it arrives, the page is transferred to your computer. When you browse the Web, you're really bringing the Web, or at least a page (with links to other pages), to yourself.

If the page you're requesting has built-in graphics—as AOL's home page does—the graphics files come to your computer, too, along with any links, which are bits of text or pictures you can click to get more information. Click a link and presto, another page comes to you, taking the place of the one you were just visiting. The browser does no more than request a page and present it to you—its formatting, pictures, and other elements ("A Page and Its Elements").

TERMS THAT CHANGED THE WORLD: URL AND HTML

A Web page is the basic unit of the World Wide Web. Every Web page has its own address, or URL (Uniform Resource Locater). The page itself is a simple text file, created in HTML (the Hypertext Markup Language), which your browser displays as a more or less polished document. Let's look closer at these two fundamental aspects of every Web page.

Where Is That Page? URLs

A URL is simply an Internet address. Every piece of information on an Internet server has its own separate address.

 *URLs always take you to a specific file on the Web. If you type in a URL without a file name (**http://www.aol.com/search/**), it's because a specific filename is assumed as the starting point in a directory, such as index.html or main.html.*

A URL such as **http://www/aol.com/search** has three parts:

1. The first bit, *http*, specifies a *protocol*. A protocol is just a set of rules for exchanging information between two computers. That may sound complicated, but it just indicates which Internet service you want to use, such as the Web (http), e-mail (mailto), file transfer (ftp), or newsgroups (news).

Note *More information about non-hypertext protocols is available in the "Your All-Purpose Browser."*

2. The next bit, **www.aol.com**, is the domain name, which tells you a little more about the site—whether it's a company and perhaps where it's located, for example. The domain name scheme used for Web domains is the same as that used for e-mail messages (see "Addresses Anatomized" in Chapter 3). Reading a domain name from left to right, you go from a specific computer to its domain. Many Web servers begin with *www* and end with *com*.

3. The final bit of the URL, */search*, is the specific page or directory path to the page you are requesting. A path is the directory or folder where the

Web page resides. On an Internet computer, a path is a series of folders and subfolders, each level separated by a forward slash (/), such as /mycomputer/myfamily/mykids/ella/circus.jpg. You can tell an actual file because it usually ends in a file "extension" such as .HTML, .JPG, or .GIF.

How Is That Page Put Together? HTML

Web pages are ordinarily formatted in the *Hypertext Markup Language* (HTML). Figure 6-1 shows a page of marked-up text, and Figure 6-2 shows the corresponding page as the AOL browser displays it.

How does HTML turn into something intelligible, even cool? The text you read is "tagged" to instruct browsers how to display it. The browser looks at the tags and displays text and pictures accordingly. If your browser sees a "bold" tag (), it displays text in bold until it's told to turn the tag "off" (). If it sees a "link" tag, it displays some blue (or some other color) underlined text that can be clicked to request another Web page from an Internet computer. If it sees a tag for a graphic, it fetches the graphic file and displays the image *inline*. And so on.

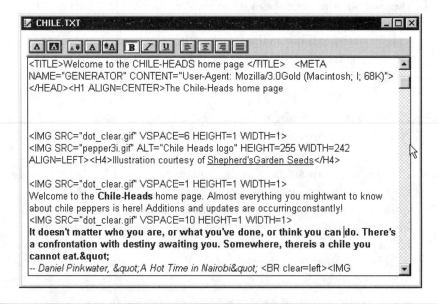

FIGURE 6-1   HTML never won a beauty contest

The Chile-Heads home page

Illustration courtesy of <u>Shepherd's Garden Seeds</u>

Welcome to the **Chile-Heads** home page. Almost
everything you might want to know about chile peppers is
here! Additions and updates are occurring constantly!
**It doesn't matter who you are, or what you've done,
or think you can do. There's a confrontation with
destiny awaiting you. Somewhere, there is a chile
you cannot eat."**
-- Daniel Pinkwater, "A Hot Time in Nairobi"

FIGURE 6-2   Figure 6-1's Web page, with a title, some text, a graphic, and
a hyperlink

Tip   Inline *means part of the page, not displayed separately. Graphics are the
most important inline elements of a Web page, but more and more you will
see video, Java, and other inline files as well.*

Different browsers will present the same Web page differently. What's graphical
about the World Wide Web is a matter of how the browser on your computer presents
a page. Netscape and Internet Explorer will take the same tag and render it slightly
differently. Some tags or Web content can't be displayed by all browsers.

HTML is easy to learn, and AOL makes it even easier using the Personal
Publisher service (keyword: PP2). Personal Publisher writes the HTML code for
you automatically. If you know even a little HTML, you can tweak and refine your
Personal Publisher page into a thing of beauty. Chapter 7 gets you up and running
with Personal Publisher.

A PAGE AND ITS ELEMENTS

A Web page can consist of any or all of several HTML elements. These are the
various parts of a Web page that you see (or hear or otherwise experience), which
together convey some content or message:

- Text
- Graphics
- Links
- Forms
- Tables
- Frames
- Java
- Multimedia

If you'll be making Web pages, good design usually boils down to choosing the right elements in the most effective layout for a given message. If you'll be exploring the Web, it doesn't take long to become a Web connoisseur!

Text

Thanks to its academic origins, the Internet was built on words, and words make the Net a feast for the mind. HTML offers many ways to present *text* for maximum effect. Your AOL browser, like any good browser, can display many text effects, including:

- Several levels of headers (varying in size and "weight"); headers, like the word *Text* in this section, show you how a document is organized
- Numbered and bulleted lists, as well as lists within lists
- Text of different sizes, colors, and fonts
- Emphasis such as bold and italics
- Alignment of text (and other elements) along the right margin or the left margin or centered between the margins
- Text links (or *hyperlinks*) to other pages

Even the modest bit of text in Figure 6-2 shows text with bold, italics, a centered head (the title), a lower-level head ("Illustration courtesy of…"), and hyperlinks!

Graphics

Pictures make the Web a feast for the eyes as well as the mind. You'll encounter several types of images on the Web:

- *Backgrounds (wallpapers)* are the colors or repeating images (*tiles*) that create a certain feeling and mood, usually to reinforce the actual content or message being conveyed. Backgrounds come in every imaginable color and pattern.

- *Inline* images are graphics files that are downloaded along with any HTML pages you fetch. Since it can take a while to download and display these images and since they don't always provide a lot of information, you can choose to turn images off. See "Turn Down the Picture."

- *Animated GIFs* look like simple movies. Some inline graphics files contain *several* images, each different enough from the previous image to create the impression of simple movement. You'll see animated GIFs all over the Web; they're the easiest way to add action to a Web page. Chapter 7 shows how to add an animated GIF to your own page using AOL's Personal Publisher 2.

- Images can themselves be *hyperlinked*; click the image and you're linked to another page. Hyperlinked images can take the form of an *image map*—click a *part* of the image and you'll go to a specific page, click another part and you go to a different page.

- Text captured as a graphic file, to create any effect.

Images of every kind are everywhere on the Web. They can add pizzazz to a page but can also slow down the time it takes to use the page. AOL offers a patented technology for compressing graphics files which speeds up their download times. And on AOL you always have the choice of turning off images altogether, though it makes the Web a less-interesting place.

Turn Down the Picture!

Browsers, including AOL's, offer a standard option of allowing you to turn off images altogether, to speed up downloads. These days, with faster modems, better graphics, and image-compression technologies, turning off the images isn't necessarily a good idea; you lose too much information. But if you have a 14.4K or slower modem, you still might want to do so, as follows:

1. With the browser open, click Prefs.

2. In the General tab, make sure there's no check in the Show Pictures box. Click OK.

 If you're using the non-Windows 95 browser and want to turn off graphics, click Prefs, and click in the No Graphics radio button.

Links, Also Known as Hyperlinks

A link is something you click to get a Web page with related content. Links are often called *hyper*links, because they make hypertext possible—the transparent linking of related information, regardless of location. "Hypertext" these days uses clickable images as well as text links. You can spot linked text because it is underlined and generally in blue, though in the "Setting Your Preferences" section, you'll learn how to adjust the color of links you have and haven't clicked.

To tell whether a word or a picture is hyperlinked, pass your mouse over the item. If it's a link, you'll see the pointed-to URL in the status bar at the bottom of your browser. Also, your mouse pointer (arrow) turns into a pointing finger, meaning you can click the link. That's the way things work on AOL, too: try passing your mouse slowly over any tool on the toolbar—the arrow turns into a pointing finger. With JavaScript or VBScript, a savvy page designer can make the status bar say just about anything.

Forms

With version 3.0 of the AOL for Windows software, forms are available to AOL members exploring the Web. A form makes a Web page into a mini-application, as in the Home Fair (Figure 6-3), a Washington, D.C.-area information service for people anywhere who are thinking of purchasing a home.

Forms give you all the standard Windows features you may know from other applications: radio buttons, check boxes, entry fields, drop-down listboxes, and buttons for processing or canceling your entries. You see forms in many places on the Web: when you register to use a site to buy something, when you customize a site, and when you take a poll or enter a contest. Forms make the Web a more interactive, less static place because with forms you're giving data to a Web site, not just passively receiving data.

Tables

Tables allow for the formatting of text and images (and anything else) in rows and columns. They're a standard presentation technique and a key enhancement of HTML version 3.2 over previous versions (Figure 6-4). The value of tables is best

6

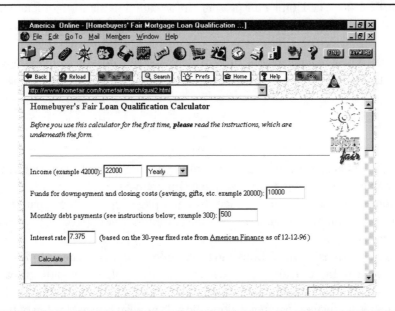

FIGURE 6-3   The Home Fair's mortgage calculator is a mini-application that takes your data, runs it through formulas, and returns useful information (see Figure 6-4)

FIGURE 6-4   The Home Fair presents information in the form of a table, for easy scanning and interpretation

appreciated when viewing a table through a browser that doesn't support them—the text is often a mess.

Frames

Netscape Communication Corp. pioneered use of frames, which AOL's browser now displays. Think of a frame as a way of dividing your browser into separate windows, each capable of displaying a different page (Figure 6-5).

If frames are set up properly, each different page appears in a separate frame. Click a link in one frame, and you're transported to a new page in that frame or another frame.

Why do you need frames? Sites can be complex, and pages can be long—longer at least than can fit vertically in a browser. Usually, a site's navigational bar—the buttons you click to get to the various parts of a site—are at the bottom of the site, though increasingly they're ranged along the side or positioned at the top of the main page. With frames, the "table of contents" (the site's navigational bar) can be made available at all times, so that it is easier to jump back and forth between different parts of a site. It is possible to have several frames at a time.

Buying Things on the Web: It's Safe!

It's a short step from being about to fill out a form that supplies a Web server with personal data to filling out an *order form* with your name, address, phone number, and credit card number. More and more companies sell products and services in this way. If the products are electronic (any publication or piece of software that can be digitized and sent over the phone lines), they can be delivered as well as purchased on the Web. All other products must use the postal or overnight services. The Internet Mall (**http://www.internet-mall.com**) collects links to thousands of merchants who sell items from jewelry to chocolates to books to CDs on the Web.

Is it safe to buy things on the Web?

The AOL browser supports an Internet security standard called Secure Sockets Layer (SSL). SSL protects your entire transaction, not just confidential data such as your credit card number. First, SSL *confirms the identity* of the company Web server from which you buy (this is called *authentication*). It also *encrypts the data* sent back and forth between you and the company Web server—scrambling the data packets so they are practically impossible to reconstruct. Finally, it *ensures the integrity of the data* transmitted between you and the server, so that tampered data will be considered invalid and rejected.

As a result of these measures, you can have confidence that your transaction is safe on the Internet. *Completely* safe? No, but nothing is. Consider the following: (1) No one has yet lost money to "robbers" on the Internet, and very big companies such as Cisco are beginning to do a major share of their overall business on the Internet. (2) Your "real-life" transactions are subject to real-life risks through phone tampering, lost credit cards, and mislaid credit card slips. Virtual transactions are subject to fewer risks and are generally better protected.

There's another aspect to your security on the Web: the *confidentiality* of what you do and where you browse. See the "Cookies" text box later in this chapter for more information.

6

Frames have other uses as well. They can present advertisements in such a way that the advertisement is always present in one frame even if you navigate somewhere else in another frame. New technologies make it possible for ads to rotate within a banner every couple of minutes. Frames can also present the site's title as

FIGURE 6-5 Frames used at the Dove Foundation's site. Note the ads (bottom frame), the fixed banner (top frame), and table of contents (left frame)

a constant feature, so you'll always know which site you're visiting. Some title frames remain visible even after you've left the site altogether, by linking to another site that's displayed in another frame.

The main problem with frames is that they can they take up a lot of space. Sometimes they leave too little space to read text; sometimes, as a result, you *must* resize them. To resize a frame, slowly pass your mouse over the frame border and, when the mouse cursor turns into a double arrow, click and drag the border to resize the two adjoining frames. Another problem with frames is that it can be tricky to navigate within a site with frames (see "Navigating Frames" a little later in this chapter). More and more, you will see borderless frames, so you don't have to resize them.

You'll also find other elements used in place of frames. A borderless table, for example, can be used to present the same information as a frame, without taking up space with borders and scroll bars.

Java

The traditional Web is static: you request a page of HTML, and your browser downloads and presents it. A page just sits there till you download another page. Since around 1994, Web developers have added active and interactive elements to Web pages, but all the processing takes place at one central computer, "serving" pages to thousands or millions of people.

When you request a Web page with a Java element, you bring life to the Web experience. The experience not only becomes more interactive, but it's all taking place at your computer—which is good for you (performance is better) and good for the Internet (you're not using scarce computing and networking resources).

Note   *To use Java and Javascript, you must be using the Windows 95 version of AOL 3.0 (with the Microsoft browser).*

You're likely to see two forms of Java while using AOL's browser. A Java "applet" is a little program that you download and play on your computer. You can simulate the Bay Area transit system, watch falling objects, play ping pong or Chinese Checkers, view a scrolling ticker tape, or try to figure out a 3D Rubik's cube. With Java, you can even chat across the Web. Sometimes applets "load" in separate windows, which are sometimes in a little box within the Web page. Over a dial-up connection, Java applets can take a couple of minutes to load and play. Hundreds of applets are available at Gamelan (**http://www.gamelan.com**).

Tip   *AOL's WebDiner (keyword: Web Diner) contains folders of information about Java and Javascript, with many links to Web sites. They're available in the Web Developers Resource Center, in the Websoup folder. The Java forum (keyword: Java) contains many links, plus message boards, software, and tutorials.*

You'll also encounter "Javascript," a computer "scripting" language that can be integrated into a page's HTML. The effect of Javascript is more subtle and less jarring than the experience of applets in their current form. You'll see some effective Javascript at work on AOL's Web site and, of course, at Netscape's site.

Multimedia Gumdrops

Java is just one of the many elements working to enliven the Web experience. These days a Web page can also play home to other elements as well, including "streaming" sounds, videos, and animations. Some of these files play in separate "helper applications" and others play right inside the browser. Increasingly, you'll encounter a Microsoft technology called ActiveX as well, which delivers specific sounds, videos, and animations directly to your computer. The "Sights, Sounds, Moving Pictures: Working with Multimedia Files" section provides a compact guide to using multimedia Web pages.

 Some multimedia effects require use of the AOL 3.0 for Windows 95 browser.

YOUR DASHBOARD: A CLOSER LOOK AT YOUR BROWSER

The Web's the same the world over—text, pictures, and any additional elements, packaged up as HTML pages. Browsers, however, behave differently, and they *display* Web pages differently. Let's take a moment to closer look at the AOL browser, which sports an AOL look but, inside, contains Microsoft's powerful Internet Explorer technology.

Browsers are becoming mainstream applications, like word processors and spreadsheets, with the difference that the "documents" they use aren't located on your own computer and could be anywhere on the globe. More and more you'll find that your Internet applications and your standard desktop applications work closely together.

Which Version Do You Have?

To tell which version you have, choose About America Online from the Help menu. You will see either *America Online 3.0 for Windows* or *America Online 3.0 for Windows 95*. If you use Windows 95 but don't have the Windows 95 version of AOL, you can upgrade at keyword: Upgrade. The system requirements for AOL 3.0 for Windows 95 are provided in Appendix A.

 This chapter focuses on the Microsoft browser, so if you're using the BookLink browser, not everything in this chapter will apply to your browser. The most important differences between the two browsers are pointed out wherever appropriate.

Opening Your Browser

The fastest way to get to the Web is to click the Globe icon of the main AOL toolbar, which spirits you directly to the AOL Web site, **http://www.aol.com**. You can also get to AOL's Web site by going to keyword: Web or keyword: WWW. The AOL Web site is automatically set as your home page, but in "Setting Your Preferences" you'll see how to start with any page you want (see "Changing Your Home Page"). Figure 6-6 shows the AOL Web site's opening page.

The Stand-alone Microsoft Internet Explorer Browser

When you install the integrated Microsoft browser (Windows 95 version of AOL 3.0), you also simultaneously install the Microsoft browser as a completely separate ("stand-alone") application. Its icon is placed on your desktop (modestly labeled "The Internet"). You can, if you want, run both the integrated and the stand-alone browsers at the same time, if, for example, a large page or file is downloading, and you want to do something else, or if you need a full-screen browser (the stand-alone version). You must be logged onto AOL to use the stand-alone Microsoft browser, since it's a "Winsock" application, as explained in Chapter 10. This chapter focuses on the integrated browser, not the stand-alone.

Naming of Parts

Notice that the integrated AOL browser is a window *within* the larger AOL window; you must be logged onto AOL to use the browser.

Tip   *While you're using the browser, it's a good idea to maximize both the AOL window and the browser window by clicking their respective maximize buttons in the upper right-hand corner. Maximizing the browser will help you see as much of a Web page as possible.*

The integrated browser, in both versions of AOL 3.0, consists of standard Windows elements.

The *title bar* shows the name of the Web site (picked up from its "Title tag" in the underlying HTML code, in case you were wondering). If the browser is maximized, its title appears in the main AOL title bar, in [square brackets], at the very top of your screen. Whenever you save a Web site in your Favorite Places folder, the site's name is based on what you see in the title bar. When you use Personal Publisher, you're prompted to provide a title.

The title bar displays the Web page's title.
The buttons give you control
over your browser.

Click the arrow to see the pages
you've visited this session.
The AOL logo spins
as a page is being
downloaded and
stops when it arrives.

The location
box displays a
page's URL.

Web page!

The status bar shows what URL a link is pointing
to and how much has been downloaded.

FIGURE 6-6   AOL's Web site is a good place to start exploring the Web and
to get an overview of AOL's broad range of Internet services

The *buttons* do pretty much what their names say (Table 6-1). These buttons
apply to what you're doing during the current Web *session*, which takes place from
the time you opened the browser to the time you closed it.

*You can open several browser windows at the same time, thus running a
couple of sessions at once, and each browser window will be subject to
its own set of buttons.*

Right below the browser's button bar is the *location box*, which displays the
URL of the current Web page. Click the little downward-pointing arrow to see a

Button	What It Does
Back	If you've seen more than one site during the current session, Back takes you to the previous page you viewed.
Reload	If a page was partially displayed or if you've changed some preferences, Reload fetches a new copy of the same page. *Note: Clicking the right mouse button and selecting Refresh does the same thing.*
Forward	If you've backtracked to a site (using Back), Forward takes you to the site viewed after that site.
Search	Brings up AOL NetFind where you can search the Web and newsgroups.
Prefs	Lets you set preferences, as explained in Table 6-2. The Preferences window differs in the two versions of AOL 3.0. See "Setting Your Preferences."
Home	Returns you to the home page, which you can set using the Prefs button.
Help	Brings up the Help area of the AOL Web site, with many pointers to help resources on the AOL service and on the Internet.
Stop	Stops a page from downloading if you change your mind or make a mistake, or if it's taking too long for all of the elements of the page to arrive.

TABLE 6-1   The AOL browser's buttons and what they do. If you linger with your mouse arrow over any button, a short description comes up

drop-down list, or menu, listing pages you've recently visited on the Web. You can jump directly to any one of those by simply selecting it and releasing your mouse.

The *spinner,* the blue AOL icon to the right of the URL box, spins while a page is downloading. The spinner stops if a page is either successfully downloaded or the download got interrupted for some reason.

 If the spinner ever stops before a page has downloaded, click the Reloadbutton to attempt to download it again, or try again later.

The largest part of the browser is the *display* window, which is where you actually look at and respond to Web pages. If a Web page is either too long or too wide to fit nicely in this window, horizontal or vertical scroll bars (or both) appear. Click the appropriate ends of the scroll bars to see content that doesn't fit.

Finally, there's the status bar at the bottom of the browser. Move your mouse over a link (word or image), and the URL of the page it's pointing to will appear in the left part of the status bar:

```
shortcut to www.aol.com
```

"Shortcut" is Microsoft's way of referring to a "link"; the URL's protocol indicator (*http://*) is left off. Click the link, and the status bar registers what's going on as the Web server is contacted, a connection is made, and the elements of a page are downloaded one at a time. You'll be notified in the status bar as each page element is downloaded, until all elements of the page have arrived and you can start clicking and browsing.

Fish and Fowl: AOL's Hybrid Browser

Across the AOL service you will encounter a customized version of the AOL browser called a "hybrid"—because it's part AOL (non-Web) "form" and part Web browser. Hybrids are used to display Web sites specially chosen for a channel. In the Kids channel, *all* the Web sites appear in hybrids:

Hybrids ensure the best performance but sometimes lack one or another of the basic AOL browser features, such as the status bar and URL box. Sometimes they can't be maximized, making the viewing area a bit cramped. But sometimes you'll get *extra* features, such as message boards and buttons pointing to related content, as at the ESPN SportsZone site (keyword: Espn).

Setting Your Preferences (Windows 95 Version of AOL 3.0)

Microsoft's Internet Explorer offers a somewhat intimidating set of ways to tweak your browser to your liking. Table 6-2 outlines the most important of these preferences. On America Online, help is available for any preference not found in the table (keyword: Nethelp).

Preferences are arranged in "tabs" ranged along the top of the window (Figure 6-7). Click a tab to see a set of related preferences you can set. The Security and Advanced tabs will be of interest mostly to technical users. Under Security you'll

FIGURE 6-7   The AOL Internet Properties window, with each tab giving access to a set of related preferences (see Table 6-2)

To...	Tab (AOL Internet Properties Window)	Option	Comments
Turn images off/on	General	Multimedia section, Show Pictures checkbox	Turning images off can speed up download time, especially with slower modems, but it can also reduce the visual interest of pages. Make sure to click Reload if you make this change after a page has displayed on your screen.
Change color of visited link	General	Links section, click Visited and select a color	Choose a color that's clearly distinguishable from the color used for unvisited links!
Change color of unvisited link	General	Links section, click Unvisited and select a color	Choose a color that's clearly distinguishable from the color used for visited links. It's usually best to leave visited and unvisited link colors as they are.
Change the font	General	Click Font Settings and make your selections	Applies only if the Web page doesn't explicitly determine the font and won't apply to fonts that are actually graphics files (GIFs).
Change background color	General	Colors section, click Background and select a color	Applies only if the Web page has no background.

TABLE 6-2   The main preferences you are likely to want to set for the built-in (Microsoft) browser

To...	Tab (AOL Internet Properties Window)	Option	Comments
Change home page	Navigation	Type URL into Address field (if the page you want to use as a home page is displayed), click Use Current	http://www.aol.com is the default. A search engine or a search page such as **http://www.aol.com/search** makes a good home page, too.
Set up a plug-in or helper application	Programs	Viewers section, click File Types and click New Type	Make sure to fill out all the information required: file type, MIME type (from drop-down list), file extension, and program to open automatically.
Receive a "warning" when you send data using a form	Advanced	Warnings section, select first check box	Placing a check in the "Warn before sending over an open connection" box will cause you to get a warning no matter what you send, even if it's not personal in any way. This control is designed to protect you if you'll be buying things over the Web. If you won't be buying things or otherwise providing confidential information, turn the option off.

TABLE 6-2   The main preferences you are likely to want to set for the built-in (Microsoft) browser (*continued*)

To...	Tab (AOL Internet Properties Window)	Option	Comments
Receive a "warning" before a cookie is created	Advanced	Warnings section, select last check box	See "Cookies" sidebar.
Set your cache	Advanced	Temporary Internet Files section, click Settings	A cache stores Web pages for speedy display when you revisit them. You can specify when the page is compared with the actual page for any changes and how much of your hard disk (in percent) you wish to use to devote to your cache. See "Get Cache Fast" sidebar.
Whether to display compressed graphics	Web Graphics	"Use compressed graphics" checkbox	Compressed graphics display faster! Applies only to images compressed using Johnson-Grace technology.

TABLE 6-2   The main preferences you are likely to want to set for the built-in (Microsoft) browser (*continued*)

also find an area called "Content advisor" that duplicates to some extent the options available under Web Controls in AOL's Parental Controls area (keyword: Parental). Actually, these and other preferences apply to the stand-alone Microsoft browser, not the integrated one.

Setting Your Preferences (Non-Windows 95 Version)

With AOL 3.0 for Windows, you can adjust three key sets of preferences. To adjust your *cache*, see the instructions in the "Get Cache Fast" box. To *set up a helper application*, see the "Setting up a Plug-in or Helper Application" section. To *change your home page*, see "Changing Your Home Page."

In addition, you have some control over the display of graphics and the appearance of your browser. Here's how to set those preferences. With the browser open, click Prefs to bring up the WWW Preferences window:

Choose one of the first three radio buttons to indicate whether you want pages to display no graphics (download as fast as possible), compressed graphics (display quickly but at a slight loss of picture quality), or uncompressed graphics (display less quickly but with the best graphics). The "Don't show graphics at 2400 bps" checkbox turns off the downloading and display of inline graphics if you sign on at 2400 bps (if, for example, your primary dial-in number is unavailable).

Your Browser's Appearance

Three checkboxes give you some control of your browser's appearance: "Show current location," "Show destination of hyperlinks," and "Use a gray background in WWW docs." The first two give you the choice of whether to display the URL of the current page (in the browser's location box) or the URL a link is pointing to (on the status bar), respectively. Removing either the location box or the status bar gives you a small bit of extra vertical space in which to display Web pages but at the cost of the vital information that URLs can provide. The "gray background" option was created before backgrounds were available—and when gray was fashionable on the Web, thanks to the look of Mosaic, the Web's first popular graphical browser.

Your Home on the Web: AOL's Web Site

When you first install the AOL for Windows software, AOL's Web site is your *home page*, the hub of your travels on the Web, providing roadside assistance, roadmaps, and tips about what's worth seeing. It comes up when you click the Globe icon on the tool bar at the top of the screen, or go to keyword: WWW or keyword: Web. When you "go home" you arrive at the AOL Web site, one of the most visited sites on the Internet. The first thing you should do is maximize the page, so you see as much of it as possible. In Windows 95, click the middle of the three boxes you see in the upper-right corner of your screen to see as much of the opening screen as possible.

Note   *In this book, a* site *is a collection of organized pages. You can get an overview of a site's organization in a navigational bar (often at the bottom of each page) or in a frame that makes the navigational bar visible at all times.*

The AOL Web site (Figure 6-6) uses a set of long buttons to simplify access to the various parts of the site. These buttons are hyperlinks and are available in the upper left-hand part of every page. Pass your mouse over a button without clicking, and a small bit of explanatory "balloon text" appears, thanks to Javascript. Click one, and you'll go to a different part of the AOL site.

Starting Out	An overview for beginners
Top Sites	New and notable Web sites
Guided Tours	The favorite Web sites of some of AOL's personalities
Rants & Slants	Opinions about the Internet
About the Company	All about AOL as a company

When you visit the "About the Company" portion of the site (where the company vision statement, corporate strategies, and press releases are located), you'll see lots of additional choices not available from the top part of the AOL site (Figure 6-8).

FIGURE 6-8   AOL, the company: vision, strategy, financials, opportunities, press releases

When AOL members acces the AOL Web site while logged onto AOL, they can click certain hyperlinks to go directly to exclusive AOL content (forums available on the service but not on the Web)! Even if they're using the "bring your own access" plan, members can access AOL content. Nonmembers who access the AOL Web site while logged onto their Internet Service Provider see Web content only and cannot link directly from the Web to AOL forums. Non-AOL browsers may not be able to display all parts of the AOL Web site.

Changing Your Home Page

A good home page is one of intrinsic interest or general usefulness. It's the place from which you choose to start your wanderings on the Web and to which you can usefully return again and again. If you frequently use a search engine such as Excite, AOL's Search page, **http://www.aol.com/search**, is a good place to call home.

Here's how to use another Web site as your starting point if you're using AOL 3.0 for Windows 95:

1. With the browser open, click Preferences. Click the Navigation tab.

2. In the Address field, type in the URL you wish to use as your home page. You can use anything under the sun: a Gopher menu or FTP directory, a search engine such as Excite, or your company's Web site.

3. Click OK.

Now, next time you click that Globe icon, or go to keyword: Web or keyword: WWW, you'll open the home page of your preference.

Changing Your Home Page (AOL 3.0 for Windows)

With the browser open, click Prefs. The Home Page box at the bottom of the WWW Preferences window lets you enter the URL of the home page you want to use as your starting point: it's where you go when you click the Globe icon or use keyword: WWW or keyword: Web. You can start at a newsgroup, Gopher site, Web site—any place whose URL you know.

GETTING FROM A TO B: HOW TO VISIT A WEB SITE USING AOL'S BROWSER

The comforts of home are necessarily fleeting on the Web, unable to compete with the pull of favorite haunts and the lure of new places to discover. America Online's browser gives you many ways to get to any site on the Web.

> *Tip* *The easiest way to get from one Web site to another is to click a link. A new feature of the AOL browser is that you can open a link in a new browser window while keeping open the page you're linking from. To do this, right-click on the link, then select Open in New Window. Use AOL's Window menu to go back and forth between multiple open browser windows.*

Here are four ways to proceed directly to any page you please:

■ Hopping with keywords—gives you the most freedom if you don't have a browser open yet.

- Skipping to Favorite Places—allows you to revisit sites you've already seen

- Chasing after channel selections—lets you go directly from your favorite channel to sites related to the channel's theme

- Jumping to new URLs—gives you the most freedom *after* you've started a browser session

---

Keeping Up with New Sites

The Web is growing so fast that you cannot *possibly* keep up with all the latest Web sites. How do you keep up with the ones of likely interest to you? Here are a few suggestions:

- The **NetGuide** forum on AOL (keyword: Netguide), *NetGuide* magazine, and the NetGuide Web site (**http://www.netguidemag. com/** all provide a good selection of the best new sites, with clearly written annotations.

- **AOL's Site of Day (http://www.aol.com/top).** Includes a directory of past favorites.

- **Netscape's What's New (http://home.netscape.com/escapes/ whats_new.html).** Uniformly high-quality Web sites.

- Three mailing lists described in Chapter 4 provide excellent updates on new Web resources: **Scout-Report, NetSurfer Digest,** and **Yahoo!'s Picks of the Week.**

- **Net-happenings.** Gleason Sackman's classic resource began as a mailing list, migrated to a newsgroup (**comp.internet. net-happenings**), and is now available on the Web as well (**http://www.gi.net/net/**)

- The **comp.infosystems.www.announce** newsgroup is used to publish notifications of new, noncommercial Web sites.

- **Yahoo! What's New.** At keyword: Yahoo, click New or Cool or whatever it's called when you get there.

6

Hop with the Keyword Window

Suppose you want to see what Disney is doing on the Internet. From the GoTo menu, select Keyword. Type in the URL, **http://www.disney.com**, and press ENTER. If you already have a page open (such as your home page, or anything else), keywording to a different page opens a *new* browser window.

AOL has assigned easy keywords to members' favorite Web sites, so that, for those sites, you don't have to know the URLs. In the Keyword window, you can type in **Pathfinder**, **Excite**, or **Disney.com** to go directly to those sites.

*Tip At keyword: Web keywords (click Web Keywords) you get a list of keywords that take you directly to Web sites, including all the major search sites (**Altavista**, **Excite**, **Lycos**, **Liszt**, **Dejanews**, **Infoseek**, **Yahoo**, **Magellan**, **Switchboard**, and **Webcrawler**), as well as popular sites such as MTV, NASA, and dozens of others. See Chapter 11 for a list of current Web keywords.*

Skip to a Favorite Place

Favorite Places give you quick access to *your* favorite things on AOL and the Internet. You can save any kind of content as long as it has a little heart in its title bar. After you've saved a number of places (they're actually *links* to places), you can organize your Favorite Places any way you want—in any order and with as many "levels" (folders within folders) as you want. To get to your Favorite Places folder, click the Favorite Places button in the tool bar:

Something like the window in Figure 6-9 comes up.

To jump to a Favorite Place, just open the folder and double-click a place.

■ If it's a Web resource and the browser is already open, double-clicking the favorite place opens up a *new* browser window.

Note On AOL you can keep open as many browsers as you want. Bear in mind, though, that the more browsers that are open, the slower your computer will work.

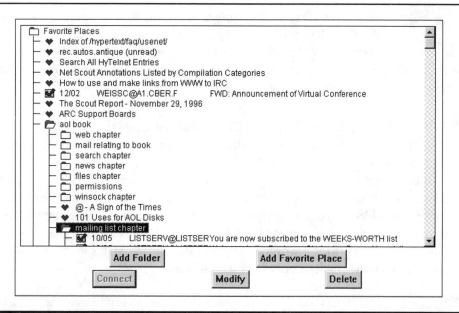

FIGURE 6-9   Favorite Places can quickly become an overgrown garden
(speaking of favorite places)

■   If you click the Favorite Place item and drag it from the Favorite Places
folder into an open browser, the Favorite Place replaces the Web site
displayed in the open browser.

Organizing your Favorite Places is a snap:

■   *To create a new folder* for related Favorite Places, just click Add Folder.
Give the folder a name and click OK. To move a Favorite Place into the
folder, just click and drag the item into the folder.

■   *To change a folder's name*, select the folder and right-click. Select
Rename, type in a new name, and click OK.

■   *To change the* name *of a favorite place,* to shorten it or associate it in your
mind more clearly with its content, select the resource and click Modify.
Make your changes in the first field (Place's Description) and click OK.
*You ordinarily don't want to touch the second field, which is the Internet
Address, or URL!*

Note *If you use AOL on several machines, each will have a separate Favorite Places folder. You can't currently copy Favorite Place folders from one machine to another. Also, if you use more than one version of AOL for Windows 3.0 (e.g., the Windows 95 and non-Windows 95 versions) on the* same *machine, each will have its own Favorite Places folder.*

Yet Another Way to Keep Track of Places You Like

Microsoft's Internet Explorer browser (the stand-alone version, on your Windows 95 desktop) offers an alternative to AOL's Favorite Places, a separate and different collection of your favorite Web sites. With a page displayed in AOL, right-click and select Add to Favorites…. The name of the page and its URL will be stored in the Favorites subfolder of your Windows folder. Whenever you use the stand-alone Internet Explorer browser, these favorites—not AOL's Favorite Places—are available to you by clicking Favorites on the tool bar. Unlike AOL's Favorite Places, Microsoft's Favorites include only Internet resources.

Tip *For that extra-special Web site: make the site a Favorite Place, then drag it from the Favorite Places folder to your desktop. In the future, clicking the icon of the Favorite Place on the desktop will prompt you to sign onto AOL. Once signed on, you go directly to the Web site! You can do something similar by right-clicking and selecting Create Shortcut: an icon for the site is placed on your desktop. For this to work, you must already be signed onto AOL. When you double-click the shortcut icon on your desktop, it's the stand-alone Microsoft browser that comes up, not the integrated browser.*

Cookies

A "cookie" is a little file that a Web site creates to track your visits to the site: which particular pages you visited, for example. The marketing uses of such a file are obvious: sites get a clear idea of your browsing preferences (without knowing exactly who you are). A possible use of cookies is to present you with customized pages, based on your past browsing preferences. Some people, however, consider "cookies" a violation of their privacy.

The AOL browser gives you the option of being warned when a cookie file is being created and having the choice of not allowing it to be made. With the browser open, click Prefs. On the Advanced tab, in the Warnings section, make sure there's a check in the "Warn before accepting cookies" box. Now, every time a site tries to create a cookie, you'll be given a choice of *not* allowing a cookie to be created for you. You may be told that a page will not display correctly if you don't use a cookie, but I have not found that to be the case.

Leap to a Web Site Integrated into an AOL Channel

All AOL channels integrate Web sites into other channel content. You'll find these sites arranged in listboxes, and "behind" buttons in your favorite channels. In the Health channel, for example, there's a large set of useful Web sites, such as:

🌐 Mayo Clinic

Keyword: Health Web takes you to the channel's best health-related Web sites. Chapter 11 provides a directory of the best of the Web sites for your favorite channels. To go to a Web site from the channel, just double-click (if the site's in a listbox) or single-click (if there's a button).

Do You Know What Your Children Are Viewing?

"If it's human, it's on the Web." This means that there may be sites, pictures, and sounds that you, if you're a parent, might not want your child to experience. AOL does not censor the Web; it *can't* censor the Web. But it does give parents the tools to limit what members of their household do on the Web. To use these controls,

1. Go to Keyword: Parental.

2. Click Custom Controls.

3. Click Web, then Web Controls. You get four levels of control for every screen name on the master account: no access to the Web; access to kid-appropriate sites only; access to teen-appropriate sites only; and full access. Make a choice and click OK.

Jump to a New URL

With a browser open, you can use your mouse to select the current URL and type a new one over it. Press ENTER, and the site you've selected is contacted, downloaded, and then takes the place of the current one. As with the use of the Keyword window, make sure you have the full and exact URL of the site you want to visit!

Tip   *Typing in the URL box can be tricky. Click once on the URL of the currently displayed Web page, and the whole address is selected, so that typing* anything *replaces the* entire *current URL. Click again to move the typing "insertion point" to any specific point of the current URL, to edit it. Thus, to jump to a new site, click once on the current URL and type a new URL. To remain within the current site but move to a different part of the site, click a second time and edit the current URL (from* **http://www.aol.com/search** *to* **http://www.aol.com/** *for example). "Backing up" a directory path in this way can be a good way to explore a Web site, especially if you've linked to a low-level page in a large site.*

MANAGING YOUR WEB SESSION

Once you start visiting Web sites, you'll invariably start visiting *other* Web sites. That's the nature of the Web and of browsing. Clicking a hyperlink—underlined text, or part of a clickable image, or image map—takes you to another site. With 100 million pages out there, linking never stops. Remember that you can tell if something's a link if a URL appears in the status bar when you pass your mouse cursor over it. The mouse pointer (arrow) turns into a pointing finger. At any point in any session, you can return home by clicking the browser's Home button.

Moving Around Within a Page

A Web page rarely fits within the browser window. To help you get around long or wide pages, vertical or horizontal scroll bars, or both, are available.

> *Tip*   *The up and down arrow keys (↑↓) are also available to help you navigate up and down a little at a time, but to use these keys you must first click anywhere on the Web page (except on a link!).*

Neither version of AOL's integrated browser currently lets you search for a specific word on a Web page, which can be a bother if you've used a search engine such as Excite, and you're not sure what the page has to do with what you are searching. But both the customized Netscape browser and the stand-alone Microsoft browser (which is automatically set up for you when you install AOL) do include this feature and allow you to search for a specific word on a Web page. The Microsoft browser is available by clicking The Internet icon on your desktop. You can read about the customized Netscape browser in Chapter 10.

Managing the Slow Page

Sometimes a page can take too long to download. This can happen because it's a badly built page, it's in great demand, network traffic is too heavy, or the page has lots of images. If you ever suspect a page has gotten "stuck" somewhere between the Internet and your PC, click Stop. Sometimes the text (the part that downloads the fastest) will already have been downloaded, but the pictures haven't yet arrived. In this case, clicking Stop may cause the text to appear on your screen—and it may be what you were trying to get in the first place. Sometimes, nothing will have arrived, and your browser will be blank. If that's the case, you can click Reload to attempt again to retrieve the page.

Use the Reload button, too, if you've changed your settings while displaying a page. For example, you're viewing a site with very big, very slow images. You turn off the images by clicking Prefs and unchecking the Show Pictures box on the General tab. The change won't take effect until you click Reload.

If you're using Windows 95, another way to reload a page is to click with the right mouse button and select Refresh. Reload and refresh mean the same thing.

Going Back and Forth Between Pages

Using the Back and Forward buttons is straightforward. "Backward" and "forward" are relative to the list of pages you've viewed in the current browser session. To see the list, click the downward-pointing arrow in the URL box at the top of the browser. You can jump to any of the pages on this list by double-clicking.

You can get direct access to your History file and from there jump to any site you've visited in the past 20 days (or however many days you want). With the browser open, click Prefs. In the Navigation tab, click View History. An alphabetized list of URLs comes up. Selecting a link calls up the stand-alone Microsoft Internet Explorer browser that was automatically installed for you when you installed AOL and is available whenever you sign onto AOL.

Get Cache Fast

Going forward and backward can be a lot faster than downloading a page for the first time—if the pages you visit are being *cached*. A cache is a place where something is stored for fast retrieval. AOL uses caches at two points while you're browsing the Web, and both uses of caches can improve your experience of the Web.

First, sites that members most like to visit are stored on AOL's computers, so that members who subsequently want to visit the same sites can download directly from the cache, instead of going out to the Internet for a new copy of the page. These caches are frequently cleared to ensure that pages are as up to date as possible. Old pages are constantly reviewed, and pages that are no longer accessed are removed.

Second, there's a cache on your hard disk that keeps track of the pages you visit most frequently during a session. Loading the page or elements of the page from the cache can be quicker than getting the whole thing "off the Internet."

If you're using the Windows 95 version of AOL 3.0, you can set the size of this cache by clicking Prefs, clicking the Advanced tab, and, in the Temporary Internet Files section clicking Settings. Now, using your mouse, slide the "lever" right or left to tell AOL how much of your hard disk to dedicate to copies of Web objects (GIFs and the like). To "purge" your cache (which can sometimes speed things up on your system), click the Empty Folder button. If you're curious about what a cache keeps track of, click View Files (if the folder looks empty, select Refresh from the View menu).

If you're using the non-Windows 95 version of AOL 3.0, follow these steps:

1. With the browser open, click the Prefs button.

2. Click the Advanced button.

3. To turn caching on or off, select or deselect the "Cache web pages and graphics locally" checkbox.

4. To set the maximum size of the cache (the number of megabytes on your hard disk), enter a number (such as *10*) in the "Maximum disk space to use for cache" box.

5. To remove information about pages you've visited, click the Purge Cache button, and click OK.

Navigating Frames

The Windows 95 version of the AOL browser keeps track of all the pages you've seen within frames. So, clicking Back and Forward takes you to *all* the previous and subsequent pages you've viewed, whether they took up the whole browser or just a part of one (a frame).

In the non-Windows 95 version of AOL 3.0, pages with frames complicate the generally neat pattern of navigating the Web by going forward and backward. If you're using that version, here's how to navigate frames.

To go back or forward *within* a frame, click anywhere in the frame to select it. Do a right-mouse click to get the popup menu, and then select either Go Back in

Frame or Forward in Frame. The browser's Back button takes you to the page you saw *before* opening the page with the frame.

THE 15-SECOND WEB SEARCH

Suppose you want to find a fertilizer for your wild roses, look into beekeeping as a career, or plan an outing in Wyoming. Where do you start? Much of your experience on the Web will probably begin with a *search*. The tools for searching have gotten dramatically better and easier to use in the past year, and changes are in store that will make for radically simpler custom-searching in the future. Chapter 9 helps you do really effective searches, regardless of where the information you need is located or how it's made available. For now, it's enough to introduce Excite, AOL's exclusive search engine and perhaps the only search tool you need.

With the browser open to any page, click the browser's Search button to go to AOL NetFind, shown in Figure 6-10. To search for information about roses, or bees, or Wyoming, enter key words in the box and click Find. *Wild roses* will do as an example. You can add more specific key words, joined (if you wish) by words such as *and* and *or*. In general it's a good idea to conduct as specific a search as possible, to avoid being swamped by tens of thousands of pages.

FIGURE 6-10   What aisle is it in? Start with the AOL Search page

After Excite has finished looking through its index of millions of URLs, it *returns* (a fancy way of saying *displays*) a list of pages that contain the word or words you've entered. To visit a site from the list, just click it!

Choosing a Search Engine

Search engines vary in many ways, including:

- The number of URLs they track (how many tens of millions!).

- Their flexibility in allowing you to ask questions and then, from there, figuring out what you want.

- Their ability to return the URLs for which you're probably looking.

- Their additional bells and whistles, such as value-added reviews of sites, editorializing of one sort or another, and features such as Excite's City.Net and its directory of selected sites.

Chapter 9 goes into the endlessly interesting and rapidly changing world of searching for information on the Net. For now, try Excite to get some sense of what searching the Net is all about.

SIGHTS, SOUNDS, MOVING PICTURES: WORKING WITH MULTIMEDIA FILES

FTP, the Net's File Transfer Protocol, was once the major way to transfer software, images, and other files across the Internet. Using FTP is like navigating someone else's hard disk, finding a file, then copying it over the Net to your computer. With FTP, however, you then have to find a word processor, or graphics viewer, or other program that can "play" the file. And all you get with FTP is files—no context, no discussion, no links to related files, nor any of the other essential content you get on the Web.

The Web has now become an important alternative way of delivering files over the Internet, by means of links to sound, audio, or video files *and* as an interface to FTP (see "Your All-Purpose Browser").

Using your browser you play, see, and hear files in two basic ways:

- The most common image and sound files are displayed automatically by your browser.

■ Other files require special "players" that are more or less well-integrated into Web pages, so the *content* of the files—the music, the video, whatever—is more or less smoothly integrated into the content of the Web page.

Letting the Browser Present Files

Some types of files can be automatically "presented" by AOL's browser, using the browser itself or a built-in Windows utility. Common image files such as GIFs and JPGs appear directly in the browser without requiring any special program. With the file displayed, you can do what you do with any file: save it on your hard disk, print it, or delete it.

Likewise, click a link to a common sound file (with the extension AU, WAV, or MID) and the file downloads and plays. AU files are based on actual music and recordings; thus, they're big and slow to download. A 100K file might play only a few seconds. In the case of AU files you may see the following icon or something similar:

When the file's *completely downloaded*, click the arrow to play the sound. Increasingly you see the following "ActiveX" control, which "floats" above the browser and can play a sound while it's downloading:

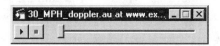

For a MIDI file, a little player comes up after you've downloaded the file:

Once again, you must wait for the whole file to be downloaded before playing it, but the beauty of MIDI is that files are small (and they download in a snap), while playing times are long. The 10K MIDI file with "Eleanor Rigby" runs for more than a minute. With AOL 3.0 for Windows, "embedded" MIDI files play automatically as a page downloads. Chapter 7 has more to say about this effect.

Note   *Nonmultimedia files can be downloaded from the Web as well. Many software companies make* executable files *(programs you can run) available over the Web. These programs can be downloaded to your hard disk, then decompressed (if necessary), installed, and run as separate programs. With AOL's Microsoft browser, you will be asked, when downloading such files, whether to open them or save them to disk. Save them to disk. While a file is downloading, you don't have to remain parked at the Web page from which you're downloading the file, but you do have to remain signed onto AOL.*

Likewise, you get *video files* in the same way: downloading and running them. Windows's built-in Media Player can handle AVIs as well as some types of MPEG. Other types of MPEG files require special helper applications. More and more, to simplify access and improve the experience, video and even audio files are being delivered through a new technology called ActiveMovie, so you never have to be concerned about a file's type.

Working with Plug-ins and Helper Applications

More and more Web sites are delivering video and audio directly to your browser. The most important type of such files requires a *plug-in* program that runs automatically *within* your browser (or at least smoothly integrated with it) when you click a link to a certain kind of file. Where do you find the programs to run these newfangled files? The best place to start is at the Web sites of the vendors who create them (Table 6-3).

The other way to play files is with a helper application, a small program *external* to the browser. These programs, called "helper apps," load when you click a link to the file. The experience of helper apps can be similar to that of plug-ins, but helper apps are not integrated with the browser experience—a video clip will always play in a separate application, not in a little box on the Web page itself. Both kinds of "player" are set up in the same way (see the next section), though more and more plug-ins are set up automatically for you "in" your browser, when you install them.

Setting Up a Plug-In or Helper Application (Windows 95 Version of AOL 3.0)

When your browser can't play a file, you'll probably have to set up a helper application or plug-in. The procedure can seem technical, but it's not. Here's the background you need.

The Net's Multipurpose Internet Mail Extension (MIME) is the standard used by e-mail programs to identify attached files so they can be properly handled by the programs receiving them. When you download a file over the Web, it has a MIME type too. AOL looks at the MIME type and launches the appropriate program. Based on a file's MIME type, the browser either plays the file itself or launches a helper app or plug-in to play it.

Tip *All the helper apps you'll ever need can be downloaded from AOL's software libraries, as explained toward the end of Chapter 8. All the plug-ins you need are on the Web, free for you to download from the vendors' sites*

6

Plug-in	What It Lets You Do	Where You Can Get More Information and Sample Files
Acrobat	View complex documents	keyword: Adobe
FutureSplash	Get mini-applications with interactive buttons, drawings, and cartoons	**http://www.futurewave.com/**
QuickTime	Experience music, audio, and video	keyword: MVD
Real Audio	Play "streaming" audio clips from sites such as Pacifica Radio	**http://www.realaudio.com/**
Shockwave and Shockwave Audio	View interactive animations and hear CD-quality audio	**http://www.macromedia.com/**
ToolVox	Play human speech	**http://www.voxware.com/**
VDOLive	View streaming video	**http://www.vdo.net/**

TABLE 6-3 Plug-ins give the AOL browser access to the multimedia Internet

(Table 6-3). A well-planned Web site directs users to the source of a plug-in if the site uses files requiring that plug-in. The great thing about Java and ActiveX is that neither requires any external software to play multimedia files.

To set up your browser so that it can read a new type of file and launch the appropriate player (plug-in or helper app), follow these steps:

1. With the browser open, click Prefs, and then click the Programs tab. In the Viewers section, click File Types.

2. Click New Type... In the Add New File Type window, you'll be asked to provide four pieces of information:

   ■ A description of the file type in your own words, such as *Real Audio*.

   ■ Extension(s) for that type (such as *.RA, .RAM* for Real Audio).

   ■ The MIME content type, which can be chosen from the drop-down list. Content types are organized by broad multimedia category, such as *application*, *audio*, and *video*. Choose from one of the items provided. If a type is not evident, consult the documentation that comes with the helper app or plug-in that you're setting up.

   ■ The program you want to automatically open when you click the multimedia file on a Web page. Click the Browse button and navigate to the place where you have installed the program on your hard disk. It's not enough to have merely downloaded the program; it must be installed as well. Programs usually have .EXE tacked onto their file names.

3. Click OK to accept your choices.

Setting Up a Plug-in or Helper App (AOL 3.0 for Windows)

You can use helper apps and plug-ins with the non-Windows 95 browser, but you must set them up manually. To add a new helper application for a new kind of file (such as Real Audio):

1. With the browser open, click Prefs. In the WWW Preferences window, click the Helper Applications button, and then in the Helper Applications window click New....

2. In the Description box, describe the file (for example, *Real Audio*).

3. In the Content Type and Sub-Type box, identify the content (video, audio, etc.), a slash (*/*), and then a MIME file type (in this case, *audio/x-pn-realaudio*). You may have to consult a FAQ at the site from which you got the helper application or plug-in to find out the Content Type.

4. In the File Extensions box, indicate the file extension(s) that launch the player or plug-in when you click them (for example, *ra, ram*).

5. In the Application Name box, specify the path and name of the plug-in or helper application using the Browse button to navigate to the folder where it is stored. Click OK, then Close.

Three Major Plug-Ins

In the future, you'll have access to a broad range of automatically installed plug-ins on both the Windows 95 and Windows 3.1 platforms, and ActiveX and Java will be delivering cool stuff without the bother of *any* external software. For now, in the Windows 95 browser, your best bets are the following three plug-ins, among the mostly popular available on the market: RealAudio, VDO, and Shockwave.

Real Audio

Real Audio is currently the most satisfying plug-in because of its ease of use, the number of sites taking advantage of it, and its relatively good sound quality. What's special about Real Audio is *streaming* sound: the sound starts playing while it's still downloading, no matter what modem speed you're using. The tiny Real Audio player (with forward, pause, and rewind buttons) runs automatically whenever you click a link to a Real Audio sound. Right-click on the Real Audio player, and you can pause, stop, and skip to a specific point in the sound clip. Real Audio offers the fidelity of AU but the good experience of MIDI.

The potential for integrating sound into Web content is great. Interviews, news commentaries, sports reporting, music—all are being delivered via Real Audio. The following RealAudio resources are all a click away from the RealAudio site (**http://www.realaudio.com**). If you're interested in up-to-the-minute news, from the Real Audio site you can link to ABC, NPR, and the Pacifica News Network. (For NPR's "All Things Considered" fans, the entire show is available via Real Audio, although a day or two after the original broadcast.) WebActive (**http://www.webactive.com/**), for activists, brings an extensive collection of Real Audio content related to social causes. TimeCast (**http://www.timecast.com**) is a *TV Guide* style directory of Real Audio sites. And for music, you'll find loads of Real Audio links at LiveConcerts (**http://www.liveconcerts.com**) and CDNow (**http://www.cdnow.com**).

VDO

What RealAudio does for sound, VDO does for video—though keep your eye out for a new technology called RealVideo! Among the sample VDO files available when I visited the VDO site were tapes of a space walk that had occurred within the last 24 hours and a Bill Gates speech devoted to Internet technologies. Here's a video clip from the Blue Note, New York's famous jazz club:

Shockwave

The coolest plug-in, Macromedia's Shockwave for Director, is the product of Macromedia, a San Francisco-based company that creates multimedia applications for use in graphic arts, education, training, and entertainment. When you click a Shockwave file, the Director program is launched automatically and plays interactive animations inside a new Web page. Shockwave also supports files that play CD-quality sound.

Links to lots of "shocked" pages are available in the Shockwave gallery at **http://www.macromedia.com/shockwave/epicenter/**. You'll find a Barney punching bag, NeuroGolf, an extreme snowboarding game, and other great stuff.

RealAudio, VDO, Shockwave—this stuff can be addictive. Over a modem, the experience is less than instantaneous, but the excitement of hearing music or watching a live broadcast must come close to the feeling of tuning into a scratchy radio broadcast in the early days of this century. The taste of the future and sense of connection with other people and places is more tangible, perhaps, than anything on the Web.

YOUR ALL-PURPOSE BROWSER

URLs beginning *http://...* (Web pages) aren't the only ones you can use with the AOL browser. In fact, the Web was originally designed to create a uniform way of viewing diverse information, not just Web pages. With your browser you can access:

- Gopher—the precursor of the Web

- FTP—thousands of sites with millions of files for the downloading

- Newsgroups—via AOL's Newsgroups window

- The Compose Mail window—from which you can send an e-mail message

- Telnet—to use the computing resources of a remote Internet computer

When you visit a Gopher or FTP site, everything takes place within the browser window; you use the browser's controls to get around. However, when you read a newsgroup, send a mail message, and play a game on a Telnet computer, everything takes place in a separate application that the browser calls up; you use the controls of these separate applications—there's no Back or Stop button. The trend in the next few years will be to integrate more and more in the browser, but for now it's good to get used to a mix: some protocols are directly supported by the browser, others launch a separate program.

Gopher's Swan Song

In 1991, after the Web was invented but before it became hugely popular, Mark McCahill and others at the University of Minnesota invented Gopher. This tool had a similar purpose as the Web—to provide easy access to different types of information located around the globe. However, while the Web used hypertext as the model for how to find and link information, Gopher used simple menus to provide access (Figure 6-11).

A *menu* is just a list. Click a menu item and you either go to another menu (directory) or to actual content (a text file, say). While the Web integrates sounds and video into text information, Gopher was designed and is still used mostly as a way of accessing information one file at a time, particularly textual information such as statistics, government reports, books, magazines, current temperatures, earthquake reports, and the like.

Gopher It on the Web

Going to a Gopher site is easy using the AOL browser. Just enter the full URL, beginning *gopher://* in the keyword window. For instance, **gopher:// spinaltap.micro.umn.edu** takes you to a big collection of public domain books, reference works, and classics available at Gopher's birthplace, the University of Minnesota.

Gopher URLs, like all URLs, abide by the domain naming system: names have several parts separated by periods. On AOL, at keyword: Gopher, you will find a list of Gopher Treasures that provide access to goodies ranging from the Congressional Record to 35 years of speeches by Castro. Be forewarned, however, that many Gophers are no longer being maintained, and many have been converted to Web sites. You'll find increasingly that Gopher menus point you to Web pages, from which you browse the Web and leave Gopher behind.

6

FIGURE 6-11   Gopher—via the AOL Web browser (Windows 95). Here's a good place to start for reference materials and public domain books

When I first discovered Gopher in 1993, I was exhilarated by the easy access it provided to all kinds of information. As a researcher at heart I didn't mind the text-only nature of most of the information.

In 1994-95, textual information was still published via Gopher, especially on university campuses. But soon the Web absorbed almost all of the energy and resources that had gone into the creation and maintenance of Gopher sites. Today, even classic sites such as Rice University's Gopher subject directory and classic resources such as Gopher Jewels are no longer maintained. If you have serious information needs, however, it's important to know about Gopher.

File This: FTP on the Web

In contrast to Gopher, transferring files with FTP (the Net's File Transfer Protocol) remains a fundamental part of the Internet—it's the principal means by which files are stored on and transmitted across the Internet. When you use FTP, you log onto a distant computer in search of a file or group of files. You search for files in directories, going in and out of directories, subdirectories, sub-subdirectories, and so on, until you find the files you're seeking.

With AOL's browser, you can visit any FTP site whose address you know by entering its full URL into the Keyword window or directly into the browser's URL box. An FTP site's URL consists of *ftp://* plus the domain name, for example, **ftp://ftp.aol.com**. Using the browser to access FTP is an alternative to using AOL's FTP gateway at keyword: FTP. Chapter 8 makes a case for the browser being a better way to search FTP than to actually download files from an FTP site.

E-Mail and Newsgroups Over the Web

Some Web sites hyperlink to newsgroups to take you to pertinent discussion groups (newsgroups). Clicking such a link brings up AOL's newsreader with the newsgroup displayed (Chapter 5 is all about newsgroups).

The URL for a newsgroup is *news:* (without the forward slashes) and the name of the newsgroup. So, if you know a newsgroup name, such as **comp.-internet.net-happenings**, you can type **news:comp.internet.net-happenings** directly into the Keyword window, click Go, and go directly to that newsgroup.

Some Web sites have hyperlinks that, when you click them, allow you to send an e-mail message to someone (the "Webmaster," the person who runs the site, for example). Clicking such a link on AOL calls up the Compose Mail window and inserts an e-mail address (for the Webmaster or whomever) into the To window. Finish the message by supplying a Subject line and writing the message body, then clicking Send. You will return to the Web site (actually you never left the page from which you linked to the Compose Mail window) so you can continue to browse.

Telnet!

With the Windows 95 version of the AOL browser, you can now link from Web pages to Telnet sites. Telnet is an Internet service that lets you log onto and use remote computer resources. Just as FTP gives you access to a remote computer's *hard disk*, Telnet gives you access to the *actual computer,* where you can run programs that reside on that computer. You use Telnet to access a university account where you might have an e-mail account, to search through the card catalogs of thousands of libraries, to play games such as MUDs and MOOs, to use community networks (Free-nets), and to use information databases of many types. If you're using the built-in Microsoft browser, you automatically get Telnet access: click a link and you're transported to the Telnet site.

 If you're using Netscape, you'll have to specify a Telnet program, as shown in Chapter 10.

A Telnet link on a Web page begins **telnet:*[address]***. That's what you see in the status bar when your mouse passes over a link to a Telnet resource. To go to the actual Telnet resource, just click. Note that you will usually need a log-in and a password to use the site, and finding out those things might take some effort. One site from which hundreds of Telnet sites are available is Hytelnet. With Hytelnet, you'll find log-in and password information for many Telnet sites, as well as loads of information about using Telnet. Another Web site that links you to hundreds of Telnet sites is MudConnector. For more on Hytelnet and MudConnector, see Chapter 10.

SAVING WEB PAGES

In the world of old-fashioned computing, "saving" meant keeping a copy of something (a program, a word processing document, an image file, or any file) for yourself, on your own hard disk, for later use or archival purposes. On the Web, *saving* a page has a broader meaning. "Saving" a page can mean one of three things:

- Saving a link to the page with Favorite Places
- Saving the page's underlying HTML
- Saving some or all of the text or multimedia elements of the page

Saving a Link to the Page with Favorite Places

With Favorite Places, you can save *links* to the places you like. Instead of saving the actual Web page, you're saving the URL and title of the page, and making it as easy as possible to return there in the future. See "Skip to a Favorite Place."

Saving a Page's Underlying HTML

You've seen what HTML is all about ("How Is That Page Put Together? HTML"). Why would you want to save the HTML file such as the one shown in Figure 6-1? For one thing, if you save the file with its extension (HTM or HTML) intact, you can open the HTML file at any time, and the browser will display the page. It's a fast way of keeping a "local" copy of any page you like. Of course, any changes made to the original file, out on the Internet, won't be reflected in the page you've saved on your own PC, and you won't be able to link to *other* pages. If you save the file with a different extension (such as TXT, for text), you can keep a copy of the underlying HTML—a great way of learning HTML if you want to design your own pages.

To save a Web page:

1. Display the page. From the File menu, select Save. Change the file name if you want. To save the file as a Web page (the way it looks in your browser), retain the HTM or HTML extension at the end of the file. To save the file as a text file in order to study the HTML, save it as a TXT file.

 If there are any inline graphics, they won't be saved in either case, since they're not actually part of the HTML file. See "Saving a Page's Elements."

2. To look at the page, go to the File menu, select Open, and look for the HTML file you've saved. Your browser opens automatically, displaying the HTML page—just as it did on the Web.

Using Windows 95, there's an alternative way to see the skeleton—the HTML—of a Web page. With a page displayed, click the right mouse button and select View Source (that is, the HTML "source code") from the menu. The HTML appears in a separate Notepad window (Notepad is a mini-word processor that comes with Windows 95). Once displayed, the page can be saved in the usual way (from the File menu, choose Save, then give the file a name and directory). If you use the

Netscape browser (Chapter 10), you can view any page's HTML by going to the View menu and choosing Document Source.

Saving a Page's Elements

More interested in the text or the art than the HTML tags? You can also save part of the text of a Web page by simply selecting it with your mouse and using the copy (CTRL-C) and paste (CTRL-V) functions. To select *all* the text on a page, click the right mouse button (in the Windows 95 version) and choose Select All. Then copy and paste the selected text manually into a word processor or other text editor, and save it.

To save an inline image, move your mouse over it, click the right mouse button, select Save Picture As, then give the image a filename and find a folder in which to store it.

Printing Web Pages

Printing's a snap with AOL's Web browser. With the page displayed, just click the Printer icon on the tool bar at the top of your screen. Of course, you'll need a printer with paper, plugged in and properly set up. Graphics will print, as well as text. If the downloading of graphics delays the display of text (and you want to print the text), click the Stop button before clicking the Printer icon. Until a page has stopped downloading, it can't be printed.

To print an HTML file, just open an HTML file that you have previously saved and select Print from the File menu.

WHEN THINGS DON'T WORK

As Web sites get more complex, as more and more people pile in (like those phonebooths in the 1950s), and as sites change owners and addresses, it is a miracle the Web works as well as it does. It's also a miracle how much better the Web experience gets from month to month. Still, things go wrong. Table 6-4 shows the details of the most common error messages you may see, and when possible it tells what you can do about them. In general, you can minimize problems by making sure the error isn't yours. Always type URLs carefully and exactly. Spelling and punctuation count.

If all else fails, try contacting the Webmaster at the site. If the Web address is something like ***http://www.xyz.com/*** then the Webmaster's address would probably be ***webmaster@xyz.com***.

Error Message	What It Means and What To Do
401- Authorization Required 403 - Forbidden	You see this error message when you attempt to access a Web page that has limited access. You may need a special password to access it. Double-check the source of your information.
404 - Not Found	The file is no longer available, is incorrectly linked, or has changed its URL. There's not much you can do except contact the person or organization responsible for the site or do a search for the new site.
500 - Server error	If the server has been incorrectly set up or is experiencing mechanical problems, you may see this message. Try again later!
Unable to Connect to Site	The browser cannot find the server specified in the URL. The URL you entered may be incorrect, the server on which the URL is located may be shut down or busy, or the URL may no longer exist. Try again, carefully. Or, click Reload if you're sure it's right.
Too much network traffic	%#$&%*%! The Web page to which you are attempting to connect has too many other people trying to access pages. Sometimes you'll get this message when there's a problem with your cache, the part of your hard disk that keeps track of the sites you visit. Use the Reload button to try to connect to the site again, or wait and try again later.
http couldn't be "parsed"	You made some mistake—adding a space, using backward instead of forward slashes, adding weird punctuation, using one forward slash instead of two, etc. Try again but type your URL more carefully!

TABLE 6-4 Things that go bump on the Web and what to do about them

AOL does not censor sites in any way. If you're ever unable to visit a site, it is never because AOL is blocking it.

FROM HERE...

This chapter covers a lot of ground, but so does the Web! The best way to get comfortable with the Web is to start browsing. It's easy, fun, fairly intuitive, and you can't break anything. You can get tangled up in it, but it will never tear. The AOL Web site is a good place to start exploring.

The next chapter shows you how to create your own Web page using AOL's Personal Publisher.

6

Chapter **7**

Publishing on the Web with Personal Publisher

One reason the Web's growing so fast is that it's so easy to create new Web pages and make them available to the entire Internet. It probably doesn't get any easier than using America Online's Personal Publisher 2, which provides everything you need to create, publish, and refine a single Web page or an entire Web *site* (a collection of linked pages).

Why would you want to create a Web page? If you own a small business, you could probably benefit from your own Web "presence." The tens of thousands of American businesses with Web presence range from the smallest one-person outfits to giants like Microsoft and Cisco. Nothing can more effectively level the playing field in business than a Web presence. If you have a large (and wired) family and want to post the latest batch of pictures for everyone to see, a Web page may be the easiest way to stay in touch with loved ones. If you want to promote your organization or keep its members apprised of group gossip and events, a Web page may be, again, just the ticket. Finally, if you have a hobby or an abiding obsession, a Web page may be the best way to display your passion and discover who in the world, literally, shares your interest.

Tip   *For large, professional, and commercial sites, AOL also offers a Web-hosting service called PrimeHost, described later in this chapter ("In Business? Let PrimeHost Maintain Your Site").*

A Web page consists merely of a simple text (ASCII) file saved in a format called HTML, for Hypertext Markup Language (for a little background, see "How Is that Page Put Together? HTML" in Chapter 6). Figure 6-1 in the last chapter shows a page of HTML that consists of text (the words you see on a Web page) and "tags" (the formatting applied to the words you see when you browse the Web). Your browser's job is to turn tags—such as <b> for bold and <i> for italics—into an informative and attractive page, with live links to other pages (Figure 6-2). In this chapter, you'll learn to create a Web page that anyone on the Internet can visit. Using AOL's Personal Publisher 2, the HTML is generated automatically for you.

This chapter starts out with a discussion of My Place—the free disk space AOL makes available to every member. It's helpful to know a little about My Place before you start storing and maintaining your Web pages there. Next, you'll learn the nuts and bolts of Personal Publisher 2, a simple way of making an attractive Web page. Then you'll learn to refine and perfect Personal Publisher 2 pages using some of the easy HTML effects possible with Personal Publisher itself or with an HTML editor such as AOLpress. Finally, and most fun, you'll see some of the cool pages created by other AOL members.

Note   *You can use Personal Publisher 2 on either version of AOL 3.0 (AOL 3.0 for Windows or AOL for Windows 95). This chapter was written for the Windows 95 version, and some AOL features (such as right-clicking on a page to view its source code) are available only on that version. Because the browsers in the two versions differ, a page made for the Windows 95 (Microsoft) browser will probably not work in the other (BookLink) browser.*

THREE WAYS TO MAKE A WEB PAGE

On America Online you basically have three ways to create a Web page:

- By hand, using a text editor such as Windows Notepad.
- Using an HTML visual editor such as AOLpress.
- Using Personal Publisher 2, which focuses strictly on the content you want to convey and not the HTML methods you use to convey it (they are automatically handled for you). Pages created with Personal Publisher can be refined using one or both of the other methods.

Making Web Pages by Hand

Many Web pages are created with nothing more than Windows Notepad, the program included with every version of Windows. You can create an HTML file with *any* text editor or word processor, for that matter, then upload it to a computer on the Internet to which other people have access (see "Publishing and Maintaining Your Web Pages in My Place"). However, to use a text editor or word processor requires that you hand-code the HTML.

Using an HTML Editor

A much easier way to make a Web page is to use an HTML editor, many of which are available on AOL in the software libraries. These graphical tools work in much the same way as your word processor. You simply type in the text, highlight it with your mouse, and apply HTML tags by clicking buttons on a tool bar or selecting items from a menu. The editing tool adds the HTML tags for you, makes sure they're correct, and usually lets you view the results as others will see them *before* you actually publish your pages. Such software makes it possible to generate a page using "visual" methods (menus, buttons, etc.), but you still need to know HTML to use the tools effectively.

 At keyword: My Place, click on HTML Software for a library of editors to download. AOLpress (formerly Navipress) is AOL's own editor, and it's free to members. It's described later in "Using an HTML Editor to Edit Your Page (AOLpress)."

Point and Click with Personal Publisher 2

The easiest way to make a Web page on America Online is with AOL's Personal Publisher 2 service. Once you've created a page, you can edit it either manually (using Notepad or other text editor) or using an HTML editor, as described in "Using an HTML Editor to Edit Your Page (AOLpress)." An additional advantage of Personal Publisher 2 is that it provides a complete publishing solution—the ability to both create and edit pages and to make them available for people on the Internet to see. The next few sections look at My Place, the publishing area on AOL's computers that makes Personal Publisher possible.

Note   *Personal Publisher 2 is closely tied to the AOL browser. Like the browser, it supports HTML version 3.2.*

PUBLISHING AND MAINTAINING YOUR WEB PAGES IN MY PLACE

 My Place is the free Internet-accessible disk space available to every AOL member. Each AOL screen name automatically receives 2 Mb of storage space on an AOL computer called **members.aol.com,** in a directory labeled called */screenname* (for example, **members.aol .com/answerman**). Since every master account can have five screen names, that makes a total of 10 Mb per account. It's not yet possible to allocate space between screen names, but it's easy with Personal Publisher to link to pages in several locations. With up to 10 Mb of disk space to store your files, you can make an awesome Web site!

Tip   *The beauty of My Place is that you can use it to publish any Web page, whether you've made it with Personal Publisher, an HTML editor, or by hand. Many AOL members create and publish Web sites in My Place without even using Personal Publisher! The member pages highlighted at the end of this chapter were made with a variety of tools, including Personal Publisher and AOLpress.*

To get to your area of My Place, go to keyword: My Place. You will see the My Place window, the useful information hub shown in Figure 7-1, from which you get access to AOL's Web-publishing services, as well as to My Place.

Click Go To My Place to directly access the 2 Mb of disk space allocated to your screen name (Figure 7-2). If you'll be using this area actively, you should probably save it as a Favorite Place by clicking the heart in the title bar. Now My Place will be available in the Favorite Places folder on your tool bar. Open the folder and click **members.aol.com/*screenname*** to go there in the future.

7

■ **FIGURE 7-1**   Start here to access your area in My Place, Personal Publisher 2

FIGURE 7-2   My Place is your storage space on an AOL computer; it's where you publish your Web pages

My Place is an FTP server (computer) that doubles as a Web (http) server. FTP is the Net's File Transfer Protocol—the chief way of storing and moving files around on the Internet (see Chapter 8 for the full story). While you ordinarily use FTP to *download* (retrieve) files from public FTP sites, My Place is chiefly used for *uploading* (copying) files from a PC to AOL's FTP server. From your area of My Place, *others* can download them as either Web pages or free-standing files (word-processed documents, sound files, programs, whatever). You can't use My Place to upload to disk space other than **members.aol.com**.

Think of your area of My Place as a chunk of hard disk on someone else's computer where you can store files. Unlike the hard disk on your PC, however, My Place can be made available to *other* people, once you publish your Web pages.

When you visit My Place (Figure 7-2), you'll find a handy FAQ (Frequently Asked Questions) document, which answers some basic questions about My

Place. Double-click the file, then click View File Now. Read the FAQ and, if you want, print it. You'll also notice a **/private** directory, where you can store files that only you have access to.

Uploading a File to My Place

When you use Personal Publisher to publish your page and any associated files (such as image and sound files), your work is automatically *uploaded* to My Place, that is, it's copied from your hard disk to My Place. You can also upload your files one at a time, when (for example) you change an image or add a sound file. And you can upload files that you want to make available to others simply as files and not as a part of a Web page.

Before you begin uploading your files, you must know the name and type of the file you want to upload and the location of the file on your hard drive.

1. Go to keyword: My Place, and click on GoTo My Place. Or, use Favorite Places if you've already saved My Place in your Favorite Places folder.

2. Open (double-click) the directory *into which you want to upload a file*. Click the Upload button. The following window comes up:

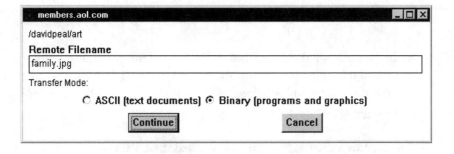

3. Type in the name that you want the file to have in My Place (yes, you first name the "target" name, then the "source" name). If the file is for your Web page, note that HTML files must end in *.HTM* or *.HTML* and that graphics files must end in *.GIF*, *.BMP*, or *.JPG*. You must also select a Transfer Mode. Select ASCII for your HTML files and Binary for everything else.

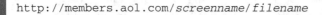 *Keep all of your filenames short and memorable. To avoid confusion and simplify management, use the same name in My Place that you use on your hard disk. If you upload a file with the same file as an existing My Place file, the existing file will be replaced by the new one.*

4. Click on Continue to bring up the Upload File window.

5. Click Select File, and browse your hard disk to select the file you want to upload. Click on OK.

6. In the same window, click Send. The File Transfer window comes up and tracks the progress of the upload. When the transfer is complete, your directory window (Figure 7-2) is updated to display the file you just uploaded.

You can now view the file you've uploaded. Its URL is

```
http://members.aol.com/screenname/filename
```

Managing My Place

Like your own hard disk, your space on My Place can easily get cluttered. If you're using large multimedia files, it can fill up. Just as you do with your hard disk files, you manage your Web files by creating directories, moving files around, and deleting files and directories as required to keep things orderly. In fact, you'll probably find it easier to manage My Place than your hard disk!

Creating a directory is useful if you either want to make individual files available to people or if you want to allow people to upload a file to you. If you want to *make files available* to anyone over the Internet, you create a **/pub** directory in your main directory. To *accept* files, you'll need to create an **/incoming** directory. Bear in mind that an incoming directory can become clogged with files and eat up the 2 Mb of hard-disk space available to you.

 *The "/" symbol separates folders from each other. /incoming is shorthand for **http://members.aol.com/incoming** and /pub is shorthand for **http://members.aol.com/pub**.*

Creating a Directory

Revisit the My Place shown in Figure 7-2 (yours will look different, of course, since you'll create it with *your* screen name):

1. Click Create Directory, to bring up the following little window:

2. Type in a directory name (in this case, *art,* because it's for graphics files), and click Continue. A message confirms the creation of the directory. Click OK. Create more directories if you want, then close the little window.

 My Place (like FTP) is case sensitive, and uppercase letters precede lowercase letters (an Art *directory would come before an* art *directory).*

Deleting a Directory (or File)

Select the directory (or file) you want to delete, click Utilities, and click the Delete button. Be sure you want to delete it because, unlike on your hard disk, you cannot undelete using CTRL-Z or any other keystroke. Once it's deleted, it's gone.

Renaming a Directory (or File)

What if you incorrectly entered the remote filename or uploaded the file to the wrong directory? If you incorrectly entered a filename, change it as follows: simply select the file, click Utilities, click Rename, and type in the correct name. If you put a file in the wrong directory, you can move it by renaming its *directory* path, as in the following example, changing

```
/spacetravl/art/venus.jpg
```

to

```
/spacetravl/incoming/venus.jpg
```

In other words, a file's full name consists of its full directory path. Changing its name from one path to another removes it from one directory and *moves* it to another directory.

USING PERSONAL PUBLISHER

Personal Publisher 2 makes it easy to create a Web page in a couple of minutes, adding images, sounds, backgrounds, and links to your favorite places using point-and-click techniques. It's also easy to edit and refine your page, using either Personal Publisher 2 or an HTML editing tool such as AOLpress or Windows' built-in Notepad editor.

Personal Publisher 1 and 2: What's the Difference?

Why the *2* in Personal Publisher 2? The original Personal Publisher allowed only for simple effects and didn't support features such as colorful backgrounds and flexible formatting. Editing was a pain.

Another difference between Personal Publisher 1 and Personal Publisher 2: pages you create with Personal Publisher 2 are stored on your hard disk, in your Personal Filing Cabinet's Web Pages folder.

Any page you made with Personal Publisher 1 is still available on the **home.aol.com** computer, while everything you do with Personal Publisher 2 is available on a different computer, **members.aol.com**. You can't edit your Personal Publisher 1 pages with Personal Publisher 2, but it is very easy to re-create your PP1 pages in PP2 and go much further in refining them.

Let's get started and see how easy it can be. Keyword: PP2 takes you to the window shown in Figure 7-3.

Click the big Create a Page button to bring up the window shown in Figure 7-4, where you choose one of three templates (Personal, Business, or Greeting) for your page. A *template* is a set of pre-defined *elements*, such as text, background, and images. All you do is "fill in the blanks" with the specific words and pictures you want to appear on your page. These elements include HTML tags, which are created for you behind the scenes. You never have to worry about the actual tags, because Personal Publisher creates them for you automatically. However, if you do want to create or edit your page either manually or with an HTML editor, you *may* need to work with the actual HTML tags.

When you choose either the Personal, Business, or Greeting template and make a page, you're guided through the process and prompted to add one element at a time. For the sequence of steps, see "The One-Minute Web Page (Give or Take)." Even when you select No Template, you're really using the same elements that are in the templates. The only difference is that with No Template you're not guided

7

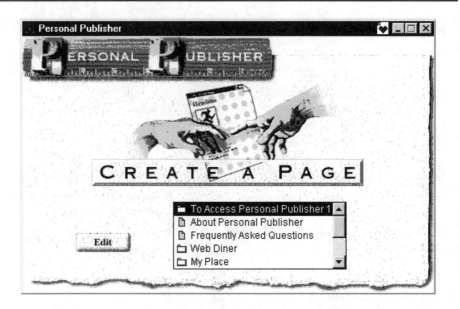

FIGURE 7-3 Here's where you start creating a page or editing one you've already made

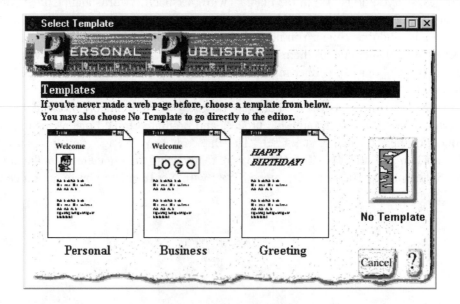

FIGURE 7-4 Choose a template and start publishing

through the process; you can choose any elements, any number of times, in any order, and you also get the choice of an additional element: HTML, which gives you the ability to add HTML code if you're comfortable with it.

No matter what template you use, you choose from the following elements in building your page. For a more complete overview of the page elements you'll *experience* when you browse the Web, see "A Page and Its Elements" in Chapter 6. You can't create every Web element with Personal Publisher, but it's a good place to start, and you can add fancier elements later, using AOLpress or another tool.

- *Title* and *heading*. A *title* is the phrase that appears in the title bar of the browser when someone looks at your Web page. A *heading* is the headline, the big bold letters on the Web page itself announcing its purpose or welcoming the reader (or whatever).

Note *In HTML-speak, a Personal Publisher heading is a level-one head (<H1>...</H1>).*

- *Background.* Ever since the release of version 3.0 of the AOL software, AOL's browser has supported "backgrounds," a color or pattern, also called *wallpaper*, that covers the entire page and against which all text, links, and images appear. Personal Publisher lets you choose a colored background from a "color wheel," which you'll use in Step 2 below. With Personal Publisher 2 you can also choose a repeating image as a background. Or, you can choose not to use *any* background.

Tip *Nothing is more annoying than an overdesigned Web page whose loud background makes it impossible to read the text. Personal Publisher 2 gives you the ability to choose type color as well as background color/pattern. If you choose any colored background or any repeating image for your page, make sure to choose a type color that will display well. That may take some trial and error. Also, if you use a background on one page, you may want to use it on all pages—to give your site (collection of pages) a common overall look and feel.*

- *Image.* Personal Publisher 2 lets you choose a graphics file from either its own library of clip art or from your own hard disk. For more about using image files, see the "Images on the Web: What You Need to Know" box. "Image" is really shorthand for multimedia file: you would also use Personal Publisher's Add Image window to add a sound file or video clip to your page.

■ *Personal information*—short bits of unformatted personal or business information about you, your business, your hobbies, or anything else you please. Depending on the template you choose, you'll get one or two small text boxes for your personal information. You can change the names of the categories if you want, *hobbies* to *favorite sports*, for example, but you can't format this text (bold, italics, etc.) unless you play with the HTML directly or use an HTML editor.

■ *Body text.* A personal statement, formatted in bold, italics, or other effects, with live links to your favorite AOL and Internet resources. If someone's viewing your page and clicks a link, he or she will go directly to the resource that you're pointing to. Of course, only members will be able to link directly to any AOL areas you link to (see Figure 7-5).

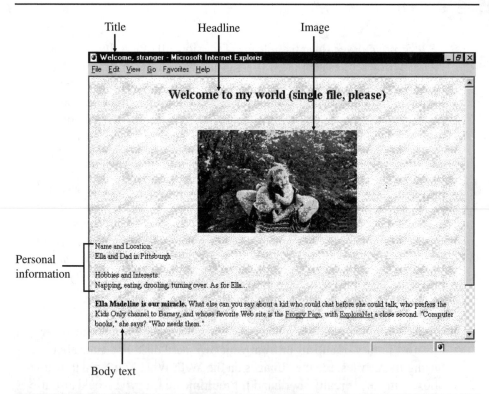

FIGURE 7-5   A personal page (my own) built with Personal Publisher and viewed from the Internet with Microsoft Internet Explorer

The three templates—Personal, Business, and Greeting—all use a mix of these elements, which differ slightly between templates. For instance, the images available in the Business template are a shade more serious than the images in the Personal template, and the Greeting template offers a box for a personal message as opposed to the more structured "personal information" (name, address, hobby…) in the Personal and Business templates. When you use No Template or when you edit *any* template, you get the option of adding "raw" HTML if you want to achieve a specific effect. The "Adding HTML" section provides the details.

Despite these differences from template to template, when you edit a page, you can change the wording, the images, and the links, and even reverse the order of elements so that you can get the same results no matter which template you choose!

Tip   *The upshot: It really doesn't matter which template you use. Pages made with the Greeting template do offer some extra images, but the Personal and Business templates give you a choice of almost identical elements. A page made with any template is easily editable into a page that could have been made by the others.*

Creating the One-Minute Web Page (Give or Take)

Let's see how easy it can be to make a personal page. Here's how I would make a personal page with Personal Publisher. I've kept the page self-contained and short; you can get as ambitious as you want!

1. Go to keyword: PP2, and click Create a Page. At the Select Template window, select Personal. The first window that comes up asks you for two pieces of information: your page's title and its heading.

You don't *have* to supply either a title or a heading, but both provide important context to anyone viewing your page. Fill them in as appropriate. Click an alignment for your heading. (I chose Center.) Click Next.

> *Note* *You don't have to save your work as you progress from step to step. As you add elements to your Web page, they are automatically saved on your hard disk, in your Personal Filing Cabinet.*

2. Add a background, use a repeating image as a background, or choose no background.

   If you want to use a repeating image, you can choose a "tile" from AOL's clip art collection or select an image of your own—a photo, say—that you have converted into a graphics file and saved on your hard disk. (See "Images on the Web: What You Need to Know.") Feeling earthy today, I'll use "Sand Tile" as my background by clicking the Image button and double-clicking on Sand Tile in the listbox. Click Next.

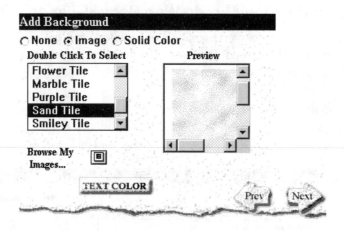

   If you choose Solid Color for a background, you get AOL's color wheel. Click any part of the color wheel to bring up Windows' color palette, from which you either choose one of 48 preselected colors or create a blend of your own by using the Define Custom Color window. Click OK when you're happy with the color for your background, then click Next.

Note *If you ever want to revisit a previous screen in Personal Publisher, click Previous. If you want to do something else and quit the current page, click Cancel. Any elements you have created are saved in your Personal Filing Cabinet even if you Cancel. You can delete unwanted images either offline (using Personal Filing Cabinet's Web Pages folder) or online (going to keyword: PP2 and clicking Edit from the main screen).*

3. Now I'm going to add an image. Again, I can choose one of AOL's clip art files or browse my hard disk for an image of my own, which is what I'll do in this case. I click Browse my files…, search for an old family picture I happen to have handy, and double-click.

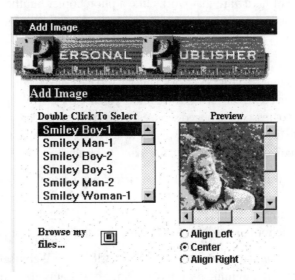

If you use your own image, you may get a message from the AOL browser asking whether you want to "open" the file or "save it to disk." If you get this message, choose to "open" the file. I click the Center button because I want the image to be centered on the page. Click Next.

Images on the Web: What You Need to Know

Your Web pages can incorporate any graphics files of the common formats: GIF and JPG, as well as the less common ART, BMP, and XBM formats. In practice, you'll just be using GIFs and JPGs, and perhaps a BMP. How do you *get* such files?

- For *clip art and generic art*, you could start at one of the AOL image archives such as the PC Graphics Art Forum (keyword: PGR) or the "quick clips" that are downloadable from the AOL Web site at **http://www.aol.com/images/public/**.

- More interested in using *your own images, especially photos*? But how do you turn those photos into files? Turning a photo that you can view into a file that a computer can use requires a scanner—a piece of hardware that works like a photocopier but that produces a file instead of a paper copy of an image. For more information about scanners and scanning, visit AOL's Digital Resource Center (keyword: Digital Imaging) and see the next item.

- If you don't have access to a scanner, a service called PictureWeb, offered through AOL, can provide everything you need. PictureWeb offers a broad range of reasonably priced services. They process film, archive photos, and create files. The service is available at keyword: PictureWeb. A link to PictureWeb is available from the main PP2 listbox.

- *Make your own art.* If you're proficient using a tool such as Adobe PhotoShop, CorelDraw, or Fractal Design Painter, you can make your own movies, graphics, and backgrounds and save them as GIFs or JPGs suitable for uploading to My Place and using in your Web page.

- *Get art on the Web.* Finally, don't overlook the Web itself as a source of free art, beginning with Web Diner host Laurie McCanna's Free Art Site at **http://www.mccannas.com/**. And Images from Planet Earth (**http://www.nosc.mil/planet_earth/images.html**) also includes files you can use in your Web page.

 Make sure not to use any image or other content that is copyrighted!

4. Now it's time to add Personal Information. For the Personal template, I get two boxes, one asking for my "name and location" and the other for my "hobbies and interests" (similar to the AOL Member Directory). I oblige:

Personal Information

Name and Location:
Ella and Dad in Pittsburgh

Hobbies and Interests:
Napping, eating, drooling, turning over. As for Ella,

If you prefer not to provide this particular information, delete the text and use one or both boxes to say anything you want. Note that formatting (bold or italics, say) isn't possible here but is possible if you later refine the page using an HTML editor such as AOLpress. Click Next.

7

5. Now I'm asked to provide Body Text—up to 32K (a lot) of freeform text, formatted more or less as I please, with any *links* I want. I'm going to keep it simple, since I know that very few people like to read lots of text on the Web. Any text I enter can be formatted in the same way an e-mail message sent to someone on AOL can. Just enter some text, highlight it, and click a button to apply bold, italics, or other effects. If it's unclear what the formatting buttons do, see "Adding Pizzazz to Your AOL Mail" in Chapter 3. The formatting "controls" are identical.

Body Text
Type text, select and drop Favorite Places:

Ella Madeline is our miracle. What else can you say about a kid who could chat before she could talk, who prefers the Kids Only channel to Barney, and whose favorite Web site is the Froggy Page, with ExploraNet a close second. "Computer books," she says? "Who needs them."

This window conveniently gives complete access to your Favorite Places folder, so you can easily create links from your personal page to one or many of your favorite places. Just type and select your text, then drag the Favorite Place from the list on the right to the text on the left. Or, drag the Favorite Place into the Body Text window, and the title of your Favorite Place becomes the clickable text on your Web page.

I've placed a check box in the "Add My E-Mail Link" box, so readers can send me an e-mail message by clicking a "mailto" link (if their browser can automatically call up an e-mail program, as the AOL browser can).

6. To wrap things up, let's view the page by clicking the View button. A mini-browser, similar to the hybrid browser encountered in Chapter 6, comes up and displays the page just created as anyone on the Web would see it. You probably won't be able to see all of your page at the same time, so be prepared to scroll.

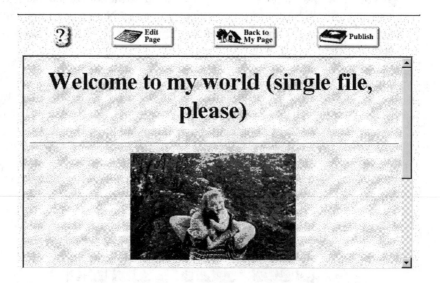

If you like what you see, click Publish. Your Web page and all associated image files are now uploaded to My Place, where your creation can be viewed by the entire world.

If you're not 100 percent satisfied with the results, click Edit Page and read on; the next sections are devoted to editing your Web pages.

Note   *Personal Publisher 1 gave you the option of publishing for AOL members only, for the Internet, or for both. With Personal Publisher 2, everyone with Web access, whether on AOL or the Net, can see your page. If you're serious about publishing for the world, you should get into the habit of viewing your page on different browsers (at least Microsoft Internet Explorer and Netscape), since there are many subtle differences in each that can cause the appearance of your page to vary. When you publish, Personal Publisher 2 names your main page **index.html**, so if you already have a page in PP2, it will be overwritten. PP2 notifies you if you're about to overwrite a page and lets you rename it.*

What's My URL?

When you create a page using Personal Publisher 2, this page and all associated files are kept in My Place, described earlier in "Publishing and Maintaining Your Web Pages in My Place." Anyone on the Internet can view this page by using your URL: **http://members.aol.com/*screenname*.** In place of *screenname*, your friend should type your actual screen name. It's not necessary to specify a file in the */screenname* directory, since browsers automatically attempt to open **index.html** if a page is not specified in a URL.

Sharing Your URL

On AOL, you can mail someone a hyperlink to your home page. The recipient must also be using AOL 3.0 or above to use the hyperlink.

1. From the Mail menu, select Compose Mail.

2. Fill in the To and Subject fields, then, in the message field, select the word or phrase that is related to your site and that you want to hyperlink.

3. Right-click the highlighted text, and select Create Hyperlink.

4. Type in your URL.

5. Click OK to close the little Create Hyperlink window, then click Send.

7

EDITING YOUR PERSONAL PAGE

One of the greatest improvements of Personal Publisher 2 over Personal Publisher 1 is the ease with which you can now edit your work. If you're at all dissatisfied with any page you have created, view it as instructed in Step 6 of the section "Creating the One-Minute Web Page" and click the Edit Page button to go to the Edit Home Page window, shown in Figure 7-6.

Note   *If you have more than one version of AOL on your computer or if you used another computer to make your page, you must edit your page using the same computer and same version of AOL you used to create it.*

The window contains two big sections: Add Contents and Edit Contents. Let's start with the Edit Contents section, on the right. This section lists the elements you created, in the order you created them. You can do two things here. You can double-click any element to tweak it—change the text, image, background, or whatever. Or you can rearrange the elements by clicking and dragging any element

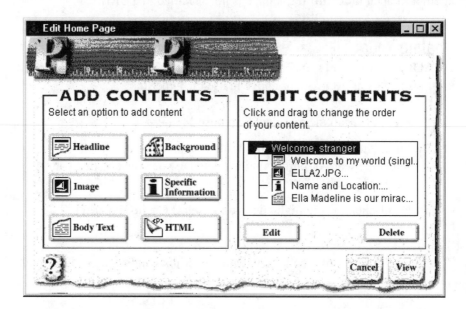

FIGURE 7-6   Add an element or double-click an element you've already created to edit it

above or below any other element. This will change their order in the actual page after you publish it.

The buttons in the Add Contents section take you to one of the windows you saw in the previous section. Here you can *add* a headline, a background, an image, or whatever. Any element you add will go at the *end* of the elements listed on the right side of the window in the Edit Contents section.

If the list on the right is getting cluttered or you've inadvertently added elements that you don't want (which is easy to do), select the unwanted elements and click Delete. If you don't delete them, they will show up on your Web page.

Click View to see your page with the elements you've added or edited. Again, if you're not quite happy, click Edit Page; if you like what you see, click Publish.

Editing a Page You Created a While Ago

You can edit anything you've ever done in Personal Publisher 2 by clicking the little Edit button on Personal Publisher's main window, shown in Figure 7-3. You'll see the following scrolling window, which gives you access to your life's work on Personal Publisher:

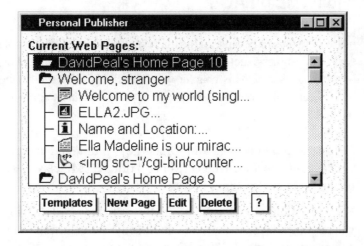

Note that even opening PP2 and closing it again will create a new Home Page folder for you in your Personal Filing Cabinet. Select any element and click the little Edit button to bring up the mini-browser (pictured in Step 6 in the section "Creating the One-Minute Web Page"), in which you view and from which you can edit or publish a page. Click Edit Page, view the page again, and either do some more editing or publish it.

Adding HTML

The HTML button of the Add Contents section of the editing window (Figure 7-6) gives you your first opportunity to add some raw HTML to your page. HTML is very simple in principle, but it can get as fancy as you want it to. It gives you the flexibility to add just about any effect you want to your page. Some of these effects are described in "Next Step: Refining Your Page."

Tip *With AOL for Windows 3.0 (Windows 95 version) and Personal Publisher 2, it's easy to get a behind-the-scenes view of the HTML you've generated. Just display your page as in Step 6 in the section "Creating the One-Minute Web Page," right-click, and select View Source. Your HTML script appears in Notepad. You can save it, study it, or revise it if you're comfortable with HTML—though bear in mind that making changes (unless they're very simple) may require that you use another HTML editor, such as AOLpress. Close the Notepad window when you're done (it's easy to open up these windows and forget about them!).*

Learning HTML on AOL

HTML is simple in concept but is getting more and more complex to master because of the many powerful features available to Web designers, such as tables, forms, precise font control, plug-ins, and Javascript. This chapter won't teach HTML because there's not enough room, but here are some places to start if you want to learn HTML on AOL.

- For instruction in person, Web Diner (keyword: Web Diner) and Web University (keyword: Web University) offer HTML classes at regularly scheduled times in chat rooms.

- For a selection of books about HTML, go to keyword: My Place, where you can click a button to go directly to a selection of tutorials and reference guides, all for sale on AOL.

- On the Web itself many tutorials and references are available. A classic place to learn correct HTML is the *Beginners' Guide to HTML,* at the following address (just type it into the Keyword window and press ENTER):

```
http://www.ncsa.uiuc.edu/General/Internet/WWW/HTMLPrimer.html
```

> And Tim Berners-Lee, one of the inventors of the World Wide Web, has written a classic called the *Style Guide for Online Hypertext*, to help you write *good* HTML—tags that convey your content as effectively as possible:

```
http://www.w3.org/pub/WWW/Provider/Style/Overview.html
```

NEXT STEP: REFINING YOUR PAGE

Now that you've created your Web page, you may want to know how to add Personal Publisher features to it that are not as obvious as the basics; or maybe you want to add features that you can't get by using PP2. For example, you may wish to add a visitor counter to your Web page. Or you may wish to add sound. Or you may want to do something as simple as bolding some of your text. The following sections barely begin to show how far you can go in building and refining a Web page. For more ideas, read the "Learning HTML on AOL" box or visit AOL's Web Diner (keyword: Web Diner), Web University (keyword: Web University), or Desktop and Web Publishers forum (keyword: DWP).

Adding a Visitor Counter

A counter is a neat gimmick many people use to keep track of the number of people who access their main Web page. Actually, it just keeps track of "hits," not unique individuals, so if someone visits your page twice, the counter will say *00000002*. To add a visitor counter to your Web page:

1. From the PP2 main window, click Edit, select the page to which you want to add a counter, and click Edit. Your page now shows up in the view window. Click Edit Page to bring up the window shown in Figure 7-6.

2. Click the HTML button in the Add Contents section and type the following text in the big box, including the quotes and brackets:

```
<img src="/cgi-bin/counter?your_screenname">
```

Substitute your screen name for *screenname*, for example:

```
<img src="/cgi-bin/counter?ellamp">
```

3. Click OK to return to the Edit Home Page screen.

Note *HTML elements go at the end of the list of your Web page elements (see Figure 7-6). You can add more than one HTML element in a single box, but the elements will be adjacent on the actual page. Thus, it's a good idea to add HTML elements separately, so you can position them on the part of the page where they will be most effective.*

This little "script" won't really work until you've uploaded (published) the revised Web page to **members.aol.com** using My Place. Once it's published, you can open your Web browser and view your counter at the bottom of your Web page. You're visitor 00000001…of many more, I hope. By the way, don't forget to add some text before the counter, saying something like "Since June 1, 1997, you are visitor number…to my site. Thanks!"

Tip *To see other counters, visit one of the sites with counters at the end of this chapter. For more about counters, visit **http://members.aol.com/wwwadmin**, where you will find more useful tips for building interactive elements such as guestbooks, counters, and e-mail links.*

In Business? Let PrimeHost Maintain Your Site.

AOLpress can be used as a stand-alone application, but it also forms part of the more complete business service offered by AOL's PrimeHost (keyword: PrimeHost). *Hosting* allows a business to lease the technology required for an Internet presence on a monthly basis, so it can focus on business while the hosting provider focuses on the technology—running the server, installing the software, leasing fast connections to the Internet, and ensuring security.

AOL's PrimeHost service offers companies fully supported publishing software (AOLpress), AOLserver software with a fully integrated database, and

> simple Web-based methods of gaining access to and information about your site. Customer service and technical support staff are always on hand to assist you with any questions you may have. PrimeHost also facilitates domain name registration if you want your own Internet address, such as **sunnyprospects.com**.
>
> For more information, visit keyword: PrimeHost.

Adding Multimedia Files

Suppose you want to share files with visitors to your Web page. They could use FTP to download the file from your corner of **members.aol.com**. However, what if you want visitors to *hear* a cool sound as part of your Web page? You can require them to click a link to the file (giving them the choice of whether to hear it) or make it play automatically in the background.

Let's say you have a WAV file on your hard drive called **beethovn.wav**. To add this file to your page as a clickable link, you follow pretty much the same steps you followed in the previous example of the counter. View your page, edit it, click HTML in the Add Contents section (Figure 7-6), and type in the following bit of HTML:

```
<a href="beethovn.wav">The sound of victory (700k)</a>
```

You've just used HTML's link tag (<a>), the standard way for linking elements on the World Wide Web! Its "argument," *href,* identifies the file being linked to (**beethovn.wav**), which is placed in quotes. The part your reader clicks is:

```
The sound of victory (700k)
```

The tag is "closed" by the </a> tag. Finally, for the link to work, you must publish the page again (view the page, then click Publish). The audio file (**beethovn.wav** or whatever) will be uploaded automatically to My Place.

 On AOL you'll find loads of audio files you can use without violating copyright at keyword: Midi. MIDI files tend to be much smaller than WAV files.

Background Sound

A variation on the theme of the clickable sound link is the *background* sound, which plays automatically when someone merely visits the page. How? The file downloads in the background and AOL plays it automatically using a built-in Windows player, which makes for a smoother experience, though some people will be startled by the sound!

To add a background sound file to your Web Page, the steps are pretty much the same as in the preceding section, but the HTML is different. So, view the Web page to which you want to add sound and click Edit Page. In the Add Contents section (Figure 7-6), click HTML and add this bit of HTML, brackets and all:

```
<EMBED SRC="mySound.wav" height=2 width=2 autostart=true hidden=true>
```

In place of *mySound.wav* put the actual filename of your WAV or MIDI file. Users whose systems can't play these sounds for some reason won't get an error message; the sound just won't play.

Adding Animation

The simplest way to add animation to your Web Page is to use an animated GIF, a file that contains several images shown in sequence when someone views the page, creating the impression of animation. There are other more advanced types of animation you could use, plug-ins such as Shockwave and VDO, but they require more advanced software to create, and it's not a good idea to assume that users around the world will have the required gear (for more on plug-ins, see Chapter 6).

Tip   *You can find animated GIFs at Web Diner (keyword: Web Diner). These GIFs are indistinguishable from regular GIFs since they have the same GIF extension. An excellent guide to animated GIFS has also been published by an AOL member:* ***http://members.aol.com/royalef/gifanim.htm***.

As in the previous sections, you view and edit the page to which you want to add the animated GIF. In the Add Contents section (Figure 7-6), click Image. Click Browse and search for the GIF file on your hard disk, then double-click to select it. Back in the Add Image window, choose the proper alignment. Now, click View again and make sure that at least one frame of your animation appears on the page. Click Publish.

Now anyone viewing your Web Page with a browser that supports animated GIFs will be able to see your creation and is sure to be impressed by your technical prowess.

Using an HTML Editor to Edit Your Page (AOLpress)

Astonishing things are possible on the Web these days—animation (from animated GIFs to VDO, Shockwave, and beyond), CD-quality audio, Java-driven ticker tapes, and much more—but many of the coolest effects require that you get comfortable with HTML code, either manually (using a text editor like Notepad) or graphically (using an HTML editor such as AOLpress).

Caution *Once you start editing an HTML page using tools other than Personal Publisher 2, you can no longer use Personal Publisher 2 with the file, so make sure you're comfortable with "going it alone" if you plan to use another tool!*

Let's take a quick look at an HTML editor you can get for free on AOL (see Figure 7-7). At keyword: AOLpress, you come to information about both PrimeHost (AOL's Web-hosting service for commercial Web sites) and AOLpress. To use AOLpress, you must download and install the program following the online instructions. Make sure to restart your computer after installing it.

To actually use AOLpress, you must have first published (uploaded to My Place) a page with Personal Publisher; the **index.html** file, the file that contains your automatically generated HTML, is only created when you upload it. For AOLpress to edit this file, you must now *download* it using My Place. (In My Place, just select the file, click Download, and find a location on your hard disk for the file.)

Now, start AOLpress. From the File menu, select Open, navigate to **index.htm**, and double-click. The page will be displayed in AOLpress (Figure 7-7). (Note that the file is stored as **index.html** on **members.aol.com** but as **index.htm** on your computer; Windows can't handle "long" file extensions such as *html*.) Here are some of AOLpress's features you might want to explore:

- A graphical tool for making multicolumn, multirow structured tables, without the hassle of coding them in HTML. AOLpress doesn't yet provide simple tools for making forms, however.

- Access to your HTML code just in case you want to tinker with it (Figure 7-7). A great way to learn HTML coding is to go back and forth between the graphical image of your page and the underlying HTML. You can edit in either mode—graphical or HTML.

- A spell checker.

- An easy way to link to other pages and anchors. Just highlight text, click the Links button, and type in or navigate to a URL. A *link* takes you to the top of a page, an *anchor* to some point you specify within a page. Although with Personal Publisher it's easy to link pages to your main page (**index.html**) using the Body Text element and dragging Favorite Places onto highlighted text, it's a bit more complex to create and link several levels of pages within your Personal Publisher site. You also can't create anchors with Personal Publisher 2. AOLpress makes it easy to create, link, and edit the links between pages in a complex site.

- Really simple tools for making bulleted and numbered lists. Just select the text and click the appropriate button. Personal Publisher 2 doesn't let you create lists unless you know a little HTML.

- Complete control of the appearance of text. For instance, the Personal Information can't be formatted in Personal Publisher 2, but you can format it in AOLpress.

FIGURE 7-7   AOLpress lets you edit your page graphically or manually, by giving you direct access to the HTML script

Some of the most powerful capabilities of AOLpress can be used with PrimeHost but not with Personal Publisher 2. For instance, with AOLpress you can save files on a remote server and edit a large complex set of pages and links directly from your desktop computer! The related ability to view the remote files as a "mini-web" is a powerful tool for remote management of a more complex site. For the full scoop on these and other features, excellent online help, including a FAQ and a tutorial, is available from the AOLpress Help menu.

TELLING THE WORLD ABOUT YOUR SITE

So, you've built a page. What good does it do if no one knows it exists? There are search engines and directories that collect the URLs of Web sites around the world; for others to find your page, it has to be available on one of these search engines. Chapter 9 is devoted to the whole topic of searching. Some search engines automatically "crawl" the Web looking for sites, but most also accept URLs sent to them by Web builders eager for promotion.

The Submit-it service lets you provide information about your site to more than 300 search engines and directories at the same time, letting you reach both the general sites (like Excite) and the highly specific ones (like SBA's Guide to Computer Vendors). You can get more information at **http://www.submit-it.com**.

Tip *In Web Diner (keyword: Web Diner), check out the Web Developers Resource Center for a great deal of additional information about how and where to publicize your Web site.*

Curious about who's actually linking to your page? Infoseek's Ultraseek (available at keyword: Infoseek) offers a "Link search" by which you can enter your URL and find out who's pointing to it! That in itself is a good way to seek out like-minded people on the Internet.

Adding a Guestbook

A guestbook gives you a way of collecting information about people who visit your site. You can find out what they think of the site, for example, or what they'd like to see you add. Making a guestbook requires the use of forms, with fields and other Windows elements. AOL now supports the *CGI* (Common Gateway Interface) capability required for members to include guestbooks in their Personal Publisher sites. For complete instructions and sample scripts, see **http://members.aol.com/wwwadmin/guestbook/guestbook.htm**.

SHARING YOUR PAGE WITH OTHER AOL MEMBERS

The most important thing to do with your new Web page is to share it with others. Many individual areas throughout AOL offer collections of home pages created by AOL members who frequent the area and share interests. Here are a few AOL areas with big collections of member home pages, to which you can add yours:

- AnswerMan (keyword: Answerman)

- Digital City, Washington D.C. (**http://www.digitalcity.com/washington/Page1.html**)

- InBusiness (keyword: Inbusiness)

- Newsgroup Scoop (keyword: Scoop)

- Web Diner (keyword: Web Diner)

If you're feeling ambitious, enter your page in the AOL Member Home Page Contest (keyword: MHP Contest). Winners get a denim shirt with the AOL logo and are admitted to the MHP Hall of Fame. The rest of this chapter is devoted to a handful of sites created by AOL members, and it shows what makes them stand out.

Learning Web Design on AOL

Mastery of HTML in itself doesn't make for good design. Here are some places on AOL where you can learn the fine points of the new art of Web design:

- Web Diner (keyword: Web Diner), led by Tim and Laurie McCanna, ostensibly focuses on designing business sites, but in fact offers abundant and free Web advice of very general interest, organized in areas with mysterious names such as "Byte of the Day" and "Blue Plate Specials." Visit Web Diner daily to figure out what the names mean—it's worth it. The tutorials are particularly useful for anyone taking the high road and writing their own HTML scripts. There's also a ton of graphics elements to download from Web Diner.

■ The Desktop and Web Publishers' forum (keyword: DWP) brings together design-minded desktop publishers and Web builders. The most useful part of the forum for Web designers is at keyword: Webmakeovers, where you can see how members' home pages have benefited from the recommendations of seasoned designers.

■ Jill Ellsworth's InBusiness forum (keyword: Inbusiness) is a great place to get pointers for making effective business pages—not *how* to make pages, but how to make them *work*.

NOTABLE AOL HOME PAGES

Here's a very small sampling of pages made by AOL members that were chosen because they exemplify one or another aspect of strong Web design. No offense to the countless excellent member pages not included here!

Out of Balance

http://members.aol.com/gerrym22

Winner of Member Home Page contest.

Creativity is the main theme of the site shown in Figure 7-8. Graphic artist and former Lockheed engineer Gerry Manacsa's home page combines rich graphic design and good readable content. The content is personal as well as creative. Manacsa, born in the Phillipines, displays his graphic art and photographs, and he shares his musings about surfing, life, and Fellini. The site has won more than 20 Website awards, including Point Communications' Top 5 percent award.

Tip   *Learning HTML? It's worth viewing the source code to see how Manacsa achieved special effects such as the links, the image map, and the Blue Ribbon graphic on the opening page. Just right-click and select View Source.*

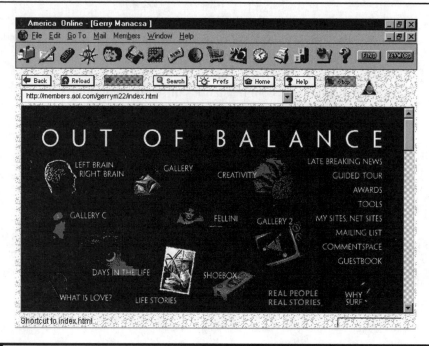

FIGURE 7-8 Gerry Manacsa's beautifully balanced—and very personal—page

This site was published in My Place. It was created with Adobe PageMill, an HTML editor.

Ovarian Cancer Links

http://members.aol.com/mind2body/mind2body.html

Winner of Member Home Page contest.

This site, created with Personal Publisher, demonstrates the Web's powerful way of delivering essential information to a specific group of people, in this case women who have experienced, or who want to learn about, ovarian cancer. The one very long page consists only of links to information about ovarian cancer. They're carefully selected, attractively grouped, and effectively centered on the page. The categories include "your medical team," "support," "legal, finance & insurance," "general cancer links," and "general health links." This is a "must see" Internet resource for both women with this disease and their families.

Womanist is to Feminist...

http://members.aol.com/nshour

This site, recommended by the good people of the Web Diner, comes from Nancy Shour, who teaches American Studies and African-American literature at Union College in Schenectady, New York. It shows how someone can incorporate the Web into their actual work, in this case, into the literature classes Professor Shour teaches.

Shour uses her Web site as a resource for her students as well as a way of reaching a broader, "virtual" audience of anyone interested in the literature she clearly loves. She uses both the Web and e-mail to make her class interactive and to publish students' work. She posts extra credit projects on her site, giving her students an incentive to explore the site and the larger Web.

A distinctive feature of the site is that it is self-contained—it has a clear purpose and just about all the content it needs to achieve that purpose—so readers aren't distracted by links that take them to other sites. Where there are links, as in the set of selected links to sites devoted to the writings of Alice Walker, they are fully annotated, so Shour adds value and probably unique content to the links themselves. Much of the site was hand-built with a text editor, then uploaded to My Place.

FROM HERE...

Browsing gives you somewhat passive access to Web sites. With Personal Publisher, My Place, and all the HTML tools and resources at your disposal on AOL, the Web comes alive. If you ever have a question about Web publishing, make sure to frequent Web Diner or another Web-related AOL forum.

FTP, the subject of the next chapter, is the final Internet service covered in this book. It's the other, more interesting side of My Place. While My Place lets you upload to a single site (**members.aol.com**), FTP lets you download millions of files from thousands of Internet sites.

7

Chapter **8**

Downloading Software from AOL and the Internet

I n human terms, the work you do at the computer consists of the letters you send people, the reports you prepare for work, and the images and videos you like to watch. You might use your PC to keep track of everything from recipes and resumes to jokes and addresses—perhaps you also play games and do your bills on it.

Files are the way your PC stores and keeps track of all this information. They make activities such as playing games and paying bills possible. Everything you do on a computer requires files, that is, discrete pieces of data and software, each with a name and a location on a hard disk or other kind of "storage medium." Even the AOL for Windows software is just a huge set of program and data files.

On the Internet, the FTP (File Transfer Protocol) service gives you access to millions of publicly available files on every imaginable subject. America Online provides everything you need to search for files available by FTP and to help yourself to files you like—images, games, software of every type, even public-domain literary classics, and much more. AOL's own software collection includes programs you can use to run the files you download via FTP.

Note   *Copying a file from a distant Internet computer to your own PC is called downloading. Uploading means moving a file from one computer to another, usually from a PC to a "larger" computer. On AOL you can upload files using Personal Publisher 2 (see Chapter 7).*

America Online has a built-in FTP program, or *client*, that enables you to go quickly and easily to any publicly accessible FTP site. AOL's World Wide Web *browser* gives you an alternative way of going to FTP sites. Which do you use? This chapter makes a case for the browser as a great tool for *finding* files to download, and the "client" as a great tool for actually retrieving them. This chapter begins with an introduction to filenames and types, and ends with an overview of the vast software libraries available on America Online itself.

UNDERSTANDING FILES AND FILE TYPES

Every file has a filename and a file type.

A *filename* is the name that a person gives a file so that others know what is *in* the file. Naming files is in fact a subjective matter and does not always simplify access. Sometimes, naming files is an exercise in shoe-horning. In the old DOS and

Windows 3.1 file-naming system, filenames had to be eight characters or less and were followed by a period and an *extension* of no more than three characters. Happily, Windows 95 allows long filenames.

A file's *type*, on the other hand, can give you a great deal of reliable information. How do you tell a file's type? An extension is the best guide, since it is usually assigned automatically by the program that created it. The extension is the part of a file's name after the period ("dot"). In *chapter8*.doc, *doc* is the file extension (a *doc* file is Microsoft Word's extension for all of its DOS and Windows versions). Not all files have extensions, but even the absence of an extension can be informative—such files are likely to be for the Macintosh or Unix operating system (and are probably not usable on a Windows computer like yours). Table 8-1 provides an overview of the most common file extensions of PC files you'll encounter on FTP. Here's what you can learn from a file's type:

- Which operating system you must have in order to use the file. Unix, Macintosh, and Windows are the primary operating systems for which files are available on the Net. Generally speaking, as a Windows user you won't have much use for non-Windows programs, although text files (see the next item) can be read on any platform.

- Whether the file is *binary* or *text*. It used to be that when you downloaded a file using FTP, you had to specify whether it was binary or text. Now, AOL's FTP program takes care of that for you. Basically, everything is a binary file except "pure" text files (ASCII). If you know a file is text, you can count on being able to use it with any word processor. If it's binary, you must use a specific program. Table 8-1 provides some guidance, as does the "Using the Files You Download: Graphics, Sounds, and Beyond" section.

- Whether the file is compressed or zipped (archived). A *compressed* file has been run through a special program to reduce its size and thus decrease the download time. A *zipped* file usually consists of several files that have been run through a program to make it possible to download the entire batch of files at the same time. When you download a file of either type, you must decompress or unzip it.

Note   *Zipping a file is a good way to reduce the size of large individual single files. Thus, a zipped file can be a single compressed file (such as a large database file) or an archive of many files (such as several chapters of this book).*

■ What the file contains. Reading a file's extension can tell you whether the file contains a program or raw program code; whether it's an image or a video file; whether it's zipped, compressed, or something else; whether it's a Word or Excel document; and more. To name the most common extensions, image files have extensions such as GIF and JPG; video files use AVI, MOV, and MPG; and audio files use WAV, AU, and MID.

File Extension	Platform	Comments and Usage Tips
	Compressed and Archived Files	
EXE	Windows	Self-extracting executable file; just run the file from the Windows Start menu or File Manager.
HQX (BinHex)	Macintosh	A binary file that's been encoded and converted into a text file; requires another program to be decoded.
SEA	Macintosh	Self-extracting archive file: run a SEA file and all its parts are automatically unzipped.
SIT	Macintosh, Windows	A zipped file produced by the StuffIT program, originally for Mac only; Windows version of StuffIT allows decompressing but not compressing.
UUE	Unix, Windows	A binary file that's been converted to a text file for transmission, especially via newsgroups; requires another program to be decoded, but can be done automatically by AOL's FileGrabber (Newsgroups only, see Chapter 5)

TABLE 8-1 Standard Mac and Windows file types, platforms, and categories, with usage tips

File Extension	Platform	Comments and Usage Tips
ZIP	Windows	A zipped file; unzip with WinZip or PKZip, or automatically using Download Manager.
Image		
ART	Macintosh, Windows	Compressed Johnson-Grace image file; requires no special software to view on AOL.
BMP	Windows	Bitmapped picture file, requires no special software to view on AOL.
GIF	Macintosh, Windows	Stands for Graphics Interchange Format, an Internet standard; requires no special software to view on AOL.
JPG, JPEG	Macintosh, Windows	Stands for Joint Photographic Experts Graphic; requires no special software to use on AOL.
PCX	Windows	Requires no special software to use on AOL.
PDF	Macintosh, Windows	Delivers highly formatted documents; requires Adobe Acrobat (freeware) to use (keyword: Adobe).
Sound		
AU	Macintosh, Windows	Play using AOL browser.
MID	Macintosh, Windows	MIDI (Musical Instrument Digital Interface) sound file, played with Windows' built-in Media Player.
VOC	Macintosh, Windows	Sound Blaster file; requires separate helper application.
WAV	Windows	Windows sound file; can be played with Windows Media Player.

TABLE 8-1   Standard Mac and Windows file types, platforms, and categories, with usage tips *(continued)*

File Extension	Platform	Comments and Usage Tips
	Video	
AVI	Windows	Windows standard; runs in Microsoft Media Player
MOV	Windows, Macintosh	QuickTime; requires a player, available at keyword: Mac video (or keyword: MVD).
MPEG	Windows	Windows standard, runs in Microsoft Media Player but some versions require special software.
	Text	
TXT	All	Text file; open in any word processor or AOL's text editor.

TABLE 8-1 Standard Mac and Windows file types, platforms, and categories, with usage tips *(continued)*

Where's It At? Files and Directories

A full filename consists of a name of the actual file and the *path* to that file. A path is the exact directory (a directory is another name for folder) where the file is located, including any directory to which it belongs, any directory to which that *parent* directory belongs, and so on up to the computer's *root* directory. A path starts at the top level of a site, or root, which is similar to the root of your hard disk—it's the directory that contains all other directories.

For example, the **wsftp.exe** file (feature-laden FTP software you can run with AOL) is itself available by FTP and is located at dozens of FTP sites around the world. Here are its directory paths on an FTP site at the University of Vienna in Austria: **ftp.univie.ac/edvz/progs/win95/wsftp.exe**. The **wsftp.exe** file is contained in the **win95** directory, which is contained in the **progs** directory…which is contained in the **edvz** directory, which is contained in the site's top level or root directory.

Why Use FTP?

FTP is perhaps most useful as a way of making available a specific file or set of files that many people want—a software product or group of sound files, for example. In projects where people live in different places, FTP can be a superb means of allowing limited access to files and keeping files secure. In addition, FTP is the only practical way of *uploading* files to a place from which they can be referenced by a Web site you are building (see Chapter 7). Lastly, it's easier to "publish" a single file (a program, say) by uploading it than to design and maintain a Web page just to make the file available. As a result of its usefulness, there are more than four million files available by FTP!

Ways of Retrieving Files over the Internet

FTP may be the most efficient way of transferring files, but it's only one of many. You can also get files in the following ways:

- **Files via Newsgroups**. Using a technique called UUEncoding, many people insert binary files into newsgroup messages by converting them to encoded text files (strings of characters that only a computer can understand). As an AOL member, you can use FileGrabber to effortlessly download and convert these files. See Chapter 5.

- **Files via the World Wide Web**. The Web has become a popular way of making files available to a broad audience—not just as files to download onto your own computer, but in *context*. A NASA Web site, for example, lets you view images based on photographs taken by the Hubble Spacecraft, together with information about the Hubble mission (**http://spacelink.msfc.nasa.gov/**). Web pages today are loaded with files—Real Audio, Shockwave, image, video, and more (Chapter 6). Many Web publishers prefer the Web as a way of distributing files, because users experience file *content* directly, without having to worry about filenames and the like.

- **Files via E-mail**. If you need to send a file to a single person or a small group of people, attaching it to e-mail can be easier than using FTP, because your recipient(s) is more likely to have (and know how to use) an e-mail reader than an FTP client. You and your recipient do need a "MIME-compliant" mail reader, however, as explained in Chapter 3.

8

FINDING FTP FILES

Unlike the Web or newsgroups, FTP was not meant for browsing. "Finding" a file usually means searching for a specific file. With FTP, browsing makes little sense, since you cannot automatically tell what's in a file from its name. Moreover, almost all FTP sites limit the number of incoming connections—the number of people who can use the file directories at that site at the same time.

 Browsing an FTP site (going up and down the directories in search of interesting files) can be bad netiquette, because it ties up limited FTP resources and can prevent access to people who know exactly what they are looking for.

On AOL, you have traditionally two ways of discovering the FTP sites where a certain file resides:

- Using AOL's FTP search technique (the Search for FTP sites button at keyword: FTP)

- Using the Net's technique, based on a neat little service called Archie

 If you're ever in desperate need of a file, start with AOL's file libraries, which are available all over the service. The files can be searched at keyword: FileSearch (see "Downloading Files from America Online," later in this chapter).

Anonymous and Non-anonymous FTP

When you use AOL or Archie to search for files, you're really searching only for publicly accessible files (of which there are "only" a couple of million). These public files are available by a method called *anonymous FTP*. All this means is that you log on to these sites with the user name **anonymous** and the password set to your e-mail address. You don't actually do this yourself, however: logging on is handled automatically by AOL if you use the FTP client (keyword: FTP).

*If you use the browser to access FTP, you may be asked to log on to anonymous FTP sites! If you are, just type in **anonymous** for the user name and your **screenname@aol.com** for the password.*

USING NON-ANONYMOUS FTP On AOL, when you use the FTP client, there's a little check box: "Ask for login name and password." (Go to keyword: FTP, click on Go To FTP, then on Other Site; it's illustrated in "Using FTP the AOL Way.") If you don't want to use anonymous FTP, put a check in the box, and, when you arrive at the FTP site, you will be prompted to supply a user name and password. This form of FTP is an excellent way of sharing confidential files with a small group of people.

AOL's Search FTP Service

At keyword: FTP, you can do a search of FTP sites by clicking the button labeled Search for FTP Sites. It seems easy, and it is. This search looks through a gigantic text document consisting of a list of FTP sites. This valuable list, maintained by Perry Rovers of the Netherlands, provides information on every known anonymous and Non-anonymous FTP site in the world: its address, location, and date last modified (see the box about "Anonymous and Non-anonymous FTP"). This list is posted in more than 20 long parts to the **news.answers** newsgroup, and it's also available by FTP at **rtfm.mit.edu/pub** (one of the "Favorite Sites" available at keyword: FTP).

Unfortunately, this document does not provide a list of the files actually available at these sites—only a characterization of the kind of files available and the names of some of the most popular publicly available directories. Here, for example, is a description of the files available at **brawls.mindlink.net**:

```
audio and textual information related to arcade one-on-one
fighting video games (Street Fighter II, etc); pictures.
```

Thus, with AOL's FTP Search service, you can search by subject, but you also have to assume that the people who run FTP sites make the same assumptions you do about categorizing files. Sometimes you'll get good results: a search for "funny" turns up three sites, while it doesn't turn up any using an Archie search (FTP's standard search service, discussed in the next section).

Here's how to go to an FTP site that you find using the FTP Search service:

1. Write down the FTP site name, then close the Search window.

2. From the main FTP window, click the Go To FTP button.

3. Click the Other Site button. Type in the FTP address in the Site Address box and click OK. An information window appears; read it and click OK. For help getting around an FTP site, see the "Navigating an FTP Site" section.

FTP Site Names

FTP site names are a type of *domain name* (see Appendix B). They consist of little bits of text separated by periods, or *dots*. For instance, the FTP site, **ftp.aol.com**, is the site name of a set of FTP computers in the **aol.com** domain. Sometimes you'll find FTP sites beginning *ftp*, just as you'll find Web sites beginning *www*. Organizations with multiple types of services are likely to follow this convention, hence **www.aol.com** and **ftp.aol.com**. But, in general, you can't tell an FTP site from its address.

Searching with Archie on the Web

Archie is an Internet search service that goes a big step further than the AOL Search FTP Sites option. It searches a list of actual files and directories available on anonymous FTP sites around the world. The list is updated approximately weekly, and is the "industry standard" method for searching FTP.

These days, the easiest way to use Archie is over the World Wide Web. The Web and your browser put an easy-to-use face on Archie and similar search services. All you do is type a keyword (part or all of a file's name) and click the Search button. The Web site contacts the Archie server, asks Archie to search its list of files, and presents the answers back to you as *hypertext*. To go to an FTP site and get the specific file at that site, just click a link, as shown in Figure 8-1. Current Web "front ends" to Archie and similar services are available at many places, a few of which are listed in "Searching FTP on the Web: A Few Starting Places."

Figure 8-1 shows a search for the **wsftp** program using ArchiePlex, an Archie service in Switzerland. For each "return" I got a link to the FTP site's top level ("Host"), to the directory containing the file I'm seeking (if I want to see what else

FIGURE 8-1 Three of many results of an Archie search for *wsftp32*, the Windows 95 version of the FTP program

is available there, including similar files and other versions of the file I'm seeking), and to the file itself, whose size and upload date are provided. What I didn't get is an estimate of how long it would take to download the file, useful information that's always available when you download a file directly from AOL (see "A Word About File Size").

Note *With earlier methods of using Archie (via Telnet and e-mail), you had to know some rudimentary commands, then type them in accurately. The commands have now been embedded into easy-to-use Web forms, though only a few of Archie's many commands have been implemented in most of these Web sites. Lists of Archie servers and key Archie commands are available at keyword: Nethelp, in the FTP area.*

Searching FTP on the Web: A Few Starting Places

The following World Wide Web sites give you a simple, point-and-click interface to Archie:

- **http://hoohoo.ncsa.uiuc.edu/archie.html**
- **http://www-ns.rutgers.edu/htbin/archie**
- **http://www.uib.no/htbin/archie.pl**
- **http://cuiwww.unige.ch/archieplexform.html**

If you're not familiar with the Web, go to the Keyword window, available from AOL's Go To menu, and type in one of the Web addresses (URLs) from this list, then click Go. Follow the onscreen instructions. Usually, all you have to do is enter a term (part of a filename) to search for and click Search. Chapter 6 provides all you need to know about using the AOL Web browser.

Archie on the Web: Common Options

As easy as it is to do an Archie search over the Web, Archie "forms" (windows with text boxes, radio boxes, check boxes, and other Windows elements) can still present some choices:

- **Type of search**. The basic choice is *exact* versus *substring*. If you do an exact search, Archie searches only for the exact characters you type in, paying attention to uppercase and lowercase. If you do a substring search, you're really doing a search for a part of a name, which makes sense if you're not exactly sure of the full filename. If you do a *case-**insensitive** substring* search, Archie ignores whether the actual filename has capital or lowercase letters.

> *In general, FTP, unlike other Internet services, is case sensitive, so when you are searching for a specific file, pay attention to its pattern of capitalization.*

- **Server to search**. There aren't all that many Archie servers in the world—only about 20—to handle the entire Internet's file-searching needs. Try to search the Archie server closest to you, which in the U.S. are the servers at ANS, Rutgers University, InterNIC, and the University of Nebraska.

- **Number of "hits."** A hit (a needlessly menacing term) is just an answer to your question—an FTP site with the file you are searching.

Doing an Archie Search on the Web

The exact way you do an Archie search on the Web will vary in the details, but usually you must do the following:

1. Enter a search term consisting of all or part of a filename.

2. Adjust other settings to make sure you are (1) searching the closest Archie server and (2) doing the most efficient search (which is usually "case insensitive substring").

3. Press Search or Submit. Archie searches its huge list and returns a list of files whose names match the characters you entered, plus their paths (see "Where's It At?").

Here, Snoopie!

One tool I like these days is an Archie-like service that's available only on the Web at **http://www.snoopie.com**. It's quick and easy to use, and, like Archie, it returns the following information for each site it returns: host (FTP site), directory, filename, size, and date of last modification. One thing Archie does that Snoopie *doesn't* do is a substring search, and this may be one reason why it's faster than Archie. According to John Matzen, Snoopie's Network Engineer, Snoopie currently indexes approximately four million files, and would do more if storage technology permitted quicker "reads" of gigantic hard disks.

USING FTP THE AOL WAY

When you search FTP using Archie-over-the-Web, search results are presented in a clickable list of FTP sites that contain the file. Usually, you'll be able to click either on the directory containing the file or on the file itself. Click, and you go directly to the site, or bring the file directly to you!

What could be easier? Well, it's not always a good idea to use the browser to access FTP sites, even if you're using a Web-based search. For one thing, it's usually slower using the browser to download files than using AOL's specialized FTP client (the one you get at keyword: FTP). For another, a browser wasn't made to access FTP; it was made to access the Web. As a result, when you use the browser, you don't get all the options you get when you use keyword: FTP (Figure 8-2).

Here are some reasons to use AOL's built-in FTP software (keyword: FTP) rather than the browser:

- AOL's FTP client gives you the ability to explicitly request non-anonymous FTP (see the "Anonymous and Non-anonymous FTP" box). The browser does not always gracefully handle anonymous and Non-anonymous FTP log-ins, and sometimes you'll even be prompted to supply a user name and password for anonymous FTP sites.

- The browser can be slow in connecting to and navigating FTP sites, and even slower in downloading files.

- AOL's FTP client lets you view a text file, that is, read it online without downloading it, thus saving your time and space on your hard disk. With the browser, the only way you can view a text file is to download it.

■ AOL's FTP client will estimate how long it will take to download a file (see "A Word About File Size").

■ Using Download Manager (from the File menu), you can (1) keep track of files you've downloaded using FTP, (2) decompress them by clicking a button, and (3) jog your memory when you forget where you've downloaded them (see "AOL's Download Manager" at the end of this chapter).

■ AOL's My Place service (Chapter 7), offered through the AOL FTP client, also lets you upload files—something you can't do using *any* browser.

Before using AOL's FTP client to download a file, make sure you have the file's exact directory path. Here's a useful exercise: searching and retrieving **WinZip.exe**, a useful program for "unzipping" compressed Windows files. An Archie search reveals that the file is available at **ftp.pcnet.com**. Follow these four broad steps below to retrieve *any* file.

1. **Connect to the site.**

   ■ Go to keyword FTP (Figure 8-2).

   ■ Click on the Go to FTP button. The Anonymous FTP screen comes up.

   ■ Click on Other Site, to go to the Other Site window.

■ In the Site Address box, type in **ftp.pcnet.com**, or whatever the FTP address is. Do *not* put a checkmark in the "Ask for login name and password" box. Click Connect.

If you know the entire file path, enter it (see "Avoiding Window Clutter"). If you enter a full path to a specific file, you can skip to the last step.

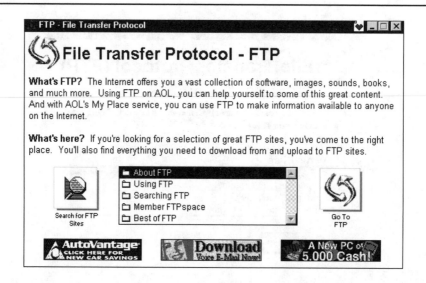

FIGURE 8-2   AOL's starting point for downloading files from the Internet (keyword: FTP)

Next, when you connect successfully with the FTP site, a message comes up from the FTP site itself. The welcoming message sometimes includes the name of someone at the site—the FTP administrator—to contact if there's a problem. This message can also provide the names of mirror sites—FTP sites with the same files as this one, if this one is busy. Read the message, then click OK.

Avoiding Window Clutter

Here's a great tip for avoiding window clutter from Bob Hirsh, who administers AOL's FTP service: In the FTP window, you can download a specific file using its "file" URL in the Site Address box of the Other Site window.

For example, typing **file://ftp.cdrom.com/pub/games/win31/jokes/fish3.zip** in that box snarfs (that's highly technical jargon for *retrieves*) the file without opening a single window! This command navigates directly through the ftp.cdrom.com FTP site, follows a path down through the *pub*, *games*, *win31*, and *jokes* directories, then finds a silly file called *fish3.zip*. (You will find *many* games here if this one's not available for downloading!) Note the inclusion of the host name, **ftp.cdrom.com**, as part of the entire address, separated from the directory path by a forward slash and no space.

Navigating directly to a specific directory such as **ftp://ftp.cdrom.com/pub/games/win31/jokes/** is also a good way to minimize the number of open windows.

8

2. **Navigate to the directory that holds the file you're seeking.**

   After getting past the welcome message, you'll find yourself looking at the top level of the FTP site—something like the "root" directory of your hard disk, the point at which you start looking for a file on your local computer. Where to start? In general, it's best to start in the *pub* directory—the publicly accessible directory of files available by anonymous FTP. In this case, however, there's a special top-level *winzip* directory with all the versions of the Winzip software in it. Open the directory by double-clicking. A new window opens with the contents of that directory.

For other searches, you are likely to have to open many directories as you burrow deeper in search of a particular file.

3. Locate the file.

Identify the file you're seeking in the directory you've opened. You'll see three pieces of information for the file: the date it was uploaded, its filename, and its size in bytes (without commas—so look closely to make sure it's 40,000 and not 400,000). For more information about file size, see the "A Word about File Size" box.

Note *Throughout an FTP site, you'll notice the dates when a file or directory was last modified. Just because a* folder *was last modified on one date doesn't mean it won't contain files with more recent dates. So, don't be put off by old dates. Likewise, if a site's README file is really old, the individual files at the site may still be more recent; it's just that no one's updated the README file. Finally, the file least likely to be changed—the opening message—can make a site seem old, even if many individual files are up to date.*

To see how long it will take to download a file, select it and click the Open button (note that you're not actually opening the file, just getting some information about it).

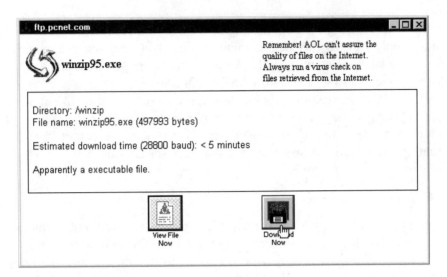

For text files, you'll be able to read the text without downloading the file; just click View File Now.

Tip   *Many FTP sites have README and INDEX files that can provide valuable information. A README file may provide advice about choosing and using files. An INDEX file usually provides a listing of files in a directory. Using AOL's FTP client (keyword: FTP), you can read both types of file right on your screen without downloading the files to your hard disk. Just select the file and click View File Now.*

A Word about File Size

A file's size matters because it determines, together with your modem speed, how long it takes to download a file. File size is also important because files take up space on your hard disk, and even a huge hard disk can be eaten up if you do enough downloading.

Files are measured in *kilobytes* (1000 or so bytes, the unit for measuring data). A thousand kilobytes is a *megabyte*.

On AOL, when you double-click a file at an FTP site to download the file, you first get a window that estimates how long it will take for the file to download. With a 28.8 modem, the estimated download for a 2 Mb file is *<18 minutes* or under 18 minutes, while for a 40K file it's under 1 minute.

In general, programs and binary files (such as sound, image, and video files) tend to be large (over 50K). Text documents are usually under that size, but you'll find Word documents weighing in at more than 100K and MIDI sound files of only 10K. Always bear in mind how much content you're getting for the time it takes to download a file. A 1 Mb WAV file might, for example, play for a minute, but so will a standard 15K MIDI file.

Using Windows Explorer (or File Manager), you can learn the size of every file on your system; you can even arrange files by their size in order to find out which ones are taking up the most space. That's the place to start if you're running out of hard disk space and need to make some room!

4. Download the file.

If you want a copy of the file, click Download Now. You'll be prompted by AOL's Download Manager to give the file a filename and directory on your hard disk. It's always a good idea not to alter the original filename and to download the file into a directory that won't be deleted. The only time to change a filename is when there's already a file with the same name in the directory where you are downloading it. After you've selected a directory on your computer and clicked OK in the Dialog Manager, you'll see AOL's thermometer box telling you how much of the file has downloaded and how many minutes are left:

Note   *Using AOL's Download Manager, you* cannot *create a list of several FTP files you want to "download later," in order to download them all at a convenient time (at the end of your session, for example). One reason for this is that FTP connections are limited: there is no guarantee that a site with a file you want will be available when you want to do a "batch" download. So, you've got to download now. You can do something else while you're downloading a single file (like read your mail or browse the Web), but if your computer seems a little sluggish, it's because downloading files is a fairly demanding task for any computer.*

AOL's Download Manager

AOL treats downloading as pretty much the same kind of activity no matter how you initiate the download—whether it's from one of AOL's many software libraries, a newsgroup, an e-mail message, or an FTP site (at keyword: FTP). Download Manager lets you adjust the way you use FTP in several important ways:

■ Whether image files you download (GIF, JPG, PCX format) are automatically displayed

■ Whether downloaded ZIP files are automatically unzipped when you log off

■ Whether the downloaded ZIP file is kept on your hard disk after it's unzipped

■ How many downloaded files are maintained in Download Manager, which gives you information such as where you download files *from* and where you download them *to*

To see your Download options, go to the File menu, select Download Manager, and click the Download Preferences window. Check and uncheck boxes as appropriate.

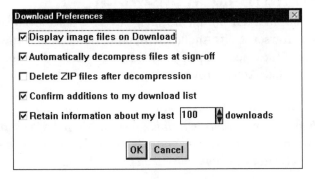

What happens if you can't remember where you've downloaded something? Choose Download Manager from the File menu, then click the Show Files Downloaded button. Find the file you've downloaded, select it, and click Show Status. Information about the file will be displayed, including its size, type, and where you downloaded it.

Where can I get more information? A large set of frequently asked questions is available in the Download Info Center (keyword: Download Info Center).

Navigating an FTP Site Using the AOL FTP Client

Navigating an FTP site means going "up" and "down" a directory path, from the top (or root) level to lower-level directories and any subdirectories. When you double-click a folder to open it, you open up a new window and go down a level. Close a window to go back up.

If you find yourself at an FTP site in search of a specific file, and the file does not appear to be where you expected, the best bet is to start with the *pub* directory and to browse downward through appropriate subdirectories. A *pub* directory is usually accessible from the root when you're using anonymous FTP.

> *Browsing FTP sites—roaming up and down the directory structure in search of interesting files to take—is not always a good idea. Many such sites are maintained as public services to the Internet, and most can support only a limited number of incoming connections. In general, it's a good idea to access an FTP site at an after-hours time, bearing in mind that the FTP site is probably in a different time zone from yours. How do you know where a site is? Do a search for the specific site from the main FTP window (Search for FTP Sites). Double-click the name of the site to read a description of the site and a mention of its location.*

NAVIGATING FTP WITH YOUR BROWSER

One reason for using the AOL *browser* to navigate FTP is that the only window that's ever open is the browser itself. Another reason is that the AOL browser itself can *play* many kinds of files (see Chapter 6), and in the future will support even more. Or, maybe you just like AOL's browser!

> *When using an FTP site from the browser, you may at some point—or perhaps at many points in a single session—be asked to supply your user name and password. If you are, type **anonymous** as the user name and your full e-mail address (**screenname@aol.com**), then press ENTER.*

To use the browser, you need to know an FTP site's address, to which you tack on an *ftp://* at the beginning. For instance, typing **ftp://ftp.winsite.com/** in the browser's location (URL) box and pressing ENTER takes you to a large FTP site at the University of Indiana (Figure 8-3).

When a file or folder is clickable, the mouse cursor turns into a pointing finger. Open a folder and it's shown in conjunction with the level "above" it, as in a family

FIGURE 8-3   A large FTP site accessed with the browser. Folder icons are used to show directories, and document icons to show files

tree. Open folders have a minus sign next to them and show you your path at a glance. You close a folder and move up a level by clicking the minus sign. The browser's Back arrow won't take you up a level, because all the levels are shown in one browser window.

To download a file, just click! Instead of the Download Manager, you'll see the familiar Windows Save As window (actually, they work the same way but have different title bars). Give the file a name and folder on your hard disk, and click OK. The browser window displays the progress of the download at the bottom of the browser window, just as it would with anything you download. When the entire file has arrived, the browser logo stops spinning. You can close the browser by clicking the Close box (the X in the upper right-hand corner) in Windows 95 or double-clicking the Control box (the little box in the upper left-hand corner) in Windows 3.1 or Windows 95.

Virus Alert

However you download a file—using the FTP client or the browser—you need to be careful about viruses! Every file you download from AOL has been checked for viruses—nasty little programs that can harm your programs, your data, or your hard disk. But no file you get from the Internet using FTP has necessarily been checked for viruses. You need to check them yourself.

For the most part, the files that can spread a virus are *programs* ("executable" files). *Documents* can be infected, but infected documents will not ordinarily hurt other files. Macro viruses, however, or "prank" viruses as they are often called, work by replacing the global template in applications like Microsoft Word with a "new" global template. *Any* document you create or open that is normally dependent on the global template will be "infected." In addition, these macro viruses can be shared unwittingly simply by opening the document or spreadsheet. In AOL's software libraries (keyword: FileSearch), you can find "disinfectant" programs to clean the affected files and replace the global templates.

AOL has excellent information in the PC Virus Information Center, at keyword: Virus, where you'll also find software for detecting and rooting out the little critters.

USING THE FILES YOU DOWNLOAD: GRAPHICS, SOUNDS, AND BEYOND

Files you download using the FTP client require an additional piece of software if you want to *use* them. Sounds require a sound player so you can hear them, videos require a video player to watch them, and so on. There's one exception: images. When you download most image files using FTP, they'll display on your screen. Even so, you may want a more sophisticated program for viewing and editing your downloaded image files.

 Chapter 6 looks at how the AOL browser handles multimedia files displayed within Web pages. More and more, the browser itself plays multimedia files.

Viewing Image Files

When you download an image file in one of the common formats, it displays automatically as it's being downloaded. (GIF and JPEG formats make up the overwhelming majority of the files for PCs available by FTP.) Actually, it's "progressively rendered," which means you gradually see more of the file until the whole thing is downloaded and the entire image is visible.

Note   *The first option of your Download Preferences gives you the choice of seeing images as they're downloading, whether you're using a newsgroup or FTP.*

Downloading an image file automatically saves it. Once a image file has been saved, you can open it again by simply going to the File menu and selecting Open. Browse to the place where you saved the file and double-click it.

Tip   *Opening a file saved to your hard disk, using the File | Open command, activates the Show Tools option on AOL's Edit menu. If you select this option, you can tinker with the colors or flip and rotate the image to see it from a different perspective. At keyword: Viewers, more powerful editing utilities, such as PaintShop Pro, are available.*

Where Do You Find Image Files on FTP?

AOL itself has great and easy-to-search image file libraries, some of which are listed in Table 8-2. If you get adventuresome, FTP has software treasures as well.

1. From the main FTP screen, click Search FTP sites and enter any keyword(s) you wish, such as **space and gifs**.

2. Double-click any FTP site that comes up for your search, and read the entry carefully. Write down the FTP address and as much file and directory information as you can glean from the site description.

3. Return to the Anonymous FTP window by closing the Search window. Click Go To FTP, then click Other Site to enter and connect to the site.

Where Do You Find Graphics Viewers on AOL?

If you want sophisticated display and editing capabilities, head for AOL's Multimedia Zone (see Table 8-2). At keyword: Viewers, too, you'll find a bushelful of recommended viewers. The viewers are screened, and like all AOL software, are guaranteed to be virus-free.

Forum (Keyword)	Software Library & Other Features
Animation & Video (keyword: Software, click Animation & Video)	Video files and utilities for AVI, MOV, and MPEG formats; includes some animations and animated GIFs
PC Graphic Arts & Animation (keyword: PGR)	Fractals, stereograms, clip art, utilities, and the like
Multimedia Zone (keyword: MMZone)	Staffed area, with message boards and software libraries
Music and Sound Forum (keyword: PC Music)	MIDI, MOD, VOC, WAV files, and much more, with sound-playing utilities and operating instructions
PC Software Center (keyword: Software)	Browsable categories of utilities: Animation & Video; Business & Finance; Desktop Publishing, etc.
Video Zone (keyword: VZ)	Message boards, a FAQ, and links to video clips on the Web
PC Recommend Viewers (keyword: Viewers)	Recommended viewers for animation, image, sound, MIME, and other file types
Windows Forum (keyword: Windows, click Windows Forum)	Computers & Software channel's Windows software library
Windows Magazine (keyword: Windows, click Windows Magazine)	Editor's picks from *Windows Magazine*
Winsock Center (keyword: Winsock)	Collection of Internet applications (see Chapter 10)

TABLE 8-2   Software treasures on AOL. Many of the files you want are already there!

Tip   *Using any stand-alone graphics utility or sound player, you can view images or play sounds when you're not online. Just open the program, go to its File menu, choose Open, and select the file you want to use.*

Hearing Sound Files

Sound files are a bit more complex than image files. For one thing, you can hear them only if you have a sound card and speakers. For another, if you do have this stuff, Download Manager does not give you the chance to hear sounds automatically as they are downloaded from an FTP site. You must find a player—a separate program—if you want to hear a sound file. You may also need a different player for different types of sound files!

Two common sound-file formats, MIDI and WAV, can be played using the Media Player, a little program that is built right into Windows. In Windows 95, this program is available from the Start menu by clicking the following menus: Programs, then Accessories, then Multimedia, and then selecting Media Player. VOC files are similar to WAV files in quality but require a separate player; many VOC players are available at keyword: PC Music.

> *Tip* *Huge libraries of sound clips as well as utilities for playing every kind of sound clip are available in the Music and Sound Forum (keyword: PC Music).*

MIDI files simulate musical instruments digitally, and they squeeze a great deal of content in some very small packages. A 15K file can run for a minute and delight any child within earshot. You play it *within AOL* by going to the File menu and selecting Open, then choosing the file. MIDI files can also be played with the Microsoft Media Player.

Finally, you may encounter AU (audio) files. Downloading and then playing such a file brings up the browser. When you see this icon, or something similar, just click the arrow to play the sound. Microsoft's Media Player can't handle this format, although it's becoming a Web standard.

Watching Video Files

The first comment to make here is that video files don't quite stack up to the quality of the video on VCR. The images are jumpy, the box in which you see them is tiny (an inch or two square), and the experience is quickly over. What Hobbes said of life—that it's poor, nasty, brutish, and short—applies to video over the Internet as well. The "streaming" effect on the Web, which lets you experience multimedia as it's downloading, without special software, is much better, but streaming video files (such as VDO) aren't widely available by FTP.

The common video file types available by FTP are MPEG, MOV, and AVI. AVI can be played with Microsoft's Media Player (included with Windows 95), which can usually play MPEG as well. MPEG, however, comes in many varieties, and you may need to explore one of the AOL forums listed in Table 8-2 if you can't run a specific MPEG file using the Media Player. For MOV videos, you'll need a QuickTime player, available on AOL at keyword: MVD.

  AOL has a special forum where you'll find answers to all your video questions: the Video Zone (keyword: VZ).

As always on the Internet, be wary of copyright violations. On a Hungarian site, I found short clips from Stephen Spielberg's movie, E.T. It may seem unlikely that the value of the movie was infringed in this way, but it's a short step from making low-quality clips available to pirating longer segments of higher quality. Were the clips illegal? Probably not. Using such files may not get you in trouble, but making them available to others is probably a bad idea.

Grappling with Compressed and Zipped Files

One common characteristic of multimedia files—sounds, images, videos—is that they're often *big*—500K, 1 Mb, and more. (See "A Word about File Size" earlier in this chapter.)

As a result of their size, they take up more and more space on servers, they can take a long time to download, and they can take up a lot of space on your computer. To deal with these problems, multimedia files are often physically shrunk, or *compressed*, before being made available via FTP. This reduces storage space at the FTP site and reduces download time. All that usefulness comes at a price, however, and you can't use compressed files until you've uncompressed them.

Often compressed files will be *zipped*, as well, meaning that several files have been packaged up in a single file, again to streamline the downloading process. With PC files, you can spot a file that's been compressed or zipped by its ZIP extension (**chap1.zip**, for example). With Macintosh files, these files usually have an extension of SIT or SEA. Zipping files also compresses them, so you'll often see individual files that are zipped to reduce their size.

There are two ways to deal with zipped files.

UNZIP THEM AS SOON AS THEY HAVE BEEN DOWNLOADED.   To do so, you'll need a program such as PKZIP (for DOS) or WinZip (for Windows). Both are freely available on America Online (keyword: FileSearch) as well as on the Internet (see the earlier downloading exercise). You'll need to download the program (itself compressed and zipped!), and install it. To install, just run the file (File | Run in Windows 3.1 or Run from the Start menu of Windows 95), and follow the onscreen prompts.

It's useful to have a program such as WinZip, especially if you'll be zipping up your own files for transfer via e-mail. But there's an even easier way to unzip a file you've downloaded: let Download Manager do it.

1. From the File menu, select Download Manager.

2. Click Show Files Downloaded, then select the file you've downloaded and click Decompress. The files zipped up together will be kept together in a new subdirectory, under the directory where the file was downloaded.

LET AOL UNZIP COMPRESSED FILES AUTOMATICALLY WHEN YOU LOG OFF.

You can set your preferences to automatically unzip files *when you log off* and even to delete the zipped file afterwards (thereby saving space on your hard disk), or both. As when you do it yourself, all the unzipped files are placed in a subdirectory with the same name as the ZIP file itself. So, if you download a file named SCOOTER.ZIP to c:\AOL30\Download and AOL unzips it, the component files will appear in your system in a new C:\AOL30\DOWNLOAD\SCOOTER directory.

Note *If you manually unzip a file before logging off, the file will again be unzipped when you log off, overwriting the files you unzipped. AOL will only automatically decompress ARC and ZIP files, not files like Z and GZIP.*

Tip *The Compression Corner (keyword: PTC, click on Compression Corner) lets you download WinZip, get help, and link to Web sites that have information relating to the riveting subject of file compression.*

DOWNLOADING FILES FROM AMERICA ONLINE

On the face of it, America Online's collection of a hundred thousand or so files is modest in comparison to the Internet's *millions* of files available via anonymous FTP. But several factors make AOL's software libraries indispensable:

■ FTP files are frequently available *in many versions on multiple sites*. The redundancy reduces the number of unique files available over FTP.

Worse, the redundancy can be confusing, since it's not always possible to know which versions of a file are the best and most recent. Many of the best FTP files are available on AOL as well—and can be downloaded more quickly.

Great FTP Sites "Mirrored" on AOL

Curious about why the same files are available in so many places? Remember that the Net is a decentralized and "distributed" network. In part there's redundancy because there's no central control, but there's also intentional redundancy in order to make sure important files will always be available in case one site is unavailable. For the latter reason, you'll find "mirror" sites of the most popular FTP resources.

AOL maintains such "mirrors" at keyword: FTP. Click on GoTo FTP. At the Anonymous FTP window, you'll see a list of Favorite Sites. The mirrors are the first ones listed, and you can tell a mirror because it has a site name *and directory path* (that is, only part of a larger site is being mirrored). One such site is **rtfm.mit.edu/pub**, a mirror of MIT's famous archive of newsgroup FAQs (described at the end of Chapter 5). Another is **ftp.simtel.net/pub**, a vast archive of DOS and Windows software, one of the treasures of the Internet. Between the sheer information locked in the newsgroup FAQs and the cool games, images, and utilities at Simtel, you'll fill up your hard disk in no time.

- ■ All of AOL's files have been subject to virus checks. You can't be sure that the Net's files have been virus checked.

- ■ Downloading files via FTP, especially when you use the browser, can be painfully slow. Using AOL's FTP client (keyword: FTP), it's reliably fast. (However, you can download only one file at a time, and performance on your computer can slow down as the processor handles the download.)

- ■ Searching with Archie or even Snoopie requires that you know a filename, or at least part of its name. On AOL's software libraries, you not only don't need to know filenames, but attempting to search by filename is sometimes the worst way to proceed! Instead, you can search by subject, author, date, file *type*, or several other criteria.

WHERE TO FIND THE GREAT FILES ON AOL

 Software, images, videos, all the utilities you need to run these files, and more, are available throughout the AOL service. Even great software such as Netscape is easily available on American Online.

Computers & Software Channel

The starting point in any search for files on AOL is the Computers & Software channel, available from the main Channel window. Here you have direct access to the Software Center and ZDNet, two large and well-categorized collections of files and utilities of every type. Also, from the Software Center, you can get help (keyword: Software Help) about every aspect of downloading files. Table 8-2 lists other AOL forums where you'll find files, utilities, and, in many cases, someone to turn to if you have questions.

Software Search

It's hard to avoid AOL's Software Search window (Figure 8-4), which lets you search an archive of more than 100,000 files. It's available in many ways:

- From the Software Center button in the Computer & Software channel click File Search

- Use keyword: FileSearch from anywhere in the service

- Click the File icon on the main AOL tool bar

Unlike Archie, with Software Search you do not search by filename but by category. Also unlike Archie, with Software Search you can (and should) search by file type, to narrow your search for specific software.

1. Choose one file release date: all dates, past month, or past week. Click the appropriate radio button. Searching for the last week's or month's files can filter out files that may be outdated or may not run on your operating system.

2. Choose several categories of files to search for by clicking the check box(es). Choosing more than one can usefully narrow the search results—checking Games and Windows launches a search for games files that run under Windows, for instance.

3. If you want, you can narrow the search further by specifying a file type or file author, if you happen to know who created the file. Type in any qualifying text of this sort in the box at the bottom.

4. Click Search to run the search. The results of this particular search appear in Figure 8-5, usefully organized by Category, Subject (short file description), and Filename. Click any result to get information about the file. From the information window, you can choose to download the file now or download it later (using Download Manager).

Note the somewhat unusual order of the files you get back. They're not listed by category or file date, but by the date when files were added to AOL's library. Also,

FIGURE 8-4   No need to use filenames to search for files using AOL's software library.

FIGURE 8-5   Software you'll find on AOL for working with AVI files

the search service looks through the text descriptions available for each file, so files may be included because their descriptions contain a keyword, even if the filename does not.

> *Tip*   *To search for a specific word in a long list of files, go to the Edit menu and choose Find in Top Window. Enter some text to search for and click FindNext.*

Double-click any file you'd like more information about (Figure 8-6). You will get information about the file's upload date and any requirements for using the file. If it's a program, you will get instructions for installing it.

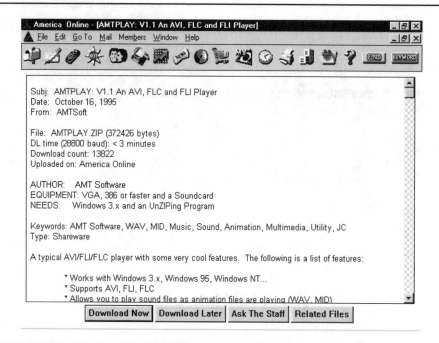

FIGURE 8-6 Descriptions of files available on AOL can include valuable information about using the file

There's No Such Thing as a Free Program

It should be pretty obvious that the software available via FTP and on AOL differs in an important way from the software available in shrink-wrapped boxes that you buy at your computer store: it's distributed directly to you, and it doesn't cost anything (at least, there's no monetary outlay)! Otherwise, commercial software doesn't necessarily differ in quality from the variety available online.

Many software creators prefer to distribute software directly to users, since it reduces their distribution costs and creates the opportunity for valuable customer feedback. However, much of this software is *shareware*, meaning that the creator expects a nominal payment of $10 to $30 or even more. Sometimes the "free" software will lack some features until you pony up some cash. Sometimes it will expire 30 or 45 days after it's installed. And sometimes the creator will rely on the honor system or forego payment altogether, in the hopes of creating a big group of enthusiastic users. Netscape (the company) got its start by giving away browser software and establishing a huge market, then selling other products (servers) plus documented and fully supported versions of the same product (browsers). Some of the best software on AOL is shareware, and many software creators both request and deserve your support (read: through payment). A rule of thumb: if you use shareware on AOL, please respect the people whose hard work makes shareware possible.

If you prefer your bits in boxes, you can buy excellent commercial software in the Marketplace channel (keyword: AtOnce or keyword: Computer Superstore). Some of the commercial software can be downloaded directly

FROM HERE...

No other Internet service is as closely integrated into America Online as on FTP. In many cases, AOL's features for working with files—Download Manager, File-Grabber, myriad software libraries, software forums—*duplicate* what's available on the Internet via FTP. The difference is that finding, downloading, and using files is easier on AOL than on the Net. The real value of AOL's file-related features is that they *complement* what you'll find on FTP; they make it easier to use the incredibly rich content available on the Internet. Since files affect everything you do on the Internet, the services you find on AOL—from the forums to the software libraries to the help resources—can enrich everything you do on the Internet.

This chapter wraps up the discussion of the Internet programs and services that are built into the AOL service. The next chapter takes a look at how to find information and people on the Internet. It moves away from *how* you use the tools to *what you do with them*, which is probably the reason for being on the Net in the first place.

8

Chapter **9**

Finding What *You* Want on the Internet

B rowsing the globe is fun, but not everyone has unlimited time to read about things they're not that interested in. When you really need information—whether it's a recipe for pie crust, a guide to raising terriers, a phone number in Iowa City, a biography of Babe Ruth, or a local movie theater's schedule this week—how do you find it? There's yet another problem: some of the information is not all that great. Unlike AOL, on the Internet there's an abundance of less-than-useful information; at any rate, it can be difficult to find information of direct use to you.

This chapter provides you with a guide to making *use* of the Internet, whether you need discrete facts or you're looking for people who have knowledge in their heads and information at their fingertips. You'll read about:

- A quick and easy search strategy ("Better Living Through Good Searching")
- Finding information on the World Wide Web
- Finding mailing lists and newsgroups, so you can get information from *people*
- Finding people's e-mail and street addresses

WHAT'S ON THE INTERNET AND WHAT'S NOT?

With so much information on the Net, many people assume everything is on the Net. It's not quite true. Here are some things you *won't* find on the Internet:

- **Books.** You *won't* find whole libraries or books that are still in print. Nor will you find free authoritative reference works (although you can pay for access to the Encyclopedia Britannica's innovative new service at **http://www.eb.com**). You *will* find a selection of public-domain books collected under the auspices of Project Gutenberg, including classics of English literature and Western civilization (**http://www.promo.net/pg/**). And you will find superb resources *about* current books and publishers (starting with BookWire at **http://www.bookwire.com**).

■ **Really private information.** You *won't* find Social Security or credit card numbers, nor will you find tax records and employment information. Mega-reams of business information are online if you do company research, but if you need employee lists and meeting minutes—don't hold your breath. However, you *will* find street addresses and e-mail addresses for tens of millions of people and businesses.

■ **Really important legal materials.** If you do legal research, you must still use a proprietary service such as Lexis-Nexis to get case law and court documentation. Although more and more of this information is going online, if you require reliable, comprehensive, up-to-date, and searchable legal records, a law library or proprietary service may be your best bet.

Better Living Through Good Searching

Sure it's easy to search the Net. But it's even easier *not* to find what you're looking for. Here are some tips for finding what you want as quickly and effectively as possible:

Step One: Ask Yourself: What do I Need? What do I Want to Know? How Will I Use the Information I Get?

■ Does it have to be authoritative or hold up in court? The Web might not be the best place to start, but people on the Internet might have advice and useful information. Ask someone in a newsgroup or mailing list.

■ Do you need software? Try FTP (see Chapter 8) or AOL's huge software library at keyword: FileSearch. Looking for image or sound files, or a *type* of file? Try Lycos or Hotbot, with their special file-searching features.

■ Is the information discrete (the number of car washes in Houston)? Search the Web. Ask someone on an AOL message board!

■ Are others likely to be interested in the question? Check out newsgroups and mailing lists, especially if your interest is long-term vs. a one-time need for a fact.

■ Just browsing? Then just browse! Use Excite's selective directory or a more comprehensive directory such as Yahoo.

Step Two: Choose the Best Tool.

Sometimes it's hard to know where to start, with so many Web search services. My advice? Get comfortable with a single tool, such as Excite, but understand the benefits of the other tools and use them when your standby doesn't return the results you need. Table 9-1 summarizes the relative strengths of the Web search indexes and directories.

Step Three: Turn your Question into a Query.

You have questions; computers understand only queries. How do you get from one to the other? The way you pose a query varies by search service. In general, use several highly specific words (from most to least specific). Use "Boolean" ANDs and ORs as necessary to expand or limit your search. Use filters to screen for specific results.

Step Four: Evaluate your Results.

If your query was specific, you can usually limit yourself to the top 10 or 20 sites returned by a query. If any of the sites returned are good, use a "More Like This" feature if it's available (as in Excite). If the results aren't useful, refine your query by adding more specific search terms or additional search terms. If *terriers* didn't work, try *short-haired terriers*!

Finding Information on the World Wide Web

The sheer size of the Web makes it a good place to start for many searches. Where exactly do you start your Web search? The first choice to make is between an *index* and a *directory*. The next choice is among indexes and among directories. Don't worry if this sounds complicated; it will become second nature in no time.

Engine/Directory (Keyword)	Strengths
AltaVista (Altavista)	Usenet searches; full-text searches of Web pages; powerful queries possible, but at the cost of complexity; speed.
Argus Clearinghouse (http://www.clearinghouse.net)	Contextual essays for serious subjects; access to all Internet resources, not just Web sites; ratings by experts and librarians; ratings of ratings.
Excite (Excite)	Excellent directory of selected and reviewed sites; concept searching; Usenet searching; "query by example" with the More Like This feature, so you can zero in on the most relevant sites.
HotBot (http://www.hotbot.com)	Easy-to-use interface and full-text searches; simple, useful filters; Usenet searches; searches by media type (images, Java, particular extensions); speed.
Infoseek (Infoseek)	Searchable FAQs; excellent "essentials"—people finder, ZIP code directory, etc.; Usenet searching and browsing (but not posting) within the browser; natural language queries; speed.
Lycos (Lycos)	Directory; ratings (Top 5%); large database; people and places searches; multimedia file searches; latest news.
Magellan (Magellan)	Ratings, annotations; Green Lights (parental controls); clear editorial standards.
Virtual Library (http://www.w3.org/vl/)	High quality; serious content; international perspective.
WebCrawler (WebCrawler)	WebSelect, a directory; customized searches for AOL channels; backward searches; More Like This feature.
Yahoo (Yahoo)	Lots of goodies: packaging of sites by city and country; customization; kids' version; latest news by subject (politics, entertainment, etc.).

TABLE 9-1 Web search services: how they differ

Start Your Search on AOL

AOL NetFind, shown in Figure 6-10, was launched too late for coverage in this book. You'll find it at Net Highlights (off the Welcome screen) and behind the browser's Search button. It pulls together the best of the Net's search services: Excite (for searching the Web), DejaNews (for searching newsgroups), and Switchboard (for finding anyone's address). You also get tons of recommended sites, plus tips for making it fun and painless to search the Net.

Which Do I Use? Index or Directory?

Think of a book. Every nonfiction book usually has a table of contents and an index. The table of contents takes you to chapters—big clumps of related information about some subject (for example, "Plants of North America"). The index takes you to highly specific references (for example, "kudzu" or "azaleas").

Or, think of AOL: Channels take you to clusters of information about a big theme such as sports or entertainment. The Find button on your tool bar near the top of the main window takes you to a specific forum of the hundreds available.

On the Web you have a similar choice. *Directories* give you access to groupings of Web sites about some large subject, such as Business or, within Business, Marketing. Directories are meant to be *browsed*, which means you can poke around until you find something interesting or something you are looking for.

Indexes on the Web give you the same kind of targeted results you get with an index in a book. They are useful when you have a good idea what you are looking for—good enough to ask a specific question. The great indexes include AltaVista, Excite, HotBot, InfoSeek, and Lycos.

Using any index is pretty much the same experience: you enter a keyword in a field and click the Search button. Most indexes also ask you to indicate *what* you want to search: the Web, Usenet, or something else. But the technique's the same: type your keywords into a box, click a button, and scan a list of "results" that can run on for many pages.

Here's an important difference between the two ways of looking for information. Indexes such as Excite are created by *computers* and are useful if you know just what you are looking for. Directories are compiled by *people* and can be excellent starting places if you need general information or are just starting to learn about something. Indexes require that you know what you want; directories assume you're willing to let someone else do some of the choosing.

Search Terms and What They Mean

Here are some terms you are likely to see on the Web when you do searches.

Boolean operators: See the sidebar, "Boolean Operators Made Easy."

Browse: In a *directory*, you browse categories of sites such as Business or Recreation for whatever strikes your fancy, instead of doing a focused search for specific information.

Database: A structured list. Each row in the list has related information, for example a URL for a Web page and all the words appearing on that Web page. A database stores information and makes it available in the form of a searchable *index*.

Directory: A catalog of selected sites, often with ratings and short descriptions, arranged into topics for easy *browsing*. A good place to get an overview of a subject.

Engine: A geeky word that usually means searchable *index*. Excite is an engine, but Yahoo is a directory. A good place to start a search for specific information.

Hit: A single item returned by *query*.

Index: A listing of URLs and associated words. Indexes make it easy to quickly find a specific URL. Search for *wild roses*, and you bring up a URL for the Web page with one or both of those words on it.

Keyword: The word or words you type at a search site to indicate what you are looking for. When you're searching the Web, a keyword is what *you* are looking for. (When you use AOL, a *keyword* is the word assigned by AOL to a forum, which you type into the Keyword window in order to go directly to that forum.)

Phrase: Two or more words that together have a special meaning, such as "League of Nations" or "home run" or "Murphy's law."

Query: What you are searching for, put in terms the computer can work with. Queries can be simple *keywords*, optionally linked by *Boolean operators* (see the sidebar). A "natural language" query is one that is expressed in *your* terms, not the computer's.

9

> **Relevancy:** The computer's best guess about whether a Web page will meet your needs. Most search engines list the most relevant sites first. Relevancy takes into consideration such factors as how many times your keyword appears on a page, how many of the words you entered are found (if you entered several words), and where the words appear on a page.
>
> **Returns:** An *engine's* answer to your *query*: a list of clickable pages with a reasonable likelihood of containing the information you are searching. Returned sites are often ranked by *relevancy*. Also know as *hits*.
>
> **URLs:** The standard way of specifying the actual location of an Internet resource, such as a Web page or Gopher menu. See Chapter 6 and Appendix B.

SEARCH ARSENAL: THE BEST SEARCH TOOLS

On the next few pages you'll find short reviews of the best search indexes and directories. The reviews compare search indexes and directories primarily by how easy it is to use them—how easy it is to turn your question into a *query* that yields good results. When you compare search services, keep in mind how big they are, how fast they are, how easy they are for *you* to use, and how well they answer your questions.

Altavista

Keyword: Altavista
http://www.altavista.digital.com/

This powerful search engine from Digital Equipment boasts a large index running on some very fast Digital computers (Figure 9-1). AltaVista does full-text searches of Web sites, and you're more likely to get good results if you follow the guidelines below. Because of its power, AltaVista is the site favored by the Yahoo directory as well as by Clnet's search.com service profiled at the end of this chapter.

Here are some tips for doing what AltaVista calls a "Simple" search; most of these tips apply to other search engines as well. For Advanced searches, help is available on the AltaVista site.

- Put phrases in double quotes, as in "guns or butter." Not putting phrases in quotes could get you in trouble in this case, since AltaVista would search for the pages with both the word *gun* and the word *butter*.

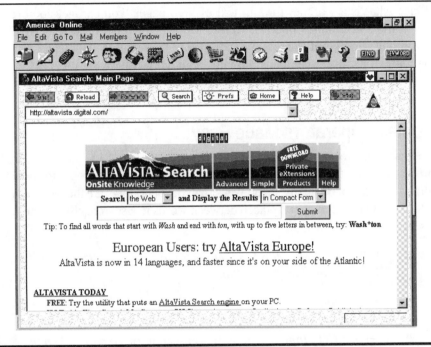

FIGURE 9-1   AltaVista, a powerful full-text searcher of either Web pages or
Usenet newsgroups

- Use several words in your query, beginning with the least common one.

- Use capitalization and punctuation to limit a search. AltaVista interprets
  small letters as either lowercase or uppercase, but any word you *do*
  capitalize returns *only* pages containing the capitalized word. A search for
  "Babe Ruth's" birthday won't return the latest "hot babes" sites.

- Precede words that must be included in the sites returned with a plus sign
  (+), as in *Babe Ruth +Yankees,* and words you definitely are not looking
  for with a minus sign (–), as in *"film noir"-pinot noir* (to use AltaVista's
  example).

*Osborne/McGraw-Hill, publisher of the book you're reading, also
publishes the official AltaVista book,* The AltaVista Search Revolution
(1996). *Ordering information is available at the AltaVista Web site (at the bottom of
the opening page) as well as at Osborne's site (**http://www.osborne.com**).*

Since AltaVista searches the full text of Web pages, you can get good results with specific and complex queries. To use "Boolean operators" such as AND and OR, you must do one of AltaVista's Advanced Queries. See "Boolean Operators Made Easy" for some general background about words like AND and OR.

Boolean Operators Made Easy

Boolean operators were named after George Boole (1815-1864), an Irish professor of mathematics who contributed fundamental concepts to modern logic and algebra. Basically, in the Web context, "operators" are the terms AND, OR, and NOT, which, when placed between words in a search, change the way a search is conducted.

 In actual searches you don't have to capitalize them; it's OK to say "and" and "or."

These terms have two effects:

- *AND and NOT **limit** a search.* If you search for *bread AND wine*, you're searching for Web pages that contain both words. If you search for *bread NOT wine*, you're searching for only those pages with *bread* that don't include *wine*. You can use these operators to get fewer irrelevant sites.

- *OR **expands** a search.* If you search for *bread OR wine*, you're searching for pages that contain either word: pages that contain *bread* and pages that contain *wine*, a much broader search than using AND.

Not all uses of AND and OR are Boolean. Sometimes, you are actually searching for the words *and* and *or*. Suppose you're looking for pages with information about the book called *Bread and Wine*, by Ignazio Silone. You'd want to package up these three words and look only for that particular phrase. You do this by simply enclosing the phrase in quotation marks:*"Bread and Wine"*.

Most search engines offer Boolean operators, and most let you search by phrase. Getting comfortable with these choices can dramatically improve the quality of your searches. *All engines differ slightly, however, so make sure to read the help text for your favorite engine.*

Excite

Keyword: Excite
http://www.excite.com

Excite is AOL's preferred search solution, and is now conveniently available in AOL NetFind (just click the browser's Search button). The Excite people urge you to use ordinary language for your keyword searches, and to do the following:

- Be as specific as possible in your query. Instead of *dogs* or *terriers*, search for *short-haired terriers*.

- Repeat those specific terms that are especially important. Instead of *terriers*, search for *terriers, terriers, terriers*.

- Precede required terms with a plus sign (+) and terms you don't want with a minus (-), as in AltaVista.

At **http://www.excite.com** you'll find a version of Excite with some advanced features. Unique among the search engines, for example, Excite offers a choice between *keyword* and *concept* searches. A keyword search looks merely for pages containing a specific word, regardless of the word's meaning or context. Excite's technology makes an attempt to figure out what you really want to know. For example, a concept search for *categorical imperative* looks for pages relating to the philosophical *concept* and not just for instances of the words *categorical* and *imperative*.

To search with Excite:

1. In the "What are you looking for?" text box, type your keyword or concept, such as **Babe Ruth's birthday**. As with other search engines, with Excite your query is not restricted to the length of the text box (keep typing and you'll "scroll" right).

2. *Below* the main text box, in the Search drop-down list, select *what* you want to search: the Web, Reviews of Web sites, Usenet newsgroups, or Usenet classifieds. In the adjacent drop-down box, indicate whether you want to search by concept or by keyword. Searching by concept is the default (pre-selected choice).

3. Click Search.

Excite is also notable in the way it returns Web addresses (URLs). It ranks them from best to worst (100% to 0%), in terms of how well the returned page matches

9

what you are looking for. Extremely useful is the More Like This feature. Every site returned by your query has a More Like This link to the right of the main link. If any site answers your query especially well, you can click More Like This to see a refined search that combines words from your original search and the result you liked. You can keep clicking More Like This until you find exactly the information you are seeking.

Excite doesn't stop at the Web. You can search newsgroups as well, looking for individual newsgroup postings containing keywords or concepts you're interested in (Chapter 5 is all about newsgroups). The clickable answers take you right to the relevant articles. As with Web searches, newsgroup results are ranked, and you can zero in on valuable content by clicking More Like This. Clicking the newsgroup containing the article brings up the AOL newsgroup window, where you can read anything you want in the newsgroup. Compared with a full-powered newsgroup search tool like DejaNews, profiled later in this chapter, your newsgroup search with Excite is limited and stops with the link to the article. You can't respond to the article or follow threads of related articles within Excite, though you can do those things using AOL's newsgroup reader.

At ***http://www.excite.com*** *you'll find additional features such as City.Net (see "City.Net: The World at Your Fingertips"). You'll also find stock quotes, the latest news, today's sports, and your horoscope.*

Excite is an index that has begun to grow its own *directory* and has hired a team of top-notch editors to select, annotate, and rate Web sites. The sites are organized in 20 categories, such as Business and Shopping, all available at Excite's opening window. Choose a category, and you can "drill down." From the Science category, for example, you can click on Planet Earth, then on Earthquakes and Volcanoes, and from there to two dozen carefully reviewed and rated Web sites.

Excite's tens of thousands of reviews can be searched. Just choose Reviews from the Search field drop-down list at the main window.

HotBot

http://www.hotbot.com/

HotBot is owned by the folks who bring you *Wired* magazine and the HotWired Web site. The underlying technology, called *Inktomi,* is the brainchild of a Berkeley professor who is trying to devise databases big enough to track the entire Web but fast enough to enable access by the entire Web community. By and large he has succeeded: HotBot is fast and easy to use. Of the search engines, it has, for now, one of the largest indexes.

Like AltaVista, HotBot does a full-text search, which in general means that if you search for very specific terms you are likely to have acceptable results. Using HotBot is a breeze. Figure 9-2 shows a sample search for information about a childhood syndrome called pervasive developmental delay. The search terms consists of a phrase (in quotes) and the acronym for the phrase, so I'll settle for pages containing either the phrase or the acronym. I'm searching the Web (not Usenet News) for a Boolean expression, *"pervasive developmental delay" or PDD*. I only want brief descriptions (as opposed to long descriptions or just URLs), and I apply a "filter"—I only want to see pages located on a North American server, because I'm especially interested in English-language resources and American organizations pertaining to the condition.

FIGURE 9-2   HotBot, from Wired Ventures, features filters and lets you search Usenet News as well as the Web

HotBot lets you use filters in conjunction with queries. With filters you specify some of the characteristics of the information you are seeking. If you're looking for information about *terriers*, you can use filters to search for information of a specific format or information more recent than a certain date.

> *HotBot is the only major search engine to allow you to limit your search to a specific domain or place (with places such as North America being defined as a cluster of domains).*

Currently HotBot offers the following filters:

Filter	Effect
Modify	Lets you build complex queries out of keywords, names, URLs, and phrases.
Date	Lets you specify how current you want the Web pages to be. A good way to filter out old or stale pages.
Location	Lets you specify a particular domain, such as **aol.com**, or a specific place, such as North America (all sites with top-level North American domains).
Media type	Requests only files of a certain format, such as Java, Shockwave, image, specific extension, etc.

> *Using the media type filter is an excellent way of tracking down Java, Shockwave, or other files that take advantage of plug-ins, as described in Chapter 6.*

Finally, HotBot, like Excite, lets you search newsgroup postings for specific words. If your query has results (and it probably will), you can bring up the full text of a newsgroup. However, you cannot read the rest of the newgroup for related postings, and you cannot respond to the posting with one of your own, at least not within HotBot. But clicking on the newsgroup name (which is hyperlinked in the newsgroup article) does bring up *AOL's* Newsgroups window, where you can browse and post as you wish. There's no "Back" to click to return to HotBot, so you'll have to use the Window menu or some other Windows technique.

Results in HotBot are ranked numerically (starting with 1) and by percentage, with the best results (in HotBot's estimation) at the top of the list.

InfoSeek's UltraSeek

Keyword: Infoseek
http://www.infoseek.com/

InfoSeek offers a simple interface and powerful underlying search technology. Let's focus on InfoSeek's especially strong UltraSeek engine (Figure 9-3), available at keyword: Infoseek.

When you use any index you want to know whether it's easy to ask your questions and whether the results are reliable. UltraSmart makes it particularly easy to ask a question by accepting "natural language" queries from you. In other words, you don't have to think up keywords (as in most other engines) but can simply ask your question in your own language; so, if you have a question, you already have a query! One strength of Infoseek Ultraseek is that it allows you to use common words (such as *a, to, an, the*) in phrases; some engines automatically ignore such words, even in phrases.

FIGURE 9-3 InfoSeek lets you ask "natural language" queries of a full-text index of more than 50 million Web sites

I compared two Web searches:

```
I'm looking for a javascript tutorial
javascript tutorial
```

and got good but different results from both and marginally better results for my own purposes from the second query. In Infoseek, capitalizing a name you are searching for automatically turns the name into a phrase (such as *Babe Ruth*, which won't return a bunch of sites about the movie *Babe* and the book of *Ruth*).

InfoSeek lets you search not just Web pages (more than 50 million of them), but also newsgroup postings, e-mail addresses, "timely news," company profiles, and Web FAQs. (Searching Usenet for *javascript tutorial* turned up an important Javascript mini-FAQ!) Unlike AltaVista, InfoSeek lets you read entire newsgroups containing the postings you are seeking. An icon shows you whether you're reading a thread or an article. Opening a thread lets you read all the articles in that thread, and you get "cross references" to other newsgroups with threads of likely relevance. Finally, when you do a Usenet search, you read newsgroups directly, as opposed to bringing up AOL's newsreader as in HotBot. You cannot post your own message to the newsgroup, though you can send e-mail to the author of a specific posting.

Like other great search indexes, InfoSeek is "growing" its own directory, with categories of selected, rated, and briefly described sites, in categories such as Politics, Sports, and Travel. InfoSeek is also putting together an excellent "information mall," complete with:

- A news center

- A people finder, with millions of e-mail addresses

- Big Yellow, the Internet version of the Yellow Pages, with 16 million entries (profiled later in this chapter)

- A ZIP code directory (you put in an address to get the ZIP code)

- A searchable *Webster's Dictionary* (the 1913 edition, alas)

- Street maps (enter *any* street address and get a local map)

- Currency exchange

- A searchable set of tens of thousands of company profiles, and more

All this good stuff is available from the main page (available with AOL at keyword: Infoseek).

Lycos

Keyword: Lycos
http://www.Lycos.com

Lycos has been around for a while, at least in "Web time." The search engine, developed at Carnegie-Mellon University, was the Net's favored Web engine for a period in 1994 (Figure 9-4). It was partly its success that paved the way for services such as Yahoo, HotBot, and InfoSeek. In the way it handles queries, Lycos hasn't kept up with the other engines, but it does still have some advantages in certain areas.

FIGURE 9-4 Lycos lets you search for sounds, pictures, and Gopher resources and browse directories of reviewed Web sites

One result of Lycos' maturity is its size. When this book was being written, Lycos was the biggest of the search indexes, with about 70 million pages indexed. Another advantage: instead of searching all the words on a page, Lycos does a statistical analysis of page contents. When it works, it's great. Keep in mind that in the opinion of some, Lycos doesn't offer the best customization choices to refine your query if it doesn't work on the first try.

Lycos accepts Boolean operators (AND, OR, NOT), but not filters (HotBot) or natural language queries (InfoSeek). One strong search feature it offers is "stemming." Adding a dollar sign ($) makes Lycos look for any words beginning (or ending) with a certain *stem*, or part of a word. For example, the search term *gard$* picks up both *gardens* and *gardenias*. (The *$* is a *wildcard;* Lycos searches for *anything* in place of it. Other engines don't yet do much with wildcards.) Add a period (.) to a keyword (*gardenia.*), and Lycos searches for exactly that stem; it won't pick up *gardenias*.

One downside to Lycos is that it strips out simple words such as *a* and *an*, even, it seems, in phrases. Sure, these words are everywhere—too common to be generally useful as keywords. But from time to time they *can* be essential to a query.

Lycos searches just the Web—not Usenet—but it does give you the option of searching for *images* and *sounds* on the Web. I used this feature to find some magnificent whale cries. To search for sounds, I used *whale* as the search term in the "Sounds and Pictures" area—not very tricky! (See "Searching for Sounds.") Also, Lycos includes FTP and Gopher sites in its indexes, unlike the other search engines.

In addition to a huge index, Lycos features a 16-subject *directory* of selected and rated sites called *a2Z*. It also offers a catalog of the "Top 5%," based on a catalog of rated sites that Lycos recently acquired (Figure 9-5). These top sites are rated for their design, content, and overall experience, and are assigned a number from 1 to 50. At the end of each description is a "Find Related Sites" link. Clicking the link causes Lycos to search its index for other sites with similar titles. (Results can be mixed. I did a search for sites related to the American Classical League and found, among other things, the *American Professional Soccer League* and *Composite Ratings for the American League*! Well, at least they're both *American* and *leagues* of some sort.)

Like the other great search sites, Lycos offers a bounty of essential information services:

- CityGuide, Lycos's answer to Excite's City.Net. Though it is more narrowly focused on American cities, it does give quick access to about 10,000 Web sites.

- PeopleFinder, using the ProCD database (also on AOL at keyword: WhitePages), which lets you find street addresses if you just type in a name (see "Finding People One at a Time").

- Roadmaps for any address in the U.S.

- The latest headlines and news stories.

- Pictures and sounds of anything you want to see and hear (if it's on the Web).

- Club Lycos, membership in which (a sort of AAA for cyberspace) entitles you to discounts on travel arrangements and automatic entries in drawings for free books from Lycos Press.

FIGURE 9-5   At Lycos you can browse some 16 categories or go right to the "Top 5%" of all sites

Searching for Sounds

Sometimes it's hard to know where to start a search. In the case of multimedia files, do you start on FTP or on the Web? More and more, the answer is the Web. If you don't find a file using Archie (see Chapter 8), you're likely to find it on the Web.

Lycos and HotBot let you do searches for files of a certain type, that is, with a certain file extension (such as MIDI or WAV). In Lycos, choose Pictures & Sounds from the main page, and follow the simple instructions for locating either picture files or sound files (you can search only one type at a time). Just click Sounds and type in **midi**, for example.

HotBot is also easy to use (**http://www.hotbot.com**). From the main window, click the Media button to bring up a set of media filters, which you search for files with specific multimedia formats. In the search window that comes up, check the box for the media types you want to retrieve, such as *Audio*. If you want, narrow the search further: in the Extensions box, enter the file extension of the audio file type you're seeking, such as **midi** or **wav**. Click Search.

Looking for good MIDI sites? Vikram's MIDI-Fest is a big collection of MIDI files located, unfortunately, on a slow FTP server, **ftp://sunsite.unc.edu/pub/multimedia/midi/midi.html**. Included are MIDI versions of most of the Beatles' music. The Classical MIDI Archive (**http://www.prs.net/midi.html#index**) contains thousands of classical MIDI clips from popular composers such as Bach and Mozart and hundreds of lesser-known composers. Smithsonian Folkways has collected hundreds of clips of folk, jazz, children's, blues, American Indian, Southern, and other American music, and made them easily available and searchable at **http://www.si.edu/organiza/offices/ folklife/folkways/genrlist.htm**.

Magellan Internet Guide

Keyword: Magellan
http://www.mckinley.com

Magellan and Yahoo are the most popular Web directories (see the description of Yahoo in a couple of pages). Yahoo came first and has always been among the most popular destinations on the entire Internet, but Magellan, from the McKinley Group, offers a more systematic editorial approach to selecting, describing, and rating sites. (Yahoo hand-picks and arranges sites, but doesn't describe or rate them.) In addition to a directory, Magellan offers a searchable database of URLs—its own index.

In 1995 Magellan assembled a large and talented editorial team, and set out to create a better directory. In mid-1996, Magellan was acquired by Excite Inc., but fortunately, the Magellan directory is still available.

Magellan can be browsed, which is the proper way to approach any directory. The two dozen or so main categories give you more starting points for browsing than the other directories. Magellan can also be searched for specific rated sites, and searches can be restricted to sites appropriate for the entire family ("Green Light" sites). Finally, you can also search Magellan's Rock Guide, created by *Rolling Stone* magazine.

Tip *Looking for kid-appropriate sites? Magellan's Green Light sites are free of objectionable material, and AOL NetFind for Kids makes it easy for you to find children's sites that are fun as well as safe.*

WebCrawler

Keyword: WebCrawler
http://www.webcrawler.com/

WebCrawler (like Excite, InfoSeek, and Lycos) wants to provide everything. It started life as a powerful search engine. WebCrawler was purchased by America Online in 1995, and the technology was merged with the Global Network Navigator (GNN) directory, a classic Internet resource that AOL purchased the same year from O'Reilly, the computer book publisher. WebCrawler and GNN were key components of the GNN service, AOL's Internet-only service, until GNN was rolled into AOL in 1996. Late that year, Excite Inc. acquired the WebCrawler technology and Excite became AOL's exclusive search engine.

AOL channels have created a series of WebCrawler "Easy Searches." For example, in the Games Channel, click Strategy and you get a listbox that includes an item *Web Crawler—Strategy*. This "canned" search is all set up for you. All you do is click for sites relating to strategy games (Figure 9-6). The links shown are from WebCrawler's reviewed sites on the topic of strategy games. Enter more terms in the Search field, and you can do an even more focused query about that subject.

9

FIGURE 9-6   A WebCrawler Easy Search creates a specific query for you—it's channel searching for channel surfers

Yahoo

Keyword: Yahoo

http://www.yahoo.com

Yahoo is the largest and most popular directory on the Net (Figure 9-7). Yahoo's categories range from "Arts and Humanities" to "Society and Culture." Sites are hand-picked, so in general you can count on the links working. However, they are neither annotated nor rated, although for some sites you'll find a short descriptive phrase.

Compiling a directory of Web sites is like building a sand castle during high tide. It seems futile because of the rate at which new sites are created. Yahoo confronts the problem by offering visitors easy access to a major search index, AltaVista. In addition, Yahoo adds many layers of value to its directory:

■ The directory itself can be searched for specific sites, so you're not forced to navigate many levels of subcategories. Pages listing some of the subcategories can be quite long, so you'll appreciate searchability—especially if you know what you are looking for or if you want to find resources scattered across several categories.

■ Two other aids to navigation: (1) For each subcategory, the number of sites is available in parentheses—a useful measure of the depth of Yahoo's contents for any area and of the length of time it will take for the page to download. (2) New sites have a special little picture by them ("New" in a starburst), as do especially cool sites (a pair of glasses).

■ Yahooligans for Kids! is a large directory of kid-appropriate sites.

■ Yahoo has created both national and metropolitan Yahoos—collections of Web sites about particular countries (Canada, France, Japan, etc.) and cities (San Francisco, D.C., Boston, etc.).

■ Powerful customization features. From the top level of Yahoo, you can create something called "My Yahoo," which can serve as your private window into the world of Yahoo—with only the current news, sports, stock, and entertainment information (and more) that you want to see each day. (Expect to see such customization throughout the Web in the near future.)

■ Yahoo offers current subject-appropriate news headlines for several categories of its main directory.

■ Unlike the other search sites, Yahoo offers an e-mail newsletter to keep you informed of the week's top new sites. It's available by choosing Weekly Picks and looking for a subscription link. Online, you can get the same information, but getting it by e-mail is a major convenience if you use e-mail more often than you use the Web.

Yahoo alone is probably not the place to do a serious search for specific information (see "Essential Directories for the Serious Searcher" for that), but it does offer nicely packaged information on a large set of topics. If you're just browsing, it's the place to start.

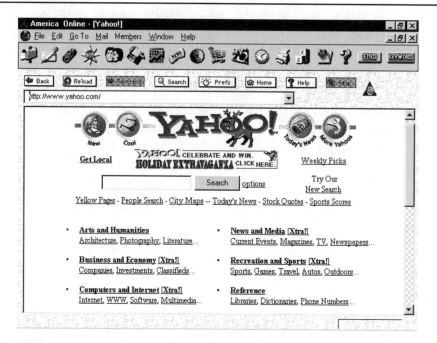

FIGURE 9-7 Yahoo, the Internet's leading directory

Essential Directories for the Serious Searcher

The **Argus Clearinghouse** (formerly the Clearinghouse for Subject-Oriented Internet Resource Guides, now available at **http://www.clearinghouse.net/**) consists of hundreds of hypertext essays, each reviewing the best resources on specific subjects. The essays were written by University of Michigan library-science students under the guidance of Lou Rosenfeld, a leading figure in the search world. Of the essays in the Health & Medicine category, for example, you will find essays dealing with AIDs, food safety, and holistic medicine Internet resources. Some of the essays are dated, but there is no rival resource as detailed and systematic.

The **Virtual Library** (**http://www.w3.org/vl/**) began at CERN in 1991 and moved to the World Wide Web Consortium in 1996. This serious directory of

Internet resources is a labor of love, and it communicates the original impulse of the Web better than any of the commercial directories.

The Virtual Library consists of well over 100 categories of information. Many of the topics are of strictly academic interest (Mycology and Vision Science, for example), but dozens of others have broad appeal as well (Recipes, Men's Issues, Games, Gardening, and the like). Unlike the commercial services such as Yahoo, the Virtual Library categories are separately maintained by experts in the various areas, all with their own approach to selecting and organizing resources. The experts live throughout the world, not just in the U.S., so you will get an international perspective on many subjects—something that's surprisingly rare on the "global" Internet. You'll also find in-depth information *about* the rest of the world, and not merely travel tips. Special categories are devoted to Taiwan, Singapore, India, and many other non-Western places.

The Virtual Library will link you to *all* the pertinent information for a subject, not just Web sites. You can find out about Telnet sites, FTP sites, newsgroups, mailing lists, and more. It's not systematic or fancy, but it makes for a true information feast.

FINDING *PEOPLE* WITH INFORMATION: MAILING LISTS AND NEWSGROUPS

Mailing lists and newsgroups provide tens of thousands of microcommunities of interest. If you raise terriers for a living, a good first stop may well be the Internet discussion group that lives and breathes the subject (such as the mailing list for "friends of soft-coated wheaten terriers"). Getting to know the people who frequent a mailing list or newsgroup, you can often find better answers more quickly, and you can stay more current about any topic than if you just used a "passive" resource like the Web.

Tip *If you're just learning about a topic, make a point to read the FAQ first. The newsgroup or mailing list may have already gathered answers to the most common questions and posted them in that document.*

Liszt: Searching for Mailing Lists

Keyword: Liszt
http://www.liszt.com

Over the years, some great mailing list *directories* have been hand-maintained to provide guidance to people searching for lists. They were maintained by individuals such as Vivian Neou, Stephanie da Silva, and AOL's own David O'Donnell. The Liszt database is the first true searchable index of mailing lists—currently more than 60,000 of them. In other words, you enter a search keyword, and Liszt searches an index for mailing lists whose name or description matches the keyword. Note that Liszt just searches through the names and short descriptions of mailing lists; *it does not search through messages posted to lists.*

Note   *A new service, Reference.com (**http://www.reference.com**), is trying to provide access to mailing list archives, but its success will depend on whether the owners and moderators of mailing lists make their archives available to the public. For now, it focuses on newsgroups.*

To use Liszt to find a mailing list about a specific topic, you enter a term as you do in any index, then click Search (see Figure 9-8).

You need to be explicit about what you want. If you want a phrase (*home run*), enclose it in quotes (*"home run"*). Otherwise, *home run* returns all mailing lists with either *home* or *run* in their title or in the short descriptions lists sometimes provide about themselves. Not only that, Liszt will return the names of mailing lists with the words *run*, *run*ning, and b*run*ch in them! Specificity can rescue any search, and not just on Liszt.

The result of your query is a list of hyperlinks of mailing lists whose names or descriptions contain the term you are seeking. Click one to bring up a description of the list.

You get two pieces of information for any mailing list. First, you get any information about the list that is archived at Liszt—the "information file," similar to the Welcome message you receive when you subscribe to the list. Such information is not always available, unfortunately. Second, you get the boilerplate How to Subscribe information shown in Figure 9-9 about the *kind* of software used to administer the list (LISTSERV, Majordomo, Listproc, etc.).

This text tells you how to get information about the list via e-mail and how to subscribe to it. Clicking the hyperlink in the How to Subscribe section brings up

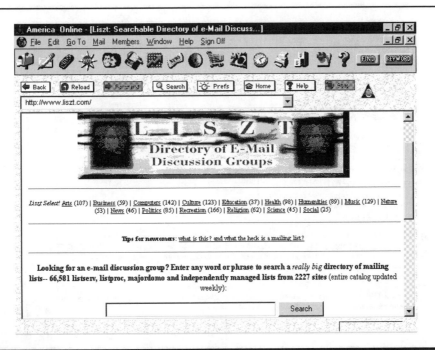

FIGURE 9-8   Liszt delivers the news (er, mail)

AOL's Compose Mail window, with the list's *administrative* address plugged into the To field. Just complete the form as instructed, then click Send to subscribe!

 Chapter 4 is devoted to mailing lists, the Internet's best service for finding groups of people who share a serious interest.

Like WebCrawler and other *Web* engines, Liszt provides a directory-like feature with the best mailing lists by subject (such as Business and Social)—a useful feature, though it's not so clear how lists make it into this pantheon.

You can also do a Usenet search on Liszt. Currently this search looks only through the *names* of newsgroups, not the actual postings; AOL's newsreader does much the same thing and searches through a longer list of newsgroups. But this Liszt feature does allow you to do all your searching for good "discussion groups"—newsgroups and mailing lists—in one place. With Liszt, you can identify all the mailing lists and newsgroups whose members share an interest of yours.

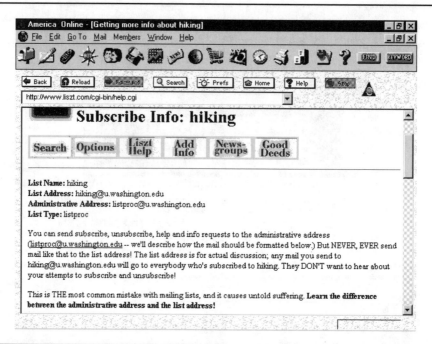

FIGURE 9-9 Liszt provides point and click subscription to mailing lists

Search Newsgroups with DejaNews

Keyword: DejaNews
http://www.dejanews.com

Chapter 5 mentioned all the ways you can "search" newsgroups:

- You can search for a *newsgroup* with a certain word in its title.

- You can search for a specific *article* (posting) within a newsgroup, by searching subject lines.

- You can search all the *text* you'll find in millions of postings by individuals.

DejaNews leads the pack of the Usenet search tools, giving you two out of three: You can search for specific newsgroups, and, more important, you can search actual content. A version of DejaNews is now available as Newsgroup Finder at AOL NetFind (just click the browser's Search button).

DejaNews boasts a database with close to 100 million articles from 15,000 newsgroups stretching back to March 1995! Despite its size, it's very fast.

From the opening DejaNews window you are presented with two text boxes (Figure 9-10). The first allows you to do a Quick Search for actual *postings* based on word or words used in them. The second lets you search for a *newsgroup* with a certain word or words in its title. To find relevant newsgroups, you enter a word in the second box ("Enter one of your interests below"), and click Find.

To search through actual articles, you enter a keyword (*banjo* or *puppies* or whatever) into the first box, click Find, and DejaNews does its magic, returning postings with your keyword. Your results are hyperlinked to actual postings. You automatically get hyperlinks to the e-mail addresses of the postings' authors as well, so you can send e-mail directly to those individuals. You can read the postings from within DejaNews, not in AOL's Newsgroups window.

FIGURE 9-10   DejaNews lets you find newsgroups and newsgroup postings about any topic. Register, and you can post to newsgroups from here

Sending e-mail to the author of the posting is easy, but sending a posting of your own to the newsgroup requires registration, which is free.

Note   *To send a posting to a newsgroup using DejaNews, you must be using the AOL 3.0 for Windows95 browser (from Microsoft). Instructions are provided at DejaNews.*

A final important feature of DejaNews is its ability to let you browse newsgroups as well as search them by title and content. This top-down approach is similar to what you do on AOL when you click Add Newsgroups and "drill down" through categories and subcategories to actual newsgroups. AOL seems to carry more newsgroups and offer faster performance, because it's not dependent on the Web or any intervening networks; it's all on AOL. But DejaNews does let you search postings and post-your-own in the same session.

SEARCHING NEWSGROUPS WITH OTHER SEARCH TOOLS

AltaVista, Excite, HotBot, and InfoSeek all do Usenet searches, searching the text of newsgroup postings for your keywords. None offers a database as old or big as DejaNews, however. Nor do they offer detailed profiles of posters or the ability to post your *own* articles in response to an article. What they *do* offer is the convenience of allowing you to combine Web and Usenet searches from the same site.

If you want to browse a newsgroup from which a posting comes or send a posting of your own, AltaVista, Excite and HotBot call up the AOL newsreader. From AOL you can browse and post to your heart's content. Only Infoseek allows newsgroup browsing *within* the browser, but it doesn't (yet) allow posting.

Of the Web engines that can search newsgroups, Excite is especially good: it allows you to do "concept" searches as well as simple keyword searches, and when you get your results you can click "More Like This" for any single result that's especially pertinent.

Yellow Pages on the Net: Finding Business Addresses

For any business, the Internet has drastically cut the costs and simplified the methods of doing competitive research. It's also easier for consumers to get contact information for both local stores and mail-order companies *anywhere*. When you're looking for business information you can use either a directory or an index; the best tools combine the two.

Big Yellow (keyword: BigYellow), from NYNEX, offers a searchable database of some 16 million businesses, plus a browsable directory of categories such as Automotive and Home Office. A strength of Big Yellow is its ability to search for all the listings for a specific type of business in a state, giving you the equivalent of a statewide yellow pages.

Switchboard (keyword: Switchboard, profiled a little later in this chapter), an AOL partner, also lets you search for a business by category (there are more than 2,000!) and by place. Unlike Big Yellow, with Switchboard you also get a huge White Pages listing of more than 100 million people. The combination of very big yellow and white page directories makes Switchboard a reliable one-stop site if you regularly need to look up a person or a business. (Big Yellow has a White Pages directory, too, but it's smaller.)

If you need more than an address for a company, **Hoover's Online** (**http://www.hoovers.com**) provides links to thousands of company Web sites as well as profiles of thousands of public and private companies. The profiles can be used by paying subscribers only, but you get free access to this information on AOL at keyword: Hoovers, with profiles nicely packaged to include links to company Web pages and stock charts for companies that are publicly traded.

FINDING PEOPLE ONE AT A TIME

A number of companies have put the real-world White Pages and similar print directories online and made them accessible via the Web.

Tip *AOL has an agreement with the largest of these services, Switchboard, to make its more than 100 million names available to AOL members. If you've got to find a phone number for that old roommate or long-lost friend, it's easiest to use the tool supported and customized by AOL, but it's also a good idea to understand the complementary strengths of other tools, such as Four11 and Bigfoot.*

The "people-finding" tools all work pretty much the same way. You:

1. Enter the name of a person or a business whose address (real or e-mail) you need. Provide as much address information as you can.

2. Click Find, or whatever the button is called.

3. Receive either an e-mail address or a real-world address for that person or business.

Caution *Searches for real addresses are likely to be a lot more successful than searches for e-mail addresses, because they're based on existing White Pages and other printed directories. E-mail addresses cannot be systematically collected or maintained, so the e-mail searches are less satisfying. All the "address finders" would love for you to add your e-mail address to their database!* ***Yet another caveat:*** *All the tools have a hard time with duplicate entries, since there is no sure way of determining whether the David Peal who lived in San Francisco is different from the one who lives where he currently lives. If the computers can't tell the difference, you probably won't be able to either! Why? If you haven't seen Harry Housebound in 20 years, there is no way to tell whether the Harry in Phoenix is different from the one in Piscataway.*

Despite these reservations, search tools have recently gotten light years better and easier to use, and they promise to continue perfecting themselves.

Switchboard

Keyword: Switchboard
http://www.switchboard.com

With more than 10 million business listings and more than 100 million residential listings, Switchboard (Figure 9-11) will almost certainly retrieve most people's street

FIGURE 9-11   Switchboard is as close as you'll find to White Pages on
                 the Internet

address; I even found my parents' address, neither of whom has ever used a
computer. To find a person, all you need is a last name, though additional information
(first name and city) will greatly improve your results. Then, just click Search.

Switchboard returns street addresses and phone numbers. If your search was a
bit too broad, you can click Modify Search to add limiting information, such as state
or city. For businesses, all you need is a business name, though, again, the more
details the better. See the "Yellow Pages on the Net: Finding Business Addresses"
sidebar for Switchboard's special Yellow Pages features.

*The power of Switchboard is now conveniently available in the new AOL
NetFind area (just click the browser's Search button).*

Switchboard also has good *security features* that protect your privacy and keep
junk e-mail out of your AOL mailbox. Your options include hiding your e-mail

address from others and showing your e-mail as *knock knock*, so that someone who wants to send you e-mail can reach you only *via Switchboard*, not directly. Being unlisted in this way does *not* mean you've been deleted from the database.

Looking for Someone on AOL?

Use the AOL Members Directory. From the Members menu, select Member Directory. Click the Advanced Search tab to search for members with the same interests and professions, even members with the same interests who live in your community! I know of someone who found a handyman in her community using the AOL Member Directory.

Search Member Directory
Member Directory   *Create or Modify Your Profile*   **My Profile**

Quick Search | **Advanced Search**

Search entire profile for the following

Optional Fields:

Member Name	Location (city/state)
	maryland

Birthdate	Sex: Female ○ Male ○ Both ◉	Marital Status

Hobbies/Interests	Occupation
bowling	

Computers	Quote

Search   **Help & Info**   ☐ **Show me only members online**

This particular search for Maryland bowlers returned more than 250 AOL members. Non-members don't have access to this directory. It's a privilege of membership!

You can find someone only if that person has filled in the Member Directory. So, it's your choice: if you don't want to be found, don't supply information about yourself. If you do want the AOL community to know about you, just click My Profile.

Four11

Keyword: Four11
http://www.four11.com/

Four11, one of the oldest Web-based directory services, claims "complete" and constantly updated Web access to U.S. White Pages as well as (at the time the book was written) ten million unique e-mail addresses. When you use Yahoo's People Finder service, you're using Four11's technology and listings. Special features include directories for the government and for celebrities.

Four11 searches for e-mail addresses as well as 100 million real-world addresses, though its real-world capabilities are stronger than its e-mail capabilities, simply because the white pages are reliable and there *aren't* white pages for the Internet. Again, I was able to find my parents' street address.

Like Switchboard, Four11 lets you register for free, then add or modify your personal information. Registering also gives you the privilege of keeping your e-mail address out of your listing and of using Four11 as an intermediary to intercept and forward mail to you. The only advantage of this particular service over Switchboard is its focus on creating a large database of e-mail addresses.

Bigfoot

http://www.bigfoot.com/

Bigfoot is notable for providing you with e-mail addresses, and it seems fairly aggressive in compiling them (with over eight million addresses when this book was written). Like other services, Bigfoot lets you edit your personal information when you move or change your preferred e-mail address. Bigfoot also lets you hide all your personal information, or parts of it such as your e-mail address, in order to protect your privacy online.

People Finders in Web Search Engines

Several of the best Web search indexes and directories have links to "people finders." Yahoo, for example, uses Four11's technology. Lycos uses a people finder from InfoSpace, which it nicely integrates with its Road Maps feature. For anyone whose street address you discover, Lycos will give you a local street map pinpointing that address. You can also link to community information and local buisnesses. Excite also offers the InfoSpace people finder.

SEARCHING THE MEGASITES:
FINDING SPECIALIZED INFORMATION

More and more, you'll find search tools being adapted to narrower and narrower subjects. Instead of searching the Web universe from this or that speck of dust, they focus on a discrete subject and aim for comprehensiveness or at least depth within that subject. Or, they search no further than a megasite, a specific, content-rich site such as ESPN (**http://espnet.sportszone.com/**), which boasts 60,000 pages! These megasites seek to be meccas—the best sites for a specific field, whether it has to do with sports, parenting, travel, or something else. What follows are short descriptions of three specialized engines, of the thousands you can find on your own.

Medline: The World's Leading Medical Database

Keyword: Medline

A standard source for doctors and all healthcare professionals, Medline is now generally available on AOL and the Internet. This database of abstracts, gathered from more than 3,000 medical journals from all over the world, was created by the National Library of Medicine in Bethesda, Maryland. It grows by about 30,000 abstracts a month, and the database goes back to 1990. It's one of the most authoritative, focused resources on the Net. You can search for an article by author, author's affiliation, title, publication date, and journal; and you can search abstracts by keyword.

Tip   *Medline, as well as related medical databases (such as MEDLARS, the Visual Human Project, and various AIDS databases), is available at the National Library of Medicine Web site* (**http://www.nlm.nih.gov/databases/ databases.html**), *but many of these databases require accounts and fees, and some are available only by Telnet. On AOL Medline is always free.*

AOL adds value in many ways. You can share your Medline findings with others in the Disabilities Forum (keyword: Dis) or on the Better Health and Medical Network (keyword: Better Health). AOL has created online help for Medline, and AOL's Medline message boards allow members to share their Medline finds.

Note   *Medline offers abstracts; you must use a document retrieval service such as UnCover to get actual articles. AOL may be offering such a service in the future.*

City.Net: The World at Your Fingertips

Keyword: City.Net

http://www.city.net

Mecca is the right metaphor for City.Net, the brainchild of a former Intel engineer in Oregon named Kevin Altis. It began as an effort to provide a comprehensive directory of place-related Internet content for travelers, students, business people, and the curious. It became the Internet's single most comprehensive geographic resource for nonscientists, and then was acquired by Excite Inc. Today, City.Net fits right in with the Excite interface (Figure 9-12).

With City.Net you can search for a specific location on any continent, and you'll get categorized sites. For example, I did a search for sites about Halifax, Nova Scotia and got sites usefully arranged in several categories, including travel and tourism, regional information, newspapers, parks and gardens, weather, and government.

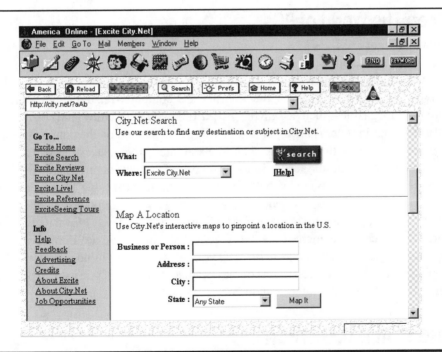

FIGURE 9-12   Leaving home on the Net

Maps were also available. Or, you can take a "top down" approach, and browse: just choose a continent and burrow down through countries, states, and provinces to local communities that interest you. Armchair travellers never had it so good.

Searchable Megasites

Some Web sites are so big or so complex that special search engines are needed just to find information at them. Search.com (see the next section, "Pulling It All Together") makes dozens of such sites available in one place. Some Web sites can *only* be used with a search engine. Jeremy Hylton's Internet classic, the searchable Shakespeare database (shown in Chapter 1, Figure 1-5), was meant to be searched, and the nicely designed search form for doing so is available at **http://the-tech.mit.edu/Shakespeare/search.html**.

Clnet: The World of PCs

Keyword: cnet
http://www.cnet.com

Everyone on the Internet has access to a computer, so it's not surprising that some of the best resources on the Internet are computer-related. Publishers of computer magazines such as CMP (**http://techweb.cmp.com**) and Ziff-Davis (**http://www.zdnet.com**) have put together large sites based on the content of their print publications, with frequently changing and interactive material as well.

The current all-around leader in the category of computing megasites is Clnet, from the same-named company that creates programming for cable TV's Computer Network (Figure 9-13). The clnet megasite brings you computer-related news, feature articles, product reviews, regular editorials, site reviews, *plus* the ability to search this excellent content. Like every good Web site, there are rich interactive opportunities as well, so (unlike cable TV) you can speak your mind and meet other people who frequent the site. It's one of the best places to begin if you want to become well-informed about the Internet industry.

PULLING IT ALL TOGETHER

Search sites are getting more powerful and easier to use with each passing month. Currently you can find Internet search services that:

FIGURE 9-13   C|net: a vibrant site devoted to the world's most dynamic industry

- Bring together links to the big search engines in one place, as AOL's Web site does (click the Search button with the browser open)

- Run queries against several search engines at the same time

- Collect hundreds of searchable megasites like C|net and City.Net in one place

Note   *Many sites are competing to provide comprehensive search capabilities. The following overview is just that—skim it, and perhaps try one or two, but don't feel like you have to master all these tools, since they overlap in many ways, and it's not clear which is going to emerge as the best.*

Sites That Link to Multiple Search Engines

An excellent resource of this type is InterNIC's **Internet Search Engines** page, which takes you to dozens of search engines by category—Web, mailing lists, FTP, "meta" search, and so on (**http://www.internic.net/tools**). Similarly, the **All in One Page** (**http://www.albany.net/allinone/**) lets you choose a search tool more by topic than by tool. Click "Desk Reference," for example, to get dictionaries, AT&T's 1-800 directory, and the like. Finally, Netscape's Web site, like AOL's, pulls together all the major search engines and offers a highly selective directory of the best sites, by topic.

Sites That Run Multiple Queries at the Same Time

Some services go a step further and run multiple searches using different engines *at the same time.* The innovative Inference search engine (**http://www.inference.com**) lets you search AltaVista, Yahoo, Lycos, InfoSeek, WebCrawler, and Excite all at once. What's unique about Inference is that it *clusters* similar items, drastically simplifying the work you have to do to scan returned sites. For example, an Inference search for *Bismarck* (the German chancellor and North Dakota capital) returns hundreds of sites, usefully grouped in categories such as Misc. European Sites, Misc. Commercial sites, Bismarck (ND), and the Bismarck Group (a Chicago-based Microsoft Solution Provider). Of course, the more specific the original query, the better the results, with Inference or any search engine. The query *Otto von Bismarck and Kaiser Wilhelm* returns sites about Imperial Germany, while the query *Bismarck North Dakota* returns sites about the American city.

Sites That Let You Search Any of Dozens of Megasites

Sites like **Internet Sleuth** (**http://www.isleuth.com/**) and **Search.com**, a part of the Clnet Web empire (**http://www.search.com**), let you do a broad range of focused searches for specific information in one place. Internet Sleuth currently lets you search any of *1,800* databases. A newer service, **WorldPages** (**http://www. worldpages.com**), pulls together people finders and business finders as well as searchable travel and business sites in the search for one-stop searching. A feature of WorldPages is the collection of White Pages and Yellow Pages for countries around the world.

Search.com is the current leader of this particular pack (Figure 9-14). Search.com looks like a directory, but it's actually a lot more. Pick a category such as Finance from the list of Search Subjects and you pull up 30 or so searchable sites such as CNN's Finance Network; SEC's EDGAR service; Hoover's online company profiles; Mutual Funds Online; and several currency converters. If you don't find what you're looking for, AltaVista is always available, as are searchable Yellow Pages (BigBook) and White Pages (Switchboard). You can also choose one of about a dozen of the major search engines, including Excite. Flight information, maps, sports scores, stock quotes—it's all a click away as well. I searched for the kitchen sink, but it's the only thing I couldn't find at Search.com.

FIGURE 9-14   Still can't find it? Visit Search.com

FROM HERE...

With these search tools and this chapter, you can start putting the Internet to *use* in your day-to-day life. Or, you can learn something new, do some armchair travelling, research your family's history, find out the capital of North Dakota, or search for the whereabouts of your favorite high-school teacher.

Everything up to this point in the book is possible with your basic AOL software. The next chapter looks beyond, to all the non-AOL software you can use with AOL, such as Netscape, Internet Relay Chat, and Telnet. It's not about software, though. In the next chapter you'll see how to extend the AOL *community* to the global Internet.

Chapter 10

Beyond AOL:
Exploring Internet
Applications

America Online provides first-rate software for browsing the Web, downloading files with FTP, reading newsgroups, and managing your e-mail, but AOL's Internet access doesn't stop there. A little file called Winsock, which is automatically downloaded and installed for you when you install the AOL software, opens an even broader world of possibilities on AOL.

This chapter takes a brief look at Winsock, and then it looks at two powerful Winsock-enabled Internet applications you can use on AOL at no additional charge:

- Netscape, if you have a yen to use the world's most popular Web browser

- Virtual Places, an AOL-inspired Internet creation that brings the pleasures of chat to the wilderness of the Web

Finally, the chapter turns to the Winsock-created possibilities for running software that's *not* included with your AOL software:

- Internet Relay Chat—chat rooms on the global Internet

- Telnet—collaborative work and play, and a thousand electronic library catalogs

These few "Winsock applications" are among the hundreds available to you. See "Where Do I Find Applications to Use with AOL's Winsock?" for a list of places on AOL and the Internet where you can find truckloads of Internet software.

ALL YOU NEED TO KNOW ABOUT WINSOCK

The little Winsock file (**winsock.dll**) makes it possible for applications such as Netscape to work with your AOL account. Most of this Winsock software is available free or as shareware.

Note   *Since version 3.0, AOL has automatically installed Winsock for you. If you use AOL for Windows 2.5, you probably want to upgrade. Otherwise, you must manually download the 16-bit Winsock file to your /windows directory, renaming other Winsocks that might be on your computer already. The instructions for downloading AOL's Winsock and renaming other Winsocks can be found at keyword: Winsock.*

Know Your Winsock: 32-Bit vs. 16-Bit

There are *two types of Winsock*: 16-bit and 32-bit. The difference between them lies in their stability, performance, and ability to work with different operating systems. In a nutshell, the 32-bit Winsock file works only with Windows 95 but runs more powerful software than the 16-bit Winsock, which works with Windows 3.1 or Windows 95 but does not run certain programs.

There are also *two types of Winsock applications*: 16-bit and 32-bit. The 32-bit Winsock applications can do more ambitious things like let you browse 3D Web sites (VRML) and play certain types of video.

The good thing about 32-bit Winsock is that it runs either 32-bit or 16-bit Winsock applications, so *if you've got 32-bit Winsock you don't have to worry about what kind of Winsock application you're running*.

The bad thing about 16-bit Winsock is that it won't run 32-bit Winsock applications. If you're not using AOL 3.0 for Windows 95, you're likely to have 16-bit Winsock.

Which Winsock Do You Have?

The answer depends on which version of AOL you have. To find out, choose About America Online from the Help menu. You will see either *America Online 3.0 for Windows* (in which case you have 16-bit Winsock) or *America Online 3.0 for Windows 95* (32-bit Winsock). In AOL 3.0 for Windows, **winsock.dll** is 11K and located in the **c:/aol30/winsock** directory. In AOL 3.0 for Windows 95, **winsock.dll** is 42K and located in the **c:/aol30/net/osr** directory. With AOL 3.0 (either version), Winsock loads automatically when you sign onto AOL. You don't have to do

10

anything! Don't move or rename your **winsock.dll** file! If you use the "bring your own access" plan, AOL's Winsock won't load if your other ISP's Winsock is loaded. I have found that a Winsock application that works with AOL's Winsock will work with another ISP's; Winsock, after all, is more or less of a standard.

Where Do I Find Applications to Use with AOL's Winsock?

Hundreds of Winsock applications are available to download from AOL and the Internet: HTML editors, browsers, and software for using FTP, Gopher, IRC, mail, and Usenet news. *With AOL you cannot yet use mail or News clients, but if you're using the "bring your own access" billing plan, you can use programs such as WinVN (News) and Eudora (mail). However, you'll be using the mail and News computers of your other provider, and you'll be using the e-mail address you use with that other account—not your AOL screen name.* Wherever you download such software, be careful to download the appropriate version—16-bit or 32-bit, depending on the version of Winsock you have (see "All You Need to Know About Winsock"). You can't go too far wrong with 16-bit applications, since they'll work with both AOL Winsocks, but they may lack some of the features and power of 32-bit applications.

On AOL, you can get Winsock applications from the following places. This software has been virus-checked, then tested with AOL's Winsock.

- ZDNet (keyword: ZD Net), click on Download. The Internet Applications category includes rated software for browsing the Web, publishing on the Web, and more.

- Winsock Central (keyword: Winsock), click on Software Library. You'll find good programs, but they're not categorized or rated.

On the Internet, several megasites provide a myriad of applications of every kind. Most of these sites highlight new arrivals and popular downloads. The following two sites focus on Winsock software, and have mirror (identical) sites around the world to make it easier to access:

- Stroud's Consummate Winsock Applications List (**http://www.enterprise.net/cwsapps/**).

■   The Ultimate Collection of Winsock Software (TUCOWS, whose logo consists of a couple of cows), at **http://www.tucows.com/**.

The following sites have enormous software collections that include substantial Winsock archives:

■   Clnet's Shareware.com (**http://www.shareware.com/**)

■   Jumbo, an AOL Member's Choice site (**http://www.jumbo.com/**)

■   ZDNet, an AOL Member's Choice site (**http://www.hotfiles.com/**)

Finally, if you have 32-bit Winsock, there's a Web site with nothing but 32-bit software to download: **http://www.32bit.com**.

How Do I Use a Winsock Application?

Using a Winsock program is like using any program—you must install it, run it, and learn what it does and how to get around. The only hitch is that you must be signed on to AOL to use a Winsock application.

You can use more than one Winsock application at the same time. You could, if you wanted, run an IRC program (such as mIRC), the Netscape browser, and a Telnet client all at the same time. You could browse the World Wide Web using more than one browser at the same time (AOL's and Netscape's, for example). You could even run more than one AOL browser and more than one Netscape browser at the same time!

If you exit from AOL or your AOL connection is broken for any reason, all your Winsock applications lose their connection to the Internet as well. If you sign onto AOL again, you will have to first close any open Winsock applications and reopen them to use them again.

NETSCAPE NAVIGATOR

America Online members can use Netscape Navigator 3.0, the world's most popular browser. Netscape Navigator has been customized for AOL. The home page has been set to the AOL Web site, and the Netscape buttons link you to AOL-selected sites. Otherwise, it's pure Netscape: fast and easy to use, a browser that supports and extends open Web standards.

10

With such a strong, integrated browser from Microsoft, why would AOL offer Netscape as well? In a word: choice. If you use Netscape at school or work, you may want to use Netscape on AOL as well. Another reason for using Netscape is its full-screen capabilities. When you run Netscape on AOL, it is a separate "Winsock" program. Instead of being confined by AOL's toolbars and menus that reduce the amount of space the browser can use, Netscape is a freestanding application with its own toolbar and menus. Finally, some applications require Netscape to work.

Tip *Once you've installed Netscape, you can devote even more of your screen to the browser by choosing not to display Netscape's Tool bar, URL (Location) box, and Directory buttons. Just go to the Options menu and deselect them.*

Downloading and Installing Netscape

Here are the steps for downloading and installing America Online's Netscape Navigator. The onscreen directions may vary slightly, but the result is identical.

1. Go to keyword: Netscape. A "hybrid" browser appears, showing the Netscape Web site inside an AOL window.

2. Click Download Netscape, a button on the right side of the form. In the Download Netscape! window, double-click Download Netscape in the listbox.

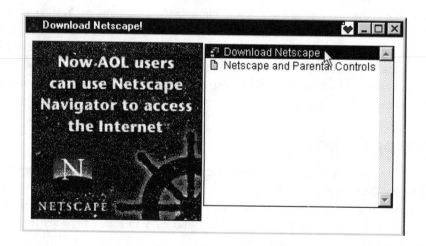

3. In the Netscape Navigator window, read the welcoming text, then click either the Windows 3.1 or Windows 95 button, depending on your operating system. Read the text and then click Next.

Note *The instructions differ, but the software is the same. They differ because Windows 3.1 and Windows 95 give you different ways to find and run files. For both versions, you get a 16-bit Netscape, which will run with both 16-bit and 32-bit Winsock.*

4. Click the Download Netscape button, then click Download Now. Select a download directory (*aol30\download* is fine—or whatever is current). Make a note of the file's "path" as it appears on top of the directories scroll box (for example, **c:\aol30\download**). The file itself is called **aolnscpi.exe** (a newer version may be available by the time you read this, though). Click OK to confirm the destination of the download and start the download.

5. Click OK when the transfer of the file is complete. Sign off America Online by choosing Exit from the File menu. In the next two steps you'll install Netscape.

6. *If you're using Windows 3.1,* double-click File Manager in the Main program group, and navigate to the directory containing the file you just downloaded. Double-click **aolnscpi.exe**.

   If you're using Windows 95, open the Start menu and select Run. Click Browse, and navigate to the place where you've downloaded the file, and select it. In the Run window, click OK.

   In either case, a dialog appears asking if you want to install America Online's Netscape Navigator.

7. Click Yes to start the quick and easy installation. Follow the prompts as instructed.

Tip *When asked whether you want to put Netscape on your Start menu (Windows 95 only), indicate "Yes," so you can conveniently launch Netscape from that menu. The installation program will also add a Netscape icon to your AOL program window so it will be available in the AOL program window in Windows 3.1 or from the Start menu | Programs in Windows 95.*

10

If You Have Already Used Netscape on Your PC

During installation you may be asked whether you want to overwrite **netscape.ini**, a file that stores Netscape "preferences" such as your home page, the color of links, the typeface Netscape uses, and any "helper applications" you have specified. You may be asked this question even if you haven't used Netscape before!

- If you do not have a previous version of Netscape, simply choose "Overwrite old Netscape.ini file." Netscape will automatically open to the AOL home page.

- If you have used Netscape, choose "Use old Netscape.ini file" for this option. You can still make AOL's Web site your home page, as follows: run Netscape, go to the Options menu, click the General Preferences tab, and type **http://www.aol.com/** in the Start With field.

To use your old Netscape bookmarks (favorite Web sites) in the new AOL Netscape, open AOL's Netscape, go to the Window menu, and select Bookmarks. The small Bookmarks program comes up. Go to the File menu and choose Import. Find the directory in which your old copy of Netscape is located, and select the **bookmark.htm** file.

Using Netscape Navigator on AOL

Once you've finished downloading and installing AOL's Netscape Navigator, follow these steps to access the Web:

1. Sign on to AOL as usual. It's OK to be signed on using the "bring your own access" plan.

2. *In Windows 3.1,* go to the Program Manager and find the America Online program window. Double-click the icon for AOL's Netscape Navigator.

   In Windows 95, select "America Online's Netscape Navigator" from the Start menu. Or, from the Start menu, select the Programs menu, click the America Online submenu, and click *AOL's Netscape Navigator.*

Note *If you click on a Web link from America Online, the integrated (Microsoft or BookLink) America Online browser launches. To access the Web with Netscape, you must manually select Navigator each time you want to go to the Web. You cannot make Netscape your default browser.*

How to Get Parental Controls to Work with Netscape

AOL gives parents the ability to restrict children to the Kids Only channel. Restricting children in this way limits the Web sites they can visit to the sites available in that channel. See "Do You Know What Your Children Are Viewing?" in Chapter 6.

The Kids Only setting will work, however, only when you use a modem to connect to AOL, not if you're connecting to AOL over a network (TCP/IP).

During installation of AOL's Netscape Navigator, you will be asked, "Do you access America Online via TCP/IP?" If you're using a network or are connecting via TCP/IP from another access provider, answer "Yes." If you choose this option, you will not be able to use the Kids Only setting. If you're using a modem, you can just accept the default, which is "No."

If you initially chose to connect through a network but later decide to connect through a modem and want to use Parental Controls, follow these steps:

1. While signed onto AOL, open the Netscape browser.

2. From the Options menu, select Network Preferences.

3. Click the Proxies tab.

4. Select Manual Proxy Configuration, then click the View button.

5. In the HTTP Proxy field, type in the following address: **ie3.proxy.aol.com**.

6. To the right of the HTTP Proxy field, in the Port box, type in **80**.

7. Click OK. You do not need to restart your computer for the change to take effect.

10

Grand Central Netscape

When you use AOL's version of Netscape Navigator, the browser opens automatically to the AOL Web site. With AOL's Netscape Navigator there's a home away from home. The Netscape button on the toolbar takes you to Netscape's home page—currently the most popular site in the universe, with over 100 million "hits" a month. When you're there, you're in the company of tens of thousands of people.

Click Netscape Destinations from the opening page of the Netscape site for one of the best starting points for exploring the Web. You'll find several hundred choice Web sites, in big categories such as Business and Finance. Click NetSearch for direct access to the best Web search tools—Excite, Yahoo, Magellan, Infoseek, and Lycos. Netscape also offers What's New, What's Cool, Yellow Pages, White Pages, and current news.

Netscape and AOL's Browser: How They Differ

Whole books have been written on Netscape, but browsing the Web with Netscape really doesn't take much explanation. If you're familiar with the basics of clicking, going backward, and jumping to a new Web page, then you'll pick up Netscape in a few minutes. Figure 10-1 gives you a quick tour of the Netscape screen.

If you are not familiar with Netscape but are familiar with the Microsoft browser integrated into AOL 3.0 for Windows 95, here are some of the more important ways in which Netscape differs.

Netscape Gives You Many Keyboard Equivalents for Core Tasks

For example, to go forward and backward, you can either click the Forward and Backward buttons on the tool bar, or press ALT-LEFT ARROW or ALT-RIGHT ARROW. Stopping a page while it's downloading in Netscape is easy: just press ESC. For other keyboard equivalents, visit the Netscape menus; the equivalents, when available, appear to the right of command names.

Netscape's Toolbar Includes a Find Button for Doing a Search *Within* a Page

Search engines are often undiscriminating, so you will appreciate the ability to look for a word on a page returned by a search. Click the Find button to search for a

FIGURE 10-1   Netscape's Destinations area, with access to the best sites

specific word! This feature is a lifesaver if, say, you use Excite to do a search for a keyword and get a long page that doesn't seem to include the keyword!

AOL Uses Favorite Places; Netscape Uses Bookmarks

Bookmarks, like Favorite Places, hold your favorite Web sites, but on Netscape you can keep track only of Internet sites—not AOL content, e-mail messages, and the like. If you discover a great site while using Netscape, go to the Bookmark menu and select Add Bookmark (or just press CTRL-A).

Remembrance of Sites Past

The Location box, just below the toolbar, is a drop-down list of sites you've visited in the current *and past* sessions (AOL's is just for the current session). Click the down arrow at the right side of the field to see all Web sites you've recently visited, in the order you've visited them; select a site from this list to visit the site.

Preferences Are Available from the Options Menu, Not the Toolbar in Netscape

Click General Preferences. As with the AOL 3.0 for Windows 95 browser, you have a healthy choice of preferences, arranged in a "tabbed" interface. Click a tab, such as Appearance and Fonts, to get a set of preferences relating to that topic. Here are two key preferences you should know about:*To change your home page,* click the Appearance tab. In the Startup section, type your preferred home page in the "Browser Starts With" box, and click OK.*To adjust your cache* (in order to devote more hard disk to your Netscape cache or to clear your cache), select Network Preferences from the Options menu and use the Cache tab. Note that AOL and Netscape use different caches.

Note   *A cache is the portion of your hard disk used to store information about the Web pages you visit, for faster access when you revisit them. See "Get Cache Fast" in Chapter 6.*

Netscape Supports Plug-ins (Integrated File Players)

What's a plug-in? Basically, a plug-in is a well-integrated helper application. When you click on a link to a Real Audio sound file or VDO video file, for example, the appropriate player appears within Netscape (or within a new Netscape window) and plays the sound or video or whatever it is. Plug-ins bring Web pages to life. See "Working with Plug-ins and Helper Applications" in Chapter 6. From the Help menu, there is a special selection called About Plug-ins, which provides information about plug-ins that are already installed in Netscape, with links that enable you to get additional plug-ins directly from the vendors.

To set up a plug-in helper application, in order to play or display certain file types you encounter on the Web:

■ From the Options menu, choose General Preferences, then click the Helpers tab.

■ Select a file type from the main list box, or create a new one (Create New Type window).

■ Select one of four things to happen: view the file in the browser; save
the file to disk; prompt you to do something (such as choose an
application or save the file); or launch the helper application. Usually,
you'll want to launch a helper application. Now click Browse, and
navigate to the directory where you've installed the player or plug-in
(**raplayer.exe**, in this case). Use Help | About Plugins to get the software
you need.

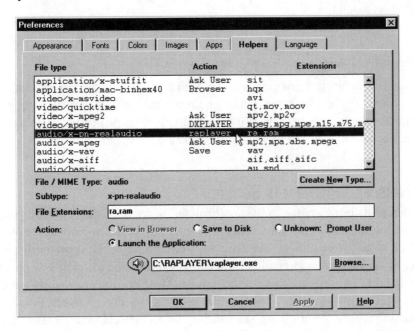

Now, when you click a link to a RealAudio file, Netscape automatically launches
the Real Audio player. See Chapter 6 ("Working with Plug-ins and Helper
Applications"). Remember, AOL's Netscape is 16-bit, so you'll want to set up only
16-bit helper apps and plug-ins. The current version of AOL's Netscape Navigator
does not support ActiveX, unlike Microsoft's Internet Explorer browser (the one in
AOL 3.0 for Windows 95). ActiveX can be a simpler experience for users than
plug-ins, since ActiveX doesn't require additional software. Pages with built-in
ActiveX "controls" may not display correctly or at all with AOL's Netscape Navigator.

You Can Open Several Browsers at the Same Time

On AOL, you open a new browser by entering a new URL in the Keyword window
or double-clicking a Favorite Place. With your mouse over a link, you can also

right-click and select Open in New Window. In Netscape, the right-click does similar magic. In addition, you go to the File menu and select New Web Browser.

In AOL, the multiple browsers are available from the Window menu—they are "document" windows within the AOL "application" window. In Netscape, however, each new browser is treated as a new *application*, so it's available by repeatedly pressing ALT-TAB (in either version of Windows) or by using the Windows 95 taskbar. AOL's Netscape Navigator is a full-scale Windows applications, which means it can take a while to load.

Frames Are Pampered by the Netscape Browser

Netscape (the company) invented frames. With a frame displayed in Netscape, you can choose to display the frame in its own (big) window: just click the right mouse button and select Open in New Window. Individual frames can also be saved as bookmarks, and frames can be separately reloaded.

The Netscape Browser Is Secure

Like the AOL browser, the Netscape browser is secure, which means you can transmit confidential information and credit-card numbers. On Netscape, however, you'll be more aware of security. The lower-left corner of the browser displays a key on a blue background to indicate a secure document and a broken key on a gray background to indicate an insecure document. Most documents—pages—are not secure, which only means they don't reside on specially secured servers. For security information about a specific page, display the page and select Document Information from the View menu. Netscape does a good job explaining its multiple security features. From the Help menu, select On Security.

Telnet Support

Some Web sites have links to Telnet resources. Later in this chapter you'll encounter two superb sites of this type, Hytelnet and the MudConnector. The AOL browser (that is, the Microsoft browser) connects you directly to Telnet sites; you don't need a separate program. Netscape, however, requires you to set up a separate program, such as Ewan (available in AOL's software libraries). With Ewan (or another Telnet application) installed, go to Netscape's Options menu, select Preferences, then click on the Apps tab. Click the Browse button adjacent to the Telnet application field, navigate to the place where the Internet software is installed, and select it. Click OK.

Now, when you encounter a Telnet link, Ewan (or another program) will automatically open and connect to the site.

VIRTUAL PLACES

The idea is simple. It can get pretty lonely on the Web, what with all those brilliant sites but no one to share them with. Chat, on the other hand, lets you schmooze with your cyber-neighbors, but in a visually dreary, text-only chat room. Virtual Places marries the best of both, allowing AOL members to chat against the backdrop of a Web page or while browsing the Web with a small group.

Virtual Places is still experimental, a technology to play with, but already the possibilities are becoming clear. Imagine learning Web design by visiting the most innovative sites with leading designers. Or discussing business issues *at* commercial sites, with business experts. Or inviting friends over to your home page. Or meeting with friends at a sports or movie site to discuss a shared interest. It's all possible with Virtual Places.

 AOL's Terms of Service applies while you're using Virtual Places. See "AOL Rules (and AOL's Rules on the Net)."

Downloading, Installing, and Running Virtual Places

The Virtual Places files can be downloaded from keyword: VP. For step-by-step procedures, follow the instructions there. The program was still being readied for release when I wrote this, so some of the details (like the name of the file you download and how you install it!) may change.

Once you have installed Virtual Places, you run VP by going to keyword: VP and following the prompts. When I tried VP, installation automatically followed downloading, and the VP program automatically started after installation; it couldn't have been easier!

Getting Your Bearings

The Virtual Places window shown in Figure 10-2 has three main parts:

- Browser

- Communication Manager, where you type and read chat messages and Instant Messages

- People Manager, where you see who's participating and observing in a room

10

Observe/Participate button   Avatars   To access Places Directory

Toolbar

Browser

People Here: 25

People Manager

Communication Manager   Tabs   Type your chat message here.   Chat pane   Gesture button   Border   Send an Instant Message.

FIGURE 10-2   The main Virtual Places window lets you chat with the people against the backdrop of a Web page

Note   *A room, in Virtual Places, is a chat-enabled Web site. A site is enabled by the mere presence of at least one person viewing the site with the Virtual Places software. Thus, if you break ranks and start browsing the Web, your "avatar" will appear on the page you're viewing, and it will be the only avatar there.*

The three parts of the window have separate but related purposes, and each part has its own buttons and controls. The toolbar at the top gives you overall controls to navigate pages, to enter and leave rooms, to fiddle with the layout, and to return to AOL.

Adjusting the Layout

If you're familiar with frames, you'll be comfortable with Virtual Places. If you're not, just think of Virtual Places as a browser in which different things are going on in different parts of the browser.

The three parts of the Virtual Places window just described are defined by the two borders shown in Figure 10-2. To move a border and increase or decrease one of the two windows sharing the border, move your mouse pointer slowly over the border until it turns into a double-headed arrow, then click and drag the border, releasing the mouse when the border's in the position you want. Virtual Places accommodates both chatters and browsers. In the View menu, choose AOL Classic to turn Virtual Places into one big chat room or Browser Only to see one big browser. VP Classic, the default view shown in Figure 10-2, gives you a little bit of everything.

Defining Your Identity

It's hard to lurk in Virtual Places, but if you want to remain incognito you can use a weird screen name and choose an *avatar* that gives you a different persona. An avatar is a small picture representing you or your persona. To change your avatar, you can use one of VP's stock cartoon images. From the Avatars menu, select Edit Identity. In the Libraries section, click Stock, and then click Change:

Make a selection and click OK. If you don't like these cartoon images, you can also use any GIF image of your own as your avatar, as long as it's 48 X 64 pixels and doesn't violate TOS guidelines or copyright laws. To use your own graphic, in the Libraries section click Personal, then click Stock and browse for the graphics file.

Add any other information you want in the Edit Identity window, but just remember that anything you enter is accessible to others using Virtual Places. The About Me tab lets you enter personal stuff such as your gender, your hobbies, and your favorite quote.

10

> *You must have an avatar in Virtual Places. If you don't want to view anyone's avatar, deselect Show Avatars on the Avatars menu. The best reason to do this is to see the page you're all supposed to be chatting about! With Avatars deselected, you'll still be able to read chat messages in the Communication Manager.*

Selecting a Place to Visit

Not every Web site is a virtual place—at least, not yet. There are millions of Web pages but only thousands of Virtual Places pioneers. To find out which sites are home to Virtual Places folk, click the Places to Chat button on the tool bar to bring up the Virtual Places Directory:

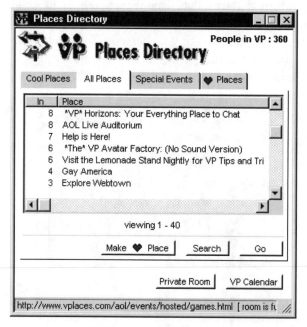

To see the different places, click one of the four tabs. *Cool Places* are chosen by the Community Administrator—the DJ, sort of, who runs one of VP's "community servers." *All Places* includes Cool Places *and* any pages currently used by Virtual Places users. *Special Events* take place in a virtual auditorium, a visual version of AOL Live, where you can listen to (and now watch) special guests ranging from Michael Jackson to Steve Case. The last tab, ♥ Places, is for *your* favorite (Virtual) Places.

Tip   *Virtual Places has the equivalent of Favorite Places. To add a place to your favorites, display the site. From the Go menu select Favorite Places, and from the submenu select Add to Favorites.*

Entering a Room: Participating vs. Observing

The unit of the Web is the page; the unit of Virtual Places is the *room,* or chat-enabled Web site. It is "enabled" simply by virtue of the fact that several people are browsing it while using Virtual Places. Virtual Places runs on several "community servers," each of them with its own set of Web rooms to visit and most of them accessible to the AOL *and* Internet communities. To see the servers available to you, go to the Virtual Places Tools menu and select Community Servers.

Once you have an identity and know where you want to go, ask yourself whether you want to take an active or a more passive part in the goings on. To take part actively means to get an avatar and chat. To merely observe, you get neither an avatar nor the chance to chat, but you do get to watch the goings-on and exchange IMs with active participants. The People Here section (on the right side of Figure 10-2) separately lists the nicknames of those observing and those participating.

Note   *Like a chat room, a room in Virtual Places has a limit of 23 people, though larger rooms can be created for special occasions. If you try to enter a room that's full, you'll be able to observe but not participate.*

Ordinarily, you automatically enter a room when you visit a Web page in Virtual Places. Entering a room makes your avatar visible and lets you chat and browse. If you don't want to join a room automatically, go to the Tools menu, select Preferences, and on the General tab uncheck the "enter a room automatically" box.

To observe, simply "leave" the room by clicking the Leave Room button on the toolbar. You can now view a page, read chat messages, and send Instant Messages to other participants, but you can't chat and you don't get an avatar. The button changes to Enter Room when you're just observing. Click it if you wish to chat.

Tip   *Anyone can see the identity of an observer by selecting the name in the People Here list and clicking the Identity button at the bottom.*

10

Finding Out Who's Who

Who's in the room with you?

- To find out who's behind an avatar, select it, right-click, and select Identity.

- To find out who's behind a nickname, select it from the list of People Here (on the right side of the display), right-click, and again select Identity.

- To find out whose avatar goes with a nickname, select the nickname; the avatar blinks a couple of times.

Chatting with the Group or Conversing One-to-One?

If you're participating and not just observing and want to send a chat message, simply type it in the message box and click Send (Figure 10-2). Your message appears both in the chat pane and the browser window of everyone in the room, as shown in Figure 10-2.

Virtual Places adds a few twists to ordinary chat. Ordinarily, there's not much room in the VP chat pane to see what others say, unless you widen the chat, reducing the browser width in the process. A several-line chat message is difficult to read. To get a larger, freefloating chat room, simply double-click the Chat Room tab to create a freefloating chat window:

This chat window can be resized into any shape you want. To close the chat window, click the Make Tab button. "Make Tab" is a another way of making chat available in the little chat pane that's available as a tab in the People Manager.

If you want your avatar to express a Smiley-like sentiment, like "Wow" or "LOL" (laughing out loud), you're in luck. You can send a *gesture* such as one of these to the group. To do so, you must first be participating and not observing. Click the Gesture icon shown in Figure 10-2. You'll see a palette of gestures:

Select a gesture by clicking it. The selected gesture now appears as the face of the Gesture button, next to the Send button. To send the gesture, simply click the Send button. To have it accompanied by some text, type in your text before clicking Send. You're sure to get everyone's attention.

SENDING INSTANT MESSAGES ON VIRTUAL PLACES   When you're on Virtual Places, you're still on AOL, so you can take advantage of the power of Instant Messages (IMs). Like chat, the IM experience is funkier and offers more features in Virtual Places. If you receive an IM, a new tab will be added to your chat window; click the tab to read the message. You can do your IMing through Virtual Places' Communications Manager!

To send an IM to someone in the same room you're visiting, simply select the person's screen name in the People Here list and click the IM button. To send an IM to someone who's elsewhere in Virtual Places, go to the Tools menu and select Send an Instant Message.

Note   *You can't send an IM from Virtual Places to AOL. You can receive an IM from AOL, but you must return to AOL to do so. Click the Return to AOL button to respond to an Instant Message from someone on AOL. Return to VP as you would switch between any open Windows program: press ALT-TAB or use the Windows 95 taskbar.*

10

Unlike ordinary IMs, you can add gestures to IMs you send on VP if the recipient is on VP too. In Instant Messages, gestures are the text versions of the pictures.

To search for someone on Virtual Places (find out what room they are in), go to the Tools menu and select Locate. Enter a screen name, and click OK. If that person's available, click Send Instant Message. This feature works like the AOL's "locate a member online," from the Members menu.

Guiding a Tour

Like a chat room, a Virtual Places room is pretty informal and involves a good deal of milling about. A Guided Tour, by contrast, has all the elements of Virtual Places except that one person controls the browser, selecting the sites to be visited by the group and acting as moderator. On a tour there's more structure than in a Virtual Places room, but it's not necessarily more formal in spirit.

To guide a tour, you select Set Up Tour from the Guided Tours menu, then provide a name and indicate a size (how many people you want to join). Every tour has an icon—a picture of a motorcycle or bus or something similar—which you can select when you set up the tour. The picture becomes *your* Guide avatar, with your personal avatar lodged in the upper left corner of the Guide avatar. You cannot guide a tour if you're merely observing.

To start a tour, you simply visit the Web site with which you want to begin the tour and invite others to join along, using IM or chat. You can kick out anyone who's interrupting your tour by selecting their avatar, right-clicking, and selecting Eject from Tour. To end a tour, simply choose End Tour from the Guided Tours menu.

To join a tour led by someone else, double-click the icon of the tour vehicle (Guide avatar). Leave a tour by selecting Leave Tour from the Guided Tour menu.

Attending an Event

Virtual Places events are like real-world events and even more like the events you may be familiar with in AOL Live. You enter a virtual room called an *auditorium*. You sit in a row and kibitz with others in the row—it's a mini-chat room; people in other rows won't be aware of your chatting (there's no "shushing" in an auditorium). A speaker or special guest addresses everyone in the auditorium. You can ask questions of the speaker, though your question may be queued up and not answered right away. The speaker may ask questions of you, in the form of a poll. It's all free, even for the big-name guests.

Auditorium events are available in the Place Directory's Special Events tab (see "Selecting a Place to Visit"). Double-click an event to enter an auditorium. Once you're there, you'll see new tabs on your Communications Manager that allow you to chat with others in your row and to participate in the event. You can switch seats and rows simply by dragging your avatar to another seat. To move to a row where friends are sitting, you'll need to use the Seat Map, available from the Auditorium menu. Click the Locate button to find your buddy, then swap IMs, change seats, exchange files, or whatever. You can leave a virtual auditorium without hurting any feelings or stepping on any toes. Just click Places to Chat and go somewhere else.

Leaving a Room and Exiting Virtual Places

To leave any kind of room (auditorium, tour, Web site) simply select another place from the Place Directory. Or, navigate to a different URL (from the File menu, select Open Location; type in a URL, and click Open). Different chat sessions appear in the same chat pane, separated by a dotted line. You can visit only one room at a time.

To keep VP open and return to AOL, click the Back to AOL button.

That's Not All Folks!

This overview only touches on the possibilities of Virtual Places and leaves out cool features such as playing games and exchanging files. The online help has everything you need.

Tip *Help is always available from the Virtual Places Help menu. There are likely to be people there too—avatars, at least—so you may be able to find a person to answer your specific questions!*

AOL Rules (and AOL's Rules on the Net)

AOL's Rules of the Road (keyword: TOS), Part II, reads: "Although AOL Inc. does not control the Internet, your conduct on the Internet when using your AOL account is subject to the AOL Rules of the Road. Because AOL Inc. wants to be a good Internet citizen, it prohibits Members from engaging in certain conduct…" Inappropriate conduct includes posting the following to newsgroups, mailing lists, and Internet Relay Chat channels: chain letters, commercial communications in noncommercial places, and copyrighted material.

Don't forget that the "real world" also has laws again sending chain letters and violating copyright.

CHATTING ON THE INTERNET WITH MIRC

Chatting on the Internet is pretty much like chatting on AOL, which is like chatting in the airport, at the checkout counter, or anywhere else. It's informal, lively, sociable, and usually has no purpose beyond itself. You'll also find rooms for serious discussion, fact finding, and emotional and moral support.

The Internet version of chat—Internet Relay Chat (IRC)—differs from chat on AOL primarily in its global reach. IRC also differs from AOL's chat in that it requires special software, and the software is more complex than AOL's. Many IRC programs are available for the PC, and one of the best of them, mIRC, is conveniently available, with installation instructions, at keyword: Internet Applications (click mIRC). AOL has licensed this software so that all members can use it for free.

Note *On AOL (keyword: FileSearch) you will find a more recent version of mIRC (4.7 when this was written). Unlike the AOL-licensed version at keyword: Internet Applications, the shareware version urges you to make a small payment after 30 days of use. The screen captures in this section are based on the powerful, stable, and very capable AOL-licensed version.*

You must first download the file from Internet Applications, then install it. You install it simply by running the file you downloaded and following the prompts.

Setting up mIRC

With mIRC downloaded and installed, you have to provide mIRC enough information for it to connect to an IRC computer at AOL.

1. From the File menu, select Setup to bring up the mIRC Setup window (if it doesn't appear automatically).

2. Supply your real name (your AOL screen name will do) and your real e-mail address (*screenname*@**aol.com**).

3. Supply a nickname. A nickname is your IRC persona: how you want others to see you in an IRC channel (chat room). It's like an avatar in Virtual Places. Unlike e-mail addresses, nicknames are not unique, and you can't prevent someone else from using the same nickname. That's why you must supply an alternate nickname. If the first one is in use when you sign onto an IRC server, it will automatically use this alternate. If the alternate is also in use, the mIRC program will ask you to enter a second alternate.

4. Enter the *server* (computer) through which you want to connect to IRC. Click Add to get the mIRC Add Server window:

10

mIRC Add Server		✕
Description: AOL		
IRC Server: irc02.aol.com	**Port:** 6667	
Group:		**Add**
Passwords are ONLY needed by special types of users.		**Cancel**
Password:		**Help**

For the best chance of reliably getting onto IRC, use AOL's server, **irc02.irc.aol.com**, with **6667** as your PORT #. Click Add to return to the Setup window.

5. Click Connect to connect to IRC. The main mIRC window is shown in Figure 10-3. From now on, when you start mIRC, all you have to do is click the Connect button on the toolbar.

Starting mIRC

First, make sure you're signed onto AOL. You can then sign onto mIRC as you do any program: double-click its icon. The mIRC Setup window comes up. Select AOL's server (the IRC computer you set up in the previous section), and click Connect. The Status window registers what's happening as you're signing on. If for some reason you can't use the AOL server, either try another server in the mIRC window or try again later.

Choosing a Channel to Join

An IRC channel may remind you of an AOL chat room. Unlike an AOL chat room or Virtual Places room, however, an IRC channel can grow to be very big; there's no 23-person limit or "self-replicating" feature, whereby an AOL chat room spawns

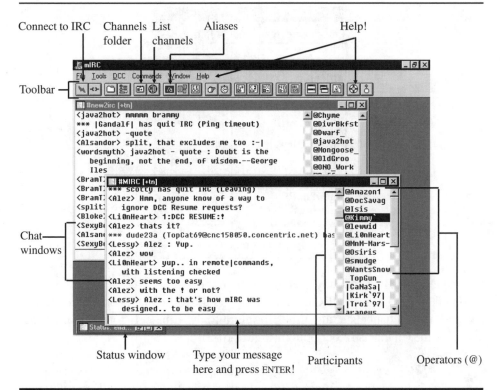

Connect to IRC Channels List Aliases Help!
folder channels

Toolbar

Chat
windows

Status window   Type your message   Participants   Operators (@)
here and press ENTER!

FIGURE 10-3   The mIRC main window, for chatting on the Internet

a new chat room if it gets too big. On average, however, IRC channels are pretty small—a lot smaller than the packed chat rooms you'll find on AOL! On IRC, you will find thousands of one- and two-person chat rooms—people waiting for the party to start. Sometimes the party never does start!

You choose a channel to join from the Channel folders window, which pops up as soon as you log on:

10

Several channels have already been included in the list.

Think of this list as the IRC equivalent of your Favorite Places on AOL. You can add and delete channels at any time. To return to the Channels folder at any time, just click the Channels folder button (Figure 10-3).

 *IRC channels are denoted by a pound sign (#) and the name of the channel. For example, **#irchelp**. Channel names sometimes start with an additional pound sign, or "bang" (!), or percentage (%) sign, in order to be listed first in the channels list (like the Yellow Pages entries beginning AAAA).*

With the Channels folder open:

- To join a channel on the list, double-click it.

- To add a channel to the folder, type in the name (for example, **#mirc**), and click Add.

- To create a channel, enter its name, preceded by a #, in the text box at the top of the window, and click OK. See "Running a Channel."

Tip *To get the hang of IRC, join a channel such as **#new2irc** or **#newbies**. It's like using the **misc.test** newsgroup if you're learning to use a newsgroup.*

Getting a List of Available Channels

Which channel to join of the thousands available? To find out what's available, click the List Channels button on the mIRC tool bar.

Note *The buttons on the toolbar are small and not always self-explanatory. You can tell a button's purpose by passing your mouse arrow slowly over it until a text description ("balloon") appears. The List Channels button is (in my version) the sixth button from the left, just to the right of the Channels Folder button.*

The List Channels window comes up:

```
List Channels                                    [X]
        List channels which match these criteria:

   Match text:                    ⌐

   |irc                              ▼|   | List! |

     □ Match text in topics              | Help  |
     □ Extract URLs from topics
     □ Do not sort channel list
                                         |  OK   |
   Number of people on a channel:

   min: |10|      max: |999|             | Lock  |


     □ Hide channels which match these criteria:

   |                                              |

     □ Hide non-alphanumeric channels
```

10

Use this window to search for channels on topics of interest to you. It's a good idea to restrict the topic by typing in some text that must be contained in a channel's name. Also, you'll probably want to screen out the smallest channels by specifying a minimum number of people you want to find in a channel (using the *min* box). Obviously, a minimum number is required for *any* conversation.

My search for *irc*-related channels with at least ten people in each one yielded four: **irc???**, **irchelp**, **mirc** (about the mIRC program), and **new2irc**. A broader search, for smaller channels (or all channels available on your server), will amaze and possibly offend you with the variety of channels available on IRC, many of which wouldn't be allowed on AOL. Double-click any channel to go there directly.

Elements of a Channel Window

Channel windows have three elements, something like Virtual Places, a place for "input," a place for "output," and a list of people doing the inputting. (See Figure 10-3.)

 You can't do horizontal scrolling with mIRC, so it's a good idea to maximize any chat window that you want to follow closely.

1. To the right, a *list of participants* in alphabetical order, beginning with the channel's operators (beginning with @). Operators are the one who create and run channels (see "Running a Channel").

2. The *chat window*, where chat text is displayed.

3. The *entry field*, where you enter either chat messages (text) or commands (preceded by a forward slash, /). Commands are discussed a little later.

When you perform a specific action, such as sending someone a message or looking up information about another user, a separate window comes up. The Status window is always present during your chat session and can get in the way; it can be useful to minimize it, as in Figure 10-3.

 If it ever appears that an action or request for information had no results, check the Status window. If you ever suspect that nothing's happening, it could be that you've been disconnected because so many people are using the server. The Status window will read "Disconnected" if this is the case. Click the first icon on the toolbar (the lightning bolt) to log on again.

Taking Part

As in an AOL chat room, in an IRC channel you can either communicate with the group or chat privately with one individual in the group. To communicate with the group, type a message in the text box at the bottom of a channel window (Figure 10-3) and press ENTER. Your message appears in colored text, *not* preceded by your nickname.

 Your messages don't have to be colored and can be preceded by your nickname. mIRC offers dozens of ways to customize the program, but these options can be a bit bewildering. mIRC is a lot more powerful and hence more complicated than AOL-style chat. To see the options available to you, choose Options from the File menu—there are 11 sets of preferences to choose from!

To communicate with an *individual* in a chat room, just double-click their name in the list of participants to start an IM-type exchange.

> *Tip*   *Something called DCC (Direct Client to Client) communication is also available on mIRC, for directly chatting with someone. Just right-click a participant's name and select DCC | Chat.*

Using Simple Commands

Commands give you the flexibility to customize mIRC and to create the equivalent of macros (chains of commands you'd like to carry out routinely). You enter a command by typing it into the chat window's text box preceded by a slash (/), then pressing ENTER. For example, if you want to type a message saying you're stepping away for a moment, the command is **/away back in a sec** (actually, */away* is the command and *back in a sec* is your argument—it's what appears in the chat window).

The most popular commands are also available from the Commands window. Table 10-1 explains what each command does.

The reason to learn these text commands is that they let you create shortcuts, or *aliases*, a powerful IRC feature that's nicely explained in the online help. Another reason to use text commands is to get access to unique mIRC commands, such as **/clear** (get rid of the text in the chat window) and **/finger** (to get additional information about a user whose e-mail address you know). Best of all are mIRC's **/help** commands, for a list of basic commands.

> *Tip*   *A neat mIRC feature gives you the equivalent of AOL's Buddy Lists but requires that you use text commands. The /**notify nickname, nickname**… command (where you replace **nickname** with the nicknames of your buddies) causes a message to appear in your Status window when one of your buddies logs onto the same IRC server as you. (Like Virtual Places, IRC is run from several servers, each of which has separate channels.)*

10

Running a Channel

Like a chat room, an IRC channel exists as long as someone is in it; the last person who leaves a channel also kills the channel automatically. So, if you try to join a channel that doesn't exist, you don't get an error message; you get a new channel! You've also appointed yourself channel *operator* of this new channel.

Every channel has at least one operator. Relations between a channel's operator(s) and everyone else can make an IRC channel a different environment

Command	To Do the Following
Join channel	Join a channel. In the window that comes up, type in *#[channel name]*.
Part channel	Leave a channel. In the window that comes up, type in *#[channel name]*. See also the Set Away command.
Query user	Send a message to someone on the channel using a special query window. In the window that comes up, type in that user's nickname, leave a space, and type a private message. Click OK.
Send notice	Send a message to a nickname (not in special window).
Whois user	Find out the e-mail address and other information (such as channels currently joined) for a nickname. Results appear in Status window.
Send CTCP	Get information about a nickname, such as how long messages take to reach that person (Ping) and the IRC software they are using (Version). The results appear in the Status window.
Set Away	To present a message to the group saying that you'll be temporarily away and can't respond to queries and messages, etc. From the pop-up menu, select On, and type a message. Select Off when you come back.
Invite user	Invite another user (nickname) to a specific channel. In the window, provide both the user's name and the #channel name.
Ban user	For channel operators only (see "Running a Channel").
Kick user	For channel operators only (see "Running a Channel").
Ignore user	For channel operators only (see "Running a Channel").
Change nickname	Change your nickname, for any reason (if you're being bothered by someone or someone else has the same nickname, for example).
Quit IRC	Same as File	Exit.

TABLE 10-1 Commands available from the Command menu and what they mean

from an AOL chat room. For one thing, an operator has considerable power in this small world and can name other operators, kick people out of a channel for any reason, ban people from a room in the first place, and define a channel's topic—the bit of optional text that accompanies a channel's description when you search for channels.

Note   *Channel operators have great flexibility in determining who they ban from their channel. They can even ban entire domains, and from time to time you will find that channels don't allow anyone from **aol.com**. Don't take it personally; it's their loss.*

Operators can also limit the number of people in a room, declare the channel invitation-only, and define the channel as either *private* (it won't appear in the list of all channels) or *secret* (a person in the channel won't be revealed by a "whois" query).

Tip   *The best way to learn about all this is to create a channel and double-click on the main channel window. In the window that comes up you can define the channel's attributes: its size, whether it's private, how big it can get, and so on. For a normal channel you join, double-clicking on the channel window brings up the same window, with the settings used by the operators listed at the top of the participants window. You can't alter these settings.*

Leaving a Channel and Quitting IRC

The easiest way to leave a channel is to close its window: in Windows 95, just click the X in the far upper-right corner. A channel remains in existence after the original operators have left, and the last person who leaves the channel automatically "turns off the light."

Leaving mIRC is like quitting any program: File | Exit does the trick, as does (for Windows 95 users) clicking the X in the upper-right corner of the main window. With mIRC, you can use commands as well: /quit and /exit. With the Quit command, you can add your own message, such as **/quit parting is such sweet sorrow**.

Finding Out More

Here are some resources for getting more information about IRC.

■ The easiest way to get your questions answered is on IRC itself. Click the List Channels button on the tool bar and search for channels with *mirc* in the name. The #mirc channel is excellent.

■ Informative Web sites are devoted to mIRC, such as (for starters) **http://www.mirc.co.uk/mirc.html.** It includes links to other mIRC Web sites.

10

- Check out the **alt.irc.mirc** newsgroup, as well as the family of newsgroups in the **alt.irc.*** hierarchy, such as **alt.irc.games** and **alt.irc.questions**. (At keyword: newsgroups, click Search All Newsgroups and do a search for *irc*.) A general IRC FAQ is available at **http://www.cis.ohio-state.edu/hypertext/faq/usenet/irc-faq/faq.html**.

TELNET

What is Telnet? When you access a Telnet site on an Internet computer, your PC becomes the terminal—a mere keyboard and display—for a distant computer (the word *remote* is sometimes used for *distant*; they both mean "out there" on the Internet). You type in commands and responses, and all the processing takes place at the distant computer, where you can do searches, make requests, and communicate with others who are also telnetting to the computer. The "results" are displayed on your monitor as old-fashioned and not very attractive courier text (Figure 10-4).

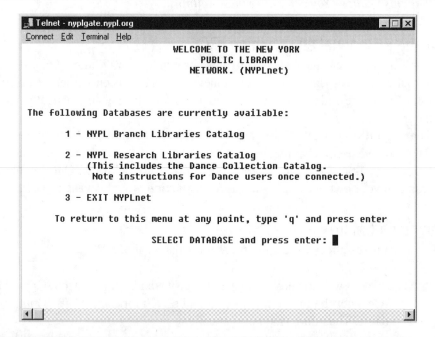

FIGURE 10-4   NYPL without the lions. The New York Public Library's CATNYP system allows you to do author, title, and journal searches of millions of titles in a fraction of a second

It may not be very sexy, but Telnet is useful and versatile precisely because of its lowest-common-denominator display.

AOL provides provides you with a choice of ways to do Telnet. If you're using AOL 3.0 for Windows 95 and are browsing a Web page that links to a Telnet site, you can click the link and go automatically to the Telnet site. Or, if you want to access a Telnet site that's *not* linked-to from a Web site, you can run any one of the many Telnet Winsock programs, such as Ewan, CommNet, and Anzio Lite, to name three of the most popular.

Telnet gives access to two essential Internet resources, which I'll introduce here, plus dozens of others you can explore on your own. First of all, Telnet lets you search hundreds of library card catalogs, saving time and money if you are doing any kind of research. Every kind of Internet-accessible library catalog can be searched: law, medical, public, community, university, and K-12. See "Hytelnet: Gateway to a Thousand Libraries."

Telnet also provides a haven for people who love collaborative games and simulated environments. A whole genre of simulation, fantasy, adventure, and learning games has grown up over the past decade on Telnet, collectively known as MUDs—multi-user dungeons, or dimensions. See "Garden of MUD."

Downloading and Installing CommNet

When you use AOL 3.0 for Windows 95, a Telnet window pops up whenever you click a Telnet link on a Web page. That's fine—when you stumble across such links. For all other circumstances, you need stand-alone Winsock software such as CommNet, Ewan, or Anzio Lite. Let's focus on CommNet, because it's licensed by AOL and is made easily available at keyword: Internet applications.

Here are procedures for downloading and installing CommNet. Note that this shareware version of CommNet lacks important features, such as the ability to function as a helper app in Netscape (so you can automatically link to Telnet sites from a Web page viewed in Netscape), and the number of simultaneous open Telnet sessions is limited. The full CommNet program offers audio, a bright interface, the capability of running more than one Telnet session, and an interface from which you can copy text (copy-and-paste). You may wish to buy the full version, as explained in the ordering document that's included in the program window when CommNet is installed. Or, you may prefer to use Ewan, a more limited but fully functioning program, also available on AOL (keyword: FileSearch).

1. Go to keyword: Internet applications, and click on CommNet Telnet.
   Read the background information, and click Continue. Click Download

10

Now and save the **cmnet21d.zip** file (the version current when this book was written) in the **aol30/download** directory. The file is zipped, so you'll need to unzip it: From the File menu, select Download Manager; click Show Downloaded Files; select **cmnet21d.zip** and click Decompress. A new directory, **Cmnet21d**, will be created in your **aol30/download** directory.

2. Install the program by running the **install.exe** program (in Cmnet21d) from the Windows File Manager (Windows 3.1) or from the Run window of the Start menu (Windows 95). The installation program creates a new directory, **Commnet**, and also creates a CommNet icon for you.

3. To run CommNet, make sure you're signed onto AOL, then double-click the new CommNet icon created in Step 2.

> *Tip*   *If you use Netscape, you'll have to define a Telnet "helper" application other than CommNet (Ewan is a good choice). From the Options menu, select General Preferences, and click on the Apps tab. By the Telnet Application box, click the Browse button and navigate to the place where you've installed Ewan.*

Hytelnet: Gateway to a Thousand Libraries

Have you noticed that card catalogs have disappeared from your public library? Throughout the world, those inefficient and difficult-to-maintain space-wasters have given way to the electronic catalog, which can be easily searched by anyone, anywhere, using a "terminal emulation" program such as Telnet. Electronic searches allow you to search for books by title, author, year of publication, and other standard criteria.

Telnet makes it possible to do such searches from a distance and to do several such searches at a sitting. The books themselves are not available by Telnet. For that, you'll need to get in the car or on the phone.

Hytelnet is a piece of software written by Peter Scott, one of those Net heroes who have contributed an essential service to the larger Internet community. Hytelnet is available by Telnet, of course, but also by Gopher and, most important, by the Web. A stand-alone version can run on your PC and give you access, from your hard disk, to the world's card catalogs. The only problem with the PC version is that it must be frequently updated to accommodate the trickle of new Telnet sites.

Other Cool Telnet Resources

Hytelnet provides more than access to library catalogs. Click the boringly named Other category at Hytelnet's top level to get direct access via Telnet to all kinds of goodies: Archie servers (Chapter 8); dozens of community free-nets (computer "online services" for small communities from Canada to Finland); a large set of NASA databases of interest to students and teachers; stores such as CDNow; and all of the world's publicly accessible Gopher servers!

Hytelnet on the Web is available at many sites, including Trade Wave (formerly EINet, in Texas, **http://www.einet.net/hytelnet/HYTELNET.html**) and the University of Saskatchewan (**http://moondog.usask.ca/hytelnet/**). With Hytelnet, you can take a top-down approach to finding a particular library, beginning with region (Americas, Europe, Asia) and "drilling down." (More than a thousand libraries are available for the U.S., which is more than for the rest of the world combined.) You can also do a search for a specific library. A word of warning, however: whether you browse or search, the Hytelnet Web sites can be slow.

Telnet 101

Logging onto a distant computer often requires that you know a password and log-in name. Hytelnet usefully provides you such information for libraries, but other kinds of Telnet sites may require that you first contact an administrator.

A key setting you may need to adjust in your software—or set at the site—is your "terminal emulation" type, which makes your keyboard behave in a way that makes sense to the distant computer. (Remember, the programs are sitting on a faraway computer; imagine that your keyboard has a 4,000-mile extension cord!) The most common terminal emulation type for PC-compatible keyboards is VT-100, though you will also see VT-102.

Once you're signed on, you'll find that navigation differs from site to site. As a rule of thumb, you use the arrow keys on your keyboard to get around, and the mouse is useless at a Telnet site. When in doubt, try to get help at the distant computer by typing a **H** or a **?** or **Help**. To end a Telnet session, you can simply close the Telnet window or (more gracefully) end the session from the File or Connect or similar menu. Pressing CTRL-] often gets you out as well. Close the Telnet application to end the session altogether.

10

Garden of MUD

Community has come a long way on the Internet. Up-to-date, graphically whizzy programs such as Virtual Places are easy to use and a pleasure to watch but are still maturing. Dig a little, and you come to IRC, a graphically simple but fully mature environment for chatting with people around the world. MUD*s* have no graphics and are nothing but text, but they offer the most creative environment for meeting and interacting with others on the Internet. MUDs require an active imagination— and good typing. Like radio in the early decades of the twentieth century, subsequent innovations have not replaced MUDs; they've emulated and supplemented them. MUDs are alive and well.

Tip   *If you're serious about MUDding, then use a Winsock program like zMUD. It offers a much easier-to-use interface than "vanilla" Telnet, makes it very easy to join any MUD, and gives you a level of control over your display that programs like Ewan don't provide. zMUD and other such MUD "clients" are available at keyword: FileSearch as well as through any of the Internet resources listed in "Where Do I Find Applications to Use with AOL's Winsock?" A program like zMUD is Telnet that's been customized for use on MUDs.*

MUD stands for multi-user *dungeon* (after the Dungeons and Dragons games popular in the seventies) or *dimension*. Unlike an IRC channel, a MUD is a structured environment in which people assume and develop online identities other than their "real" identities. The "avatars" in Virtual Places owe a lot to MUDs. Author and MIT professor Sherry Turkle considers MUDs a profound tool for exploring the parts of one's self that aren't fully expressed in day-to-day life. There are enough MUDs—hundreds of them—for you to find a comfortable place to try on a new persona. MUDs have been used in the workplace as a powerful collaborative tool and in the classroom to create virtual learning and role-playing opportunities. But they're mostly used for creative and interactive (not arcade-style) games.

MUDs tend to fall into two big classes. Traditional MUDs are devoted to adventure. You assume an often elaborate identity, defined by a set of traits you can choose. You name your character and join a specific clan or guild. You're now ready to interact with other personas, developing the characters and story in the process, in pursuit of giants, the Grail, evil, whatever. With practice comes recognition, advanced levels of play, and prestige. Characters engage in activities such as whispering, walking, fighting, and flying, and action unfolds in elaborate imaginary places, with rooms and neighborhoods. Bored with what's going on in one room? Try another.

The "social" MUDs—with names like Mush, Muck, and TinyMUD—have more in common with an AOL chat room than with Dungeons and Dragons. They're sheerly for socializing, although, with their objects, role-playing, and invented spaces, they have more structure than a chat room. But the goal is benign.

Learning about MUDs

All MUDs are different. Where do you start? Harley Hahn's chapter on MUDs in the *Internet Complete Reference, Second Edition* (Osborne/McGraw-Hill, 1996) is an excellent place to start. What Hytelnet does for library resources, the MudConnector (**http://www.mudconnect.com**), created and maintained by Andrew Cowan, does for the world of simulated environments. The searchable list of annotated MUDs includes every variety of MUD, from aggressive galaxies to peaceable kingdoms, from Age of Dragons to New Age. It's the place to find crisp descriptions of more than 600 MUDs, as well as usage statistics and links to MUD home pages on the Web. Most important, Telnet links take you directly to any MUD you want to explore.

Newsgroups on MUDs abound, starting with two major families of newsgroups, **alt.mud.*** and **rec.games.mud.*** (where the * stands for *announce*, *diku*, *tiny*, and others). Dozens of general MUD-related Web sites, plus the home pages for hundreds of individual MUDs, are available from MudConnector. Finally, an informative MUD FAQ is available at **http://www.math.okstate.edu/~jds/ mudfaq-p1.html**.

The best way to learn about MUDs—like anything on the Net—is to jump right in. You can't break anything, and you will never be alone. Welcome to the Internet community!

10

Chapter 11

The AOL 300 Directory

The AOL 300 was designed to bring together in one place, *by channel*, the best Internet resources you'll find on AOL. For each of 19 channels, you'll find 15 Web sites and newsgroups closely related to the channel's theme. Most of the sites you'll find in the AOL 300 are integrated into channel listboxes. Some were added here to complement the integrated sites. The AOL 300 opens with some sites that AOL members like the best—AOL Members' Choice (which you can get to with the Hot button on the tool bar). It's a pretty remarkable list. Welcome to the feast!

HOW CHANNELS USE INTERNET RESOURCES

Web sites are everywhere on AOL, tucked into hundreds of listboxes. You'll see Web sites indicated in listboxes in different ways, as shown here.

Clicking any listbox item with one of these icons or the WEB label will usually take you directly to a Web site. Sometimes you'll first go to an AOL screen describing the site.

Some of the Web sites in the AOL 300 are siblings to AOL forums. What's the difference between a Web site and an AOL forum? The Web sites tend to be splashier, but as a rule the AOL forums will download *much* faster and offer more ways and more consistent ways to interact with others. The spectacular Rollingstones Web site (MusicSpace), for example, takes forever to download for mortals using a normal-to-fast modem (28.8K) compared to the corresponding AOL forum. AOL forums have the additional advantage of linking you directly to the *most useful* parts of the Web sites, as you'll discover in the Personal Finance forums run by Charles Schwab, Dreyfus, and Fidelity.

From section to section you'll notice some overlap in content. In fact, AOL's channels overlap in lots of ways. Sometimes it's fun to watch the border skirmishes. For you, it means more choice but also a little less clarity. That's just the way it is.

The most popular sites have their own keywords, to simplify access. So, instead of typing **http://www.pathfinder.com**, you just type **pathfinder** in the Keyword window. Following is a list of "keywordable" Web sites. The most up-to-date list of such keywords is always available at keyword: Web keywords (click on *Web keywords*).

adobe.com	Garden.com	Nasa.gov	Travelocity
AltaVista	Gateway2000.com	Nascar.com	Treasury
American Photo	Go Florida	Navy.mil	Tribune.com
Angelfire	HBO	NBA	Tripod
Apple.com	Home PC.com	NBC.com	U Iowa
Atlantic Financial	HomeArts	NetGuide Live	U Mich
Big Yellow	Homes	NetGuide.com	U Penn
BigBook	HotWired	Netscape	U Texas
BingoZone	HP.com	Nintendo.com	UIUC
Boston Globe	IBM.com	Novell.com	UMD
CBS	IDSoftware	NY Times.com	United Media
CDnow	iGuide	ON.com	Universal
Census	Indiana University	Pathfinder	Urban Desires
City.Net	Infoseek	Purdue	USAToday.com
CNN.com	Intel.com	Quantum Group	Vacations.com
CNNfn	Intellicast	RealAudio	Warner Bros.com
Compass.com	Internet Movie	Riddler	Washington Post
DejaNews	Database	RIT	Washingon
Digits	Ivanhoe	Rockwell	University
Discovery.com	Jumbo	Automation	Webcrawler
Edmunds	LA Times.com	Salon	Webtivities
Electronic News	Link Exchange	Sci Fi.com	White House.gov
Elle.com	Liszt	Search.com	WinMag.com
Epicurious	Look up	Sierra.com	Wisc
ESPN	Macromedia.com	Slate	WSJ
Excite	Magellan	Sony	Yahoo
Family Tree	Mapquest	Sportsline	ZD Net
Firefly	McDonnell Douglas	Stanford University	Zippo
FoodTV	Microsoft.com	Switchboard	
Four11	Monster	TechWeb	
GA Tech	MSU	The Weather	
Gameplayers	MTV.com	Channel	
Gamespot	Nando.net	Total NY.com	

11

In the future you'll see more and more channels and forums creating their own Web sites, to reach a broader audience and tap some of the power of the Web. Digital City is already beginning to "aggregate" sites for major metropolitan areas such as Washington and Chicago, for example, and the Travel section of the AOL 300 includes a site created by the channel itself.

WHAT'S MISSING?

Missing from this guide are the Web sites integrated into the "subchannels" you'll find within AOL's channels: the Your Business subchannel within Personal Finance, for example.

> *Tip* *The Internet is an unparalleled source of information about business as well as a place to do business. If the subject interests you, visit the InBusiness forum, led by Jill Ellsworth. Dr. Ellsworth provides a sampling of the best business resources on the Net (keyword: InBusiness).*

Also missing are two AOL channels that as yet have no parallel on the Web. First, the People Connection channel is primarily a place—hundreds of places, actually—to *chat*. If you want to chat on the Web, you can visit Virtual Places, as described in Chapter 10, where you'll find lots of Web pages where you can chat with Net people as well as with AOL members. Second, the Marketplace channel is a unique AOL offering. Marketplace is a hundred-story mall, a marvelous maze of stores to browse, with opportunities to purchase books, steaks, flowers, and notebooks computers, among a myriad of other things. The Net's still pretty much a flea market, though electronic commerce on the Internet is coming on very strong and will likely reshape consumer habits in the next 3-5 years. For now, it's nowhere as convenient or as safe to purchase *anything* as on AOL.

The sites in the AOL 300 are missing something even more important. They're missing the context AOL provides to make a coherent whole out of diverse content. Channels add descriptive text, attitude, a point of view, chat rooms, message boards, leading personalities such as NetGirl and the Motley Fools, and *much* faster download times. Members take all this content and turn channels into communities, creating a mix more compelling than anything the Internet yet has to offer.

In a channel with *many* communities, such as Life, Styles & Interests, the best idea is to find your niche (whether it's writing or birdwatching) and explore *all* the AOL and Internet resources for that niche. It's a good way to meet people on America Online.

HOW DO I USE THE AOL 300?

As a starting place.

These 300 sites are a very small sampling of what the Internet has to offer. New sites are cropping up daily, some, no doubt, as good as what you'll find here. Begin with sites of personal or professional interest, and see where they lead you.

■ If you're looking for something that's not here, Chapter 9 provides plenty of guidance in finding exactly what you're seeking.

■ If you're looking for a way to stay up to date with new sites devoted to your interests, subscribe to the appropriate mailing lists, as discussed in Chapter 4.

One final thing, to repeat a point made in Chapter 1: the Web's not the Net. The AOL 300 brings you primarily Web sites because they're fun and easy to use. In the search for good, cool, and even practical information don't forget the other core Internet services: FTP, Telnet, and mailing lists.

Tip   *Osborne/McGraw-Hill publishes two resource directories for your reading and Web-browsing pleasure:* Harley's Hahn's Internet and Web Yellow Pages, 1997 edition, *and Jean Polly's* Internet Kid's Yellow Pages, Second Edition *(1997).*

FEEDBACK

If you ever encounter problems with a site—because its address changes, or the site disappears, or anything else—please send a message to **inetbook97**. Please use the same address to recommend sites for inclusion in the next edition of this book. Thank you!

AOL MEMBERS' CHOICE

City.Net

http://www.city.net/

This site is a must-visit for travelers. Here you can find extensive information on any major city in the United States and the world, and you can search for other cities, too. If you are planning a trip soon, check out Concierge, a listing of resources on arts and entertainment, food and drink, travel and sights, and the weather for any particular city or region. In addition, **City.Net** offers a free interactive, customizable mapping service.

11

DC Comics

http://www.dccomics.com/

DC Comics fans frequent this site to find high-quality graphics, stories, and games. WeirdWeb, for instance, offers original and colorful online comic strips. If you enjoy interactive multimedia, explore the Toys and Games section to listen to the Superman radio serial and check out the digital trading cards. In addition, you can find original DC Comics fiction, complete with beautiful painted images, for adults, teenagers, and children.

EXTRA

http://www.extratv.com/

If you are an entertainment news addict, check out EXTRA, an insider's guide to Hollywood, fashion, business, and pop culture. Here you can read celebrity interviews, find exclusives on television shows and movies, and chat live with the stars. Movie buffs will appreciate the EXTRA film release schedule. If you are a fan of a particular celebrity, check out the Superstar Library to find specific information, images, and multimedia files.

Firefly

http://www.ffly.com

When the WWW first started to gain popularity, one of the biggest complaints was that it was "static." Surfers would access a page, look at it, and move on. There was no real interactivity. That's changing fast these days, and Firefly is one of the sites that is making the change. At its heart, Firefly is another database of movies and popular music, but the interface makes all the difference. Here you can rate music, and Firefly makes suggestions based on your ratings. You also have a special Firefly mailbox, where you can send and receive notes to other Firefly browsers. You can spend hours here.

HomeArts

http://www.homearts.com/

Welcome to the premiere Web magazine devoted to home life. This value-added compilation of resources brings together the best content of popular magazines such as *Country Living, Good Housekeeping, Popular Mechanics,* and *Redbook.* Here you can find news and features on home improvement and decorating, crafts, family life, health, romance and relationships, and food. Some of the best features here include the extensive Recipe Finder database, the weekly horoscope, and the Botanica gardening newsletter.

iGuide

http://www.iguide.com/

A rich source of information—news, listings, and searchable databases—on television, movies, soap operas, music, and sports. If you enjoy interactive media, check out the TV show- or movie-specific games, quizzes, bulletin boards, and live chat auditorium. The features and databases are updated all the time, so keep visiting iGuide to stay abreast of the entertainment industry.

Jumbo

http://www.jumbo.com/

This is a huge—yet carefully organized—repository of free downloadable software available on the Net. Here you can find up-to-date software for various purposes, such as business (databases and finance), desktop (wallpaper and icons), education (tutorials and vocabulary-builders), and games (3D and adventure). The software runs on various platforms, and there's an archive of programs based on ActiveX and Java. Jumbo also offers value-added services, including What's New, to help you stay abreast of new software additions; the Resource Center to access a directory for Web sites; and Starter Kits for newbies.

Magellan Internet Guide

http://www.mckinley.com/

This Internet directory includes FTP, Gopher, Telnet, and resources, as well as Web sites. Unlike other directories (including Yahoo), Magellan's resources are described and rated; a Green Light rating means a site's OK for kids. The directories, plus the Internet as a whole, are searchable. Magellan's People Finder helps you find long-lost friends. Surfers who want to sneak a peek at others' search entries will enjoy watching the automatically updating Search Voyeur.

MapQuest

http://www.mapquest.com/

Why spend money on a new road atlas when you can access MapQuest for free? This service allows to you customize your own interactive atlas and create a personalized home page. After entering address or city information, you can view detailed road maps of the area, zoom in and out, and identify points of interest for travel and business services. If you are planning a road trip, check out TripQuest, an easy-to-use, door-to-door mapping service.

MTV Online

http://www.mtv.com/

If you're an MTV fan, you'll love this site. MTV Online offers the latest in music news as well as information on shows such as *Real World, Road Rules,* and *Beavis and Butt-Head.* You can also find data, graphics, and audio clips of your favorite bands and vocal artists. The Java-enriched version offers live news and hot graphics. If you have a slower connection or prefer a more straightforward approach to surfing, you'll appreciate the Decaf version.

Riddler

http://www.riddler.com/

If you enjoy games and puzzles, check out Riddler, one of the most popular game sites on the Web. Riddler offers word searches, a solitaire game, and a trivia sampler to members and non-members alike. Membership registration is free, and once you are registered you may play the Daily Riddle, crossword puzzles, and a variety of trivia games. You may even win a prize!

Salon

http://www.salon1999.com/

This popular Web e-zine is one of the best reads on the Net. Salon offers a rich mix of feature articles, including some by famous writers or celebrities. Here you can also find updated comic strips by Tom Tomorrow, Carol Lay, and others. The most popular feature of this site may be Table Talk, Salon's interactive bulletin board, in which you can participate in discussions about books, television, movies, digital culture, music, politics, and more.

Switchboard

http://www.Switchboard.com

Welcome to America Online's official people and business directory. This is a way to search for companies, addresses, and telephone numbers that's faster than your hardcopy telephone directory book. Your search is not limited by your own geographic region; Switchboard lets you search people and businesses in any city and state. Within its database, Switchboard contains additional contact information, such as e-mail addresses, affiliations, and personal comments. You may add and modify your own listings free of charge. If you wish, Switchboard will not make your actual e-mail addresses publicly known, but will forward any messages to you.

11

Tripod: Tools for Life

http://www.tripod.com/

Some Web sites focus on a particular subject; this one takes "life" as its subject. This appropriately named, practical Web publication is akin to an all-purpose guide to how to improve your life in a variety of areas: money, politics, community, living, and travel. The information is delivered in the form of how-to guides, bulletin boards, and interactive tools such as the Resume Builder and Retirement Planner. If you are a surfer and just want to relax and have fun, check out the Tripod Toybox for multimedia games, animations, and other goodies.

Warner Brothers Online

http://www.warnerbros.com/

The central information hub for WB media and services, including television, movies, music, videos, stores, and DC Comics. (Warner Brothers is also available on AOL at keyword: WB.) The site is chock-full of colorful graphics, cartoons, and animations. Kids will especially enjoy viewing WB Animation, which includes Looney Tune animations, downloadable media files, games, puzzles, and other goodies. The Warner Brothers Kids Page features Looney Tunes Karaoke.

COMPUTERS & SOFTWARE

C|Net's Product Reviews

http://www.cnet.com/Content/Reviews/

Nearly everyone knows about C|net's Web site. It's one of the absolute best sites about computing and the Internet. The folks at AOL's Computing and Software channel have singled out the Product Review page though, and rightly so. Here you can read informed opinions on hardware and software. The page is updated often, so you'll want to check back regularly. The design is the typical confusing jumble that C|net uses everywhere on their site, but what the heck—you're here for the information, and there's plenty of that!

comp.os.ms-windows.win95.setup

http://www.comp.os.ms-windows.win95.setup

So you're having a little trouble getting Windows 95 to work the way it's supposed to? Well, you're not alone. While Win95 sets up easily for most people, there are enough differently configured computers out there to ensure that a fairly sizable minority will be beset with problems. Here's where many of them come with their

11

troubles. Stop by and ask your questions, then stick around and read your answer. You're just about guaranteed to learn more than you bargained for, without paying a consultant's bill.

Computer Virus Help Desk

http://www.indyweb.net/~cvhd

The Macintosh Utilities (MUT) forum on AOL is one of the best resources for Mac users around. One of the things they do very well is disseminate information about computer viruses. Their link to the Computer Virus Help Desk is one of their nicest features. The site provides visitors with guidance in preventing, detecting, and eradicating computer viruses. One thing to note about this site is that it is heavily Java-dependent. If you aren't using a Java-enabled browser, such as the one that comes with the Windows 95 or Macintosh version of AOL 3.0, you may not have access to all the features of the site.

Design & Publishers Center

http://www.graphic-design.com/

This online center for visual communications includes information and links for anyone involved with graphics, writing, typography, printing, publishing, advertising, signs, displays—in short, for anyone in the design and publishing fields. The site includes Web chat, interviews, and links to online versions of several desktop publishing magazines. It also actively solicits submissions: "Guess what? Talent scouts cruise our Gallery all the time! They're looking for your masterpieces!"

FamilyPC on the Web

http://www.zdnet.com/familypc

This electronic counterpart to the Ziff-Davis print publication is devoted to family computing and features reviews of hardware and software and recommendations of family-friendly places to visit on the Internet. For kids, there are stories, projects, and contests.

Guide to Computer Vendors

http://guide.sbanetweb.com/

From SBA * Consulting, this simple guide provides a searchable and browsable directory to all the major and many of the minor vendors of software and hardware. Plus, there are links to dozens of computer magazines.

Microsoft Windows

http://www.microsoft.com/windows/

No list of computing and software Web sites would be complete without mentioning Microsoft. Running the gamut from press releases and self-promotion to HTML tutorials, informative overviews of ActiveX, and free software downloads (including tons of plug-ins), the Microsoft Web site is so extensive that it may be hard to figure out exactly where to start with it. An excellent spot to begin is right here, with their Windows page. You'll find industry news and links to pages for Microsoft Office, Microsoft BackOffice, and the Microsoft Internet Explorer (now integrated into AOL for Windows). The site has a clean professional look. It loads quickly and looks great, particularly if you are using Internet Explorer, the browser that is not built into the AOL software for Windows and the Mac.

MIDI City

http://www.berkshire.net/~malancar/midicity.htm

A favorite of the PC Music & Sound Forum. MIDI is the Musical Instrument Digital Interface, a cool technology for simulating instruments, and then putting a lot of music into very small files. Chapter 8 has more to say about MIDI. Dedicated to MIDI music by songwriters and developers, MIDI City provides original artists' MIDI songs, compatible with PC sound cards. It includes links to a dozen or so sites where you can find bluegrass, big band, and light jazz tunes sequenced for MIDI. Best of all, if your browser allows it, it will play selections for you while you browse. The site comes in three flavors: frames, no frames, and free-flying frames. The last choice works properly only with Netscape Navigator 3. You can try it with the Microsoft Internet Explorer, but you will end up with several open browser windows.

11

Modems, Modems, Modems

http://www.rosenet.net/~costmo

The Costmo Modem page was created to be a hub where you can find links to just about any modem information that might be available on the Web. It succeeds. Here you can find links to over 50 modem manufacturers, links to other sites about modems, initialization strings for all occasions, and the site-creator's personal experiences with a variety of different modems. The page design is very simple. Virtually all the links are on the same page, so you can either use the handy alphabetic buttons or simply scroll down until you find the modem manufacturer you want.

The Pixel Foundry

http://the-tech.mit.edu/KPT/KPT.html

Formerly known as KPT Online, The Pixel Foundry has a wealth of information for users of Adobe Photoshop. It includes an interactive message forum and tips from Kai Krause, Tom Karlo, and Swanson Technical Support. There are also dozens of background tiles you can use for your Web pages or desktop. The design is clean and uncluttered, allowing you to move from page to page and get the information you want without delay. If you're a Photoshop or Kai's Power Tools user, this page should be one of your Favorite Places.

Print Magazine Online—1995 Regional Design Annual

http://www.printmag.com/

Print is America's leading graphic design magazine, and its online version shows you why. It includes every page of the printed design annual. Winning images are indexed and can be searched by category, designer's name, design firm, art director, client, and region. You can also click through the pages as though you are looking through the paper version of the book, or you can take a guided tour. It's a good thing they're so organized, because there are 2,000 images on this site! This may be one of the best-looking sites on the Web.

RealAudio

http://www.realaudio.com/

If video is the Web's future, then RealAudio is the present. Anyone who has tried to look at a video clip on the Web over a 28.8 kbps connection knows that we have a way to go before the technology is really useful. Sound is another matter. RealAudio has created a quiet revolution. You can get high-quality sound (near CD-quality over a fast connection) from a Web page without having to wait for the file to download. This is the Progressive Networks' home page, and you can either download your free RealAudio player here or purchase an enhanced player or server (the software that allows you to put RealAudio sound clips on your page). The best thing about this Web site is that it contains links to a dozen or so pages with interesting sounds. You can listen to live music at the House of Blues, hear the latest news being reported by ABC, or check National Public Radio's "All Things Considered."

Shareware.com

http://www.shareware.com

Shareware.com is a tremendously popular site for downloading software on the World Wide Web. By dividing the software up into easy-to-use categories (games, Internet, multimedia, etc.) and then writing short, breezy, and informative reviews of each offering, the Clnet folks make it easy for you to find what you want and then decide if you really want it. Like the rest of the Clnet site, the design here is busy, busy, busy. It is filled with advertisements, button bars, tables of contents, and search windows. Still, it loads quickly and is very easy to use. If you haven't seen any of the pages on Clnet's Web site, this is a great place to start. It is also updated regularly, so you will probably want to bookmark it.

Windows Magazine

http://www.winmag.com/

Windows Magazine is for everyone who lives with Windows, from the blackbelt programmer to the clueless user of the latest application, from manager to consumer. At this Web site you'll find the best of the magazine's tips, features, product reviews, and commentary, plus the stuff you get only on the Web (free software, a searchable archive, links to related resources, and plenty of chances to interact with editors and writers).

DIGITAL CITY

Alaska Internet Travel Guide

http://www.alaska-online.com/travel/alaska.htm

If you're planning to travel to Alaska, you'll want to explore this travel guide first. Here you can find statewide information on accommodations, adventures, hunting and fishing, cruises, parks, travel agents, and more. Say you're planning to visit Kodiak or the Kenai Peninsula. No problem—just click the particular region on the imagemap of Alaska to get more detailed information. Look over Alaska Lingo to learn fun terms like "bush pilot" (a pilot of small aircraft providing transportation to isolated Alaskan areas), *cheechako* (a newcomer to Alaska), and "outside" (anywhere outside of Alaska).

Atlanta Traveler

http://www.georgia-traveler.com/

An excellent service for both Atlanta residents and travelers, this Web site offers a broad range of pointers to Atlanta information, including entertainment, professional sports teams, city sites, cultural events, and community services. The transportation section is especially useful and features continually updated maps of real-time traffic and a map of the Atlanta area freeway system, as well as information on public transit, MARTA parking, and route planning. Also, check the Atlanta project section to read about why Atlantans are the first to use the Intelligent Transportation Systems (ITS) to ease the stressed metropolitan transportation system.

Boston Online

http://obi.std.com/NE/boston.html

An impressive and well-organized directory of Boston area community services, organizations, education, entertainment, culture, health care, environment, sports, and much more. While you're browsing the directory, you can learn something about Boston as the capital of Massachusetts, why Boston is called the "Athens of America" and the "Hub of the Universe," a bit about cod, and Roger Williams' recipe for Boston baked beans. Boston lovers won't want to miss Adam Gaffin's Good Guide to Boston English, where you can learn Boston pronunciation, place names, and neighborhood variations, as well as peruse an extensive glossary of vocabulary.

California Highway Conditions

http://www.dot.ca.gov/hq/roadinfo/

Everyone in California is affected by highway conditions; this Web site offers a reliable way of previewing road conditions before you start the car. Here you can get immediate information on all the interstate, state, and U.S. routes (listed by route number), an hourly compilation of all current reports, winter driving conditions, and alternate routes for damaged highways. If you'll be traveling through Nevada, check the data at the bottom of the main page, which is provided by the Nevada Department of Transportation.

11

Chicago

http://chicago.digitalcity.com/

A visually attractive combination of a Web directory and metropolitan magazine for Chicagoland. Here you can find interesting articles on things like spas, Brenda Starr comics, and ballroom dancing. The Go Guide to recreational sports is jam-packed with helpful information on finding a local pickup game of basketball, billiards, or bridge. Similarly, the entertainment section provides calendars, club information, and tons of ideas for going out on the town. If you live in or are planning to visit a suburb of Chicago, check out Digital City's guide to Arlington Heights, Crystal Lake, Evanston, Hoffman Estates, Naperville, and Schaumburg.

Colorado, Arts to Zoo

http://www.artstozoo.org/

"The ultimate source for arts, culture, and science information" in Colorado, from A to Z. The Events, Organizations, Directories, and Resources sections contain a huge listing of arts, dance, music, theater, and other cultural and educational information. If you're interested in staying abreast of the Colorado arts scene, check the news section to read press releases that are posted at least several times a week. Also, you can jump to Star Attractions to find a listing of events during the current month.

Destination: Washington, D.C.

http://www.washingtonpost.com/wp-srv/local/longterm/
tours/guide2.htm

Here's a unique tourist guide to Washington, D.C. provided by WashingtonPost.com. Some interesting virtual tours you can take include the Scandal Tour ("a glimpse of Washington's seamy underbelly"), Black History and Latino Culture Tours (museums, schools, and historical houses), The Smithsonian and the National Mall, the Theater Guide, and the Restaurant Guide. Other fun stuff you can find here includes the Washington Trivia Quiz, a public golf course guide, an outdoor recreational guide, and a music calendar.

Experience New Orleans

http://www.neosoft.com/~bigeasy/acquaint.html

A virtual tour of the city famous for jazz, Mardi Gras, the Orpheus Parade, cemeteries, swamps, the Saints, and Cajun cuisine. You can learn about these and other facets of New Orleans culture and history at this Web site; it also provides a live Netcast from Mardi Gras (as well as a gallery of photographs after the event), authentic Creole and Cajun recipes, a useful shopping guide, and information on New Orleans celebrities such as Harry Connick, Jr. and Anne Rice.

Honolulu's Internet Café

http://www.aloha-cafe.com/

The aesthetically appealing Web site of "the World's First 24-Hour Cybercafé," which is physically located in Honolulu. This Web site is kindly offered in light (text), medium (text and graphics), and heavy (Java, Quicktime, and audio) versions. Here you can read news about both the café and about the Internet. If you're a serious news addict, click Brief to find a well-compiled index to famous columns and newspapers around the United States. Art lovers will want to visit the Gallery to view images of works by local Hawaiian artists.

Houston Entertainment Network

http://www.steppingout.com/culture/maincu.htm

An interesting and useful collection of cultural, entertainment, and community information for the Houston area. In the attractions section, you can find information

11

on such sites as the American Funeral Service Museum, Six Flags Waterworld, the Houston Space Center, and the Beer Can House—and everything in between. Ballet lovers will want to peruse the Houston Ballet page to read about productions like *Swan Lake*, *The Nutcracker*, *Dracula*, and *Don Quixote*.

Las Vegas Leisure Guide

http://www.pcap.com/lasvegas.htm

A complete guide to Las Vegas, one of the world's most popular vacation destinations. In addition to everything you need to plan your vacation—tours, hotels, shows, restaurants, recreation, night life, shopping, transportation, attractions, and maps—you can also find an extensive guide to conventions and business services in the area. The main page offers news about casinos and hotels, which makes it easy to stay abreast of new attractions.

Meet Minneapolis

http://www.minneapolis.org/

Well-organized guide to the "City of Lakes." The Discover Minneapolis section is chock-full of fun and useful information, including "Minne-facts" about business and the economy, medicine, the quality of life, and trivia; original cartoons by Paul Davies in Minnesota Sights; and a message from the Mayor. If you need more information, you can fill out the Tourism Information Request Form to have pamphlets and guides sent to you via the postal service.

Pittsburgh Net

http://www.pittsburgh.net/

The official site of the city of Pittsburgh. Here you can find a variety of useful materials, such as the online Yellow Pages, visitors information, and residential and business relocation information. In addition, this site offers some fun stuff, like a special welcome message from Mayor Tom Murphy and a Quicktime video of Pittsburgh. Visitors will especially appreciate the Special Events Calendar and the Top Ten Reasons for Visiting Pittsburgh.

Seattle P-I Plus

http://www.seattle-pi.com/

The official Web supplement to the printed *Seattle Post-Intelligencer* newspaper. Here you'll find four main sections: Getaways, Neighbors, Golf NW, and Classified. Although there isn't much news at this Web site, these four sections offer some worthwhile local information. In Getaways, for instance, you can find a multitude of materials on outdoors recreation, travel, and the natural environment. In addition, the Neighbors section profiles a different neighborhood or Seattle region once a week.

11

TotalNY

http://www.totalny.com/

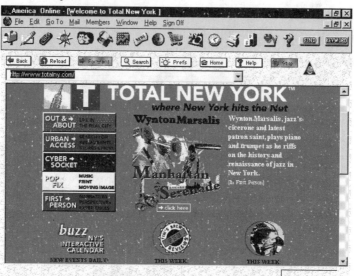

The motto "Where New York hits the Net" is a fairly accurate description of this site. Here you'll find five main sections—Out & About, Urban Access, Cyber Socket, Pop Fix, and First Person—all of which are chock-full of detailed information, reviews, and guides. In Out & About, for example, you can peruse Buzz, the event calendar; NY Essentials, a guide to eating, clubbing, and Web surfing; and NY Solutions, a quick-and-dirty collection of advice for real estate, fashion, and holiday problems and issues.

ENTERTAINMENT

alt.days (newsgroup)

http://www.io.com/~jlc/alt_days/

An alternative version of NBC's *Days of Our Lives,* **alt.days** has been in production since 1993 as a Usenet newsgroup and has been on the Web since 1995. While many of the same characters who appear on the television show also show up here, the plot is independent of the broadcast show. You can keep up with the episodes each week in the newsgroup, or you can check this Web site (where episodes are uploaded biweekly) and read the complete series in the archives. The Web site has additional features such as cast lists and a readers poll.

Café Utne

http://www.utne.com/cafe

The magazine *Utne Reader* is a progressive version of *Reader's Digest*. The Utne Café has taken the concerns and interests of *Utne* readers and created a Web site with over 40 conferences with hundreds of topics. As they say of their site, it is "a place in cyberspace where ideas and community intersect." Although it is free, you must register to use this service, and, because of Utne's concern about the male/female ratio of contributors to their site, men may find themselves waiting a few days.

Celebrities On-Line

http://www.mgal.com/links/celeb.html

Subtitled "Cool Links to Celebrity Sites," Celebrities On-Line delivers the goods. It has over 70 links to specific celebrity sites as well as links to *People* magazine online, the Official Interactive Guide to the Academy Awards, information on autographs, and a TV index offering information on what celebrities are doing on the tube this month. There is one oddity here: among the links to pages for Christian Slater, Sharon Stone, and Madonna is a link to a Web page for jailed Native American activist Leonard Peltier. Here you'll find not just the "manufactured" stars but the people you want to know about.

Centre for the Easily Amused

http://www.amused.com

Your best bet for trivia and time-wasting tips, this site is an exercise in uncomplicated frivolity. The Centre's Short Attention Span Site of the week (SASS) offers truly useless Internet resources ranging from **RubberChicken.com** to the Home Lobotomy Kit to really awful sites. They'd also like to sell you stuff: T-shirts, poly white caps ("not just for bad hair days"), and a CEA mousepad.

Dilbert Zone

http://www5.zdnet.com/yil/comics/dilbert.html

The engineer-as-hero and management-as-obstacle-to-progress. That's *Dilbert* in a nutshell, one of the most popular comic strips in the country, especially among nerds.

11

Read Dilbert at this site daily, but be aware that the strip is delayed a week before making it to the Web. Still, it's worth it, since you can read months of the cartoons at a time. You can read the original Dilbert strips submitted to syndication and see some of Scott Adams' pre-Dilbert attempts here as well. There are also contests, games, and a Dilbert store. On AOL, check out keyword: Dilbert.

The Doonesbury Electronic Town Hall

http://www.doonesbury.com/

News, opinions, real-time chat, and message boards—all with the flip but critical Doonesbury point of view. Curious about how the characters have aged? Check out a Doonesbury strip from 16 years ago. Want your own Zonker T-shirt? You can get that here, too. You'll also get some astute political commentary, a very amusing biweekly poll, and lists of activist organizations.

Graceland

http://www.elvis-presley.com/

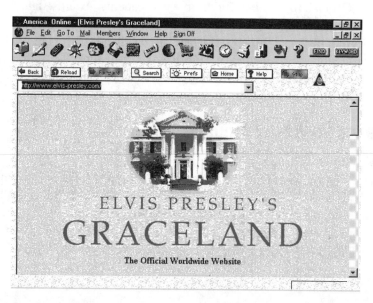

If you're planning a pilgrimage to the estate of the late Elvis Aron Presley, plan your trip here, the official Web page for Graceland that includes ample information on tours and hotels. You will also find a discography and filmography of the King here. Even if you aren't planning to visit Memphis any time soon, there's still a good reason to see this site. It's the home of the Graceland Shopping Mall, which claims to have "the finest selection of Elvis Presley merchandise" anywhere. Finally, a source for the much-sought-after Elvis doll!

Hollywood Online

http://www.hollywood.com/

The, um, blockbuster site devoted to the quintessentially American industry of making movies. They don't leave much out, and you'll find reviews, box office statistics, video catalogs, gossip, multimedia clips from your favorite flicks, and a big source of information about (and samples of) soundtracks. Of course, you'll also find stuff to buy. It's owned by Time Mirror and beautifully complements AOL's version at keyword: Hollywood.

Internet Movie Database

http://www.imdb.com

One thing the Internet is good at is making available simple databases, enabling you to get the specific information you need. Take this site: it's got information about more than 80,000 movies and an even larger number of actors and actresses. Type in, say, *Fearless Vampire Killers*, and you get the plot summary, director, complete cast, some trivia questions, and a chance to rate the movie. For many actors and actresses, you'll get a biography and hyperlinks. You can search by keyword as well as movie name, making this site a superb research resource if you have serious film interests. Other goodies: local cinema schedules (they aim to cover the world, so it's not quite complete yet), info about movie-related mailing lists, a trivia quiz, and "This Day in the Movies." Bring some popcorn.

Mr. Showbiz

http://www.mrshowbiz.com/

Are you a Hollywood junkie? If so, this online magazine, brought to you by Starwave (the same people who produce the popular ESPNet), is for you. Updated daily, Mr. Showbiz brings you entertainment news, film reviews, interviews, biographies, fun polls, contests, a real-time chat area, and more. For a real hoot, try playing in the Plastic Surgery lab, where you can mix and match famous features to create bizarre new celebrities.

Personalized Shakespearean Insults Page

http://kite.preferred.com/insults/

Plug in a name and out comes an insult: "Thou art a knotty-pated beslubbering pignut, Jon!" "Thou art a bat-fowling currish pumpion, Vick!" The erudite way to insult a boss or in-law, more dignified than "I told you so."

rec.arts.tv.soaps.misc (newsgroup)

If you just can't get enough conversation about soap operas, there's a place for you in the Usenet newsgroups. In the **rec.arts.tv.soaps.misc** newsgroup, you can discuss the relationship between Josie and Gary on *Another World* or the machinations of Sami and Kate on *Days of Our Lives*. You'll even find the occasional posting from writers and others close to the shows who give hints about future developments and the background stories of characters. If this isn't enough, you might also want to check **rec.arts.tv.soaps.abc** and **rec.arts.tv.soaps.cbs**.

Scrolling Mystery Theater

http://www.fiction.com/

The Advanced Fiction Workshop explores the literary, creative facets of network-centric computing. Its first project is the launch of the Scrolling Mystery Theater, which brings groundbreaking detective fiction and thrillers to the World Wide Web. SMT's first production, "The Moving Face," written by the site's Webmaster Robert Richardson, premiered on February 20, 1996, and can be read here in its entirety.

The Squat

http://www.thesquat.com

The Squat is one of the world's first online comedy shows. It began as a satire of The Spot (a Web site that created a fictional situation similar to MTV's *Real World*) but has taken on a life of its own. Instead of a young, attractive, upwardly mobile group living together in a beach house, you have homely, incredibly stupid people living together in a trailer. Its clever animations and art are worth the price of admission (free, by the way), but it is the continuing comedic adventure that will keep you coming back. So pick up some Whup A** beer and join Earl, Woody, Val, Cleitus, and Elvis in their trailer park home.

Worldwide Internet Live Music Archive (WILMA)

http://wilma.com/

WILMA includes a database of concert schedules for over 3,000 musical performers. You can search for concerts by artist, map location, city, or venue. There are also sound clips, music reviews, and articles about bands, singers, and songwriters. You can join in the conversation in their musical chat room, or join the Intergalactic Freak Club to win free prizes. WILMA also has a mailing list that can be joined from here.

GAMES

Avalon

http://www.avalon.co.uk/

A beautifully designed role-playing game with a faraway, mythological feel. At this Web site you actually engage in and play the game, but the site also contains everything you need to get started and maintain the game's logical structure. The Introduction is a step-by-step tutorial that teaches you about creating a character, getting help, the geography of Avalon, cityports and guilds, and communicating with other players.

The Big List of Puzzle and Riddle Pages

http://huizen.dds.nl/~mahulsma/biglist.htm

A huge and well-organized compilation of puzzle and riddle pages on the Web. If you're a regular here, you can simply check the front cover page of this site to find new listings. Many of the listings are rated, and they all have reviews. For more lists, check Archives to find an index of **rec.puzzles** archives in North America, Europe, and Asia. If you like Escher, you'll find a handy list of optical-illusion sites.

Bridge on the Web

http://www.cs.vu.nl/~sater/bridge/bridge-on-the-web.html

Mecca for bridge aficionados. This is a simple, straightforward site where you can find just about anything pertaining to the popular card game. For fans, there's information about recent and upcoming tournaments all over the world, and, for players, there are laws and rules. For enthusiasts, there are bridge-related companies, periodicals, and even arguments for making bridge a new Olympic sport. There are several sections devoted to electronic bridge resources, such as bridge software, live bridge games online, FTP sites, Usenet newsgroups, and indexes of other bridge Web pages.

Chess Space

http://www.redweb.com/chess/

An award-winning resource for chess enthusiasts. Chess Space offers tons of links to chess sites on the Internet—and these links are impeccably organized, so you can easily find what you're looking for. Categories include Internet Archives, Audio Sites, Commercial Sites, Databases, E-mail Chess Games, and anything else you might want. Or you could skip all that and go directly to BEST, where you can find the most valuable and well-designed chess sites.

Computer Gaming World

http://www.zdnet.com/gaming/

If you enjoy playing games on your computer—any type of game—you've come to the right place. This is an excellent resource for not just staying abreast of the computer gaming industry, but for getting insider information on good gaming computers, peripherals, and networking connectivity. Here you can find news and features; reviews; sneak previews; strategies, tips, and cheats; worthy opponents; and interactive discussions on action, adventure, role-playing, simulation, space, sports, strategy, war, and online games, as well as discussions on classics and puzzles.

CyberLink Web Games

http://www.cyber-link.net/games.htm

Simple, straightforward index of interactive, multimedia Web-based games. Here you can find everything from puzzles and board games to casino gambling and

11

horror-genre games. If you are drawn to the bizarre, check out Find-the-Spam and Piercing Mildred. Otherwise, the "normal" games are well represented: Tetris-style motion puzzles, racing games, crosswords, trivia and matching games, virtual construction sets, Yahtzee, Mastermind, Spirograph, scavenger hunts, and even the Sony PlayStation Web Game.

Dream League

http://www.dreamleague.com/

The Dream League is the original promoter of fantasy sports in the United Kingdom and Europe, as well as throughout the world. This is one of the best sources for easy Dream Team selection. Here you can find information on Gaelic Football, Cycling, Cricket, Golf, Tennis, and Motor Racing Dream Leagues, as well as daily updates during live events. The Football (*soccer*, in the U.S.) League is available on World Soccernet. Check out the competition results for the European Champions League and the U.K. Snooker Championships.

duJour

http://www.dujour.com/

New games, puzzles, and contests every day. Here you can play MondoTrivia, The Labyrinth (a maddening multidimensional maze), Jacques du Jour (casino card games), WordAngst (lexicon games), BigByte (brain twisters), and play the Online Sphinx in Riddle du Jour,. If you win a game, your name will be prominently displayed on the front page of duJour, and you may win some cool prizes. Just for the heck of it, check out Ce Jour to learn what is so special about today's date in history, including birthdays, death anniversaries, significant events, and holidays from around the world.

Games Domain

http://www.gamesdomain.com/

An internationally mirrored meta-index of gaming resources on the Net where you can download scores of free games for all personal computer platforms and check out hundreds of demos and previews. You can also run a sophisticated search for specific game information which covers a wide range of resources, such as commercial sites, game hints and cheats, and online gaming help. Families will be pleased with the Kids Area, where there's kid-appropriate software, contests, desktop decorations, and FAQs.

11

GameSpot

http://www.gamespot.com/

Home to a mountain of computer games of every stripe—action, adventure, role-playing, sports, simulation, and strategy. Each page provides in-depth review and test results according to game play, graphics, sound, learning curve, and difficulty. Shopping for a 14-year-old or closet gamer? Check out the Game Spot Top 10—or jump directly to GameSpot's Product Index to find an extensive alphabetized list of computer games.

House of Cards

http://www.sky.net/~rrasa/hoc.html

A central hub of card game information, with a focus on the different types of solitaire card games. Here you can find downloads and support for shareware solitaire games, including Solitaire Suite, Simple Pleasures, Four Seasons, FoxFire 13, Pyramid Deluxe, Poker Squares, and Chinese Solitaire. If you enjoy playing cards with others, this site is also a good resource for a variety of multiplayer card games. If you need more information, check the index of links to information on card game online rulebooks, books, newsgroups, e-mail lists, archives, and other shareware card games.

The Internet Role Playing Society

http://feeds.engr.ucf.edu/irps/

Official Web site of the Internet Role Playing Society (IRPS), a club "dedicated to the advancement of role-playing over the Internet." Here you can register to become a club member; it's free. Once you are a member, you may access a large user database of other players and subscribe to a monthly newsletter. In addition, you can conduct club business, read about the IRPS, engage in Internet-based role-playing games, learn about upcoming conventions and tournaments, and find other resources such as e-mail lists and organizations.

The MUD Resource Collection

http://www.clock.org/muds/

Extensive index of Multi-User Dungeon (MUD)-related informational and gaming links. Both MUD users and researchers who study the communications and sociology of MUDs will find many useful resources here. For general information, jump right to the FAQs page to find a huge list of FAQs and Usenet newsgroups. Academic students and teachers may want to explore Research-Oriented Links first. Other resources you can find here include MUDlists and MudWHO, Web interfaces to games, FTP Archives, and lists of Multi-User Shared Hallucinations (MUSHes).

POKERwwwORLD

http://pokerwwworld.com/

There are many poker informational and gaming resources here, although the Web page interface is a bit off-putting with its avant-garde design. Once you start roaming the site, though, you'll find an impressive compilation of links to poker-related newsgroups, rulebooks, and Poker IRC Web sites. Serious poker enthusiasts won't want to skip Razzo's Poker Archive, where they can uncover images and biographies of famous players, reference materials, and descriptions of poker events. And they'll appreciate the rule books provided for the varieties of poker.

Video Game Yellow Pages:
Your Guide to Computer and Video Games

http://www.gamepen.com/yellowpages/

Like the name says, this is a comprehensive reference to computer and video gaming sites on the Internet. It's your guide to electronic gaming mailing lists, online

11

archives, publications, and documentation. There are specific sections for action, adventure, flight simulation, strategy, role-playing, and sports games. In addition, you can ponder indexes for cheats and hints, demos and downloads, multiplayer online and network games, fan sites, patches and fixes, commercial sites, and much more.

HEALTH & FITNESS

Achoo Online Healthcare Services

http://www.achoo.com

It's hard to dislike or overlook a site named Achoo, especially since *Consumer Reports* (keyword: Consumer) recently singled it out as one of the most useful Internet resources for people who need reliable medical information. Achoo aims to be the comprehensive directory of health-related resources, included 8,000 Web sites and hundreds of newsgroups, all helpfully arranged for both browsing and searching. The site is a service to the Internet from a company that (among other things) designs Web sites for companies and organizations in the healthcare sector.

American Cancer Society

http://www.cancer.org/

An award-winning Web site with information and support for medical professionals, cancer patients, and their families. You'll find information about ACS programs, events, offices, and meetings, and you'll find a large set of links to the growing number of Net cancer resources. You can also access news on cancer research and cancer prevention. This is also a great place to learn how you can donate money or time to this cause and to find out exactly how your contribution helps.

American Diabetes Association

http://www.diabetes.org/

Start here for information on both diabetes and the American Diabetes Association itself. It's also a good source of health-conscious recipes, with a new offering each day and a review of the past week's recipes. A self-test for diabetes is offered as a way of learning more about the disease. A state-by-state listing helps you find the nearest ADA office, or you can search for specific medical information.

America's Housecall Network

http://www.housecall.com/

Some sites bury their treasure. On the Housecall Network, the treasure is the invaluable drug reference from U.S. Pharmacopeia, based on USP's consumer pamphlets, which contains reliable information about prescription drugs: warnings, usage advice, and the like. (In the Health Information section, click Medications.) The American Academy of Family Physicians also makes its pamphlets available, with information on dozens of common ailments such as nosebleeds and ulcers. (The link is in the Dictionary section of Health Information.) Two dozen bulletin boards let you ask questions and perhaps get answers via the Web.

Blindness Resource Center

http://www.nyise.org/access.htm

A Web site dedicated to making the Net accessible for the sight-impaired, it's available, naturally, in a large-print format. Tools and information for helping low-vision users to access the Web are readily available, along with discussions of considerate design. Learn about "talking" programs for the visually impaired and how blind people use computers. Other fascinating links offer information about organizations serving the visually impaired and an archive of the mailing list Blind-L, which discusses computer use by and for the blind.

CNN Interactive Health

http://www.cnn.com/HEALTH/

CNN offers top health-related stories in a format that allows you to either scan headlines or plunge in for more depth. Prominent parts of the site promote CNN shows such as *Parenting Today* and *Your Health*. This is a great way to check the programming schedule for future shows that might be of interest to you and to check out transcripts of shows you may have missed or in which you have a particular interest. Direct access to the rest of CNN Interactive makes for a great way to get your minimum daily information requirement.

HospitalWeb

http://neuro-www.mgh.harvard.edu/hospitalWeb.nclk

Created and maintained by the department of Neurology at Massachusetts General Hospital, HospitalWeb is a small but growing list of hospitals on the Web, working

11

towards offering a way for patients, medical researchers, and physicians to get information on any hospital in the world. Geographically arranged information makes finding your hospital Web site easier. HospitalWeb offers an "Interesting Medical Site" of the week, medical school listings, and links to the sites of healthcare businesses.

Interactive Food Finder

http://www.olen.com/food/

Based on the book *Fast Food Facts* by the Minnesota Attorney General's Office, the Interactive Food Finder aims to break you of the fast-food habit. In a special form, you select a fast-food restaurant, type in your favorite dinner, and click Fire Up the Deep Fryer. You'll find out, if you can bear the truth, the number of calories and amount of fat, sodium, and cholesterol in your favorite fast foods. Not for the timid or those who won't pass up the fries.

KidsHealth

http://kidshealth.org/

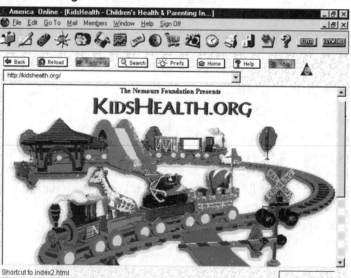

The medical experts at the Nemour's Children's Clinic at the duPont Hospital for Children bring you KidsHealth.Org. This site is devoted to the health of children and teens and features information on growth, food and fitness, childhood infections, immunizations, and more. The interests of parents and professionals are nicely served. The Nemours Foundation also includes some fun for kids, with games, Shockwave animations, and cool activities. One area even covers kid's health questions, such as, "What makes you sneeze?" Big fun!

MedicineNet

http://www.medicinenet.com/

A free medical resource, presenting news and information on medical and health issues for the consumer. Included in the useful content in this site is a medical dictionary, pharmacy information, an alphabetical list of diseases and treatments, and *a state-by-state listing of 24-hour poison control centers*—a particularly valuable resource for families with small children. Here's a tip: print out a hard copy of your state's centers and keep it by your phone.

Medscape

http://www.medscape.com/

This site, one of the few health-related sites recommended by *Consumer Reports*, features full-text articles from leading medical journals, plus free searchable access to both Medline and the National Library of Medicine's AIDSLINE. Medscape caters to the needs of patients as well as physicians, even offering Continuing Medical Education credit. Click to subscribe to Medscape's mailing list, MedPulse. The simple, low-graphic tabbed interface makes it easy to get around.

Mental Health Net

http://www.cmhc.com/

Mental Health Net's award-winning site offers links to over 4,200 individual resources covering information on disorders such as depression, anxiety, panic attacks, chronic fatigue syndrome, and substance abuse. Linger in the "Reading Room," browse resources for professionals and administrators, and spend some time with the self-help resources. These areas offer links to magazines, discussion forums, polls, news, a Managed Care glossary, and a Clinician's Yellow Pages.

Oncolink

http://cancer.med.upenn.edu/

Oncolink is the University of Pennsylvania's award-winning Cancer Center resource Web site. There is a search facility available, but many topics of immediate interest are available at a glance. Information on cancer can be found via the site's Disease Oriented

Menus and FAQs. Issues of concern to patients and their families, such as psychosocial support and financing, are conveniently available. Links such as their Conferences and Meetings, Clinical Trials, and Journals will attract the medical professional.

Special Education Resources on the Internet

http://www.hood.edu/seri/serihome.htm

This is a massive directory whose resources cover more than special education. The topics are of interest to any parent or professional concerned about children whose educational needs aren't met by the existing system. The topics covered include learning disabilities, attention deficit disorder, autism, assistive technologies, and legal resources.

Women's Health Resources

http://sunsite.unc.edu/cheryb/women/resource/health-int.html

A clearinghouse of information about women's health concerns relating to breast cancer, pregnancy, and HIV. Also available are facts on homeopathy, caffeine, and computer-related repetitive strain injuries and their effects on women. More general guides to women's health resources can be found here, as well as a link to a women's health Gopher and several Web publications addressing these concerns.

THE HUB

AFU and Urban Legends Archive

http://www.urbanlegends.com/

Fun site to learn about a wide variety of urban legends as well as what an "urban legend" is. Here you can read the **alt.folklore.urban** FAQ and a few defining features of an urban legend: It "appears mysteriously and spreads spontaneously in varying forms," "contains elements of humor or horror," "makes good storytelling," and "does not have to be false." Among the list of categories, you'll find urban legends about animals, celebrities, drugs, food, language, politics, and religion; each legend page contains a lot of source material.

AIDS Research Information Center

http://www.critpath.org/aric/

Based in Baltimore, the AIDS Research Information Center (ARIC) aims to help people with AIDS (and those close to them) sort out the dizzying array of medical terms and data into understandable, medically accurate information. ARIC's Web site provides a comprehensive glossary of AIDS-specific terms, such as "antiretroviral," "prophylaxis," "maintenance therapy," "thrush," and "viral load." In addition, here you can read "The DIRT [Direct Information on Research and Treatment] (on AIDS)," a quarterly newsletter.

Amnesty International On-line

http://www.amnesty.org/

The official site for Amnesty International (AI), a renowned organization devoted to promoting awareness of human rights violations around the globe and taking action to stop them. To read news alerts and country political profiles, go directly to Stop Press. The AI Library is an excellent compilation of materials, including annual and campaign reports, an index of publications (by country and region), and 1994-1997 country reports (by year and continent). If you want to learn more about the organization and mission of AI, click About AI to read a FAQ on AI's stance on the death penalty, 15 Steps to Protect Women's Human Rights, and the 12-Point Program for the Prevention of Torture.

Archive X, Paranormal Phenomena (WWW Virtual Library)

http://www.crown.net/X/

Compelling site in which you can explore the real X Files—that is, personal and news stories of paranormal phenomena. Here you'll find a wide range of fascinating tales of ghostly encounters and hauntings, angels, channeling, near-death experiences, and UFO sightings. There are over two hundred ghost stories alone. If you find yourself addicted to reading these stories, you can submit your e-mail address to the convenient service that automatically notifies you of Web site updates.

Center for Democracy and Technology

http://www.cdt.org/

In the aftermath of the telecommunications and Internet explosion, it's important that civil liberties are protected online as well as offline. The Center for Democracy and Technology is an organization committed to this cause. Under Headlines (at the top of the main Web page), you can read a number of continually updated news alerts on House and Senate hearings, FCC actions, FBI surveillance, and Supreme Court decisions. You can also browse Issues to jump to more in-depth reading material on Net censorship, cryptography policies, electronic privacy, Congress' impact on the Net, international cyberspace relations, and public digital access.

11

David Bowie: The Official Web Site

http://www.davidbowie.com/

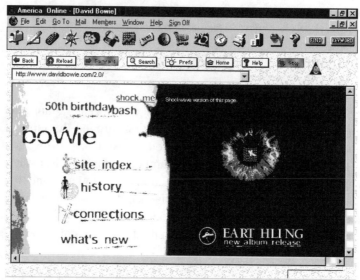

A visually enticing, multimedia-rich guide to this world-renowned and unique artist. Here you can find a gallery of Bowie's 50th Birthday Bash, including photographs, video from the Madison Square Garden concert, and a transcript of his America Online chat session. Another cool feature is the "EARTHLING" section, which includes RealAudio track samples and an interview. If you're a serious David Bowie fan, you'll appreciate the History section, complete with a biography, a discography, the Best of Bowie page, "OUTSIDE" album data, and song lyrics.

The GIG

http://www.thegig.com/

The Global Internet Gathering (GIG) is where the worlds of music and Internet technology meet. For a solid week, musicians, technicians, photographers, and journalists met online and in real life to form "the world's largest music festival." At this Web site, you can review the event and get information on the ongoing GIG. Check out Going GIGging, for instance, to access schedules, sponsors, and press releases. Musicians can submit audio samples to the Interactive Gallery. Other sections you won't want to miss include Digital Club Network (an index of GIG venues everywhere), The Bands (data on over 600 bands), and Show Reviews & Photo Pass (editorial features and high-quality graphics).

MoJo Wire: Mother Jones Interactive

http://motherjones.com/

Here's a content-rich and exciting complement to the print edition of *Mother Jones* magazine where you can find a bunch of articles, tools, and goodies for those on the left side of the political fence. For example, check out MoJo 400, a searchable database of America's biggest political donors and their recipients. In addition, Hellraiser offers a variety of interesting features: HOT!media (reviews and profiles of good and bad films, television, books, music, and Web resources), Sideshow (illuminating and sometimes amusing analyses of pop culture, politicians, and big corporations), and Cartoon Alley (original comics by Mr. Fish and Callahan).

News of the Weird Archives

http://www.nine.org/notw/archive.html

As you might guess from the title, here you can find a large collection of extraordinary, amusing, and downright bizarre news stories. These stories—about news headliners, business, schemes and scams, politics, and even undignified deaths—are gleaned from a collection of Chuck Shepherd's News of the Weird articles. The index page lists the archives by month, and you can peruse over a year's worth of stories, all of which are displayed in a straightforward text format.

Poet's Corner

http://www.lexmark.com/data/poem/poem.html

A huge, organized collection of over 1,700 poems written by over 300 poets. Here you can run a Boolean search of the poetry database, browse the alphabetical index of poets, or view the sampler of outstanding poetry. If you are looking for other poetry resources, try the Elsewhere section to find a list of links to events, magazines and journals, contests, collections, and other types of resources—or jump to the bibliography page to view a neatly compiled list of hardcopy poetry books and anthologies.

Safer Sex Page

http://www.safersex.org/

A very important page that explains a range of information along the safer-to-riskier sexual activity spectrum. Some materials you can find here include Safer Sex, AIDS Proofing Your Kids, Sex Myths, and How to Talk with a Partner About Smart Sex—all of which are written in a straightforward, down-to-earth, and sex-positive way. In addition, you can find information on women and safer sex, condoms, birth control, and HIV and AIDS. If you need more information, check out the Multimedia Gallery, the archive of Safer Sex newsletters, and research data and resources for counselors.

Sierra On-line

http://www.sierra.com/

Sierra Entertainment produces hot software, including many game and multimedia titles. Here you can get information on Sierra software products, technical support, and hardware devices (like the 3D video card). Sierra fans will appreciate the Free Stuff section, where you can download PC and Macintosh demos, the Johnny Castaway and Sierra Diving Adventure screensavers for Windows, Internet games, sheet music, game utilities, hints, recipes, audio files, computer wallpaper, Windows desktop theme packs, and more.

Surflink.com

http://www.surflink.com/

Surfing this Web site is possibly the second best thing to surfing the ocean waves. Here you can find a number of Surf Cams—cameras taking continually uploading pictures of the California Pacific waves at Cardiff, Huntington Pier, Malibu, and Manhattan Beach. Each Surf Cam page displays data on surf height, air and water temperatures, high and low tide times, and wind. In addition, you can explore Just Surf to find articles and interviews, and the Gallery to view photographs of Kelly Slater, Shane Beschen, Long Boarding, and other surfers.

Swank-O-Rama Cocktail Revolution Page

http://www.cyborganic.com/People/jpmckay/

If you're too tired to go out to a hip cocktail lounge at night, stop by this page for the cyberspace equivalent of the experience. You can start by enjoying a virtual

11

mixed drink in the cocktails section; here you'll find recipes and reviews of various drinks and serving manners. Similarly, the Fabulous Lounge Sound section offers interesting reading material on such famous lounge musicians as Frank Sinatra, Sergio Mendes & Brasil 66, and Tony Bennett. Lounge lizards will also appreciate the style and dance sections.

Zipper: Gain a Voice in Washington

http://www.voxpop.org/zipper/

A handy tool to keep on your permanent Web page bookmarks list. You simply type your five-digit ZIP code into a form, and you can view all the contact information for your Representatives and Senators, including their e-mail addresses. If you're really in the mood to take some political action, check out Netgrams, another easy-to-use system for sending a message to your Representative, Senators, the President, and members of a variety of Congressional committees.

INTERNATIONAL

Afghan Cultural Info Center

http://www.gl.umbc.edu/~hqurba1/Afghanistan.html

Excellent resource on Afghanistan—its culture, religion, and history. Some unique features of this site include an index of Islamic resources for Afghans and information on other Muslim countries; downloadable movies of an animated Afghan flag, civil war in Tajikistan, and Tajikistan Muslims at prayer; and audio files of contemporary popular Afghan music. In addition, here you can find the *Jantari* (Afghan calendar), and traditional recipes.

Africa Online

http://www.africaonline.com/

A visually appealing and content-rich guide to Africa. Here you can read continually updated news from Kenya, Uganda, and Tanzania. One particularly interesting feature here is Griots Talk. A *griot* is a storyteller in traditional West African culture; Griots Talk continues this tradition by providing information on African films, writing, and other media through cyberspace. Young Web surfers will enjoy exploring the Kids Only section, where you can read *Rainbow Magazine,* a Kenyan magazine for children; play interactive games and decode messages; learn about the various languages in Africa (over one thousand!); and meet African students.

Argentina!

http://www.middlebury.edu/~leparc/htm/argent2.htm

A collection of interesting and useful information about Argentina, all of which is written in English. Here you can find a compilation of encyclopedic articles on Argentine government, economy, transportation, communications, and other

11

categories of country facts. Check out the Culture section to learn about *Yerba Mate,* a South American tea-like beverage; *Los Gauchos,* Argentine people of mixed ethnic backgrounds; *Lunfardo,* Argentine slang; *Tango,* the most well-known Argentine dance; cuisine; and sports. You also won't want to miss the Geography page, which includes a map, photographs, and data on cities and regions, as well as the People section, which has information on Jorge Luis Borges, Evita Peron, and the Argentine Soccer Team, among others.

The Bahamas

http://microstate.com/bahamas

Straightforward, easy-to-use index to an information database on The Bahamas, "the country of islands." If you are traveling to The Bahamas soon, this is an excellent resource to use for quick facts about the country, pictures, cultural information, maps and travel information, and important telephone numbers. Other data you can find here includes the local time, a historical timeline, educational information, Bahamian folklore and myths, facts about the government, business and industry information, a list of holidays, and a bibliography.

The Brasil Page

http://charlotte.acns.nwu.edu/rio/brasil.html

Central hub of Brasilian information on the Internet. The Web Index is an organized list of pointers to sites pertaining to Brasilian business, culture, education, government, media, sports, and tourism. Each pointer has a one-line description and is marked with a "Portuguese-only site" or "exceptional site" symbol when appropriate. The coolest feature of this site is the Great Brasil Web Tour, which takes you on an automatically running, multimedia virtual tour of a variety of Brasilian culture, music, cuisine, and much more.

Discover Turkey

http://www.turkishnews.com/DiscoverTurkey/

One of the best Web resources for Turkey. Read the introduction on the front page to get a brief history of this globally significant region. In addition to standard reference material (society and culture, business and economics, tourism and travel, geography, sports, etc.), here you can find entire sections devoted to Turkish poetry, carpets, and Turkish/Cyprus unrest. Or you can peruse the Anatolia page to read about ancient Anatolia, the Hittites, the Byzantine Empire, the Seljuks, the Ottoman Empire, and finally, Turkey.

J-Links Meta-Index (Japan)

http://www.islandtel.com/j-links.html

A true meta-index of pointers to information on Japan and Japanese culture. For your convenience, each resource is accompanied by a symbol denoting text in English, Japanese, or both. A sampling of what you'll find here includes the Nihongo Yellow Pages, Internet Service Providers in Japan, Colleges of Technology in Japan, Anime (Japanese animation) and cartoons, ramen links, Furyu's Web Guide to Budo Sites, sumo links, The Anti-Japanophile Japan Page, and The Unofficial Shizuoka Home Page.

Madagasikara (Madagascar)

http://www.cable.com/madagas/madagas.htm

Central Web site of Madagascar information for the Malagasy community. Besides typical reference material, such as government, politics, and travel data, here you can find an interesting section on academic studies conducted in and about Madagascar as well as a page of Malagasy music. A very fun resource here is the section devoted entirely to lemurs, the most talked-about animal from Madagascar; from here you can explore galleries of photographs and lemur data.

New Zealand

http://nz.com/NZ/

Interactive tour guide to New Zealand. Here you can peruse the Aotearoa Guidebook to find recent New Zealand news stories, an automatic virtual tour, an illustrated gallery, travel and tourist information, and relocation information (immigration, job, and housing data). Or you can go directly to WebNZ: New Zealand Business on the Net to jump to commerce information on gold, platinum, and real estate. To meet other New Zealand travelers or residents, check out the Akiko Meeting Room, KiwiChat (a threaded discussion BBS), and real-time chat forum.

Peru

http://www.latinworld.com/countries/peru/

Latin World's guide to Peru. Some information is provided in English, some is in Spanish, and some in both languages; each pointer in the guide is denoted with the

11

language of the text. In this guide, you can find general information (in Spanish), business data (companies, exporters, organizations, products, and services), cultural information (art, magazines, music, and traditions), economy, education, politics, news, sports, and travel. The front page displays a beautiful photograph of Machu Picchu.

Portugal Home Page

http://s700.uminho.pt/homepage-pt.html

Everything you want to know about Portugal can be found through this Web site. Most of the information is provided in both English and Portuguese; check out the running marquee exclusively in Portuguese at the top of the front page. Immediately underneath the marquee is a large clickable imagemap of Portugal, from which you can learn more about specific cities and regions, including Braga, Porto, Aveiro, Coimbra, Lisboa, and Faro. If you need more information, peruse the indexes to general and cultural information about Portugal.

The Tonga Page

http://user.cs.tu-berlin.de/~minibbjd/tonga/

A compilation of materials on the Kingdom of Tonga, a group of islands in the South Pacific. Some unique features here include texts on King Taufa'ahau Tupou (the King of Tonga), the Royal Family, human rights in Tonga, an article about Pacific Islands Independence, and Tonga in the newspapers. In addition, you can find other such useful data as maps of Tonga and Polynesia, an excerpt from the 1994 *CIA World Factbook* about Tonga, a bibliography, and a list of Internet resources.

Ukraine FAQ Plus

http://www.std.com/sabre/UKRAINE.html

Excellent reference to educational, financial, political, and other types of information about the Ukraine. Here you can find everything you've always wanted to know about this region, including business and commerce, culture, economics, history, language, law, and more. Some of the most useful and interesting features here include maps, entries from the Encyclopedia of Ukraine, information on the Ukrainian Diaspora, the Directory of Business Contacts, the Country Marketing Plan for Ukraine, and an exclusive preview from *The Ukrainian Weekly*.

Virtual Tour of Israel

http://dapsas.weizmann.ac.il/bcd/bcd_parent/tour/tour.html

Just as the title describes, this site is a virtual tour of this unique Middle Eastern country. Here you can follow the guide through Galilee (Western, Upper, and the Sea), Mount Carmel, the Negev desert, Golan, Tel Aviv, the Sharon Valley, Jerusalem, the Coastal Plain, and the Dead Sea. Each section offers color photographs, data, and often a sensitive map. You can also learn a lot of general and historical information about Israel just by reading the introduction page.

Welcome to Mexico!

http://mexico-travel.com/mex_eng.html

Make this your first stop on the Internet before traveling to Mexico. Here you can find a searchable compendium of resources and information geared towards the tourist looking for a high-quality vacation. If you need travel ideas, you can explore the Showcase to find content-rich brochures on beach destinations, archaeological zones, copper canyons, and colonial treasures, all provided by the Ministry of Tourism of Mexico. Other information you can find here includes travel tips, fiestas and events, Mexico states, and much more.

INTERNET CONNECTION

Beginner's Guide to HTML

http://www.ncsa.uiuc.edu/General/Internet/WWW/HTMLPrimer.html

This is the premiere source for learning HTML. Although the presentation is simple and straightforward, this guide is chock-full of material—in fact, it contains everything you need to get started making your own Web pages. Here you can learn what HTML is; what the differences are between head, title, and body tags; when it's appropriate to use headings and preformatted text; how to link and arrange graphics; how to create a table, and much more. Consult this site while you're making *your* site; you may not need a book!

Electronic Frontier Foundation

http://www.eff.org/

This is the home page of the Electronic Frontier Foundation (EFF), an organization famous for championing Internet-related civil rights and advocating a global cyber-community. In the EFF library, you can find a huge collection of online civil liberties material. In addition, you can stay abreast of new civil rights issues by checking the EFF Alerts regularly. Another way to learn about your rights online is to participate in EFF's "Know Your CyberRights Sweepstakes."

Gamelan

http://www.gamelan.com/

The Web's premiere Java directory, this site sports a nicely organized collection of thousands of useful and fun Java applets for entertainment, business, and development purposes. There is even a category for related technologies, such as ActiveX, JavaScript, VRML, and Castanet Channels. Java enthusiasts will appreciate EarthWeb Direct, a supply of professional development tools, class libraries, and applets, as well as EarthWeb Chat, a live forum for meeting other developers and users. Be sure to check out Special Features to find Our Favorite Games, Java Jolt with BackWeb, Gamelan Staff Picks, and other goodies.

HotWired

http://www.hotwired.com/

One of the first and most famous e-zines, HotWired is exemplary of the best digital publishing on the Internet. This home page is now the center of the HotWired Network. If you want to browse the contents, you must register for free membership to the HotWired Community. Once you are a member, you can explore the gamut of HotWired content, including Dream Jobs (opportunities, especially in multimedia), Netizen (Internet-related politics), Cocktail (cultural events and information), Ask Dr. Weil (health alerts), and The Rough Guide (virtual travel guide), as well as subscribe to a number of e-mail news services and participate in live forums.

HTML Bad Style Guide

http://www.earth.com/bad-style/

There are plenty of HTML how-to guides available on the Web. In contrast, this is a guide to what you should *avoid* when designing your Web pages. Here you can learn to avoid sloppy and ambiguous HTML coding, keep your page design consistent, and create Web sites that are readable and look good on any platform and in any browser. The author of this guide may seem to be a bit obsessive about proper HTML code, but if you follow the instructions, you're guaranteed to produce clean, inoffensive Web pages.

Internet Index

http://www.openmarket.com/intindex/

How many Brazilian orphans were available for adoption over the Internet in October 1996? How many copies of Mosaic were downloaded per day from NCSA in 1994? You can find answers to all kinds of obscure questions here. Published several times a year since 1993, the Internet Index provides a "collection of facts and statistics about the Internet and related activities." Win Treese, the editor, painstakingly organizes these factoids into bite-size statements. These trivia questions and answers convey something of the Internet's astonishing scope and growth.

Internet Service Providers

http://thelist.iworld.com/

Now that AOL offers the "bring your own access" plan, you can access the service using the plain-vanilla access offered by an Internet Service Provider (ISP). This iWORLD service from Meckler provides an updated directory of several thousand ISPs. Here you can search for an ISP by commercial name or domain name, and you can browse the list by country, state, or area code. International users can check the World Wide Listing and browse by country or country code.

Internet Society

http://www.isoc.org/

The official Web site of the Internet Society, an organization that works to ensure the viability and scalability (growth) of global networking and to promote networking in developing countries. Go directly to Information Services to find Internet-related conferences and forums, *The ISOC Forum* (the Internet Society's newsletter) archives, press releases, a global connectivity map and table, articles on the history of the Internet, and international Internet news. In the Papers and Presentations section you can find a statement on cryptographic technology, Vinton G. Cerf's "Truth and the Internet," and the Internet Code of Conduct.

Internet Tools

http://www.december.com/net/tools/

A must-visit (and must-frequent) site for Internet developers. Here you can find abundant information about tools for network information retrieval (NIR), computer-mediated interaction (CMI), and computer-mediated communication (CMC). Learn the nitty-gritty of "ping"; tools such as Archie, FTP, and Telnet; interfaces such as Netscape; and much more. This material can be displayed in three views, each providing different amounts of detail.

JavaScript Authoring Guide

http://home.netscape.com/eng/mozilla/Gold/handbook/javascript/

What is JavaScript, how does it differ from Java, and how might you use it? The answers begin here, at the official Netscape guide to creating your own JavaScript code. If you are ready to begin scripting, just follow the guide. Start with JavaScript Basics to learn Netscape Navigator scripting, objects, and using windows and frames. Then, explore Language Concepts to learn about values, expressions, operators, objects, and functions. For additional help, the Reference section provides information on methods, properties, event handlers, statements, reserved words, color values, and more.

11

Net-happenings

http://www.mid.net/NET/

(also available as a newsgroup at **comp.internet.net-happenings**)

Every day's a feast on the Internet, and here's your menu. Moderated by Gleason Sackman, this is an announcement service in which you can read recent postings about new Internet resources. It's one of the best ways to stay informed about new Web and Net resources. For your convenience, each message is categorized to indicate the type of resource being announced: CONF (conferences and event calendars), EMAG (electronic magazine, or e-zine), K12 (educational), LISTS (mailing lists), MISC (miscellaneous), NETLINK (list of Web pointers to similar resources), NEWSLTR (online periodicals), RESOURC (useful resources on the Net), and SOFT (software). Together with Netscout (a mailing list mentioned in Chapter 4), this resource will keep you apprised of the best serious new content on the Internet.

TUCOWS: The Ultimate Collection of Winsock Software

http://www.tucows.com/

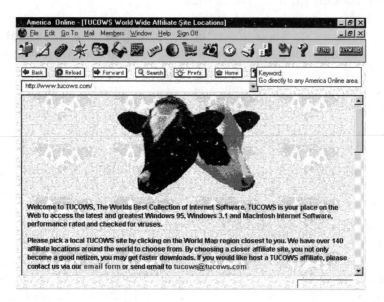

A must-visit for all personal computer users. Here you can find gigabytes of Internet-related shareware for Windows 95, NT, and 3.x platforms, as well as for the Macintosh. In fact, this site contains so much and is so internationally popular that it is mirrored all over the world and throughout the U.S. TUCOWS contains software for Web page editors, network phones, Internet connection adapters, compression utilities, log analyzers, Java applications, and much more. Check back often to find new additions to the repository or to view the Pick of the Week.

Unofficial Netscape FAQ

http://www.sousystems.com/faq/

The Unofficial Netscape FAQ, nicknamed "The UFAQ," offers a wealth of useful, often witty information on browsing the Web and developing pages with Netscape Navigator. Here you can learn ways of dealing with font problems, get tips on using Netscape applications (the newsreader, mailer, etc.), figure out how to connect to the Internet from specific platforms, and implement workarounds for Netscape product bugs. Further assistance you can find here includes a descriptive list of pointers to official Netscape sites and newsgroups as well as other useful FAQs.

Web Developer's Virtual Library

http://www.stars.com/

If you're involved in any way in creating Web content, bookmark this site, a one-stop compendium of information and tools for Web developers. Here you can find a massive set of links to technical information about site development, including entire pages of resource links on meta tags, Web page style, VRML, HTML, graphics, CGI programming, Perl scripting, Java, and browser plug-ins. You can also jump to other Internet information, such as legal issues, news, and glossaries. Check the Top 100 to find out what are the most widely used—and often the most important—sites for developers.

Web Diner

http://www.webdiner.com/

The Web sibling to AOL's popular Web Diner forum (keyword: Web Diner), Web Diner aims to teach "people how to use the Web to enrich their lives and their businesses." Jump directly to Web Utensils to find useful templates for Web pages, a collection of classes and tutorials, graphics tips, galleries of free graphics, and Web

11

Diner links. The bibliography points you to high-quality books on business, HTML, graphic design, and the Web.

KIDS ONLY

Bill Nye the Science Guy

http://nyelabs.kcts.org/goodies/goodies.html

Can't pry the kids from the TV set when Bill Nye the Science Guy is on? Just show them this site, which offers videos in the Screening Room, still graphics in the Photo Album, and sounds in the Sounds of Science. If you've ever seen Mr. Nye's popular children's science show, you know that it manages to impart as much information as Mr. Wizard used to but with all the kinetic energy of an MTV video. It's not surprising, then, to find that the Web page is goofy and fun but also simple to use. The videos and sound files themselves come from the television show.

Blue Dog Can Count!

http://kao.ini.cmu.edu:5550/bdf.html

Who is Blue Dog? If you haven't seen or heard of her yet, you probably will soon. Thanks to this Web page, the dog that appears in the surreal paintings of the Cajun artist George Rodrigue has taken on a life of her own on the Internet. Click on the painting of Blue Dog, and she will bark at you. Fill in numbers in the arithmetic form on this page and she will bark out the answer. Typing *2+2=4* elicits a bark. This page is a top choice for pre-schoolers and kindergartners, but with over 1,000 hits a day, it looks suspiciously like moms and dads are getting help with their addition and subtraction, too!

Boy Scouts of America

http://www.bsa.scouting.org/index.htm

The BSA home page offers information about scouting for boys ages 7 to 20 and scout-leading for adults. A link to BSA activities lists links to their High Adventure bases, Jamboree pages, and Learning for Life program for schools. Check out official BSA gear such as the Pinewood Derby kits and order an official catalog. Family Fun offers ideas for engaging and educational activities for the scout and his family. The Index takes you to scouting and other related sites for more in-depth information, and the Local Councils link will help you to find active scouting groups near your home.

CollegeNET

http://www.collegenet.com/

So it's time to go to college and you can't figure out where to start? Well, there's always the guidance counselor, but if you want to search for yourself, CollegeNET is a good place to start. You can get information on colleges and universities based on geography, tuition levels, and the size of the student body. There is information on financial aid and graduate programs, too. You can search through the MACH25 Scholarship Search Engine and can even try for a $5,000 CollegeNET scholarship by sending in your application electronically!

Cyberspace Middle School

http://www.scri.fsu.edu/~dennisl/CMS.html

The Cyberspace Middle School is designed for students in the sixth, seventh, eighth, and ninth grades who are using the World Wide Web for educational assistance with their science fair projects. It includes lists of possible science fair projects, links to libraries, and personal help from the Web author. There is also an excellent list of educational Web sites on any number of science-oriented subjects.

11

Empowered Young Females

http://www.eyf.com/

Here is the electronic edition of *XX Empowered*, a magazine dedicated to helping teenage girls grow up into well-adjusted women. With articles on subject such as "No, I Am Not Anorexic" and "The Inner Beauty Contest" and topics like judo, it's pretty clear where they're coming from. This is a magazine with an attitude, and that attitude is expressed with clear writing and good graphics. EYF includes surveys, archives of earlier issues, e-mail, and regular features on games, television, and films.

ExploraNet

http://www.exploratorium.edu/

This Exploratorium is as good as science museums get. In the coolness and hands-on department, it rates a solid ten. The museum's Web site brings some true magic to the Net. The Exploratorium "teaches" about the senses by playing tricks on your sight and hearing. At this site you can hear the Doppler effect and view the Golden Gate Bridge live from a Web cam on the museum's roof. Or, learn about the world. You can dissect a cow's eye and imagine a nuclear bomb. Each month the

Exploratorium presents ten cool Web sites, some of which are as good as the Exploratorium itself. The Learning Studio features links to the current project there, as well as favorite recent projects. One visit offered a look at planets outside our solar system, satellite images of the earth, information on auroras, the ozone, and electronic versions of popular exhibits from the Exploratorium itself. The Exploratorium's Science Snackbook Series offers ideas and plans for fun and educational science projects that can be built and enjoyed in the classroom or home.

FishNet

http://www.jayi.com/jayi/

How many sites on the Web are called "FishNet"? There are probably quite a few, but this site is especially designed for teens. It includes a college guide, message boards, a quarterly e-zine, daily "weird facts," and a discussion of street language. It also has a random link and a list of age-appropriate links so kids can browse safely. FishNet is the free portion of a subscription service called Students Online, which gives kids the opportunity to set up their own Web pages, run forums and surveys, and much more.

Girl Scouts of the U.S.A.

http://www.gsusa.org/

Girl Scouting is open to girls between the ages of 5 and 17, and scout leading is open to men and women over the age of 18. The GS USA home page offers information on membership, history, publications, council sites, and, of course, cookie sales. This page should be particularly helpful for families looking to get involved in Girl Scouting as well as for those with girls already involved, with information on volunteer opportunities, current news, forthcoming events, and a product catalog. For those with questions about Girl Scouts, a click of a button will send e-mail directly to the Girl Scouts' U.S. administrative offices.

Homework Tools

http://www.zen.org/~brendan/kids-homework.html

The Kids on the Web: Homework Tools is just the place to go when you've put off that assignment until the library has closed and your bike has a flat tire. Links on

11

the page will take you to electronic versions of *Webster's Dictionary*, *Roget's Thesaurus,* the *Encyclopedia Britannica, The Elements of Style,* and *Bartlett's Familiar Quotations,* but the electrons weigh a lot less than all those books! Other assorted links such as Researchpaper.com can give you a jump-start on your project, with ideas and assistance on school-related research projects.

The National Zoo

http://www.si.edu/natzoo/

Washington, D.C.'s National Zoo now has a state of the art Web site (as if a real, free, world-class zoo weren't enough). It has all the bells and whistles including a lecture center with streaming audio and Web cameras set around the zoo so you can see what's going on while you're visiting the site. It also includes a flashy marquee that moves randomly, changes color, shrinks, and grows. Pictures of animals are the mainstay, but there is much more here. Just like the National Zoo itself, there's no way to see everything here in just one visit.

Seussville

http://www.randomhouse.com/seussville/

For Dr. Seuss fans of all ages, this bright page opens spattered with color and Seussian critters. Information about Theodore Geisel can be found on a link right out front, but kids will want to go right for the "Say, Let's Play" area. You will need to have the Shockwave plug-in to play Grab the Grinch, but other games need nothing more than agile speaking for the tongue twisters. Humorous pictures, contests, events, and special holiday sections round out this site full of fun for kids.

Teen Movie Critic

http://www.dreamagic.com/roger/teencritic.html

When someone is talking about a movie critic named Roger these days, they probably mean Roger Ebert. At some point in the future, though, they may well mean Roger Davidson. Roger's a teenager who loves films and shows it by reviewing a movie a day every week on this Web site. His reviews aren't just for kids either. From classics like *It's a Wonderful Life* to the latest releases, he always has something interesting to say, and he's often insightful.

Theodore Tugboat

http://www.cochran.com/tt.html

Web sites for small children must be hard to build. How else can we explain why there are so few good ones? Cochran Communications' Theodore Tugboat comes to the rescue with a site that is loads of fun for little kids. It includes an interactive story, postcards to be sent, and coloring book pages to be printed. Theodore Tugboat is the star of his own children's television show (which appears to be in rather limited distribution at the moment), but even if your kids have never seen it, they will enjoy this Web site.

Yahooligans

http://www.yahooligans.com/

Yahooligans is the Web directory just for kids from the folks at Yahoo. This bright and cheerful site features a special content-filtered search that was designed with the young user in mind. Kids can choose special search topics such as "Around the World" for culture, politics, and history; "School Bell" for educational programs and some homework help; and "The Scoop" for comics, daily news, and the weather. A link to "Stay Street Smart on the Internet" brings up the Yahooligan's rules for online safety, a document every young surfer should read and discuss with his or her parents. Resources for parents concerned about their children's safety on the Internet are also provided.

LEARNING & CULTURE

American Memory

http://rs6.loc.gov/amhome.html

The key contributions by the Library of Congress to the National Digital Library are available at the American Memory Web site. Here you will find photographs, documents, movies, and sound recordings from various times in American history. The format of this site is a little confusing (you sometimes have to work your way through four or five intermediate pages to get from the main screen to the actual text of a document), but all the pages on the site load very quickly, and the information is wonderful.

Ansel Adams

http://www.adamsgallery.com/

The photography of Ansel Adams is immediately recognizable by most Americans. Once seen, the magnificent black and white shots of Yosemite cannot be easily forgotten. It's readily apparent that a lot of people with Web sites haven't forgotten Adams' art—there are dozens of pages devoted to him and his photographs. This one is operated by the Ansel Adams Gallery in Yosemite. You can see examples of the artist's work here and can even buy quality prints for yourself.

Art on the Net

http://www.art.net/

Art on the Net is a virtual space where artists join together in sharing their art with others on the Internet. One hundred artists from around the world—poets, musicians, painters, sculptors, digital artists, performance artists, animators, and others—create and maintain studios and rooms in this virtual gallery. Because this site is graphics-intensive, some pages may be a bit slow to load, but it can be well worth the wait. Each area of the gallery contains thumbnails or descriptions of the art, allowing you to view larger representations simply by clicking. Beautiful.

ArtSource

http://www.uky.edu/Artsource/artsourcehome.html

If you are interested in art or architecture, this award-winning Web site is a great place to start looking for things. Although, as the Web owner points out, "For help in locating specific art-related information, the *BEST* source of information is your local art librarian," this isn't bad either! The site, regularly updated, features links to museums, image collections, online exhibitions, art journals, and vendors.

BookWire

http://www.bookwire.com/

A true mecca for anyone with *any* kind of interest in books, whether you write, work for a print or electronic publisher, or just like to read. You'll find reviews of the books you like to read, including poetry books, high-brow books, novels, and computer books. Get a schedule of author tours. Link to hundreds of publishers, big and little bookstores, and all manner of libraries. Follow the *Publishers' Weekly* bestseller lists. Learn about new book-related sites. Or, just have a look at the cartoon of the day.

Carnegie Library, Pittsburgh

http://www.clpgh.org/

With Andrew Carnegie's help, Pittsburgh was the center of industrial America in the early 20th century. The Carnegie libraries and museums he left behind remain the cultural center of Pittsburgh today. Carnegie, who dreamed of using his millions to make cultural treasures "free to the people," would be pleased with this Web site. From here you can search all public (Carnegie) libraries of the Pittsburgh area. Or, you can link to any of Pittsburgh's great Carnegie museums: the Carnegie Museum of Natural History (where they keep the dinosaurs), the Carnegie Museum of Art (with a superb contemporary collection), and the Andy Warhol Museum. You'll also find much of the current edition of *Carnegie Magazine*.

Fine Arts Museums of San Francisco, ImageBase

http://www.thinker.org/imagebase/index.html

Maybe it was the earthquake of 1989 that gave Bay Area curators an inkling of mortality or at least a sense of the immense value of the fragile cultural treasures stored by the DeYoung Museum and Palace of the Legion of Honor. At any rate, they are currently digitizing their entire collection, including all the paintings, sculpture, jewelry, and furniture *not* on public display. Search for your favorites, including great works by Cassatt, Durer, Blake, and Homer. In respect to the artists represented and the museums who are supporting this endeavor, no images seen here should be reproduced without permission.

Franklin Institute Science Museum

http://sln.fi.edu/

The Franklin Institute in Philadelphia is one of America's best science museums. Here at the official Web site you can tour virtual versions of some of the exhibits currently on display at the museum and get brief exhibit summaries of the rest. There is also a publications library and the information you need to plan a visit.

Guide to Museums and Cultural Resources

http://www.lam.mus.ca.us/Webmuseums/

Every self-respecting museum has a Web site these days, and many museums exist *only* on the Web. Start here for a nearly comprehensive directory of such real and virtual museums. Each museum in the directory gets a brief review, and, for most, an e-mail contact person is also provided (useful if you need permissions and further information). The guide, created as a service to students, scholars, and the public by the Natural History Museum of Los Angeles County, can be indispensable for anyone planning a trip, even to less-traveled places like Tunisia and New Zealand. In your own area, you can use the site as a handy source of hours and directions.

The Hopi Way—Cloud Dancing

http://www.timesoft.com/hopi/

The songs, speeches, prayers, and stories of the Hopi Nation make moving reading. You can learn the history of the Hopi at this site and savor excerpts from their rich culture. This is not just a tourist site, although anyone visiting here will come away entertained and enlightened. It's also for the Hopi themselves, and included here is a mailing list and points of contact for various outreach programs for members of the Hopi community who need them.

The Nine Planets

http://seds.lpl.arizona.edu/nineplanets/

Did you know that the moons of Uranus were named after Shakespearean characters? That tidbit and countless more are available to you here on the Nine Planets Web site. This site has the modest goal of providing an "overview of the history, mythology, and current scientific knowledge" of our solar system which includes not only the nine planets, but also our moon, the moons of the other planets, and other celestial bodies such as comets and asteroids.

Online Reference Book for Medieval Studies

http://orb.rhodes.edu/

The Online Reference Book for Medieval Studies was put together by scholars to create a source on the Internet for papers and articles about Europe in the Middle Ages. It includes original essays, teaching resources, links to other related sites, and graphics. One area of particular interest is called Media. It discusses how the Middle Ages are represented in film, on television, and in literature.

The Smithsonian Institute

http://www.si.edu/newstart.htm

When most people think of the Smithsonian, they think of "the castle," the strange red-brick building on the Mall in Washington, D.C. that housed the original Smithsonian collections 150 years ago. The Web site conveys the sheer scope of the organization, which encompasses more than two dozen museums and research centers, including the Museum of Natural History, the National Museum of American Art, the Air and Space Museum, and the Museum of Native America. All of the museums, plus *Smithsonian Magazine*, can be accessed from this site. Plan to spend hours here, and don't worry about the parking!

Sundance Film Festival

http://www.sundancefilm.com/festival/

Actor-director Robert Redford created the Sundance Festival in 1981 to "develop new talent and preserve the voice of independent film." The festival itself is interesting because the search for exceptional independent movies has led to a few films—most notably *Sex, Lies and Videotape*—that have made quite a bit of money at the box office. You can cruise through the festival on this Web site, checking out past festivals, studying this year's entries, and reading a note from Mr. Redford.

Victoria and Albert Museum

http://www.artnet.co.uk/30VandA.html

Founded in 1852, at the height of Victoria's reign, the Victoria and Albert Museum is today the largest museum of the decorative arts in the world. The beautiful Victorian and Edwardian buildings house 145 galleries containing some of the world's greatest collections of sculpture, furniture, fashion and textiles, paintings, silver, glass, ceramics, jewelry, books, prints, and photographs. At this site you will also find masterpieces from their watercolor collection, including works from William Blake and Dante Rossetti.

LIFE, STYLES & INTERESTS

The AARP WebPlace

http://www.aarp.org/

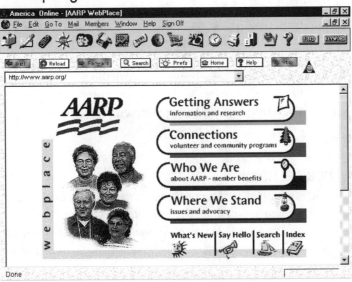

The AARP Web site is a place for "wired" seniors to hook into one of the most important resources for retired people. Folks who are new to the AARP can learn more about this organization and find chapters and resources close to home with abundant information provided in their "Connections" section. Issues of importance to seniors are presented and discussed in "Where We Stand," featuring news releases and advocacy for members. "Who We Are" details the benefits of AARP membership, while the "Getting Answers" section helps members to more deeply understand the concerns of family, health, money, and other issues central to senior Americans. If you like the site, make sure to visit SeniorNet on AOL.

Backpacker Magazine

http://www.bpbasecamp.com/

Here's the view from base camp. There are articles here on cooking, grizzly bears, and just about anything else that would be of interest to a person walking alone through the woods. This electronic edition of the popular Rodale Press magazine has most of the features of its print sibling, plus the encyclopedia (a database of useful information on the wilderness), gearfinder (a guide to equipment retailers), an online store, and an archive of past issues. There are also message boards available in the Trail Talk forums for backpacking enthusiasts to discuss matters with one another.

Black Information Network

http://www.bin.com/

From its directory of African-American businesses and employment opportunities to its lists of available real estate and information on missing children, the Black Information Network is a Web site that packs in a ton of information. As if the information offered isn't enough, nearly every page of this site includes the enjoinder to "Add Yours!" This sense of being a cooperative project, along with its striking layout, makes the Black Information Network an engaging place to visit.

BoatNet

http://www.boatnet.com/

There's just something about being out on the water that—if you can get past the motion sickness—speaks to something deep within many of us. If you've been bitten by the boating bug, sail on over to BoatNet. It contains information on new and used boats for sale, charter yachts, marine supplies and services, maritime art galleries, and boating magazines. You'll also find information on weather, tides, and navigation, as well as online yacht clubs and links to related Web sites.

Cat Fanciers

http://www.fanciers.com/

The cat fanciers' Web site offers general information about cats and descriptions of virtually all cat breeds. You will find a wide selection of cat shows, clubs and registries, the latest news on veterinary medicine, and much more. This is a great place if you're thinking about buying a purebred cat. The breeders registry lists hundreds of Internet-connected breeders of pedigreed cats. This site is run by the same people who moderate the excellent Cat Fanciers Mailing List.

Comparative Religion

http://Weber.u.washington.edu/~madin/

Mike Madin's page on Comparative Religion is a directory of Internet resources for the academic study of religion. Links to directories and pages on world scriptures, religious tolerance, and studying religion in the electronic age can be found here, as well as information on less well-known religions such as Baha'i. Other religions are presented with directories, reference tools, and links to online publications. The Academic Departments of Religion in universities from many countries are accessible through links found here. This simply presented page can be a great starting place for personal research into the religions of the world.

Fly Fishing Broadcast Network

http://www.fbn-flyfish.com/index.htm

You might expect a Web site on fishing to be of limited interest to anyone who isn't an angler, but the Fly Fishing Broadcast Network (or FBN as they like to call themselves) works hard to change that expectation. Not only are there intriguing articles such as "The Wonders of Fly-fishing in Ireland," there are also some great pictures of beautiful scenery and some games to play. Of course, if you are the sort of person who thinks the characters in *A River Runs Through It* were too casual about their fishing, there's a lot of great information for you, too! Fishing reports, a yellow pages directory, and a real-time chat room are just the beginning of the wealth of information you can find here.

11

foodwine.com

http://www.foodwine.com/

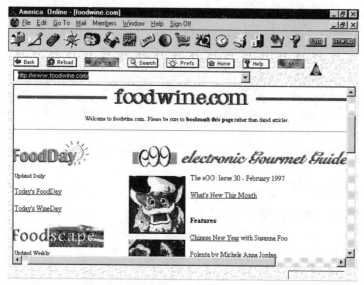

Foodwine.com is the Electronic Gourmet Guide's home on the Internet. eGG is one of AOL's premiere food resources (keyword: eGG), and this Web version handles the subject with the same cheerful and colorful flourish. The daily FoodDay and weekly Foodscape columns ensure that this site is one that you will want to visit often. You'll find recipes, of course, but there are also plenty of tips and tricks guaranteed to make you a better (or at least more interesting) cook. Drop in and take the trivia quiz or shop at the eGGbasket gourmet store.

Genealogy Home Page

http://www.genhomepage.com/

Here is a resource for people who are beginning to research their family history. The Genealogy Home Page includes help files, guides, libraries, maps, deeds and photographs, lists of associated newsgroups and mailing lists, and links to other online genealogical information, home pages, and resources. You will find commercial services, software, and lists of genealogical societies here as well. This is a great place to visit after dropping by AOL's own Genealogy Forum (keyword: Genealogy)!

HouseNet

http://www.housenet.com/

This Web version of Gene and Katie Hamilton's popular HouseNet AOL forum (keyword: Housenet) might fool you at first glance. It has the same pleasant graphics as the AOL forum, but there is plenty of additional great information. The daily tips are a treasure trove for people who are interested in home repair and home remodeling, and the message board and Do It Together projects allow homeowners to discuss their work with each other. The genuinely useful Paint Calculator lets you enter the dimensions of the walls you want to paint, then figures out how much paint you'll need. If that isn't enough, there is also the Handy Homeowner contest where you can win Craftsman tools.

11

NetNoir

http://www.netnoir.com/

NetNoir is a popular America Online forum dedicated to and run by African-Americans (keyword: Netnoir). This Web site expands many of the popular NetNoir forum features, such as Club NetNoir and interview archives, to reach people who are not yet AOL members. It also has plenty of material that is different from AOL's offerings. The information here is "presented in such a way that anyone, from any walk of life, that has any interest in Afrocentric culture, can participate..." The site's clean, fast-loading design is appealing and makes browsing a breeze.

rec.antiques.marketplace (newsgroup)

Are you looking for a place to advertise grandma's old griddle? Or maybe you're trying to find the piece of Depression-era glass that will complete your collection. If you're interested in buying, selling, or just pricing antiques and collectibles, the Usenet newsgroup **rec.antiques.marketplace** can be an invaluable resource. This is a fairly high-volume newsgroup, but the signal to noise ratio is also fairly high, which means you're almost certain to find useful postings, whatever your collecting pleasure. This is a friendly and informative newsgroup, but as with any electronic forum where money changes hands, you should make sure you know who you are dealing with before parting with money or a precious heirloom.

ScubaWorld Online

http://www.scubaworld.com/

Sport Diver Magazine's Scuba World Online opens with a bright watery scene offering links of interest on every facet of this sport. A fascination with scuba diving can be explored here with magazines, club information, bulletin boards, and more. Photos and videos are available, as well as links to online catalogs produced by dive retailers. An area on science and the environment addresses issues of importance to divers and presents information on organizations such as The Cousteau Society and The JASON Project. A click on the sidebar of links will bring information on training, travel, and weather, or you can choose to take a virtual expedition to follow the work of teams of explorers on location. Data and findings are posted as they are available to make it possible to share them with enthusiasts everywhere and also to involve other experts out on the Net.

Softworld's Sewing Resource Guide

http://www.softworld.com/sewing/sewdir.htm

Sewing enthusiasts on the lookout for patterns, instructions, and ideas need look no further than this wonderful site. There are dozens of links to resources here. You can find information on equipment and, in many cases, follow links directly to the manufacturers. There is advice for beginners as well as challenging projects for more accomplished sewers.

World Wide Quilting Page

http://ttsw.com/MainQuiltingPage.html

This isn't just information on quilts, although there is plenty of that. There are intriguing features, such as the "worst quilts in the world" contest and overviews of changes in quilting styles here as well. This site is chock-full of photos of quilts. Whether you are an experienced quilter or are just thinking of trying your hand at this traditional craft, this site will get you thinking about piecing together your next masterpiece.

11

MUSICSPACE

Addicted to Noise

http://www.addict.com/

This is a hip and professionally designed electronic magazine covering the world of new rock and alternative music. This excellent resource will help you discover reviews of new albums, musician interviews, columns, features, and hype. If you're an audiophile, skip the text and go directly to Radio ATN, where you can listen to song samples by a variety of musicians, interviews with bands or individual artists, and exclusive programs. Film addicts may want to jump right to Cinemachine—Addicted to Noise's movie review search engine—to access thousands of film reviews.

All Music Guide

http://allmovie.com/amg/music_root.html

"A complete online database of recorded music." After you search for music information by artist, album title, or musical style and sub-style, you'll find a multitude of data, tidbits, and charts, including artist biographies, detailed discographies, chronology, ratings, and reviews. New Releases contains a long listing of new music and ratings, and Reissues provides the same information for rereleased music. Check out Monthly Columns to find features chock-full of links to artists and albums. Got a question about music itself? Browse the Music Glossary.

American Music Center

http://www.amc.net/amc/

The official Web site of the American Music Center (AMC), an informational and promotional resource for American contemporary music and jazz. Find out about the AMC itself as well as its information services (general as well as specifically for jazz, AMC publications, scores, grants, and more). Musicians may be able to network with each other and find new opportunities every month in Opportunity Update. If you want to know more about what AMC has to offer, be sure to read the FAQ.

Antidote

http://www.spiv.com/antidote/

If you're tired of the Top 40, check out Antidote. This is a visually appealing resource for underground and independent music. Rant, Gig, and Pulse contain in-depth reviews and features on a variety of bands and independent recordings. Ranarium is where you can find weekly music and culture information from specific cities, including Louisville, Chapel Hill, Portland, Seattle, hip-hop Chicago, and New York City. You can also select from an extensive list of music samples in the Gramophone online listening center.

Classical Chat

http://members.aol.com/hostbri/classicalchat/index.html

This is the official Web site of AOL's Classical Chat (keyword: Classical). In addition to finding information about the forum (chat schedules, rules, an archive of chats and interviews), you can find a number of other important classical music resources here. In Composer Biographies, for instance, you can research birth and death dates, teachers, compositional media, and items of interest about the great composers. In Recommended Recordings and Music Website Links, you'll discover related resources.

Guitar World

http://www.guitarworld.com/

Impressive Web magazine where you can find guitar information, product guides and resources, and news and gossip about famous guitarists—all complete with high-quality photographic images. Here you can find features on a variety of guitarists and bands,

11

from recent artists like Smashing Pumpkins to classic groups like The Who. If you are a guitar player, you won't want to miss the Lessons section, where you can read advice, tips, and techniques on soloing, playing rhythm guitar, improving your riffs, making the most of power chords, and using alternative string tuning.

History of Rock 'n' Roll

http://www.hollywood.com/rocknroll/

The Web companion to the television rockumentary series *The History of Rock 'n' Roll.* If you're interested in the television program, click Show Buzz to find an episode guide, performers, behind the scenes, and a local station listing. The rest of the site is a multimedia gallery of such rock legends as Bono of U2, Bruce Springsteen, Quincy Jones, Green Day, Pete Townshend, Alice Cooper, Van Halen, Aerosmith, and many others. You can read entertaining nuggets in Quotables, listen to interviews in Sound Bites, view photographs in Sights, and watch mini-movies in Video Vault.

The Internet Beatles Album

http://www.primenet.com/~dhaber/beatles.html

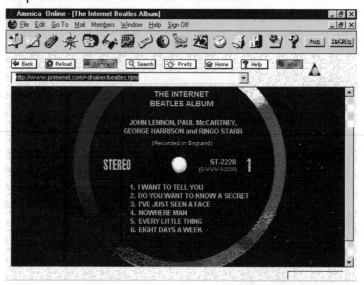

When you visit the front cover of this site, you'll see a simple image of a Beatles LP vinyl record. Click any of the songs or names listed on the record, however, and you'll access a huge compilation of Beatles facts, trivia, history, and much more.

Here you can also find a complete portfolio on each of the Fab Four. Other gems you won't want to miss include the photo gallery, trivia game, Today in Beatles History, and the entire section devoted to the Paul Is Dead mystery.

Music Previews Network
http://www.mpmusic.com/
Preview new recordings in just about any style of music, including rock, alternative, jazz and blues, classical, spiritual, rap and hip-hop, country, R&B, and more. Each music sample is provided in several sound formats and is displayed with a record cover image and a brief review and description of the album. You can search the entire database for something specific or check out the weekly list of picks.

National Anthems
http://world.std.com/~clm/anthem.html
Whatever national anthem you're looking for, you'll find a link to it here. The types of resources vary, but you can check the key to find out which links offer English or French translations of lyrics, historical notes, original lyrics, musical sound files, sheet music, and other national songs. Check the top of this home page to find links to the National Anthem of the Month, synthesized national anthems, and national flags.

Peeps Republic
http://www.peeps.com/
This is an entertaining source of R&B and similar contemporary music. Check out the Celebrity Guest Book to get an insider's perspective of vocal artists in a recording studio. The Book offers such fun tidbits as samples of musical free-styling, recordings of casual conversations, and autographed pictures. Peeps News is where you can read the latest about Grammies and other awards, movie soundtracks, a variety of vocalists and other musicians, and new albums. If you live near or are attending a university, visit Peeps Posse to find information on local music and cultural events.

resrocket
http://www.resrocket.com/
You'll feel as if you're in outer space when you're exploring this site, although this is really a gathering area for musicians. Players and artists of all levels meet in this online world to exchange ideas, chat, and—best of all—jam. Once you register,

11

you'll get an avatar (little picture representing yourself) and a locker (personal space to store your tools and data). Then you can meet hundreds of other creative souls from all over the world to engage in this unique forum.

Rock and Roll Hall of Fame and Museum

http://www.rockhall.com/

Jerry Leiber, John Lennon, Bob Marley, Led Zeppelin, Frank Zappa—they're all here, in Cleveland's extravagant museum of rock, design by I.M. Pei. Each year, half a dozen or so new inductees are enshrined in the museum, chosen by a panel of rock historians. Every inductee is represented at this site by a biography with pictures and audio clips (in Real Audio, AU, and WAV formats). Every Web museum of any worth has a museum shop, and at this one you can purchase T-shirts, caps, and rock and roll ball-point pens. Well worth a visit, and the best way to plan a visit to the real museum.

Rollingstone.com

http://www.rollingstone.com/

An interactive, multimedia companion to *Rolling Stone,* the print magazine that pioneered rock music journalism. Here you can find new music reviews, opinions and regular columns, news from the university campus music scene, music award charts, critics' picks, contests, and an impressive photo gallery. Media addicts will appreciate the up-to-the minute music and pop culture news in Random Notes Daily and the audio interviews with musicians and writers in Raw Tape.

TAXI

http://www.taxi.com/

Online service in which unsigned musicians and songwriters can network with major record label companies, publishers, and television, and film music supervisors. Here you can learn all about the TAXI service, including how to become a member, who the A&R staff is and what their credentials are, and what new recording companies are looking for in a variety of musical styles. Visit The A&R Insider to find monthly articles on A&R staff perspectives, industry advice, interviews with artists, and vocal techniques.

NEWSSTAND

Amazon.com

http://www.amazon.com/

Megasource of books; bigger than any physical bookstore— you can find a selection of over one million books. Don't be overwhelmed by the volume, though; it's easy to search the entire database by author, title, subject, and keyword. You can also browse the "shelves," which are logical categories of book types. If you're looking for a suggestion, peruse Editors' Favorites and Customer Reviews. An automatic search agent, Eyes, will send you e-mail notifying you of a requested title.

The Atlantic Monthly

http://www.theatlantic.com/

The Web companion to *The Atlantic Monthly,* a magazine devoted to politics, society, the arts, and culture. Here you can find excerpts from the print publication, and you can also read Atlantic Unbound, the Web-only exclusive edition. Atlantic Unbound contains features about Internet and digital culture, arts and entertainment, food, and books. To engage in The Atlantic Monthly community, go to Post & Riposte to join interesting discussions on a number of topics.

Better Homes and Gardens

http://www.bhglive.com/

Online companion to the *Better Homes and Gardens* print magazine. The best resource here is the Home Improvement Encyclopedia, where you can find advice and instructions for home improvement basics including plumbing, landscaping, house structure, electrical and telephone, decks, and yard structure. The encyclopedia also contains a handy tool dictionary and home improvement glossary. If you need help with the holidays, check out the Holiday Entertaining Guide, which contains interactive guides to cooking and planning, as well as recipes and holiday decorating tips.

Car and Driver

http://www.caranddriver.com/hfm/

Companion to *Car and Driver* print magazine. The most valuable feature here is the Buyers Guide for this year and last, where you can get information on over 400 cars and trucks. Simply search the database by manufacturer, vehicle type, or price range; then check the list of winners. You can also read excerpts from the print publication, such as road tests, previews, and favorite articles from the past. Check the Daily Auto Insider to find continually updated news and information about the automotive industry.

Dell Magazines Daily Crossword Puzzle

http://www.bdd.com/puzzl/bddpuzzl.cgi/puzzl

A must-visit for crossword puzzle addicts. Dell Magazines offers a different original crossword puzzle every day. If you're stumped on yesterday's puzzle, sneak a peak at the solution. The crosswords are presented in Adobe Acrobat format, which makes the puzzles look clean and professionally published. From the puzzle page, you can explore other areas of the Dell Magazines Web site, including the catalog, new releases, author of the week, young readers section, daily horoscope, and forums.

Electronic Newsstand's Monster Magazine List

http://www.enews.com/monster/body.html

Jumpstation to a huge list of magazines on the Web. The types of magazines are divided into many categories, some of which include the arts, business and economics, computers and Internet, education and academia, entertainment and pop culture, health and medicine, hobby and craft, kids and family, news and politics, science and nature, sports and leisure, recreation, and travel and destinations. Check out the Enews Top 20 to find the most popular periodicals. You can conveniently search for a specific magazine or article.

Elle

http://www.ellemag.com/hfm/index.html

High fashion Webzine. What you can find here that you can't get in the print version of *Elle* is the Online Exclusive, a special fashion features section produced only for this Web site. If you want to see beautiful pictures of supermodels, check out the model gallery to find the likes of Claudia, Naomi, Cindy, Linda, Christy, and Elle. There is always new information on fashion trends in TrendReports as well as next season's fashion predictions. If you're a fashion buff, try your hand at Woody Hochswender's fashion quiz.

Forbes Magazine

http://www.forbes.com/

Extensive online companion to the print magazine. Business readers will appreciate the company databases, including the 500 Largest Private Companies, the 200 Best Small Companies in America, and the Forbes Four Hundred, which allows you to create a customized list. Other useful tools include the stock fund calculator, which helps you manage money between tax-sheltered and taxable accounts, and the investment primer, a collection of advice for investors from past issues. Also hosted here is Forbes ASAP and Forbes FYI.

Inc. Online

http://www.inc.com/

"The Web site for growing companies." Here you can read exclusive articles and interviews from *Inc. Real Time, Zinc, Online Entrepreneur,* and *Between the Pages.* Also, check out Virtual Consultant, a collection of interactive worksheets, searchable databases, and other online business references. Registered Inc. users can create, publish, and announce a Web site free of charge. If you're a regular Inc. visitor, you can create and modify a customized view. Don't miss the daily highlights and interesting questions posed in the weekly chat forum.

Life Magazine

http://pathfinder.com/Life/lifehome.html

Beautifully designed Web companion to *Life Magazine.* Here you can read *Life* features, a FAQ, and This Day in Life, as well as view the Picture of the Day and photo essays. A fun feature is the Time Machine, which allows you to search for a specific *Life* cover by date, photographer, or subject and view it in a high-quality graphic image. You can also participate in an interactive forum or check out articles on subjects like alternative medicine, the 50 most influential baby boomers, and the band called Phish.

National Journal

http://www.politicsnow.com/news/NJournal/

Journal of political news and analysis. This site offers a ton of feature articles conveniently indexed on one page. Check back each week to find a new collection of articles. There is a year's worth of material stored here, and you can peruse the article titles, which are sorted by month. By reading this Webzine, you can stay abreast of a vast assortment of political information, including news and opinions about the President, government agencies, laws and regulations, legislative branches of the government, and more.

Osborne/McGraw-Hill

http://www.osborne.com/

Timely source of Internet development news and information. Here you can find press releases on new telecommunications products, software releases, programming language and protocol developments, security tools, and Internet business and culture. The Busy People Series includes timesaving tips and information on Microsoft business applications, America Online, the Internet and Web publishing, PCs, Intuit Quicken, and Windows 95 and NT operating systems. There are also previews of Internet development and computing books with ordering information.

Scientific American

http://www.sciam.com/content.html

One of the premier journals of scientific research and discoveries. Here you can read current and past articles; news and analyses; reviews; commentaries; the "50, 100, and 150 Years Ago" editorial column; the "amateur scientist" column; and letters to the editors. One of the most valuable sections is Weekly Web Features, where you can find large collections of explorations and exhibits on genetic and subatomic research, questions on quantum mechanics, famous scientists like Carl Sagan and Mary Leakey, and more.

11

Swoon

http://www.swoon.com/

Fun publication all about "dating, mating, relating." Here you can read stories and advice on cohabitation, coping with loss, friendships, pets, and of course, sex. Some of the original columns include "Jan's Makeout Music," "Jane Err," "Cheap Date," and the "Who's Doin' Who?" gossip column. There are other fun areas, such as the Meet and Greet community area, personal ads, horoscopes. Don't forget to add your two cents to the Daily Scoreboard.

Time

http://pathfinder.com/time/

The Web wouldn't be complete without *Time* magazine online, and here it is. Readers visit this site to find excerpts from the print magazine and special reports found exclusively online. Time Daily provides news highlights and photographs every day. In the Community area, you can participate in a discussion with others; the most popular forum is All Politics. You can also read transcripts of online discussions with celebrities and leaders. Don't miss the special multimedia section, which presents cool features in a variety of multimedia formats.

PERSONAL FINANCE

Best Rates from the Bank Rate Monitor

http://www.bankrate.com/

If you're shopping around for a new bank or consumer financial institution, you can't afford to miss this site. Here you'll get easy access to up-to-date rates on mortgages, credit cards, home equity loans, auto loans, personal loans, bank fees, and more. Other services offered here include the automatic e-mail interest rate alert for mortgage, deposits, and federal discount rates, as well as the handy monitor for personal stock, bond, and mutual fund portfolios.

Career Magazine

http://www.careermag.com/

This is an excellent resource for anyone looking for a new job or profession, graduating from college or graduate school, or climbing the corporate ladder. Here you can find articles on networking with colleagues, improving social skills in the office, and legal issues in the workplace. If you need specific job-seeking services, check out the Job Openings Database, Resume Bank, Employer Profiles, and Career Forum. You can keep abreast of *Career Magazine* by subscribing to the e-mail announcement list.

CNNfn Stock Quotes

http://cnnfn.com/markets/quotes.html

Stockholders frequent the Cable News Network, Inc.'s Financial Network (CNNfn) to find a reliable source of updated stock quotes provided by Standard & Poor's ComStock. Simply enter a stock's ticker symbol into the form or look it up in CNNfn's directory of company Web sites and symbols. In addition, you can keep abreast of the financial world by reading Breaking News and This Hour's Top Business Stories.

11

401(k) Retirement Calculator

http://www.awa.com/softlock/tturner/401k/

Have you calculated the estimated return on investment of your 401(k) retirement plan lately? If you haven't, or if you find the prospect daunting, check out this online retirement planning tool. After inputting some simple data such as your current age, current salary, 401(k) balance, and planned retirement age, the calculator does all the work for you and allows you to experiment with different figures. You can also download a Macintosh or Windows version of the calculator, which includes more features.

Home Buyer's Fair

http://www.homefair.com/home/

If you are planning to buy a home or you are interested in noncommercial real estate, stop by this Web site. Here you can find Popular Exhibits—interactive tools for calculating your salary required for relocation, moving expenses, mortgage qualifications, and more. Be sure to check out the Main Booths, which offer extensive guides and resources for first-time homebuyers, mortgage finance resources, relocation information, and free services available to homebuyers.

Insurance News Network

http://www.insure.com/

If you have questions about Auto, Home, or Life insurance, you can find answers here. This insurance news resource provides reliable news about natural disasters' effect on insurance, automobile safety tests, and pending litigation against insurance companies, as well as guidance on how to best protect yourself. The comprehensive Insurance Glossary can help you make sense out of the confusing array of insurance terms. For further assistance, be sure to check out the InfoSources section to find insurance-related informational groups and trade associations.

IRS's Digital Daily

http://www.irs.ustreas.gov/prod/cover.html

This is a free publication brought to you by the IRS. When you visit this page, you'll see that tax information doesn't need to be dry and boring; this publication is colorful, easy to read, and even fun. Here you can find tax information for both individuals and businesses, as well as tax forms, educational publications, and electronic services. If you're interested in how taxes work on a national scale, check out the proposed tax regulations and statistics.

misc.invest.stocks (newsgroup)

This immensely popular newsgroup is a gathering area for stock investors. Here you can meet other stock holders and potential investors to exchange market tips and advice; discuss brokers and investment firms; find online stock tickers, investment Web sites, and software; and debate about what is currently hot on the market—and what is not. This is also a good forum for discussing mutual funds, precious metals, and currency trading.

misc.taxes (newsgroup)

If you need tax help or advice, this free resource is available to you. Here you can meet with others to discuss a variety of tax strategies, including vesting, gifts to children, tax shelters, and IRAs. You can also find questions and answers about avoiding and dealing with audits, determining the appropriate tax forms to use, and using tax software. Other discussion threads focus on tax codes and regulations and how they may affect you.

Money Online

http://quote.pathfinder.com/money/

This is the online version of *Money Magazine.* Like the print publication, Money Online is an excellent resource for news, features, and tools to help you manage your money and increase your wealth. This Webzine, however, offers some useful services which are impossible to get from the print magazine, such as the Financial Tool Kit, which helps you calculate your debt, investment portfolio return, mortgage, retirement savings, and net worth, as well as a stock lookup service and online portfolio tracker.

Motley Fool

http://fool.web.aol.com/

Welcome to one of the most popular America Online forums. This is an online resource devoted entirely to stocks; you won't find information about any other type of investments here. Appropriately named, Motley Fool is entertaining when it serves up its timely stock investment information. Check out The Fool's School, Fool!Wire, Lunchtime News, Evening News, and The Fribble for news and advice. If you enjoy playing games, try your hand with Today's Pitch and Foolball.

Networth's Insider: Mutual Funds
http://networth.galt.com/www/home/insider/fund.htm

If you invest in mutual funds, check out this site. The Insider provides an extensive index of Web-based information on mutual fund in the United States, Canada, Great Britain, and other countries. You can explore the NETworth Mutual Fund Market Manager to find the Fund Atlas (a directory of mutual funds), Net Asset Values (recent and historical fund prices), Morningstar Profiles, and Top Performers, as well as feature articles and a mutual fund search tool.

Retirement Zone
http://www.bookpage.com/kiplinger/

You have a good chance of finding answers to your retirement questions here. In the Zone, Kiplinger Retirement Services offers several free publications and tools, including an easy-to-use worksheet for calculating your retirement needs, a table to help calculate and build your nest egg, retirement guidance for members of the baby-boom generation, and a countdown-to-retirement to-do list. While you're here, check out the other publications by Kiplinger for money management, education, and career guidance.

Social Security Online
http://www.ssa.gov/

This is the official Web source of Social Security information. One unique application you'll find here is a Personal Earnings and Benefit Estimate Statements computer, which incorporates the annual cost-of-living adjustment. You'll also find a compendium of government publications including everything you need to know about Social Security, FAQs for various services, tax information, Medicare information, and forms. Some publications are offered in Spanish. To access information quickly, use the search tool.

Taxing Times
http://www.scubed.com/tax/tax.html

This is a convenient index of tax information available on the Web. Here you can find all the forms you need, including federal tax forms and instructions, state tax forms and instructions (with specific information for the California Franchise Tax Board), and Revenue Canada Taxation forms. In addition, you can find links to the entire tax code, The Tax Digest, the tax newsgroup, IRS Code & Subject Telephone Directory, and other sources of tax help.

REFERENCE

Acronym Dictionary

http://www.ucc.ie/info/net/acronyms/acro.html

Database of definitions of acronyms—abbreviations made from the first letters of each word of a phrase. Simply enter an acronym into the form; the results are displayed with links to more information about your entry. Two options for searching are available: either search for an acronym and see its expansion, or search for a word in the expansions and view the related acronyms. You can also use e-mail to access the Acronym Dictionary; check the Mailserver page for information on the acronym and dictionary/thesaurus automatic e-mail services.

Biography

http://www.biography.com/

Provided by A&E Television Networks, this beautifully designed site features biographical information on over 15,000 people. You can read reviews of biographies, view a calendar of biographical television programs, and participate in a discussion forum with other biography fans. If you're a serious biography addict, try your hand at the Biography Quiz and Biography Anagrams, both found in the Play area. For quick access, go directly to the Find section to search for a name or to check the alphabetical listing.

CIA 1995 World Factbook

http://www.odci.gov/cia/publications/95fact/index.html

Complete reference of country facts and information published by the Central Intelligence Agency. Every country in the world is listed here, from Argentina to Zimbabwe, and each entry contains a map and information about geography, climate, terrain, land use, and more. Another huge resource here is the Notes, Definitions, and Abbreviations list, which defines terms and explains how each fact is acquired. For further information, check the appendices and reference maps.

Familiar Quotations

http://www.cc.columbia.edu/acis/bartleby/bartlett/

Online edition of Bartlett's Familiar Quotations. Here you can browse indexes of authors listed both alphabetically and chronologically. Within the huge list of literary works, you can find selected quotations from the complete works of Shakespeare and the Bible. Each author or written work in the list is linked to a page of quotations in straightforward text. Also provided here is information taken directly from the book, including the bibliographic record, front matter, and preface.

FAQ Finder

http://ps.superb.net/FAQ/

Searchable database containing a comprehensive list of approximately 1,800 links to FAQs on a wide variety of subjects. You can also read the FAQs by specific topic, including animals, art, audio, comedy, computers, countries, education, food, games, health, hobbies, Internet, lifestyles, literature, movies, music, people, personal finance, politics and law, programming, religion, science, social science, software, sports, technology, television, and video. Whether you are looking for a FAQ on birds, books, or toys, you'll find a link to one here.

11

FedWorld Information Network

http://www.fedworld.gov/

Central source of federal government information and documentation. Some examples of the many available resources here include Federal Aviation Administration service, training and regulatory information; the federal job announcement search service, IRS tax forms and instructions, Bureau of Indian Affairs law enforcement services information, the EPA Clean Air Act database, United States Treasury information, and U.S. Customs Service information. From this Web site, you can access the Telnet service and FTP site.

Internet Public Library Reference Center

http://ipl.sils.umich.edu/ref/

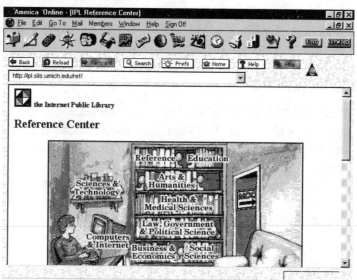

University of Michigan's virtual public library reference desk. You have the option of clicking the straightforward text links or using the cool imagemap of a library reference area. The selection of main topics includes arts and humanities, business and economics, computers and Internet, education, entertainment and leisure, and health and medical sciences. Then choose from a list of subcategories to find a descriptive list of resources. Be sure to stop by the Multi-User Object Oriented (MOO) environment for some live interaction.

iTools Research-it

http://www.itools.com/research-it/research-it.html

Instant research tool for many purposes. You can input strings of text into forms to look up language translations, biographical information, religion-related information, maps, facts, telephone numbers, financial information, postal and shipping addresses, and e-mail discussion groups. The snazzy table interface is cool and easy to use; simply type in an entry and click the Action button, and you'll get instant results. Each reference is listed with a link to the original Internet resource, so you'll know exactly which tool you're using.

My Virtual Reference Desk

http://www.refdesk.com/outline.html

A convenient and well-organized jumpstation of a variety of useful Web resources. The most valuable features are First Things First, which is a list of recommended sites to visit first thing in the morning; My Favorite Applications and Utilities; My Search Engines, which is an organized compilation of over 150 search engines; My Virtual Encyclopedia; and My Virtual Newspaper. Here you can also find a huge list of computer and Internet links. Be sure to check out the current time, United States national debt, U.S. population clock, world population clock, and online calculator.

Periodic Table of the Elements

http://mwanal.lanl.gov/CST/imagemap/periodic/periodic.html

11

Graphic periodic table. Not only is this chemistry reference colorful and beautiful to look at, it's fully interactive. Because it's one big imagemap, you can click any element to find out its atomic number, symbol, and weight, as well as its electron configuration. You can also read an extensive history of how each element was discovered and used. Each page contains a link to other useful chemistry reference sites.

Roget's Thesaurus

http://humanities.uchicago.edu/forms_unrest/ROGET.html

Simple interface to this useful reference. Unlike the hardcopy edition of *Roget's Thesaurus,* however, you can use programming techniques to search for a word with multiple endings. For example, if you look up the word "drive," you'll find synonyms for this word; however, if you add an asterisk to the end of the word ("drive*"), you'll get a list of synonyms for "drive," "driving," and "driver." You can also search for headwords.

U.S. Census Bureau

http://www.census.gov/

Official online source of social, demographic, and economic data. Here you can check out Census news to find press releases and tip sheets, recent economic indicators, radio broadcasts, statistical briefs, this year's economic census, Census 2000, Web clips, and upcoming events. The Data Access Tools page is a handy index of applications for generating maps, viewing profiles, and extracting data. Another important feature of this site is the Subjects A-Z index, an extensive encyclopedia and jumpstation.

WWW Bible Gateway

http://www.gospelcom.net/bible

Complete Bible lookup service. You can use the simple form here to find any passage, search by word, and do a restricted search in the Bible. You can also select from a list of common Bible versions. A cool feature is the "What The Bible Says About" search, where you can find passages relating to over 22,000 topics. This reference is offered in German, Swedish, Latin, French, Spanish, and Tagalog.

WWWebster Dictionary

http://www.m-w.com/netdict.htm

Web edition of *Merriam-Webster's Collegiate Dictionary*. Use the simple interface to look up the definition and synonyms of any word. If you want to conduct a more powerful word search, read the Help page. Here you can learn about wildcard searches, search results, cross-references, spelling, inflected forms, and illustrations and tables, as well as pronunciation guides, symbols, and keys. To expand your vocabulary, click Word of the Day to read a new word's definition and interesting fact.

Zipcode lookup

http://www.usps.gov/ncsc/

Official U.S. Postal Service (U.S.P.S.) ZIP code lookup and address information. Even more convenient than your trusty hardcopy ZIP code directory, this resource offers everything you need to complete the most important part of an address. Here you can use the ZIP+4 Code Lookup tool, which provides the entire 9-digit ZIP code for any address; city, state, and ZIP code associations; the Address Management Systems Office Locator, which finds the office that can correct local address and ZIP code errors in the U.S.P.S. database; and the list of official abbreviations, which are U.S.P.S. preferences of abbreviated address components.

SPORTS

Balance: Health and Fitness on the Net

http://hyperlink.com/balance

This high-quality online magazine about sports, health, and physical fitness is an excellent source of a wide variety of materials, including articles on sports injuries, the effects of exercising upon diseases, and sports equipment and clothing. You can also learn how to tailor a physical fitness program to fit your needs, from beginning a simple morning aerobic routine to training for a marathon. Special sections include Fe-mail (devoted to women's health), articles in Spanish and German, and The International Directory of Personal Trainers.

11

ESPNET SportsZone

http://espnet.sportszone.com/

A rich complement to the ESPN television channel, the SportsZone boasts more than 60,000 pages within its Web site. In addition to professional sports information and front page news headlines, you can read columns by Peter Gammons and Dick Vitale and check out the Extreme Sports section to find out about the Winter X and ESPN X games. You'll also be entertained by such fun stuff as "The Science of Sports," a monthly series by Bill Nye the Science Guy; the ESPN Multimedia Gallery; and goodies such as Sports Trivia, Players Directories, and LineTracker.

GolfWeb

http://www.golfweb.com/

The premiere golf resource on the Web. Here you can get the latest on such golf pros as Tiger Woods, Karrie Webb, John Daly, Annika Sörenstam, Kelli Kuehne, and Nick Faldo, as well as the LPGA and PGA tours. If you need some golf instruction, you can take the Lesson Tee. Avid golf players will appreciate OnCourse, an impressive database of courses. You can throw in your two cents in Tiger Talk, Architecture/Golf Courses, Women in Golf, and other discussion forums.

Major League Baseball

http://www.majorleaguebaseball.com/

Official site of Major League Baseball (MLB). The Kids section is particularly fun; here you can create your own Dream Team, get tips from the pros (such as Barry Larkin and Bret Boone), and explore the World of Card Collecting. To view vintage pictures of World Series games and famous players, check out the MLB Library. Other important features of this site include The Arizona Fall League, Major League International, and The Business of Baseball.

NandoNet's Sports Server

http://www.nando.net/SportServer/

Authoritative news source for professional sports, including football, basketball, baseball, and hockey. At this site you can read daily news and view high-quality photographs in the Photo Galleries. If you're interested in other professional sports, check out Racing Circuit (auto racing), Corner Kicks (soccer), Aces (tennis), Fairways (golf), In The Ring (boxing), and the Olympics. In addition, there are tidbits of news on horse racing, cycling, Nordic and alpine skiing, yachting, track and field, swimming, cricket, rugby, biathlons, and more.

11

NASCAR Online

http://www.nascar.com/

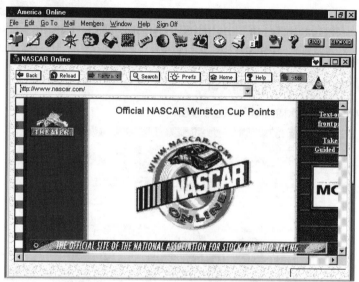

The official site of the National Association for Stock Car Racing (NASCAR). You can get the lowdown on the Winston Cup and Craftsman Truck Series, including information on the teams, tracks, schedules, and standings. You can also keep up with your favorite driver by reading Inside NASCAR. If you want to stay abreast of NASCAR news, you can subscribe to the weekly e-mail newsletter which includes information on every race weekend and announcements of NASCAR Online's new features.

National Basketball Association

http://www.nba.com/

The official site of the National Basketball Association (NBA). Here you can get continually updated news about games, teams, and players. If you're a serious basketball fan, you can try your hand at Trivia Today and send your fan e-mail to basketball stars. Be sure to check out the Top 10 Teams in NBA History to find in-depth bios of the best teams. The NBA at 50 section contains articles on the original NBA teams (Celtics, Knicks, and Warriors) and the Top 10 Coaches in NBA History.

National Football League

http://www.nfl.com/

Official home of the National Football League (NFL) on the Web. Every day, you can get NFL.com highlights, including divisional players of the week, player acquisitions, and Kevin Hardy's Rookie Journal. You can also find in-depth information on your favorite team, the complete season schedule, post-season recaps and previews, and the injury report. If you can't keep your opinions to yourself, you can add your predictions to the weekly Gatorade Dunk of the Week poll and chat with other NFL fans.

NHLPA

http://www.nhlpa.com/

The official site of the National Hockey League Players' Association (NHL). Here you can check out Player Stats to find complete playoff and final regular season stats indexed by player name. If you're curious about how much money these guys earn, sneak a peak in Player Compensation to view salaries indexed by defencemen, forwards, and goalies, as well as by team. Other fun stuff includes trivia, World Cup information, NHL Picks, and a handy *Be a Player: The Hockey Show* schedule.

The Olympic Movement

http://www.olympic.org/

The Web home of the International Olympic Committee, provided in both English and French, at this site you can get Olympic news highlights, read the Olympic Charter, check the official IOC Medical Commission's medical code, and explore the Olympic Museum in Lausanne, Switzerland. If you're a devoted Olympics fan, you'll appreciate the International Olympic Federations section, where you can find a new page for each International Olympic Summer and Winter Federation. This site also hosts the official countdown clock for Salt Lake 2002.

Professional Rodeo Cowboys Association

http://www.prorodeo.com/

Rodeo die-hards will not want to miss the world champions section, PRCA record book, hall of fame, and circuit information. Here you can also find a weekly news release and Today's Rodeo Fact. If your heart is on the animals' side, you might find solace in the Humane Facts section, where the PRCA Animal-Welfare Guidelines are located. This section also includes a FAQ on rodeo equipment.

SnowLink

http://www.snowlink.com/

Popular information source for "on-snow" sports, mainly skiing and snowboarding. If you jump directly to the Hot News/Cool Tips section, you'll find the New Products report, articles featuring on-snow trends, and seasonal snowsports news. Avid snowsporters will appreciate the listing of current snow conditions throughout the United States, Canada, and Europe. In addition, you can view informational calendars on lessons and demos as well as descriptions and contact information for clubs, teams, and organizations.

The Tennis Server Home Page

http://www.tennisserver.com/

Information resource for tennis players. A prominently displayed tidbit on this page is the huge listing of countries from which Web surfers visit—an interesting statement on the global appeal of tennis and the global reach of that other Net, the Internet. There's tons of tennis information available here, for both fans of professional tennis and tennis players. You can subscribe to the free Tennis Server INTERACTIVE e-mail newsletter and read exclusive columns by David Higdon, John F. Murray, Ron Waite, Emma Peetz, and tennis pro John Mills.

U.S. Soccer

http://www.cs.cmu.edu/~mdwheel/us-soccer

A Web site "for soccer fans by soccer fans." Here you can find U.S. soccer news, information on media resources for soccer fans, and numerous links to the sites of professional leagues, including Major League Soccer, the American Professional

Cosmetics Cop

http://www.cosmeticscop.com/

Everyone who uses cosmetics—which leaves few people out—should read this page. The author, Paula Begoun, a.k.a. the "Ralph Nader of Rouge," has done years of research on many aspects of the cosmetics industry, so she'll give you the low-down on what goes into popular products and which products make false claims. This Web site provides some excerpts from Ms. Begoun's books, as well as the *Cosmetics Counter* newsletter, the "Dear Paula" column, and Paula's Choice Skin Care System.

Diet and Weight Loss/Fitness Page

http://www1.mhv.net/~donn/diet.html

Inspiring and content-rich resource for anyone who wants to lose weight and get into better shape. Here you can read "The $1,000 Challenge," "A Powerful But Spooky Technique," "The Three Day Habit Breaker," and other articles written by a nonprofessional, self-taught expert from personal diet and fitness experience. Then move on to the huge collection of useful links, divided into categories of general information, diet and food, exercising and fitness, newsgroups, and health and fitness indexes.

Fashion Internet

http://www.finy.com/

Second best thing to attending a runway fashion show. The site has a New York focus, looking at the show rooms, design trends, and influential personalities in the fashion district. It's not parochial, though; start here to identify the ethnic and international influences on the best American designs. With Fashion Internet you'll stay a season ahead and find out what Isaac's up to.

Fashion Net

http://www.fashion.net/

Central search tool and directory of fashion-related Internet sites and services. Here you can find professionally compiled lists of message boards (fashion, beauty, modeling, and health and fitness) and top sites (magazines, shopping, fashion houses, beauty, modeling, and shows). You can also browse the industry-specific annotated guides for message boards, yellow pages, directories, trade publications, and shows and exhibits. There's hardly any fashion content per se within this site, but it is a comprehensive jumpstation to anything that may interest you.

Fashion Page

http://www.charm.net/~jakec/

Fashion maven Lynda Stretton produces this award-winning page, bringing fashion sense, style, and predictions to the Web world. For quick access, go directly to the table of contents to find new articles on current and past seasons as well as reviews of fashion television programs, magazines, books, and movies. If you're in the fashion industry, you'll appreciate the index of modeling agencies and fashion bibliography.

The Fragrance Foundation

http://www.fragrance.org/

The official Web site for The Fragrance Foundation. Here you can read about the history and mission of this organization and get perfume tips, fragrance trends, and information about the Olfactory Research Fund. The Features section offers articles that explore the importance of aromas and fragrances, such as using scent as a memory device and giving gifts of perfume. After touring The Fragrance Foundation, you'll wish that scents could be transferred over the Internet.

HairNet

http://www.hairnet.com/

Popular opinion asserts that hair is never unimportant. HairNet is dedicated to that proposition. Here you can find advice and services that help you make the most of your hair. Some of the features offered include *Beauty Online,* a Webzine devoted to beauty; *American Salon,* a leading beauty industry magazine; Salons Online, a database of beauty salons throughout the United States; HairNet Hotline, a community forum; and Beauty Schools Online, a database of beauty schools in a number of states.

The Lipstick Page

http://www.users.wineasy.se/bjornt/lip.html

Imagine an entire Web site devoted to lipstick: it would probably be full of color, advice, beauty tips, and pretty pictures. You're right—it is. Welcome to the Lipstick Page, where you can find everything you need to know about lipstick. The Lipstick Library provides a detailed catalog of colors, from "coral, peach, and apricot" to "reddish browns, brick, and terracotta." Learn who wears what lip paint in Lipstick of the Stars. Other useful sections include Cosmetics around the World, Tips and Consumer Issues, and the *FashionStance* mini-magazine.

11

Look Online

http://www.lookonline.com/

Insider perspective of the fashion industry. If you're interested in real fashion news—not just PR campaigns and ambiguous advice from waffling fashion critics—start here. Read about recent fashion shows (who showed up, who sat next to whom, and who was wearing what) and fashion politics (AIDS benefits and anti-fur and anti-exploitation demonstrations). Here you can also find interviews with designers, runway photos, and an updated list of Who's Who in New York Fashion Public Relations.

Lumiere

http://www.lumiere.com/

High-quality fashion Webzine; from funky and floral to shiny and sheer, you can read about it here. Every month, you'll find a variety of features on new seasonal fashions, trends, designers, models, photographers, fragrances, makeup, hair, and fashion in the entertainment industry. The site is chock-full of beautiful photographs, so you can see exactly what the authors are talking about. If you'd like to share your opinions with other fashion addicts or read about upcoming industry events, check out the message board.

Maximum Exposure

http://www.maxxp.com/

Webcast of Maximum Exposure, a live fashion industry event. This event is a charity benefit for Design Industries Foundation Fighting AIDS (DIFFA) and Photographers + Friends United Against AIDS. When Maximum Exposure is Webcasted, you'll be able to access live interviews with many celebrity models, photographers, performers, and actors. Some of the co-chairs of this event include Giorgio Armani, Fabien Baron, Kelly Klein, Peter MacGill, Isaac Mizrahi, Todd Oldham, and Anna Sui.

Redbook's Best Beauty Buys

http://homearts.com/rb/beauty/11bestf1.htm

Straightforward and down-to-earth guide to buying beauty products that are easy on your face and on your wallet. The pages on this site are divided into short advice blurbs on why some prices are so high, what to look for and what to avoid, which products can be substituted for more expensive brand products, and where to find the best deals on common products. Each blurb is presented with a photograph of the product and listed retail price.

Work Style

http://www.workstyle.com/

Where professional men and women come to get useful fashion advice for the working hours. Some fun features include Tip of the Day, Question of the Week, What They're Wearing in the [Music, Publishing, Computer, Legal, etc.] Industry, the Ask Kim advice column, the What to Wear column, and the Guess My Job? multiple-choice quiz. You can also read about a makeover and view "before" and "after" pictures of someone just like you!

TODAY'S NEWS

Campus Newspapers on the Internet

http://beacon-www.asa.utk.edu/resources/papers.html

A huge index of college and university newspapers, hosted by the University of Tennessee, Knoxville. You can browse the site listings by categories of how often the newspapers are published (daily, almost daily, or weekly, biweekly, and monthly). You can also find prototypes, demonstrations, and experimental newspapers which are still being developed. If you work on a student-run newspaper,

11

you'll want to check the college journalism resources to find valuable Internet sites for editors and advisors.

Capitol Steps

http://www.capsteps.com/

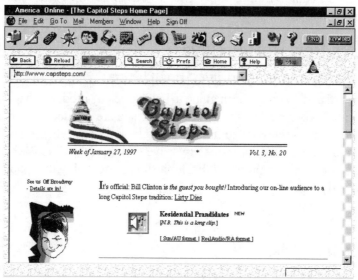

An irreverent look at Washington. This site is produced by a group of current and former Congressional staffers who monitor events and personalities on Capitol Hill, in the Oval Office, and in other typically serious places of political action. Audiophiles will love the satirical collection of songs about former Speakers of the House. You also won't want to miss the New Year's Radio Special about Ross Perot.

The Chicago Tribune

http://www.chicago.tribune.com/

Web edition of Chicago's renowned newspaper. You can start your morning by reading the main page, which contains daily headlines and top stories. In addition to the typical sections found in a print newspaper—national and local news, weather, business, sports, culture, special features, and editorials—the online Chicago Tribune offers some unique features, such as sports career profiles and archives; a search tool for finding homes for sale or rent; a real estate transactions database; and a database of Chicago-based community profiles, statistics, directories, and school information.

The Christian Science e-Monitor

http://www.csmonitor.com/

A distinguished source of international and U.S. news, cultural reviews and features, editorials, and more. Readers of the *Christian Science Monitor* (*CSM*) will appreciate Our Place, an organized directory of *CSM* articles and related links; you can browse by arts and entertainment, kids resources, travel, poetry, and other categories. Special areas include Mixed Media, where you can find stories about cyberspace, crossword puzzles, e-mail from international bureaus, the Mega Movie Guide, the Bringing Down a Gang series, and a reader forum; a collection of *CSM* Pulitzer Prize-winning stories; and an Internet radio broadcast featuring hourly newscasts and a daily show.

Editor & Publishers Directory of the World's Online Newspapers

http://www.mediainfo.com/ephome/npaper/nphtm/online.htm

Directory of international online newspapers, compiled by the *Editor & Publisher Interactive* research staff. An interesting table of information here is the online newspapers statistics, which provide data on Internet publications by news source type (dailies, weeklies, business, alternatives, etc.) and by continental region. You can also find descriptive listings of links to online newspapers from around the world. If you want to attend journalism industry events, check the Conferences and Calendar of Events section.

The Heritage Foundation

http://www.heritage.org/

The official Web home of this conservative research and educational think tank. Some of the best features of this site include Real Audio samples from Heritage's monthly "Talk of the Town"; the online edition of *Policy Review: The Journal of American Citizenship,* The Heritage Foundation's bimonthly flagship magazine; the 1997 Index of Economic Freedom, a guide to international growth and development; an online edition of *Issues '96: The Candidate's Briefing Book;* and the Tax Reform NOW! news source.

11

Los Angeles Times

http://www.latimes.com/

The renowned daily news source features continually updated top news stories. Check out the Business Review and Outlook section for entertaining business features, high-tech industry stories, the year in review, and future predictions. Destination L.A. contains a bunch of fun and interesting features for Southern California residents; check out the daily puzzle and information about seismic activity, as well as the guides to local restaurants and coffeehouses, Tinseltown, biking, shopping, and visitor and beach information.

National Public Radio

http://www.npr.org/

A Web complement to National Public Radio. You can listen to new broadcasts of NPR news every hour and find station listings, program information, and transcripts here. Jazz lovers will want to visit NPR's Jazz Profiles page to listen to a weekly one-hour jazz documentary series hosted by Nancy Wilson. You can also listen to other NPR shows, including "All Things Considered," "Morning Edition," "Talk of the Nation," "Making the Music," "Performance Today," and "Seasonings: Food." This is a great companion to the NPR forum on America Online (keyword: NPR).

The New York Times

http://www.nytimes.com/

Web edition of one of the most widely-read newspapers in the world. Some of the features available only on the online New York Times include the "CyberTimes Extra" column, Political Points Internet resource directory, Issues '96 (a joint project with National Public Radio), the Business Digest, the Business Connections financial resources guide, and the Arts & Leisure guide to the week's cultural events in New York. You can also search the real estate database, try your hand at the crossword puzzle and trivia quiz, and explore the Web Specials showcase.

the Onion: Number One in the News

http://www.theonion.com/

Weekly Webzine of satirical news. Nothing is sacred here; the Onion pokes fun at everyone and everything. Read "news" stories about strikes, mergers, and disasters that haven't really happened and are unlikely to occur. The Editorials are even worse—these are fake columns about so-called diseases, holidays, and controversies, among other topics. If you have ever thought the real news was a waste of time, you'll be pleased with this nonsense.

San Jose Mercury News: Mercury Center

http://www.sjmercury.com/

Online newspaper based in Silicon Valley. Go directly to the Breaking News section to read top news stories from the U.S. and around the globe. Mercury Center also offers extensive news and feature articles specifically about Silicon Valley and the high-tech industry. There are tons of useful services available here, including the Free Agent resume database, Family Cyberspace, the NewsHound automatic e-mail news service, and the searchable *San Jose Mercury News* library.

U.S. News and World Report Online

http://www.usnews.com/

A widely-read source of U.S. and international news based on the print magazine. You can view either a straightforward text or multimedia-enhanced version of this online magazine. Special sections include News Watch, Washington Connection, News You Can Use, Colleges and Careers, Town Hall, This Week's Issue, and Corporate Links. Specific highlights are provided with each section. Be sure to check out the exclusive excerpt of 24 Hours in Cyberspace.

U.S. Newspapers on the Net

http://www.naa.org/hot/hot.html

Top Internet newspaper picks by the Newspaper Association of America. Newspaper Online Services, Contacts, and URLs is a complete index to every newspaper on the Internet. You can look at the Feature of the Week to immediately see the most recent top choice, or you can find the past winners in the Feature of the Week Hall of Fame. If you're looking for a newspaper in a particular state, click the imagemap graphic of the United States. You can also peruse the Alphabetical Listing of Dailies; a Weeklies, Business Papers, and Alternative Press directory; and Select International Editions.

The Wall Street Journal Interactive Edition

http://www.wsj.com/

Premiere business and financial newspaper on the Web. The main sections are the Front Section, Marketplace, Money and Investing, and Sports. You can use Personal

11

Journal to customize your view of The Wall Street Journal Interactive Edition. Each company listed is linked to a Briefing Book, which provides a complete business profile. The most popular pages include Heard on the Street, Personal Technology, Editorials, U.S. Stocks, and Personal Finance. Be sure not to miss the award-winning Index to Market Data as well as the 14-Day Searchable Archive.

WashingtonPost.com

http://www.washingtonpost.com/

Widely read newspaper based in Washington, D.C. *WashingtonPost.com* consists of three parts: The Post, which presents straightforward news stories in plain text; WashingtonPost.com sections, which feature articles enhanced with related information, discussions, and graphics; and Washington World, which contains news, sports, recreation, restaurant, economy, and entertainment information pertaining to the Washington, D.C. area. Readers around the United States explore the WashingtonPost.com sections to find business, interaction, international, national, sports, and style pages.

TRAVEL

Airlines of the Net

http://w1.itn.net/airlines/

An award-winning, impartial jumpstation of Web-based airline information. Here you can find links to anything relating to air travel, including frequent flyer programs, airline stock quotes, medical airline transports, cargo airlines, manufacturers and suppliers, aviation organizations, airline Usenet newsgroups, airline toll-free numbers, and real-time airline reservations. In addition, there are listings for passenger carriers in all the continents of the world as well as carriers no longer in service (if you still haven't found that lost suitcase). Frequent travelers will appreciate the listings of the best fares, schedules, and travel agents.

AOL travel.com

http://www.aoltravel.com/

The Web site of AOL's Travel Channel. One of the most valuable features here is the interactive imagemap of the United States. Click any state to find information on state parks, museums, colleges, airports, and city sites. You can also learn each state's bird, flower, nickname, motto, and capital. In addition, there is a useful compilation of travel links, including the top ten most useful trip-planning sites, the airline reservations service at Preview Travel, a handy distance calculator, and the Olsen and Associates currency converter. Of course, if you're a member, you can link directly back to the Travel channel itself to get most of the travel-planning resources you need from one place.

Destinations Magazine

http://www.travelersguide.com/destinations/

Elegant publication devoted to vacation travel. You can find important U.S. State Department alerts on overseas travel in the Intelligence section, travel tips and tidbits in FYI, and fun events going on around the country in Happenings. If you're planning a trip soon, check out Travelogue to find Eateries (a dining, café, and bar guide) and Retreats (off-the-beaten-track vacation ideas). The Expressions section offers personal stories, complaints, and recommendations. Don't miss the special on airfare wars, hotels, and resorts.

Eurolink

http://www.syselog.com/eurolink/

A directory of voluminous travel information about 16 European countries. Simply click the flag of the country you're interested in, and you'll jump to a straightforward list of links on cities, tourism, entertainment, sports, business, government, and other types of information. This site's especially useful for aggregating travel and other information about small countries such as Hungary, Ireland, and Denmark. General European travel resources provide information about Eurail and the European Parliament.

Lonely Planet

http://www.lonelyplanet.com/

Collection of travel ideas from the successful publisher. If you have a specific destination in mind, go to Destinations to access an interactive imagemap of the world or use Text Express, a straightforward index. You can also click Take a Mystery Tour to randomly select a travel guide. Truly unique is the Postcards section where thousands of travelers' reports from every region around the world are compiled into a database of information on visas, border crossings, highlights, scams, and tips and warnings of various sorts.

National Park Services's ParkNet

http://www.nps.gov/

This huge and wonderfully informative site gives you a glimpse into the essential public services provided by the National Park Service, from maintaining the National Registry of historical buildings to acting as steward of our national parks. An Excite-powered search facility lets you plan a trip to national parks. I looked up Antietam National Park in my state and got phone numbers, maps, a copy of the Emancipation Proclamation, local weather conditions, driving instructions, and recommendations for what to wear! From ParkNet you can also link to related resources in the state park systems and the U.S. Fish and Wildlife Service.

Travel & Entertainment Network— Internet Operations (TEN-IO)

http://www.ten-io.com/

A directory of major travel and entertainment organizations and industry trade associations. These organizations are divided into categories such as accommodations, business travel services, cruises, destinations, entertainment, sports and recreation, transportation, travel agents, and travel-related information. If you click the button for any of these categories, you'll view an index of services. Each service offers an image-rich and descriptive catalog; from there, you can get contact information and make your reservations.

Travel Health Online

http://www.tripprep.com/index.html

A central source of travel health information, updated daily. Here you can peruse the alphabetized Directory of Country Summary Profiles to find health precautions, a disease risk summary, official health data, current health concerns, and the recent U.S. Department of State Advisory Consular Information Sheet. In addition, you can locate a travel medicine provider and read information on general travel health concerns, preventive medications and vaccines, and travel illnesses.

Travelocity

http://www.travelocity.com/

Complete information about the places you want to go and the ways you want to get there, with tips for having fun the whole time. Before you go anywhere, check the

Weather page to get the latest travel forecasts and airport reports. Ocean travelers will appreciate Travelocity Cruises by Cruises, Inc. You might be able to save some money by scanning Last Minute Deals. Points of View offers such goodies as the Trivia with Riddler game, a monthly contest, the Travelive chat forum, and the discussion bulletin boards. And don't miss the Spotlight feature or whale-watching column.

TravelWeb

http://www.travelweb.com/

You don't have to leave your home or office to make airline and hotel reservations; simply make a stop at this attractive site. If you're traveling this weekend, click the big button at the top to get the best hotel deals in major U.S. cities. Business travelers should go directly to the Business Traveler Resource Center to find information on special offers, ground transportation, overnight delivery, and computer services. Check the Press Office for recent travel news and features.

TheTrip.com: Flight Tracking

http://sapphire.thetrip.com/

Before leaving for the airport, stop by this site. This is an online real-time flight tracking service. Here you can get immediate data on current flights between major cities within the United States. Simply search for flights by airline, flight number, city, and time, and you'll get up-to-the-minute estimated local takeoff and landing times, status, destination distance, distance to the closest city, altitude (in feet), speed (miles per hour), and airplane equipment.

21st Century Adventures E-zine

http://www.10e-design.com/centadv/

Monthly publication containing a variety of travel features. Travelers on a budget will appreciate PennyWise. World traveler Kaye Madsen provides a valuable tips sheet on saving money while touring the world. You can also take virtual tours via the beautiful photographic galleries of Hawaii, the Rockies, the Grecian Islands, the Alps, Ancient Ephesus, England's Warwick Castle, and Ancient Olympia, as well as a sailing and balloon ride adventure. Don't miss the fun Adventurers Quiz.

USA CityLink

http://usacitylink.com/

The USA CityLink Project is a comprehensive directory of travel, tourism, and relocation information for most U.S. states and cities. You can immediately "visit" a city—or rather its page—to find an organized listing of links to valuable Web sites. The U.S. Information page offers a unique collection of tidbits and features, such as the current approximate census, the Pledge of Allegiance, a sound file of a child singing "The Star Spangled Banner," and the history of the national flag.

Vacations.com

http://www.vacations.com/

This complete guide to vacation planning comes to you from Preview Travel, an AOL partner and AOL-approved merchant whose vacation-booking service is available on AOL at keyword: Reservations. If you don't have a specific vacation in mind, you can use this Web site's Find-A-Trip to explore vacation types (such as romantic, family, singles, beach, casino, city, cultural, or weekend getaways) or regions (such as North America, Central America, or the Pacific Islands). One benefit of the Web over the forum is that you get VDO (video) clips such as "Kayaking on Kauai," to help you make your plans (Chapter 6 has a section about VDO).

World Travel Guide

http://www.wtgonline.com/

An encyclopedia-like database of regional information. If you're curious about a particular place, check the A to Z Country Fact Finder to learn about a country's area, population, population density, capital, geography, language, religion, time zone, electricity, communications, history, and government. From each country's fact page, you can access further information on accommodations, addresses, business, climate, essentials, resorts, social, and travel as well as view its map on the Map Page.

Appendix **A**

Your AOL Connection

So, you got an AOL disk in the mail or packaged with a magazine, or maybe even with this book. What do you do first? How do you get from having a disk to exploring the global Internet? It's a short trip, with three legs:

■ *Installing* AOL means putting a copy of the AOL software on your computer's hard disk.

■ *Setting up your phone connection* means letting the software figure out your modem speed and type, and your choosing the local telephone numbers you want to use to access the AOL network.

■ *Setting up your account* means connecting with AOL and providing the information required to give you full access to AOL and the Internet.

Note   *You can access AOL using a local network or another Internet Service Provider (ISP), instead of by modem connection to AOL's network, as explained in "Using AOL with a Network or Internet Service Provider." However, you must still install the AOL software and register with AOL following the steps in this appendix.*

Once you've installed the AOL software and registered with AOL, it's an easy matter to upgrade your software—get new versions. It's free, and sometimes automatic, and never requires putting another disk into your computer!

For all the "variables" involved—computer types, modem types, software versions, access numbers, service types, and billing plans—AOL has done an amazingly good job providing a simple reliable way of installing and registering. Just in case you do have a question along the way,

■ If you have general questions, you'll find useful information in the Help menu, which is available even if you've installed AOL but haven't yet registered.

■ If you've registered and have questions about your connection or your account, try keyword: Help and keyword: Quick Answers.

■ If you *can't* install or register for some reason, call one of the numbers in the "Numbers to Call if You Have Trouble" box at the end of this appendix.

If you are online and have questions about your connection, go to Member Services (keyword: Help). For help upgrading, go to keyword: Upgrade. For help using AOL, go to the Discover AOL area (keyword: DiscoverAOL) or Member Services (keyword: Help). For help with the Internet, go to keyword Nethelp—or, use this book!

Keywords

Once you're online, the fastest way to get to a specific AOL area or Internet address is using the Keyword window. It's always available from the Go To menu. To use it,

1. Sign onto AOL.

2. From the Go To menu, select Keyword. Enter a keyword in the box.

3. Click GO.

Some keywords you might want to get to know:

- keyword: Help

- keyword: Quick Answers

- keyword: Billing

- keyword: Access

- keyword: Nethelp

WHAT YOU NEED

The disk is the key to getting online, but it's not all you need to use AOL. You'll also need:

- A modem and phone (even if you plan to access AOL over a network)

- An amply equipped PC (see the "Recommended System" box)

- A credit card or other payment means

- A password and screen name (it's good to think of these things before you start)

AOL 3.0: Two Versions

There are two versions of AOL 3.0: AOL 3.0 for Windows 95 and AOL 3.0 for Windows (for either Windows 3.1 *or* Windows 95). The Windows 95 version includes the Microsoft Internet Explorer browser for using the World Wide Web, while the other version uses the older, BookLink browser. If you install AOL 3.0 for Windows and have Windows 95 on your computer, you can easily upgrade, at no cost, to the Windows 95 version at keyword: Upgrade. The system (PC) requirements for the two versions are listed in the "Recommended System" box.

This book focuses on the Windows 95 version but calls attention to the more important features of AOL 3.0 for Windows along the way.

Which Version Do I Have?

If you already have AOL on your system, it's good to know which version number you are running. Open the AOL program. Choose About America Online from the Help menu. You'll see either

America Online 3.0 for Windows 95

or

America Online 3.0 for Windows

To get even more information (specific version number), move the mouse arrow over the window and press CTRL-R. Click OK twice.

A Connection: Dial-up or Network

You can access the America Online service in two ways: using AOL's network (normal dial-up access using a modem); or *not* using AOL's network, which means either:

- Running AOL with a local "TCP/IP" network, such as you find in companies and organizations. If you have any questions about your network or need any help, ask your system administrator. If you can access the Internet over your work network, it's probably a TCP/IP network.

or

■ Running AOL with a dial-up SLIP/PPP connection to an Internet Service Provider.

 Appendix B, this book's glossary, explains terms such as SLIP and TCP/IP.

Dialing into the AOL Network

Dialing into AOL requires a modem. A modem lets your computer send and receive data over the telephone lines, which in turn are connected to AOL's data network. Your modem can be installed inside your computer (internal) or plugged into a jack in the back of the computer (external). And it can be low-speed (9,600 bps or lower) or high-speed (14,400 bps or higher). Unlike ordinary Internet Service Providers, with AOL you will usually never need to worry about the details of your modem: parity, baud, hardware handshaking, and stuff like that. The AOL software figures out what modem you're using.

If you don't yet have a modem, buy the fastest one you can afford. External modems are easier to install, but they do take up space on your desk. Once you're online, you can find more information at keyword: Modem. You can always buy a better modem on AOL at keyword: AOL Store (click on the AOL Modem Shop).

If you'll be using a modem and dialing the AOL network, you'll also need a **phone line**. In using an Internet service such as AOL, you incur two costs: one is your monthly phone bill from your phone company, which may reflect your calls to AOL if they are toll calls or local calls above "basic" service. The other is the monthly or annual bill from AOL.

Connecting over a TCP/IP Network or ISP

To use AOL over a TCP/IP network or Internet Service Provider (ISP) you must have access to a local TCP/IP network or an account with an Internet Service Provider such as AT&T's WorldNet, Netcom, Mindspring, or any of the hundreds of local ISPs. You'll find a directory of ISPs in Chapter 11 ("Internet Connection").

Recommended System

If you're new to Windows, welcome to the era of *big software*. Packing a ton of features into a "graphical user interface" (GUI) requires what a couple of years ago would have been a mainframe computer. Now the "recommended system" for AOL 3.0 is just about average for running a Windows application:

AOL 3.0 for Windows

- Windows 3.1 or Windows 95

- 486 or Pentium

- Mouse

- 8 Mb RAM

- 30 Mb hard disk

- 640 × 480 pixel monitor, displaying at least 256 colors

- 9,600 bps modem (14.4 or 28.8 kbps recommended for optimal performance)

AOL 3.0 for Windows 95

- Windows 95

- Pentium

- Mouse

- 16 Mb RAM

- 50 Mb disk space

- 640 × 480 pixel monitor, displaying at least 256 colors

- 14,400 bps modem or faster

Means of Payment

AOL bills you monthly or annually, and you must provide credit-card information (type, number, expiration date) when you register. AOL can also debit your checking account directly, but adds a fee to your bill in order to defray the costs of providing this service. Once you're online you'll find more information about this topic at keyword: Billing. You must provide this information even if you'll be signing on via a network other than AOL's.

Way of Identifying Yourself

During registration with AOL, you'll be asked for a screen name and password. Your *screen name* is how other people on AOL and the Internet will recognize you; a *password* is how AOL keeps track of your unique account.

Note　　*When you start registration for the very first time, you use the registration number and password provided on the AOL software package; during registration, you choose your own screen name and password.*

SCREEN NAME　　A screen name is how AOL members and people on the Internet will know who you are—it forms the personal part of your e-mail address, as you'll see in Chapter 3. You can choose any combination of letters and numbers between three and ten characters, but can't use punctuation marks. Screen names on AOL must be unique. They are not case sensitive, though AOL displays your screen name, in e-mail messages and elsewhere, with an initial capital letter and any other capital letters *you* use during registration. On the Internet you'll see the term *user name* more than *screen name*. It doesn't matter; they're the same thing.

Tip　　*When you register, you might not get your first choice, so be prepared with several alternatives. Many people use their first initial plus last name (HHoover) or first name plus last-name initial (FranklinDR).*

PASSWORD　　A password ensures that only you can sign onto AOL with your screen name. You enter a password every time you sign on. On AOL you'll need a password that is hard to guess if someone has any *other* information about you. So, it's a good idea to make your password different from your name and the name of anyone in your family. Nor should it contain your birthdate, mother's maiden name, or Social

Security number. Creating a password that consists of arbitrary and alternating numbers and letters is a good way of making your password unguessable.

> *Caution* *Never, in any circumstances, tell anyone your password, even if someone claiming to work for AOL asks for it. As a policy, no one who really works for AOL will **ever** ask you for your password. If someone does ask for your password, say no, then write an e-mail message to AOL's Community Action Team (CAT). Here's how: If the solicitation occurs when you're online (via an Instant Message) go to keyword: GuidePage, then click on Password and follow the instructions. If the solicitation occurs via an e-mail message to you, forward the message as proof of the incident to TOSemail1 or TOSemail2. Display the message, click Forward, type **TOSemail1** or **ToSemail2** in the To box, and click SEND. In Chapter 3 you'll learn everything you need to know to use e-mail.*

With a modem installed and turned on, with your computer turned on, with the phone line free, with a credit card at hand and a screen name and password in mind, grab that disk and follow the instructions on its package!

SIGNING ON

Once you're registered with AOL, signing on is simple. "Signing on," also known as "logging on," means connecting to the AOL service and from there to the Internet.

> *Note* *Signing onto AOL is not like flipping a light switch. First of all, you have to open the AOL program. The program itself is large, so it may take a moment or two between the time you double click its icon and AOL displays on your screen. Then, when you sign on, the modem has to be "initialized," the AOL number dialed, a connection established, and your password verified. Things can go wrong: the number can be busy (in which case the second number will be dialed) or your password could be mistyped (you'll be asked to reenter it). If you do have to wait—it'll be worth it.*

If you have Windows 3.1, an America Online "program window" is automatically created for you during installation and placed in your Program Manager (your main view of the Windows program and all the applications you've installed). The window includes the AOL icon. If you have Windows 95, an icon is created for you and placed in the following folder:

```
c:/windows/start menu/programs/America Online
```

This makes AOL available from Windows 95's Start menu, the menu that pops up when you click on the Start button on the Windows 95 taskbar. Click Programs and you'll come to the America Online folder, where you'll find the AOL program you just installed.

To create a Windows 95 icon on your desktop:

1. Use the Windows 95 Explorer to open the **c:/windows/start menu/ programs/America Online** folder. Click the America Online 3.0 program to select it.

2. From Explorer's File menu, select Create ShortCut.

3. Use your mouse to drag the shortcut you've just created to your Windows 95 desktop. You may have to minimize or close other windows to get them out of the way.

Here's the ordinary way you sign on to AOL. Other ways are discussed a little later.

1. Double click the AOL icon, whether it's in a Windows 3.1 program window or on the Windows 95 desktop. The AOL program may take a moment to display—it's a big program. When it does display, the Welcome window appears, and the cursor (where you type something) *should* be blinking in the Enter Password field. If it's not, move the mouse arrow there, and click.

2. Type your password in the Enter Password box.

3. Click the SIGN ON button. AOL now looks for the modem, dials the local phone number you chose during registration, establishes connection with the AOL network, verifies your password, and...you're ready to navigate the Internet!

 Chapter 2 picks up the story from here: what you do when you sign on, and how you sign off.

USING AOL WITH A NETWORK OR INTERNET SERVICE PROVIDER

If you already have a SLIP or PPP connection with an Internet Service Provider, you can run AOL with of that connection. SLIP and PPP are defined in Appendix B. In a word, what SLIP or PPP lets you do is connect to the Internet using a modem.

How do you know if you have such an account? If you have Internet access through a commercial service such as AT&T's WorldNet and pay a monthly fee for dial-in access (using a modem), you probably have a SLIP or PPP connection. If you're using a modem and use a graphical Internet program such as Netscape or Eudora, you almost certainly have such a connection.

AOL's new "bring your own access" pricing plan makes it easy and cost-effective for subscribers of other services to use the content on the America Online service, but dial in through *another* network. The main advantages to this plan are that it's faster to sign onto AOL (at least after you've connected to your ISP) and you're less likely to encounter a busy signal.

To do so, you create a special *location*. Here's how:

1. Sign onto your SLIP or PPP connection with your Internet Service Provider. You'll probably have to provide a username and password just as on AOL, and for good measure you should make sure they're different from the ones you use on AOL.

2. Open the AOL program. Click on Setup on the Sign On screen.

3. Click Edit Location.

4. Select TCP/IP from the Network drop-down box. In the Location box at the top of the window, type in a name for the "location." It doesn't have to be a place, just a way of remembering the fact that it's your network connection. Call the location *Work* or *WorldNet* or whatever you want. Click Save, and then click OK to return to the Sign On screen.

5. Type in your password and sign on to America Online as you normally would.

With TCP/IP selected as your network type, modem information becomes irrelevant to AOL. Even if you're using a modem to access WorldNet, for example, you're still using TCP/IP to access AOL. Any problems with your modem or connection should be pursued with the provider through whom you're getting access.

Caution *You can stay logged onto AOL only as long as your connection is active; if you're disconnected from your ISP, you'll be disconnected from AOL as well. On the other hand, signing on through an ISP won't keep you from getting disconnected from AOL if you are inactive for a long period ("long period" varies with time of day). In that case, getting logged off AOL won't disconnect your underlying ISP connection, and you'll be tying up your phone line (and maybe incurring phone cost or ISP fee, or both) as long as the connection to the ISP is active.*

Why Create Special Locations?

If you access AOL from different places or by different methods (a TCP/IP network vs. dialing into AOL's network), you may want to creation different "locations." On the Sign On window, the location you're currently using is in small letters underneath the password field:

Why create different locations?

■ If you encounter a busy signal (in the evening, say), a different location can make access easier, even if the dial-in number is slower, or further from your house.

■ If you're frequently on the road, you may want to keep a separate location for each place you visit, complete with a local dial-in number.

■ If you use AOL at work or over a SLIP/PPP account from another Internet Service Provider, you might want to create a special location for those occasions.

Procedures for changing locations are provided in this section. To change locations, click Setup at the Welcome screen, select a location, and click OK.

Signing On as a Guest

From time to time you may find yourself using America Online on someone else's computer. Your computer might be in the shop, or you might be travelling without your own computer. For these times, you start to sign on as normal, by double clicking the other-person's AOL icon.

At the Select Screen Name box, click the downward-pointing arrow, select Guest, and click Sign On.

You'll connect as you do normally. What's different is that you'll be asked for your screen name and password *after* you connect. Once AOL verifies this information, you'll be able to see your Buddy List, send and receive e-mail, and use the core AOL features, but you won't be able to do things requiring access to the hard disk of the person whose machine you're using—you won't be able to use Favorite Places, Download Manager, or Personal Filing Cabinet.

Signing On While Travelling

If you take your portable on a business trip or vacation, you can still access AOL even if your ordinary local access number is halfway across the country. Start the AOL program. At the Select Screen Name box, click the downward-pointing arrow, select New Local#, and click Sign On.

As during registration, you'll be asked to supply your current area code and then to select from a list of the access numbers closest to your temporary location. You might want to save the new number as a new location if you'll be in the new place for a while or must return there often.

You can also get a number using the 1-800-827-6364 Customer Service number. Alternatively, you can use AOL's 1-800 access number. For more information, go to keyword: Access.

If you are on the road, make sure to bring along a phone cable (RJ-11 cord), and make sure to stay in a hotel room with a jack to plug it into!

If you're travelling abroad, you can still sign onto AOL using the AOLGlobalNet network, which carries a variable surcharge depending on the location from which you're calling. The current surcharges are available at keyword: AOLGlobalnet. With this network, AOL is currently available in more than 200 cities in over 80 countries around the world.

AOLGlobalNet is quite a different thing from the new international channels popping up on AOL. Think of AOLGlobalNet as a physical network. Think of the new international channels as communities, in league with AOL's other channels, except that they serve the full range of needs of members in different countries. Currently, there are international channels in Germany, France, England, Italy, and Canada. Each has sports, entertainment, news, and more. These channels are available free to AOL members by going to the Channels menu and clicking International, then clicking World of AOL.

Information about all of AOL's international services—the International channel and AOLGlobalNet—is available at keyword: International.

MODIFYING YOUR SETTINGS

What if you get a new modem, or change your address, or want to change your screen name? With America Online, it's easy to change the information you provided during registration.

IF YOU WANT TO DIAL IN USING A DIFFERENT PHONE NUMBER. While *offline*, start the AOL program and select New local# from the Select Screen Name drop-down list. Click Sign On. AOL dials a 1-800 number and connects. It prompts you for an area code. Type in an area code and click CONTINUE. Choose two access numbers, as during registration, then confirm your choices. You'll be returned to the Welcome screen. Re-select your actual screen name in the Select Screen Name box, type in your password, and click Sign On.

IF YOU GET A NEW MODEM. While *offline*, start the AOL program and select Setup at the Welcome screen, then click Setup Modem. Select a new modem from the long list that comes up. If you're adept technically or know someone who is, click Edit Commands to adjust the commands your modem uses.

TO CHANGE YOUR PERSONAL INFORMATION (NAME, ADDRESS, ETC.). While *online*, go to keyword: Billing. Click on Modify Name or Address, or Modify Billing or Price Plan, and follow the instructions.

IF YOU WANT TO CHANGE YOUR PASSWORD (WHICH YOU SHOULD DO FROM TIME TO TIME). While *online*, go to keyword: Password and enter both your old password and the new one (twice, for verification). Write down your new password.

Tip   *With so many Web sites asking you to register these days, and each of them giving you a separate password, it's easy to forget your password! Find a special place to keep all your passwords.*

IF YOU WANT TO ADD A SCREEN NAME. First of all, you can't delete or change the main screen name on your "master account" (the one you registered with). It's your unique identifier on America Online. Together with your password, it's how AOL knows who you are. But you *can* use up to four additional screen names in your account, and sign on using one of them instead. Each of these additional screen names gets its own password. Keyword: Screen Name has all the details; you can add screen names there too.

Only one screen name for an account can be used online at the same time and screen names must be unique.

Why Would You Want Separate Screen Names?

- If other people in your household use AOL, each person may want a separate screen name, in order to have their own mailboxes. Yes, each screen name gets its own set of mailboxes (described in Chapter 3), and everybody gets their own storage space (2 Mb worth) using AOL's My Place service, as described in Chapter 7.

- If you like to hang out in chat rooms, you may want different screen names for your various online personas.

- If you subscribe to many mailing lists (Chapter 4), you can manage your mailboxes better by subscribing to lists from different screen names. If you ever delete a screen name, make sure to first unsubscribe from any mailing lists.

You'll probably find your own reasons for establishing multiple screen names. Parental Controls—which let parents control their children's access to the Web, e-mail, newsgroups, and other AOL or Internet features—can be set for each screen name on a master account (keyword: Parental).

UPGRADING AOL

Upgrading AOL means getting a new version of the AOL software. Software upgrades used to be a big deal. Now, you will encounter "incremental," more or less automatic upgrades when a single tool or feature gets upgraded.

For big upgrades (such as when the version number changes, like from version 2.5 to version 3.0, or version 3.0 to version 4.0), you must first get yourself a new **setup.exe** file and run that program. Where do you find this software? Keyword: Upgrade. For lesser upgrades, the process takes place automatically. Let's look at each of these types of upgrade.

A

MAJOR UPGRADES (WITH A NEW VERSION NUMBER)

Making a big upgrade is a two-step process: downloading the **setup** file and running the file. Since you've already registered with AOL, you needn't provide again information such as your Visa number and street address. Further, the Setup program makes note of any preferences you've established for earlier versions (they're stored on your computer) and transfers them automatically to the new version.

 Major upgrades give you a whole new set of AOL files but retain the AOL files you previously had on your system. If you want to continue accessing AOL using the same icon you used for your previous version of AOL—the icon will be in a program window (Windows 3.1) or on your desktop (Windows 95)—you'll have to change the settings for that icon so that it "points to" the upgraded AOL program. You do this by changing the icon's "properties." Click (once) on the AOL icon. In Windows 3.1, select Properties from the File menu; in Windows 95, right click, select Properties, and click on the Shortcuts tab. Now, change the "target" field (the Command Line in Windows 3.1) to match the name of the new AOL file: C:\AOL30K\AOL.EXE, for example. You can either type in the filename and path if you know it or (a better idea) click Browse to find the target.

You can get the new software online, but must install it while you're offline.

MINOR UPGRADES (SAME VERSION NUMBER, NEW TOOL)

AOL has a powerful new way of giving you "incremental" software releases. When a new service is added or an existing one enhanced, AOL automatically delivers the new software "on the fly" the first time you attempt to use it. Alternatively, when there's new software, you will be asked (in a little window) to update your AOL software automatically when you sign off. For example, if the browser's been spiffed up and you try to go to a Web site, you'll be asked to first wait for the new software to be downloaded, during which time you'll see:

These "tools on the fly" are either AOL-specific software, such as the charting tool, or AOL's Internet software, such as the browser.

While the software is downloading (in under a minute or two, usually), you will see a New Features window describing why you are getting the software. After the software has been downloaded, you may be asked to allow the AOL software to restart itself (automatically). Click OK. You will *not* be asked to sign on again.

Numbers to Call if You Have Trouble

1-888-265-8001	To receive information on AOL Products or Services
1-888-265-8002	Upgrade to the current version or to order an AOL Membership Kit
1-888-265-8003	For billing information or to reactivate a cancelled account
1-888-265-8004	Screen name or password assistance
1-888-265-8005	Obtain a new access number
1-888-265-8006	AOL for Windows technical support
1-888-265-8007	AOL for Macintosh, AOL for DOS, or other technical assistance
1-888-265-8008	To cancel an account

Appendix B

Indispensable Terms

Two excellent glossaries are available on the Internet if you want more detail about any listing in this glossary, or if you want to know about something that's *not* here. *Matisse*, from the Internet Literacy Consultants, has clean and compact definitions of the most important Internet terms (**http://www.matisse.net/files/glossary.html**). Fuller definitions, with links to actual content, are available in the *Webopaedia*, from Sandy Bay Software (**http://www.sandybay.com/pc-web/index.html**). On AOL, Answer-Man's Glossary (keyword: AM Glossary) provides short, crisp definitions of just about anything you'd want to know about the Internet.

address   There are several kinds of addresses on the Internet. An e-mail address, such as **answerman@aol.com**, is used by people to send mail to each other. An Internet address, or *URL*, such as **http://www.aol.com**, is used by people to request information from a computer. An *Internet Protocol (IP)* address, such as **206.139.24.100**, is used by computers on the Internet to send each other data. Gopher, Web, FTP, and e-mail addresses all follow the *domain name* system, and computers are set up on the Internet to "map" domain names to unique *IP addresses*.

address book   On AOL, your Address Book lets you keep track of the people to whom you most frequently send *e-mail* messages. It also lets you assign easy-to-remember names to those hard-to-remember Internet e-mail addresses. With your Address Book you can even maintain simple mailing lists, assigning a single name to a series of e-mail addresses of people you frequently write at the same time.

agent   Software used to perform some task automatically. Currently, many agents are being developed to automate the process of looking for information on the Internet.

Anonymous FTP   *See* **FTP**.

ANS   Stands for Advanced Network & Services, Inc., a company established as a non-profit organization in 1990 to serve as the principle architect of the NSFnet, the U.S. network that was the immediate forerunner of today's Internet. Since 1991,

ANS has been a pioneer in providing commercial access to the Internet. In 1995, AOL acquired ANS in order to provide reliable, fast, and affordable Internet access to a rapidly growing membership. As an AOL company, ANS continues to provide private networking services to hundreds of American companies. For more information, go to keyword: ANS.

AOLnet America Online's proprietary high-speed, high-capacity data network, which provides access by modem and network (*TCP/IP*) in hundreds of cities in the U.S. For more information, go to keyword: Access.

Archie Used for finding files available via anonymous (publicly accessible) *FTP*. Archie uses a program that regularly visits known anonymous FTP sites, makes a list of files and directories at those sites, and makes the index available to people on the Internet to do searches of the resulting database of files. Searches can be done by e-mail or Telnet, but the easiest way is via the World Wide Web. There are approximately 20 Archie sites around the world; all maintain the same database of files available by anonymous FTP. *See* Chapter 8.

ASCII Short for American Standard Code for Information Interchange; in practice, simple letters and numbers, unformatted so they can be read by computers on any operating system (Mac, Windows, Unix, etc.). All *HTML* files are available in ASCII format, to make them as widely available as possible.

asynchronous vs. real-time communication Asynchronous is jargon for "not at the same time." Electronic mail and newsgroups are asynchronous types of electronic communication. You send a message to another person, or to a mailing list, or to a newsgroup for someone else to read later or not at all. "Synchronous" is the opposite of asynchronous, though the more common technical term is "real time." Chat, Instant messages, IRC, and Virtual Places all take place in real time, that is, with another person reading your message almost instantly after you've typed and sent it. Asynchronous communication is often more "serious" than real-time communication, which is more personal and direct. For more information, *see* Chapter 3 (e-mail), Chapter 5 (newsgroups), and Chapter 10 (IRC and Virtual Places).

avatar From the Sanskrit (really!), for an embodiment of a concept, often in human form. On *Virtual Places*, an avatar is a little picture you choose to represent yourself—it can represent how you want others to see you or it can be just a picture of something you like.

B

bandwidth The amount of data that can be transmitted over any communications medium (phone line or network) in a period of time, for example bits per second (bps).

BCC (blind carbon copy) In e-mail, a copy of a message sent to someone without the direct recipient's awareness. The direct recipient is the person whose e-mail address (screen name) is in the To field. Using AOL, to send a BCC to someone, you put their e-mail address *in parentheses* in the CC field. You can send BCCs to any number of people by separating their e-mail addresses by commas. *See* Chapter 3.

binary In *FTP*, a mode for transferring any *file* that requires a special program to use it. Basically, all files that aren't text are binary. AOL's FTP client doesn't require you to indicate whether a file is binary or text, but any *Winsock* FTP client you use, such as WSFTP, will require you to make this choice. When in doubt: use binary, since a text file can be transmitted in binary mode but a binary file can't be transmitted as text unless it's been encoded using a technique such as *MIME* (*see* Chapters 3, 6).

bookmark Hot lists, bookmarks, Favorite Places, and Favorites all have the same purpose: to give you a means of keeping track of your favorite sites so you can easily return to them. *Bookmark* is Netscape's term for a list of favorite Web sites, while *Favorite Places* is AOL's term for your list of favorites available anywhere—on AOL, on the Web, in e-mail, newsgroups, etc. Microsoft's Internet Explorer browser, which is installed for you when you use the AOL 3.0 for Windows 95 software, refers to them as Favorites, and keeps them in the **c:/windows/favorites** folder. *See* Chapter 6.

BPS *See* **bandwidth**.

browser Software used for displaying an HTML *page*, part of the World Wide Web. A browser takes a plain HTML page, which you download from the Web, and presents any images, formatting, and links contained on that page. AOL 3.0 for Windows 95's browser is a customized version of the Microsoft Internet Explorer browser. Your browser is always available by clicking the Globe icon of the main AOL tool bar or using keyword: Web or keyword: WWW. In addition, with *Winsock* you can run other browsers, such as Netscape Navigator. *See* Chapter 6 on using the integrated browser and Chapter 10 on using the Netscape browser.

button A small graphic on AOL or the Web that can be clicked to either link to related content or to process something (for example, in Marketplace, a Click Here To Purchase button would process an order if you're buying something). The AOL tool bar consists of buttons.

CAT AOL's Community Action Team, responsible for enforcing AOL's Terms of Service (available at keyword: TOS).

CC (carbon, sometimes *courtesy,* copy) In AOL's e-mail program, you send anyone a CC if you want the direct recipient to be aware of the CC. The direct recipient's e-mail address goes in the To field of the Compose Mail window, while people CC'ed go in the CC field. You can send CC's to any number of people by separating their e-mail addresses by commas. You can send CCs to people on AOL or on the Internet, or both. *See* Chapter 3.

channel **(1)** On AOL, communities and forums are organized into channels, based on either subject or the actual location of the communities. The subject-based channels are Computers & Software; Entertainment; Games; Health & Fitness; the Hub; the Internet Connection; Kids Only; Learning & Culture; Life, Styles & Interests; MarketPlace; MusicSpace; Newsstand; Today's News; People Connection; Personal Finance; Reference; Sports; Style; Travel. The two place-based channels are Digital Cities (with content about large U.S. metropolitan areas) and International (with content for AOL "affiliates" in foreign countries—Canada, England, France, Germany, and Japan). Within channels, there are clusterings of content as big as some channels—Digital Cities Washington, the International channel affiliates, and Your Business (within Personal Finance), for example. The best way to find content within and across channels is using the Find area (click the Find button in the main window). **(2)** On *IRC*, the equivalent of a chat room, which can be formed by anyone and must have at least one person present to remain in existence. Unlike a chat room, a channel has an operator, with broad powers to set the channel's topic, name other operators, and kick people out. *See* Chapter 10.

chat Chat is a form of real-time communication, meaning you communicate with a group of people by sending messages, which they can read almost as soon as you send them. On AOL, chat rooms are available in the People Connection channel and throughout the other channels. The closest thing to chat on the Internet is *Internet*

B

Relay Chat (IRC). *Virtual Places* allows you to chat with others while browsing the Web. For more information about IRC and Virtual Places, *see* Chapter 10.

check box   In Windows programs such as AOL, the little square check box gives you the ability to specify a choice (as in the Software Search area shown in Figure 8-5). You can check more than one box (or no boxes). With *radio buttons*, you can (and must) select only one choice. You select a check box by clicking in the little square.

client   The software you run on your computer, such as an e-mail client or FTP client. On the Internet, client software interacts with *server* software. Clients receive, package, and transmit requests for information stored on servers. The whole Internet is built on client/server principles, with applications distributed across a network and many clients accessing the programs and data available on a much smaller number of servers.

compress   *See* **file compression**.

cookie   A small text file created by a Web server and stored on *your* computer to keep track of the sorts of things you do on the server. Web administrators create cookies in order to get information about users' browsing habits and to modify their site accordingly, or to present users with a customized view of the site. The cookie file can trace a user's "click path" through a site, but not between sites. Using the AOL 3.0 for Windows 95 software, you can set your preferences to be "warned" when a cookie is being created on your computer—you can then refuse to let the cookie be created. Some people consider cookies an invasion of their privacy. *See* Chapter 6.

directory   **(1)** The same thing as a folder—a place to keep files together. Your computer has directories, as do FTP sites and Web servers. **(2)** In the context of searching the Internet, a directory is a catalog of resources arranged into subjects such as Business and Medicine. A directory is different from a search *index* in that it is created by people and hence it is selective, more or less subjective, and often annotated (with site descriptions, ratings, and comparisons). The major directories are Yahoo!, Magellan, and the Virtual Library. Some of the indexes, such as Excite, have their own directories. *See* "Search Terms and What They Mean" in Chapter 9.

domain name   People use *domain names* to identify and communicate with computers connected to the Internet. Domain names consists of several parts, separated by periods ("dots"), proceeding from specific to general. Your domain name is *aol.com*. The general part of the name (*com*, for example) identifies the domain *type*. The main domain types in the U.S. are *edu, com, mil, net, org*, and *gov*. Other countries usually have a "top-level" domain of two characters, such as *ca* for Canada and *nl* for the Netherlands. But you'll see three-letter non-U.S. domains (such as **www.corel.com**) and two-letter U.S. domains (such as **mcps.k12.md.us**). The domain name is the key part of every Internet address (URL). Every domain name "maps" to a unique numerical IP address.

download   To send a file from a generally accessible computer (*server*) to another, usually private computer (*client*), over networks such as AOL and the Internet. You download files from the Internet in many ways: e-mail, FTP, newsgroups, and the Web. AOL's *Download Manager* "queues" files to download when you use e-mail or one of AOL's file libraries. AOL's browser handles Web downloads. *Uploading* is the opposite: it means copying a file from a PC to another computer, where (often) it can be made available to others. On AOL some file libraries allow you to upload files. Using Personal Publisher 2, you can upload files to your *My Place* area. Chapter 6 (on the Web browser) and Chapter 8 (on FTP) have information about downloading files with AOL.

Download Manager   A program available only on AOL that manages files you download from newsgroups, files attached to e-mail messages, and files you download using FTP and AOL's dozens of software libraries. It *doesn't* keep track of Web site downloads. Using Download Manager you can download several files at a time (except via FTP), automatically decompress files you download, and keep track of when you downloaded them and where you saved them on your computer. Download Manager is available from the File menu, even when you are offline, but offline use is limited to decompressing files and keeping track of where you downloaded files. Additional information about the Download Manager is available at keyword: Download Info Center and at keyword: Download 101.

electronic mail   Or *e-mail* or just *mail*. The main way to communicate with other people on the Internet. E-mail is an example of *asynchronous* communication, meaning it's not instantaneous; the other person may not see the message for days (or ever). AOL offers choices such as hyperlinks and highly formatted text when you send e-mail to someone else on AOL. Most of these features will be stripped out of mail sent to people on the Internet, however. Using AOL, you can send the same piece of mail to several people on AOL or the Internet at the same time, and you can choose to have one or more indirect recipients (*CCs* and *BCCs*). *Mailing*

B

lists are a way of communicating with a group of people. For more information, *see* Chapter 3.

emoticon   *See* **smiley**.

encryption   A way of scrambling sensitive information to prevent others from accessing it. AOL's browser allows you to encrypt information like your credit-card number when you wish to purchase a product or service from a vendor on the Web. The integrated browser automatically uses an encryption technique called *SSL*, for Secure Sockets Layer, which not only encrypts data but guarantees the authenticity of the other party and ensures the integrity of the data transmitted. *See* Chapter 6.

engine   *See* "Search Terms and What They Mean" in Chapter 9.

explorer   The name of the file management program that comes with Windows 95 (it replaces Windows 3.1's File Manager). Internet Explorer is the name of the Microsoft Web browser, which has been customized for AOL and integrated into AOL 3.0 for Windows 95. *See* Chapter 6.

extensions   *See* **file extensions**.

e-zine   Also known as a *'zine*, *zine*, and *Webzine*, an e-zine (short for electronic magazine) is a publication that appears exclusively on the Internet, on a more or less regular publishing schedule, with its own editorial staff, writers, purpose, audience, and point of view. E-zines exist for every Internet service, including e-mail (where they're distributed by mailing lists), Gopher, and these days especially the Web (*Webzine*). E-zines have a reputation of being "alternative," but some are devoted to mainstream topics as well. An excellent source of information is John Labovitz's searchable E-zine List at **http://www.meer.net/~johnl/e-zine-list/**.

FAQ   Short for Frequently Asked Questions. Sometimes pronounced as a word ("FAK") and sometimes as F-A-Q. In newsgroups, a classic format for answering questions about the scope of the topic and about the newsgroup itself (what's acceptable and what's not). The original idea was to get everyone up to speed and to keep newcomers from asking the same questions on a newsgroup. Usually, an individual maintains a FAQ, but everyone in a newsgroup can recommend modifications, giving many FAQs the status of authoritative, community-based documents. A FAQ is usually posted to the newsgroup in question as well as to

news.answers. The **news.answers** archive, with hundreds of FAQs, is available at the **rtfm.mit.edu** FTP site, which is one of the FTP "Favorite Sites" available on America Online at keyword: FTP (click Go To FTP). The FAQ format has been adopted elsewhere on AOL and the Net. *See* Chapter 5.

Favorite Places   An AOL-only feature that allows you to keep track of the "places" you like best, whether they're AOL forums, Web sites, Internet newsgroups, or individual e-mail messages. You add to your Favorite Places folder by clicking the heart in a window's title bar. You access your Favorite Places folder by clicking the Favorite Places icon (the folder with a heart) on your tool bar. With Favorite Places you can easily create folders in order to group related resources for easy access. *See* Chapters 2 and 6.

file   PCs use files to keep track of programs and data. A file has a location (a specific directory or folder), a name (its filename), a type (or format, such as GIF), and a size (measured in bytes and kilobytes). Windows 95's *Explorer* lets you view the files on your hard disk. *FTP* is the Internet service you use to *download* (retrieve) files from the Internet. AOL's many file libraries let you download files from AOL, including the programs you need to work with the files you download from the Internet! *See* Chapter 8.

file compression   A technique for making a file smaller, so it takes up less space on a computer and can be uploaded and downloaded more quickly. Compressing and decompressing files requires a special program such as WinZip. AOL's *Download Manager* can be used to automatically decompress some files. *See* Chapter 8.

file extensions   In DOS and Windows, the part of a filename that follows the period, as with the **avi** in **vertigo.avi**. Extensions can tell you whether a file is compressed (*see* **file compression**), what operating system it's for (Macintosh or Windows), and what program you need to use the file. For more information, *see* Chapter 8.

FileGrabber   Only on AOL! Newsgroups can be used to distribute files, such as software and sounds, but the files must first be converted from a *binary* format (computer code) into a text file (*ASCII text*). The text is meaningless to people, but at least it can be inserted into newsgroup postings and distributed across the Internet. To decode the text and turn it back into a computer code (a usable file), the file must be decoded. AOL handles this for you automatically with a program called

B

FileGrabber, which is accessed whenever you try to download a newsgroup posting containing such a file. *See* Chapter 5.

flame   In Internet mailing lists and newsgroups, a heated and unproductive discussion. Flaming can be considered a form of hazing on the Internet, or it can serve a rhetorical purpose, or it can be considered merely abusive and rude—a result of not respecting the other person because the communication seems "anonymous." Flaming can be counter-productive insofar as it inhibits others from taking part in the communication. Special newsgroups are devoted to flaming. From the Newsgroups window (keyword: Newsgroups), click Search All Newsgroups and do a search for newsgroups with the word *flame* in their name. *See* Chapter 5.

FlashSession   America Online gives you many options for quickly and automatically carrying out tasks online, so you can do the reading and composing offline. Many of these tasks can be done using FlashSessions: reading and posting to newsgroups, reading and sending e-mail, and downloading files. With FlashSessions (available from the Mail menu), you choose the activities you want to automate, then choose the times when you want these activities to occur (or you can do them "on demand"). With FlashMail, for example, you can compose e-mail throughout the day but only go online once a day to *send* all your messages at the same time. Similarly, you can *receive* mail and newsgroup postings either according to some regular schedule or "on demand"—go online once a day, say, and run an automatic FlashSession, then sign off. Once your mail or newsgroups have been downloaded, you can sign off and read everything offline, at your leisure and without online cost. For more information, *see* Chapter 4.

form   In Windows programs and Web pages, a window giving you the opportunity to state your preferences or indicate a choice, as when you are taking a survey or buying a product. The standard elements of a form are a *text box* (where you type in something), *check boxes* or *radio buttons* (where you select from pre-determined choices), and different kinds of lists. Forms make the Web interactive, not just a means of passively getting information. *See* Chapter 2.

forwarding e-mail   Sending a message you've received to someone else. On America Online, if you select nothing in the original message to you, you automatically forward the entire message. If you select any part of the message, editing and excerpting as you please, you'll forward only what you've selected. In either case, you can precede the message with your own comments as well. When you forward a message on AOL, the Subject line is automatically picked up from the original message; all you have to do is supply an address in the To box. Any files attached to the message you received will be forwarded as well; you can't detach them.

frames Frames divide a Web browser into several windows, each of which displays a separate page. The benefit of frames is that they allow certain parts of a Web site to remain constant, such as the title, the table of contents, an ad, or the navigation bar. *See* Chapter 6.

freeware and shareware Freeware is software that doesn't cost anything—as opposed to shareware, which is software you're expected but usually not required to pay for. Freeware can be a "crippled" version of full-blown commercial software, or it can be the older version of such software. Freeware and shareware are available on AOL (keyword: Software Center), via FTP, and on the Web at sites such as **http://www.tucows.com**. *See* Chapter 8.

FTP The Internet's File Transfer Protocol service, the most efficient way of moving a file from one computer to another across a *TCP/IP* network. Using FTP is like having access to someone else's computer: you browse directories and you help yourself to (download) files you want, copying them to your own computer. "Anonymous FTP" sites are publicly available. ("Anonymous" means that you automatically log in as **anonymous** and use your e-mail address as a password.) On AOL you can use both the *browser* and the built-in FTP *client* software at keyword: FTP to search and download files. Generally, the browser is better suited to searching, while the built-in client is better for downloading. The principle means for searching FTP for specific files is *Archie*. America Online offers excellent resources for using the files you download via FTP, and many of the files themselves are available on AOL. For more information, *see* Chapter 8.

Fwd: *See* **forwarding e-mail**.

GNN Short for Global Network Navigator. AOL's freestanding Internet service, which offers a special home site (**gnn.com**) and its own software (GNNworks). GNN was originally created in late 1993 by O'Reilly, the computer book publisher, as one of the very first commercial Internet services on the Web. AOL's GNN service was folded into the AOL service in late 1996, when AOL began to offer flat-rate pricing in addition to hourly pricing.

B

Gopher   An Internet service created in 1991 to permit easy access to Internet resources. Gopher simplified access in several ways. It organized resources in numbered lists, or menus, for easy selection. It provided English names instead of cryptic filenames, for clarity. It provided access to different types of resources, such as images, textual documents, Telnet sites, and FTP sites. The World Wide Web provides these same benefits, with the additional benefits of being able to directly display files of every kind and thus providing a better viewing and publishing platform. You search for Gopher resources using a program called *Veronica*. With AOL's browser you can access Gopher sites, and keyword: Gopher provides all the information and help you need to use Gopher on AOL, with a selection of the best sites. Most Gopher servers are not being maintained any longer, and few new ones are being created. *See* "Gopher's Swan Song" in Chapter 6.

helper app   A small program, or utility, used to present an image or sound or video file. Before integrated *plug-ins*, AOL's browser used helper apps. Microsoft's Media Player is an example of a helper app.

hierarchy   *See* **newsgroup**.

home page   (**1**) A home page, or personal page, is the creation of an individual, a way of sharing text or images via the World Wide Web. (**2**) A home page is also the first page, or top page, of a Web site, the page from which you begin exploring a site or get an overview of its contents. (**3**) On AOL, your home page is the page your browser opens to automatically when you start it (or go to keyword: www or keyword: Web). You can have the AOL browser open to any home page you wish. For information about the home page your browser opens to, *see* Chapter 6. For information about Personal Publisher, the free AOL service that lets you create your own home page, *see* Chapter 7.

host   (**1**) On the Internet, a computer that is "addressable" by (can exchange data with) another computer; it can accept and send *packets*. Sometimes (not quite correctly) used as a synonym for *server*. (**2**) To *host* a Web page means to make disk space available for it and to make it available to others on the Internet.

hot list   *See* **Favorite Places**.

HTML   Short for Hypertext Markup Language. When you use the Web, you download HTML files from Web servers to your computer. HTML files are made up of text that has simple instructions telling a browser how to display formatting (centering, type size and type styles, and so on). HTML is the common language of the World Wide Web: all browsers understand how to read basic HTML, though they vary in their techniques of representing more advanced HTML. The HTML language is regulated in practice by the big software companies, such as Microsoft and Netscape. HTML is simple to learn, especially with editing tools such as AOLpress that create the "tags" automatically. AOL's Personal Publisher tool frees you from having to know any HTML to create a page, but for certain effects you may need to use an HTML editor. *See* Chapters 6 and 7.

http   The *protocol* used on the World Wide Web governing the exchange of messages and files between Web *servers* and *browsers*. When you enter a URL into your AOL browser, you are sending an http message to a Web server asking it to send a specific Web page.

hyperlink   An image or piece of text on a Web page, e-mail message, AOL forum, or elsewhere that is linked to related content. On a Web page, you can tell a textual hyperlink because of its color and underlining. When you pass your mouse over any hyperlink (without clicking), the mouse arrow turns into a pointing finger, meaning you can click on it, and the address (*URL*) of the pointed-to resource appears in the status bar at the bottom of the browser window. You link to that resource by clicking the hyperlink: move the mouse's pointer over the link and click once with the left mouse button. The browser lets you return to the place from which you linked using the Back button. However, you cannot go "back" when hyperlinking from an e-mail message or AOL forum.

hypertext   On the Web, a text document in which some phrases and individual words are hyperlinked to enable easy access to information related to the content of the document. Hypertext can function as a glossary linking to definitions of words; as a bibliography linking to related articles about the same subject; and as a way of getting related information that documents, qualifies, or amplifies a particular point. Writing hypertext is an art, requiring selection of the best words and phrases in a way that doesn't intrude on the reading experience.

Hytelnet   A resource, available via Telnet, the Web, and in a stand-alone PC version, that provides access to more than 1,000 *Telnet* sites, particularly library catalogs. Hytelnet can be browsed or searched, and using AOL 3.0 for Windows 95, the Web version takes you to actual Telnet sites. A more detailed discussion can be found in Chapter 10.

B

icon In Windows, a small graphic that stands for, or links to, a program. Double click the icon to run the program. Icons are stored in program windows, which are created automatically during *installation*.

installation Preparing a program for use on your computer. Installation usually involves "unzipping" a file consisting of many files and running a "setup" file, which creates a new directory for the program, changes any Windows settings as required, and makes an *icon* and program window so you can start the program. Installing usually means setting up a program for the first time. With AOL, you must also "register"—provide AOL with some personal and billing information—before actually using the software and the service, as explained in Appendix A.

Instant Message An AOL-only feature that offers direct, one-to-one communication between two members who are signed on at the same time. Similar to *chat*, which allows two or more people to communicate at the same time.

Internet The world's newest and fastest-growing country, possessing neither borders, nor immigration restrictions, nor formal government, nor regulatory apparatus; a self-governing entity with a strong but benign commercial sector and a disputatious population, yet no standing army or formal legal system. English is the most frequent language, but communication takes place in dozens of other languages. A place to spend a vacation or a lunch hour, a place where privacy is as important as the right to assume another identity. A place to find information and to publish it. Home to millions of chatters and info junkies. Yes, it's also a network of networks. *See* Chapter 1.

IP Short for Internet Protocol, a technical term. IP is the core of *TCP/IP*, the standard that specifies how files are packetized and how packets are addressed to reach any other computer on the Internet. Every computer on a *TCP/IP* network is identified by a unique *IP address*.

IP address IP addresses provide instructions to packets as they travel to other computers on the Internet. IP addresses consist of four numbers separated by periods ("dots"), each smaller than 255 (for example, 199.4.102.1). When you enter a *domain name* such as **www.aol.com**, it is converted behind the scenes into an IP address.

IRC   Short for Internet Relay Chat. IRC offers the closest thing to chat rooms on the Internet. IRC is available on America Online through *Winsock* programs such as mIRC, which is available on AOL at keyword: Internet Applications. IRC is organized in channels. Communication in IRC channels is informal, as in chat rooms. *See* Chapter 10.

ISP   Short for Internet Service Provider. A company that provides access to the Internet, usually by modem, and provides little or no selection or programming of content. America Online is generally considered to be more than an ISP because it provides not only Internet access, but also its own tools, content, and community.

Java and Javascript   Two different technologies from Sun Microsystems that deliver interactive content over the Internet. Java is a programming language used to create small applications, or "applets," over the Internet. The technology is still experimental but promises a high degree of security and "platform independence" (it runs on any operating system, unlike competing technologies such as ActiveX). Javascript is a computer "scripting" language that can be incorporated into HTML to allow for certain effects such as balloon text and context-sensitive graphics. *See* Chapter 6.

Johnson-Grace   A company bought in 1996 by AOL, and the name of the technology created by the company for compressing (reducing the size of) sound and graphics files for faster distribution across the AOL network. Supported by the AOL browser but not yet widely used on the Internet.

library   On AOL, files and programs are available throughout the service, arranged in software libraries. You can search for files located in any library using keyword: FileSearch. *See* Chapter 8.

listbox   In a window, a box with a list of items that can be selected and linked to: programs, text articles, Web sites, AOL forums, etc. Chapter 2 covers listboxes as well as other things contained inside windows.

listproc   *See* **mailing list**.

LISTSERV   *See* **mailing list**.

B

mailing list   A group of people who communicate with each other about a shared interest by sending e-mail messages to a single e-mail address. Special list software distributes the message to everyone in the group. Lists range in size from a handful of subscribers to more than 100,000. Joining a list requires a subscription process that consists merely of sending an e-mail message to the software *administering* the list. The major varieties of software used to manage lists include LISTSERV, Listproc, and Majordomo. Lists can be *moderated* or *unmoderated*. Lists can also be distribution-only (newsletters) or true interactive discussion lists. *See* keyword: Nethelp, keyword: Mailing lists; Chapter 5.

Majordomo   *See* **mailing list**.

master account   In AOL, the account belonging to the screen name set up during registration. This screen name has the ability to create up to four additional screen names. It's the screen name responsible for paying bills and restricting the other screen names' access to certain areas and features. *See also* **Parental Controls**.

menu   A standard part of a Windows program, menus are usually arranged in a row at the top of an application's main window. A menu consists of a list of "commands" or things you can do. Most programs have File, Edit, Window, and Help menus. In addition, AOL has Go To, Mail, and Members menus. To use a menu, move your mouse over it and click; to select from a menu, move the mouse down the menu to the command, and click on it. Many menu commands have keyboard equivalents—shortcuts to the same command using the keyboard. When there are equivalents, the keys are displayed to the left of the command name (for example, in AOL the keyboard equivalent of Edit | Copy is CTRL-C); however, the menu commands tend to be more reliable than their keyboard equivalents.

message   A message is the unit of *electronic mail*. It originates from one person and is sent to one or more people, or to *mailing list* software, for distribution to a group. The elements of a message are **(1)** the To/CC field, where you specify direct and indirect recipients of the message; **(2)** the Subject field, where you indicate the content of the message; and **(3)** the body of the message—the content. Messages can contain attached files. In sending e-mail to someone on AOL, you can include clickable hyperlinks and formatted text (bold, centered, text of different sizes, etc.). On AOL, newsgroup postings are called messages, though on the Internet the term for newsgroup term is *article*.

Message board   An AOL-only feature available in many forums throughout the service; the AOL version of newsgroups. A place for members to ask questions and share information with each other and forum leaders. Internet-related message boards are available at keyword: Answerman and keyword: Nethelp.

MIME   Short for the Multipurpose Internet Mail Extension, designed to simplify the transfer of files through the "gateways" that separate different e-mail systems. AOL's e-mail program supports MIME. To send someone a file attachment over the Internet, your recipient must also be using an e-mail program that supports MIME. Basically, MIME works by converting your *binary* document (formatted word-processed file, for example) into a text document, then telling the recipient's e-mail program how to handle the attached file.

modem   Short for MOdulator/DEModulator. A piece of hardware that takes your computer's ("digital") signals and converts them into a form that can be sent over ordinary ("analog") phone lines. Modems dial AOL when you want to sign on to the service, and transmit data in both directions when you want to use the service or the Internet. Internal modems go inside your computer; external ones go on your desk. They also differ in speed: a "14.4" modem is capable of sending data at the rate of 14,400 bits per second (a bit is a small unit of data); a "28.8" modem transmits data at twice the speed—or more, if a compression technique is used. Modems are important when you install the AOL software because AOL needs to know exactly what kind of modem you have, but the AOL installation software usually detects this information automatically. More information is available online at keyword: Modem.

moderated   A newsgroup or, more commonly, a mailing list that has a human moderator who keeps track of things. A moderator's responsibilities can range from deciding who can join a mailing list or newsgroup and what can be discussed there, to making sure that the mailing list software is working properly, to breaking up arguments or keeping the discussion on topic. An unmoderated mailing list has no one charged with monitoring people's messages. Most newsgroups are unmoderated.

mouse   Not the rodent that drowns in toilets and gets trapped in heating vents in the winter, but the piece of plastic, molded to fit your hand, attached to the back of your computer with a cable, and used to control your computer. Your basic mouse

B

has two mouse buttons, which you can press quickly, or *click*. The basic mouse actions are the click, the double click, the right click, and the drag-and-drop. The mouse lets you do everything involved in getting around a Windows (or Macintosh) program: selecting from listboxes and menus; clicking on buttons and tool bars; selecting radio buttons and check boxes; using a scroll bar; dragging things around the desktop; and highlighting (selecting) text in order to cut, copy, and paste it. *See* Chapter 2.

MUD   A multi-dimensional dungeon (or dimension), an electronic place where people assume fictional characters and interact with others to create identities and invent another social world. Some MUDs are peaceable, while others are more warlike. MUDs have applications in business and education as well. Originally available only via *Telnet*, some MUDs are moving to the Web as it becomes more interactive. The Web has also become a good source of information about MUDs, and a way of accessing them. An excellent source of information about MUDs is the MudConnector (**http://www.mudconnect.com**). *See* Chapter 10.

My Place   An FTP-based service, available only on AOL, that allows you to *upload* files from your computer to one of AOL's FTP computers (**members.aol.com**), where they can be referenced by any Web pages you create using *Personal Publisher 2*. Every AOL screen name is allotted two megabytes of space to store uploaded files. For information about My Place and Personal Publisher 2, *see* Chapter 7.

Net   *See* **Internet**.

AOL's Rules of the Road on the Net

From AOL's Rules of the Road: "The Internet is not owned, or operated by, or in any way affiliated with, AOL, Inc. or any of its affiliates; it is a separate, independent network of computers and is not part of AOL. Your use of the Internet is solely at your own risk. When using the Internet and all of its components, Members must conduct themselves responsibly according to the Internet's own particular code of conduct. Participating successfully on the Internet is really a matter of common sense. Although AOL, Inc. does not control the Internet, your conduct on the Internet when using your AOL account is subject to the AOL Rules."

netiquette   A collection of guidelines for using Internet services and interacting with people on the Internet. Some netiquette guidelines are meant to promote a good civil experience for everyone on the Internet—such as the admonition to avoid humor that could offend or be misunderstood on newsgroups. Other guidelines are meant to protect the physical, networking environment—such as the FTP customs of using nearby servers, logging on after hours, and not browsing or staying logged on too long. Every Internet service—e-mail, newsgroups, FTP, Telnet, and the Web—has netiquette guidelines. Breach of netiquette can have assorted negative consequences, from social disapproval, to getting kicked off your Internet service, to getting included on a "black list." AOL's Terms of Services require members to respect netiquette or risk removal from the service. AOL's Terms of Service are available at keyword: TOS (Part II of Rules of the Road). For a clear and complete Net-centric statement of netiquette guidelines, *see* **ftp://ds.internic.net/ rfc/rfc1855.txt**. For an AOL introduction to the subject, *see* keyword: Netiquette.

Netscape Navigator   A *browser* made by Netscape Communications Corp., and available to AOL members (keyword: Netscape). Currently, Netscape is the world's most popular browser by virtue of its early appearance in the browser market (it is based on the Mosaic browser, popular in 1993-94), its great features (summarized in Chapter 10), its pricing (free to non-commercial users!), and its availability on all major platforms (Windows, Macintosh, Unix). Netscape has pioneered or been an early adopter of Internet technologies such as *frames, plug-ins,* and *Java.*

network   A group of computers connected by cabling, telephone wire, radio wave, or other medium, so that they can exchange data. Networks need not be restricted to a specific location, and they can themselves be networked. In a way, the Internet is a radical extension of the idea of networking, because it could ultimately include all computers and enable communication among all people with access to a computer.

newbie   Someone new to the Internet or to a specific Internet service, such as FTP or MUDs. With the very rapid growth of the Internet, more than half of all people "on" the Internet in the last year or so have been newbies.

newsgroup   An Internet discussion group, organized by topic and intended for broad public access and participation. AOL carries more than 20,000 Internet newsgroups, which are arranged in categories, or *hierarchies.* The whole newsgroup

B

system is called Usenet, which is less a network than a classification scheme. A newsgroup name indicates the category and any subcategories to which it belongs, as well as the specific topic to which it is devoted (for example, **rec.sports.baseball** is about the topic of baseball, available in the sports subcategory, within the main *rec*reational category). You can search for newsgroups at keyword: Newsgroups (click Search All Newsgroups), and you can search for specific newsgroup postings at keyword: DejaNews. *See* Chapter 5.

offline   Otherwise know as RL (real life). AOL offers many ways for you to do routine online tasks while you're offline, to keep your online costs down. With *FlashSessions*, you can read e-mail while you're offline, and compose new messages offline as well. You can also read and write newsgroup postings while you're offline.

online   Traditionally, being online meant being signed onto a commercial online service such as America Online, as opposed to *both* offline and "on the Internet." Today, there are plenty of activities that can be done offline as well as online, and, on America Online, going online is required to get onto the Internet. Signing onto AOL makes it possible to use the Internet; nothing else is required, and no additional expense is incurred.

packet   The unit of data transmitted over a TCP/IP network such as AOL or the Internet. (Actually, *packet* is the generic term, and the actual *IP* unit is *datagram*.) Files, such as Web pages in the form of HTML files, must be broken up into tiny packets of data before they can be transmitted across networks. Every packet carries information about its source, its place in the sequence of all packets, and its destination. *See* Chapter 6.

page   A Web page and the HTML file on which it is based. A collection of pages is a Web site. A *home page* is the top page of a site and also the page your browser automatically opens to. *See* Chapter 6.

Parental Controls   America Online offers many ways for parents to control the experience of children who share their account. (The *master account* is usually in the parents' name, while the associated screen names belong to children in the household.) On the AOL service, parents can restrict kids' access to *chat rooms* and other features, as described throughout the book. Parental Controls vary by Internet service. For *newsgroups,* parents can block access to specific newsgroups and downloads. For *e-mail*, parents can prohibit kids from receiving attachments. For the *Web*, kids can be restricted to sites deemed appropriate for children or teenagers.

Using Parental Controls, parents can also restrict children to the Kids Only channel. Parental Controls are available from the Members menu; click on Parental Control.

password   To sign on to AOL you must have a password and screen name, both of which you choose for the *master account* when you first register your AOL account. Once signed on, a master account holder can change, add, and delete up to four screen names, but the screen name used to register can't be changed. Your screen name and password identify you unmistakably to AOL's computers. It is vital to keep your password secret and to choose a password that others won't be able to guess. Tips for choosing a password and a form for actually changing it are available at keyword: Password.

Personal Filing Cabinet   Using your Personal Filing Cabinet (PFC), you can automatically save a copy of every e-mail message you send and receive. You can also save copies of every newsgroup posting you send and receive using FlashSessions. Click the File Cabinet icon for access and more information (and to set your preferences).

Personal Publisher 2   Also known as PP2, a free service available on America Online for creating your own Web *page*. Personal Publisher lets you upload files using My Place, then create a page and link the files without knowing any HTML. Chapter 7 is devoted to PP2, and the service itself is available at keyword: PP2.

plug in   Software that allows a browser to smoothly handle and present multimedia files. Plug-ins were developed for the Netscape Navigator browser, and they're fully supported by AOL's Netscape Navigator (Chapter 10). The Microsoft Internet Explorer browser (which you get with AOL 3.0 for Windows 95) supports both plug-ins and a Windows-centric technology called ActiveX. Some of the major plug-ins you can use with AOL are Real Audio, VDO, and Shockwave. Real Audio and VDO are examples of streaming technology; they allow you to hear sounds and watch little video clips before the files have finished downloading. Other plug-ins can be downloaded from the Web and installed for either the Microsoft or Netscape browser (*see* Table 6-3). Using the older technology of helper applications (*helper apps*), browsers used independent programs and viewers that waited for files to finish downloading before playing them. *See* Chapters 6 and 8.

PPP   Point-to-Point Protocol, a way of accessing the Internet using a modem and the phone lines, preferred by many Internet Service Providers (ISPs). Connecting directly to AOL does not require a PPP connection, but AOL's new Bring Your Own

Access pricing plan allows ISP subscribers to run AOL while using another ISP's PPP connection. *See also* **SLIP**.

protocol   A set of rules that computers follow when exchanging data. The Internet is built on widely shared networking protocols called *TCP/IP* and a set of application protocols that underlie the basic Internet services: the Web (*http*), Usenet News (nntp), e-mail (smtp), and FTP (ftp).

quoting   In e-mail and newsgroups, the practice of selectively choosing bits of a person's message to provide context for your response. In responses, by Internet tradition, each line of a quoted passage is preceded by a vertical line (|) or greater-than sign (>). On AOL, you can choose to use this style in your e-mail responses (click on MyAOL and set your e-mail preferences to "Internet"). Unfortunately, you cannot yet automatically quote when responding to an newsgroup article, but must manually copy and paste or use a third-party utility such as QClip.

radio button   In Windows programs such as AOL, a radio button gives you the ability to specify a single choice (as in the Software Search area shown in Figure 8-5). With radio buttons you *must* click one (and only one) of the buttons. With *check boxes* you can select as many as you want (or no choices). You select a radio button by clicking in the circle, and a check box by clicking in the square.

Re: This tag is automatically tacked onto the beginning of an e-mail or newsgroup message when someone is responding to someone else's message. It can be edited out, but other people won't realize that your message is part of a *thread*—a collection of messages about the same theme.

real time   *See* **asynchronous vs. real-time communication**.

Search Terms

Chapter 9 has a text box, "Search Terms and What They Mean," explaining the technical or technical-seeming terms you'll encounter while using search tools, such as *Boolean operator, directory, engine, hits, index, query, relevance,* and *returns*.

server   A computer that makes a program, database, file, or other data available to other computers, called *clients*. The various Internet services—the Web, FTP, Gopher, e-mail—each use their own servers for controlling access to and distributing data to clients.

shareware   *See* **freeware and shareware**.

SLIP   Short for Serial Line Internet Protocol, SLIP makes it possible for Internet Service Providers' subscribers to access the Internet using their modems. AOL does not provide a SLIP connection, but if you have a SLIP account with an *ISP*, you can log on to it, then run AOL: at the Sign On screen, click Setup; click Edit Location; in the Network listbox, click TCP/IP.

smiley   A way of indicating your intention or emotion by using characters requiring you to tilt your head to the left. Smileys save people the time of expressing their thoughts and feelings intelligibly ;-) If you want a big list of smileys, do a search for **smiley.txt** or **smiley.zip** at keyword: FileSearch.

spam   Unsolicited e-mail or newsgroup postings, generally considered to be a waste of time, *bandwidth*, and disk space.

Spinner, AOL   In both the AOL browser and the Netscape browser customized for AOL, the rotating AOL logo to the right of the URL box at the top of the browser window. The spinner displays the progress of a page as it's downloading, stopping when a page has been downloaded.

SSL   Short for Secure Sockets Layer, an industry-standard method of securing Internet transactions by encrypting them (scrambling them so they can't be read), authenticating them (making sure the other party is legitimate), and ensuring their integrity (making sure the data doesn't get tampered with).

status bar   In a Web browser, the line of information at the very bottom of the window that gives you information about what you are doing. It indicates whether your mouse is pointing to a hyperlink. If it is, you'll see the URL of that link in the status bar. It also tells you what's going on while the elements of a Web page are downloading one at a time.

surf   To browse the Web or the Net, jumping from link to link, page to page.

B

TCP/IP   The networking protocols on which the Internet is based. TCP/IP specifies how complex data is broken into pieces (packets) of the same size and structure, sent safely across many networks, then reassembled at the other end. TCP/IP requires several "layers" of protocols to carry out the various tasks of taking an application's data, breaking it into packets, addressing them, passing them off to physical networks, and (at the receiving end) reassembling the packets into a useful form.

Telnet   The protocol, and the applications based on the protocol, that let you use programs, games, and databases on a distant computer. With Telnet, your keywork and monitor become "dumb" terminals that allow you to communicate with the distant computer. Telnet makes it possible for people to play real-time simulation and adventure games on the Internet. Telnet also makes it possible to use electronic catalogs of libraries located all over the world. On AOL, the built-in (Microsoft) browser allows you to connect to a Telnet site. Or, with AOL's Winsock you can use a program such as Ewan to access Telnet sites. *See* Chapter 10.

text box   In Windows, an element in which you type some text or numbers to tell a program your preferences, or to order a product, or to register at a Web site, or to enter your keyword when using a search service such as Excite.

thread   In newsgroups, mailing lists, and e-mail, a set of messages about the same subject, or at least with the same Subject line. A thread is like a conversation. AOL's newsreader lets you follow all the messages that comprise a thread, but AOL's e-mail program doesn't let you sort messages in this way. Whenever you see *re*: before a subject, you're looking at a response to another message, and thus part of a thread.

TOS   *See* **CAT.**

upload   To send a file from a PC or other *client* to a *server*, where it can be used by others or referenced by a Web page. On AOL, the My Place service allows members to upload 2Mb of files per screen name for use in Web pages or for other purposes. *See* Chapter 7. *See also* **download.**

URL   Uniform Resource Locator. The standard Internet scheme for specifying the address, or location, of an Internet resource (such as a Web page or Gopher menu). A typical URL is **http://members.aol.com/jennlt1**. URLs have three parts: the *protocol* (**http**), the *domain name* (**users.aol.com**), and the file name with full directory path (**jennlt1**). File names are sometimes implicit; omitting a file name causes the browser to look for a default page, such as *index.html, main.html,* or something similar. *See* Chapter 6.

Usenet   The organizational scheme for keeping track of *newsgroups*—widely accessible bulletin boards devoted to specific topics. Newsgroups are arranged into categories (or *hierarchies*), and the two major hierarchies are the standard (or traditional) hierarchy and the alternative hierarchy. Usenet is not really a physical network so much as the naming scheme used by Usenet News servers. AOL's Newsgroup feature is available at keyword: Newsgroups. *See* Chapter 5.

Veronica   The search engine used for finding information available by Gopher. Only a handful of Veronica servers are being maintained in the world today, and not all of them are being updated. When you do a Veronica search, you can choose "searching Gopherspace," which means to search an index consisting of all the files pointed-to by all the world's public Gopher servers. You can also choose "search Gopher directories," which is similar to using a directory to find clusters of resources grouped under some subject head such as Business, Humor, or Recipes. On AOL, a Veronica server is available from the search page of the AOL Web site (just click Search on the AOL browser). *See* Chapter 9.

Virtual Places   Software for chatting on the Web, based on technology developed by Ubique, an Israeli company acquired by AOL in 1995. In Virtual Places, you see a Web page in one window and chat in another. On the Web page, you are represented by an *avatar*—a small picture representing yourself. Virtual Places enhances basic AOL features by providing chat rooms on the Web, a graphical version of AOL's auditorium events, and "gestures" in both chat and Instant Messages. *See* Chapter 10.

virus   A small program or "macro" intended to create unwanted changes to someone else's computer. Some effects can be destructive, others just annoying. Viruses work by latching onto programs or application templates, then causing programs to act in unexpected ways. The best way to avoid a virus is to scan all files downloaded from the Internet for viruses. Keyword: Virus center has information, current alerts, and anti-virus programs you can use to prevent or eradicate viruses. All software available from AOL at keyword: FileSearch or any other software library on the service has been virus protected.

B

WAIS Short for Wide Area Information System, a technique for indexing large collections of text documents to make them easier to search. WAIS is now rarely used because so few resources have been indexed and because other search tools have taken its place.

Webzine *See* **e-zine**.

Winsock Short for Windows sockets. Winsock is an emerging standard for developing Windows programs that can communicate with other computers over a *TCP/IP* network (that is, the Internet). To work, such programs require a small file called **winsock.dll**. Winsock applications let you browse the Web, search Archie, create Web pages, use FTP, and much more. For each Internet service built into AOL, several Winsock alternatives are available; Winsock makes it possible to use the Netscape browser, for example. In addition, you can run Winsock applications (such as a Telnet client) that have no equivalent on AOL. When you're using Winsock, it's important to know whether your version is "16 bit" or "32 bit," as explained in Chapter 10. Since the release of version 3.0 of the AOL software, Winsock is automatically installed when you install AOL. When you use the Bring Your Own Access plan, you're using your ISP's version of **winsock.dll**, but in most cases, this will make no difference in how Winsock applications work. *See* Chapter 10.

World Wide Web Millions of *pages* of information, arranged in more or less complex sites, on every subject, connected by *hyperlinks,* and navigated and viewed with a *browser*. *See* Chapters 6, 7, and 10.

zipped file A file that contains several other files, so the zipped files are simpler to send and receive over a network. Zipped files are usually *compressed* as well. Special utilities such as WinZip can be used to zip files, while AOL's *Download Manager* can be used to unzip them.

Zine (or 'zine) *See* **e-zine**.

A

AARP WebPlace, 445-446
Achoo Online Healthcare Services, 412
Acronym Dictionary, 468
Acronyms, 9
Addicted to Noise, 452
Address Book, 72-74, 516
Addresses
    defined, 516
    e-mail, 63-65
    finding, 75
    Internet, 175
    mailing list, 113
    newsgroup, 139
Afghan Cultural Info Center, 422-423
Africa Online, 423
AFU and Urban Legends Archive, 416
Agent, 516
AIDS Research Information Center, 416-417
Airlines of the Net, 490
Alaska Internet Travel Guide, 394-395
All Music Guide, 452-453
AltaVista, 304-306
Alt.days (newsgroup), 400
Alternative Usenet newsgroup hierarchies, 139, 141,
    144
Amazon.com, 457
American Cancer Society, 412
American Diabetes Association, 412
American Memory, 440-441
American Music Center, 453
America's Housecall Network, 413
Amnesty International On-line, 417
Anchor (link), 254
Animated GIFs, 179
Animation, on your Web page, 252-253
Anonymous FTP, 268. *See also* FTP
ANS, 516-517
Ansel Adams, 441
AnswerMan, 22-23
AnswerMan Internet Extra, 120
Antidote, 453
AOL
    finding the Internet on, 56-59
    finding people on, 330

    and the Internet, 12
    vs. ISPs, 11-12
    upgrades, 512-514
    using with other Windows applications, 60
    versions, 501
    what you need, 500
    Windows 95 version preferences, 191-194
AOL areas, 53
AOL channels, 10, 36, 203, 380-382, 519
AOL community, 13-15
AOL Community Action Team (CAT), 80
AOL connection, 498-509
AOL forums, 53-55
    elements of, 53
    finding, 53-55
AOL FTP Client, 282
AOL Internet Mailing List Directory, 108-109
AOL Internet Properties window, 191
AOL Marketplace newsletter, 119
AOL Members' Choice sites, 383-388
AOL policy on mailing lists, 121
AOL preferences, 49
AOL screen names, 37, 64, 504, 511-512
AOL spinner, 189, 537
AOL 3.0 versions, 501
AOL 300 directory, 379-496
AOL tool bar, 50-52
AOL travel.com, 491
AOL upgrades, 512-514
AOLGlobalNet, 510
AOLnet, 517
AOL's browser. *See* Browser (AOL's)
AOL's mailing lists, 119
AOL's Rules of the Road, 361, 532
AOL's Search FTP service, 269-270, 274-282
AOL's Web site, 56, 58, 188, 196-197
Applications, using AOL with, 60
Archie, 270-274, 517
Archive X Paranormal Phenomena, 417
Argentina!, 423-424
Art
    on the Net, 441
    on the Web, 242
Articles (newsgroup), 138
    listing, 156
    netiquette, 164-165
    parts of, 156-159

INDEX

read vs. unread, 155
reading and posting offline, 162-164
responding to, 159-162
saving and printing, 169
scanning, 154-156
ArtSource, 441
ASCII, 517
ASCII files, 263
Asynchronous vs. real-time communication, 517
At (@) sign, 63
Atlanta Traveler, 395
Atlantic Monthly, The, 457
Attachments to e-mail, 78-80, 83-84, 86
Auditoriums (Virtual Places), 360-361
Authentication (Web purchases), 183
Avalon, 406
Avatars, 15, 517

B

Background sound, for your Web page, 252
Backgrounds (wallpapers), 179
Backpacker Magazine, 446
Bahamas, The, 424
Balance: Health and Fitness on the Net, 473
Bandwidth, 30, 518
Bank Rate Monitor, 462
Bartlett's Quotations, 9
BCC (blind carbon copy), 518
BCCing (e-mail message), 68-70
Beauty Net, 480
Beginner's Guide to HTML, 427-428
BELIEF-L (newsletter), 122
Best Rates from the Bank Rate Monitor, 462
Better Homes and Gardens, 458
Big List of Puzzle and Riddle Pages, 406
Bigfoot, 331
Bill Nye the Science Guy, 434
Billing plans, 18
Binary, 518
Binary document, 79
Binary files, 79, 165, 263
Biography site, 468-469
Black Information Network, 446
Blindness Resource Center, 413
Blue Dog Can Count!, 434-435
BoatNet, 446-447

Body Electric, The, 480
Body (of a newsgroup article), 156, 158-159
Bookmark, 518
BookWire, 441-442
Boolean operators, 306
Boston Online, 395
Boy Scouts of America, 435
Brasil Page, The, 424
Bridge on the Web, 407
Browser (AOL's), 172, 186-210, 518
accessing the Internet, 216-219
buttons, 188-189
going back and forward, 205
going to a newsgroup, 153-154
help on, 22
keyword window, 200
location box, 188
managing a session, 204-207
navigating FTP, 282-283
vs. Netscape Navigator, 348-353
opening, 186-187
opening several browsers at once, 351-352
presenting files, 209-210
session, 188, 204-207
spinner, 189, 537
title bar, 187-188
visiting a Web site, 198-199
Browser versions, 186
Browsing, 55
Browsing newsgroups, 146-147, 149-150
Bubble text, 44
Buddy Lists, 13
Bulletin boards, global, 58
Business, doing on the Net, 31-32
Business addresses, finding, 327
Business newsletter, 121-122
Buttons (clickable), 44, 519
Buying from the Web, 183

C

Clnet, 334-335
Clnet's Product Reviews, 389
Caching, 19, 205-206
Cafe Utne, 401
California Highway Conditions, 395
Campus Newspapers on the Internet, 485-486

Cancelling a message, 71
Capitol Steps, 486
Car and Driver, 458
Career Magazine, 463
Carnegie Library (Pittsburgh), 442
CAT (Community Action Team), 80, 519
Cat Fanciers, 447
Categories (AOL News), 140
CC (carbon or courtesy copy), 68-70, 519
CCing (e-mail message), 68-70
Celebrities On-Line, 401
Center for Democracy and Technology, 417
Centre for the Easily Amused, 401
Channels (AOL), 10, 36, 203, 380-382, 519
Channels menu, 36
Chat, 13, 362-372, 382, 519-520
Chat rooms in Virtual Places
        attending an event, 360-361
        chatting in, 358-360
        entering, 357
        exiting, 361
        guiding a tour, 360
Chat window, 17
Chatting on the Internet, 362-372
Check boxes, 43, 520
Chess Space, 407
Chicago, 396
Chicago Tribune, The, 486
Christian Science e-Monitor, 487
CIA 1995 World Factbook, 469
Cities, sites about, 394-400
City.Net, 333-334, 383
Classical Chat, 453
Clickable button, 44, 519
Client, 520
Client software, 19
Clip art, on the Web, 242
CNN Interactive Health, 413
CNNfn Stock Quotes, 463
CollegeNET, 435
Colorado: Arts to Zoo, 396
CommNet, 373-374
Communicating with e-mail, 61-101
Communications, 24-26
Community Action Team (CAT), 80, 519
Community (AOL), 13-15
Community of the Net
        doing business, 31-32

global, 29-30
self-governance, 31
Comparative Religion, 447
Composing and sending an e-mail message, 65
Comp.os.ms-windows.win95.setup, 389-390
Compressed files, 263, 288-289, 523
Compression technology, 19
Computer Gaming World, 407
Computer and software sites, 389-394
Computer Virus Help Desk, 390
Computers & Software channel, 291
Connecting to AOL, 34, 498-509
Connecting over TCP/IP network or ISP, 502
Context (AOL), 15-17
Contributing to the Net, 2
Cookies, 202, 520
Cosmetics Cop, 481
Culture sites, 440-445
Custom Controls, 21
Customer service, 21
CyberLink Web Games, 407-408
Cyberspace Middle School, 435
Cycling through open windows, 59

D

Data encryption, 183
Data integrity, 183
David Bowie: The Official Web Site, 418
DC Comics, 384
Decoded document, 79
Dedicated connection, 24
DejaNews, 324-326
Deleting e-mail messages, 92, 99
Dell Magazine's Daily Crossword Puzzle, 459
Design & Publishers Center, 390
Destination: Washington D.C., 397
Destinations Magazine, 491
Dialing in the AOL network, 502
Dial-up connection, 501-502
Diet and Weight Loss/Fitness Page, 481
Digest (e-mail), 105
Dilbert Zone, 401
Directories, 266, 520
        in My Place, 233-234
        for the serious searcher, 320-321
        Web, 303

Directory of the World's Online Newspapers, 487
Discover Turkey, 424-425
Discussion lists, 106
Discussion threads, 129, 140, 157, 161-162, 538
Distant computer, 372
Distribution lists, 106
Domain Name System (DNS), 65
Domain names, 63-65, 270, 520-521
Doonesbury Electronic Town Hall, 402
Dove Foundation, 184
Download, 60, 521
Download Manager, 84, 280-281, 521
Download preferences, 280
Downloaded multimedia files, using, 284-289
Downloading, 261-295
Downloading files, 230
Downloading files from AOL, 289-290
Dragging and dropping a window, 40
Dream League, 408
Drop-down lists, 42-43
DuJour, 409

E

Editing your Web page, 246-248, 253-255
Effective e-mail messages, 96-100
Electronic Frontier Foundation, 428
Electronic mail. *See* E-mail
Electronic newsletters, 15, 106, 119-122
Electronic Newsstand's Monster Magazine List, 459
Elle, 459
E-mail, 61-101, 521-522. *See also* Messages (e-mail)
    accessing, 218
    adding clickable hyperlinks, 76-78
    AOL vs. Internet, 68
    file attachments, 78-80
    filtering incoming, 86-88
    formatting, 75-78
    managing mailboxes, 85
    managing mailing list mail, 115-117
    reading, 81-88
    retrieving file attachments, 83-84, 86
    retrieving files via, 267
    sending/receiving, 57
    unsolicited, 80, 88, 537
    using the Address Book, 72-74
    using FlashSessions, 116-118

E-mail addresses, 63-65
E-mail digest, 105
E-mail flame, 30, 98, 524
Emoticons, 99
Empowered Young Females, 436
Encoded files, 165
Encryption, 522
Engine, 522
Entertainment sites, 400-412
Error messages, 221-222
ESPNET SportsZone, 474
Essential Internet resources, 5
Essential keywords for using the Net, 47-48
Eurolink, 492
Events in Virtual Places, attending, 360-361
Excite, 307-308
Experience New Orleans, 397
ExploraNet, 436-437
Explorer, 522
Extensions, filename, 231, 262-266, 523
EXTRA, 384
E-zine, 522

F

Familiar Quotations, 469
FamilyPC on the Web, 390
FAQ Finder, 469
FAQs, 167-169, 522
Fashion Internet, 481-482
Fashion Net, 482
Fashion Page, 482
Fashion and style sites, 480-485
Favorite Places, 48, 95, 152-153, 200-202, 220, 523
FedWorld Information Network, 470
Feedback on sites in this book, 383
15-second Web search, 207-208
File attachments to e-mail, 78-80, 83-84, 86
File compression, 19, 263, 288-289, 523
File formats, handling, 167
File name extensions, 231, 262-266, 523
File size, 279
File Transfer box, 79
File types, 262-266
FileGrabber, 166-167, 523-524
Filenames, 231, 262-266, 523
Files, 262-266, 523

downloading from AOL, 289-290
finding FTP, 268-282
finding great AOL, 291-294
getting from newsgroups, 165-167
multimedia, 208-210, 251-252, 284-289
newsgroup article, 156, 159
retrieving over the Internet, 267
sending in newsgroups, 167
uploading and downloading, 230
uploading to My Place, 231-232
using downloaded, 284-289
Filtering incoming mail, 86-88
Finance-related sites, 462-468
Financial management, 10
Find button, 53
Find window, 54
Finding. *See also* Searching
an address, 75
AOL forums, 53-55
a business address, 327
FTP files, 268-282
great AOL files, 291-294
information on the Internet, 297-338
information on the Web, 300-303
a mailing list, 108-109
newsgroups, 144-147
people, 321-326
people on AOL, 330
people one at a time, 327-331
Fine Arts Museums of San Francisco, 443
Firefly, 384
FishNet, 437
Flaming (e-mail fight), 30, 98, 524
FlashSessions, 116-118, 162-164, 524
Fly Fishing Broadcast Network, 447
Foodwine.com, 448
Forbes Magazine, 459-460
Formatting e-mail, 75-78
Forms (Web page), 180-181, 524
Forums (AOL), 53-55
elements of, 53
finding, 53-55
Forwarding e-mail messages, 90-91, 524-525
Four11, 331
401(k) Retirement Calculator, 464
Fragrance Foundation, The, 482

Frames (Web page), 182-184, 525
navigating, 206-207
in Netscape Navigator, 352
Franklin Institute Science Museum, 443
Freeware, 525
FTP (File Transfer Protocol), 262, 525
finding files, 268-282
finding graphics viewers, 285
finding image files, 285
using, 267
FTP site names, 270
FTP site navigation
using AOL browser, 283
using AOL FTP Client, 282
FTP sites
accessing, 218
mirrored on AOL, 290
Fwd, 90-91, 524-525

G

Game sites, 406-412
Gamelan, 428-429
Games Domain, 409
GameSpot, 410
Genealogy Home Page, 448-449
Getting online, 34
GIG, The, 418
Girl Scouts of the U.S.A., 437
Global bulletin boards, 58
Global community, 29-30
GNN, 525
Go To menu, 45-46, 48
GolfWeb, 474
Gopher, 216-218, 526
Gopher sites, accessing, 217
Graceland, 402
Graphics file name extensions, 231
Graphics viewers, finding on FTP, 285
Graphics (Web page), 179-180
Group Name, 74
Guest, signing on as, 509-510
Guestbook, 255
Guide to Computer Vendors, 391
Guide to Museums and Cultural Resources, 443
Guitar World, 453-454

H

HairNet, 483
Header (e-mail message), 132
Header (newsgroup article), 156-158
Health and Fitness on the Net, 473
Health and fitness sites, 412-416, 473
Help
    getting, 21-23
    with mail, 69
    numbers to call for, 514
Help menu, 50
Helper applications, 210-215, 526
Heritage Foundation, The, 487
Hierarchies, Usenet newsgroup, 139-144
History of the Internet, 27-29
History of Rock'n'Roll, 454
Hollywood Online, 403
Home Buyer's Fair, 464
Home Fair's mortgage calculator, 181-182
Home pages, 196-198, 526. *See also* Web page; Web
  site of your own
    changing, 197-198
    notable AOL, 257-259
HomeArts, 385
Homework Tools, 437-438
Honolulu's Internet Cafe, 397
Hopi Way—Cloud Dancing, 443-444
Horizontal scrolling, 40
HospitalWeb, 413-414
Host, 526
Hosting (Web presence), 250-251
Hostmaster, 133
Hot list, 526
HotBot, 308-310
HotWired, 429
House of Cards, 410
HouseNet, 449
Houston Entertainment Network, 397-398
HTML Bad Style Guide, 429-430
HTML Editor, 227, 253-255
HTML elements, 177-186
HTML file name extensions, 231
HTML format, 124
HTML (Hypertext Markup Language), 175-177,
  526-527
    adding to your Web page, 248
    Beginner's Guide to, 428

    learning, 248-249
    saving a Web page's, 220-221
Http, 527
Hybrid browsers (AOL), 190-191
Hyperlinks, 59, 180, 527
    adding to e-mail, 76-78
    saving, 220
Hypertext, 172, 270, 527
Hytelnet, 374-375, 527

I

Icons, 50, 528
Identifying yourself, 504-505
Ignoring e-mail messages, 92
iGuide, 385
Image files
    finding on FTP, 285
    viewing, 284-285
Image maps, 179
Images
    clip art and art, 242
    inline, 176, 179
Inc. Online, 460
Indexes, Web, 303
Indispensable Web sites, 3-11
InfoSeek's UltraSeek, 311-313
Inline images, 176, 179
Installation, 528
Instant Messages (IMs), 14, 528
Insurance News Network, 464
Interactive AOL channels, 36
Interactive elements of windows, 43-44
Interactive Food Finder, 414
Interfaces, 28
International WWW Schools Registry, 3
International-interest sites, 422
Internet address, 175
Internet addressing, 65
Internet applications, 26-27, 58-59, 339-377
Internet Beatles Album, 454-455
Internet community, 31-32
Internet Connection, 56
Internet Explorer, 186-210
    changing the look of, 195-196
    setting preferences in, 191-196
Internet Index, 430

Internet Mail, vs. AOL Mail, 68
Internet Mailing List Directory (AOL), 108-109
Internet Movie Database, 403-404
Internet (Net), 2, 528
    accessing, 216-219
    am I on it?, 12
    AOL's stake in, 24
    chatting on, 362-372
    essential keywords for using, 47-48
    finding information on, 297-338
    finding people on, 327-331
    history of, 27-29
    programs needed to use, 26-27
    retrieving files from, 267
    what it is, 23-26
    where on AOL is it?, 56-59
    yellow pages on, 327
Internet Properties window, 191
Internet Public Library Reference Center, 470
Internet resources, essential, 5
Internet Role Playing Society, 411
Internet Society, 431
Internet Tools site, 431
Internet-related menus, 44-46
Internet-related sites, 427-434
IP address, 528
IRC (Internet Relay Chat), 362-372, 529. *See also* Chat
IRS's Digital Daily, 465
ISPs (Internet Service Providers), 11-12, 430-431, 529
    connection, 502
    using, 507-509
iTools Research-it, 471

J

Java, 185, 529
Javascript, 185, 529
JavaScript Authoring Guide, 431
J-Links Meta-Index (Japan), 425
Job searching, 6
Johnson-Grace, 529
Joining and using mailing lists, 124-133
Jumbo, 385
Jumping to a new URL, 203-204
Junk e-mail, 80, 88, 537

K

Keeping e-mail messages as new, 91
Keyboard alternatives, 45
Keyboard equivalents (Netscape Navigator), 348
Keyword window, 45-46, 200
Keywordable Web sites, 381
Keywords, 7-8, 46-48
    using to find newsgroups, 149
    for using the Net, 47-48
Kids sites, 434-440
KidsHealth, 414-415
Kilobytes, 279

L

Las Vegas Leisure Guide, 398
Library, 529
Life Magazine, 460-461
Lifestyles and interests sites, 445-451
Links (Web page), 59, 180, 527
    adding to e-mail, 76-78
    saving, 220
Lipstick Page, The, 483
List moderator (editor), 106
Listboxes, 42, 529
Listing your Web page, 255
Listproc commands, 131
Listproc mailing lists, 110, 131. *See also* Mailing lists
Lists (drop-down), 42-43
Lists (mailing). *See* Mailing lists
LISTSERV mailing lists, 110, 125-130. *See also* Mailing lists
Liszt Directory, 109, 322-324
Locations, creating, 509
Logging on, 34
Lonely Planet, 492
Look Online, 484
Los Angeles Times, 488
Lumiere, 484
Lycos, 313-315

M

Madagasikara (Madagascar), 425
Magazines, 7

Magellan Internet Guide, 316-317, 386
Mail. *See* E-mail; Messages (e-mail)
Mail Center, 22, 48-49
Mail controls, 86
Mail help, 69
Mail menu, 48-49
Mail preferences, 71
Mailboxes, managing, 85
Mailing lists, 103-134, 530. *See also* Newsletters
    addresses of, 113
    AOL's, 119
    commands for, 111-112
    discussion and distribution, 106
    finding, 108-109
    finding who owns, 132-133
    in HTML format, 124
    index commands, 116
    joining and using, 124-133
    managing mail from, 115-117
    moderated and unmoderated, 106-107
    netiquette, 113-115
    vs. newsgroups, 137-138
    noise on, 115
    parental control and AOL policy, 121
    sampler, 118-122
    searching for, 322-324
    subscribing to, 110-113
    what you need to know, 105-106
Major AOL upgrades, 513
Major League Baseball, 474-475
Majordomo commands, 132
Majordomo mailing lists, 110, 131-132
MapQuest, 386
Marketplace newsletter (AOL), 119
Master account, 530
Maximizing a window, 40
Maximum Exposure, 484-485
Medical information, 6-7
MedicineNet, 415
Medline medical database, 332
Medscape, 415
Meet Minneapolis, 398
Megabytes, 279
Megasites, searching, 332-334, 336-337
Members menu, 49-50
Mental Health Net, 415
Menus, 44-50, 530
Message board, 531

Message headers, 132
Message queue, 70
Messages (AOL News), 140
Messages (e-mail), 63, 530. *See also* E-mail
    cancelling, 71
    CCing and BCCing, 68-70
    composing and sending, 65
    deleting, 99
    deleting or ignoring, 92
    emoticons and Smileys in, 99, 537
    forwarding, 90-91
    keeping as new, 91
    keeping track of, 98
    making easy to read, 100
    managing, 88-92
    to more than one recipient, 67
    parsing, 97
    personalizing, 97-98
    quoting in, 90
    replying to, 89-90
    responding to, 100
    rewriting offline, 99
    saving and printing, 92-96
    searching saved, 94
    sending, 70
    shouting in, 96
    stating the point of, 100
    Subject line, 67
    tips for effective, 96-100
    unsending, 70, 72
    whispering in, 97
Messages from mailing lists
    managing, 115-117
    off-topic, 115
Microsoft Windows, 391
MIDI City, 391
MIDI files, 287, 293
MIME standard, 79, 211, 531
Minimizing a window, 41
Minor AOL upgrades, 513-514
mIRC, 362-372
Mirror, on the Internet, 116
Mirrored FTP sites, 290
Miscellaneous Usenet newsgroup hierarchies, 139
Misc.invest.stocks (newsgroup), 465
Misc.taxes (newsgroup), 466
Modem, 531
Modems Modems Modems, 392

Moderated mailing lists, 106-107, 531
Moderator (mailing list), 106
MoJo Wire: Mother Jones Interactive, 419
Money Online, 466
Motley Fool, 466-467
Mouse, 531-532
Mr. Showbiz, 404
MTV Online, 386-387
MUD Resource Collection, 411
MUDs, 376-377, 532
Multimedia, 208-215
Multimedia files, 208-210
    adding to your Web page, 251-252
    using downloaded, 284-289
Multimedia plug-ins, 213-215
Music Previews Network, 455
Music-related sites, 452-457
Mutual Funds, 467
My Place, 228-234, 532
    managing, 232-234
    uploading files to, 231-232
My Virtual Reference Desk, 471

N

NandoNet's Sports Server, 475
NASCAR Online, 476
National Anthems, 455
National Basketball Association, 476
National Football League, 477
National Journal, 461
National Park Service's ParkNet, 493
National Public Radio, 488
National Zoo, The, 438
Net. *See* Internet (Net)
Net Highlights, 56
NetGirl newsletter, 120
Net-happenings, 432
Net.help, 22
Netiquette, 30, 533
    mailing list, 113-115
    newsgroup article, 164-165
NetNoir, 450
Netscape FAQ, Unofficial, 433
Netscape Navigator, 343-353, 533
    vs. AOL's browser, 348-353
    Destinations area, 349

    downloading and installing, 344-345
    frames, 352
    plug-ins with, 350-351
    preferences, 350
    recently visited sites, 349-350
    using on AOL, 346
    using parental controls with, 347
Network, 533
Network connection, 501-502
    signing off from, 38
    and using AOL, 507-509
Networth's Insider: Mutual Funds, 467
New Mail window, 39
New York Times, 488
New Zealand, 425
Newbie, 533
News sites, 457-462, 485-490
News (Usenet), 136
News of the Weird Archives, 419
News.answers, 523
Newsgroup addresses, 139
Newsgroup articles, 138
    listing, 156
    netiquette, 164-165
    parts of, 156-159
    read vs. unread, 155
    reading and posting offline, 162-164
    responding to, 159-162
    saving and printing, 169
    scanning, 154-156
Newsgroup postings, 138
Newsgroup Scoop, 147
Newsgroups, 58, 135-169, 533-534
    accessing, 218
    browsing, 147, 149-150
    browsing for, 146
    creating, 141
    finding, 144-147
    getting files from, 165-167
    keeping a list of, 150-152
    vs. mailing lists, 137-138
    organization of, 138-141
    and Parental Controls, 142-144
    regional, 143-144
    retrieving files via, 267
    searching, 146, 324-326
    sending files in, 167
    tracking, 147-149

using browser to go to, 153-154
using keywords to find, 149
Newsletters, 15, 106, 119-122
Newspapers, 7
NHLPA, 477
Nine Planets, The, 444
Noise (off-topic messages), 115
Non-anonymous FTP, 268-269
Numbers to call for help or service, 514
NYPL's CATNYP system, 372

O

Offline, 534
Olympic Movement, The, 477
Oncolink, 415-416
Onion (The): Number One in the News, 488-489
Online, 534
Online Reference Book for Medieval Studies, 444
Osborne/McGraw-Hill site, 461
Out of Balance, 257-258
Ovarian Cancer Links, 258-259
Ownership of mailing lists, 132-133

P

Packet switching, 25
Packets (of information), 24, 28, 534
Page, Web. *See* Web page
Pane (window), 15
Parent directory, 266
Parental Controls, 49, 534-535
for incoming mail, 86-88
on mailing lists, 121
and newsgroups, 142-144
using with Netscape, 347
Parsing e-mail messages, 97
Password, 504-505, 535
Path (to a file), 266
Payment, means of, 504
Peeps Republic, 455
People, finding, 321-331
Periodic Table of the Elements, 471-472
Personal Filing Cabinet, 93-94, 535
Personal Finance channel, 10
Personal finance-related sites, 462-468

Personal Publisher 2 (PP2), 225-259, 535
editing your page, 246-248
and My Place, 228-234
one-minute Web page, 239-241, 243-244
vs. PP1, 235
templates, 235-236
using, 234-245
Personalized Shakespearean Insults Page, 404
Personalizing e-mail messages, 97-98
Peru, 425-426
Pittsburgh Net, 399
Pixel Foundry, The, 392
Plug-ins, 210-215, 535
with Netscape Navigator, 350-351
Real Audio, 213-214
setting up, 211-213
Shockwave, 215
VDO, 214, 215
Poet's Corner, 420
POKERwwwORLD, 411
Portugal Home Page, 426
Postmaster, 133
PPP, 535-536
Preferences (AOL), 49-50
Preferences (AOL Mail), 71
Preferences (Internet Explorer), 191-196
Preferences (Windows), 50
Preferred Mail, 88
PrimeHost, 250-251
Print Magazine Online, 393
Printing e-mail messages, 95-96
Printing Web pages, 221
Professional Rodeo Cowboys Association, 477-478
Protocols (in URLs), 28, 139, 175, 536
Publishing information on the Web, 172
Publishing a Web page. *See* Personal Publisher 2; Web
site of your own
Puzzle and Riddle Pages, 406

Q

Queue (message), 70
Quick Start, 55
Quotations, 9
Quoting in e-mail messages, 90, 536

R

Radio button, 43, 536
Re:, 536
Read My Newsgroups, adding to, 150-152
Read vs. unread newsgroup articles, 155
Reading e-mail, 81-88
Reading and posting newsgroup articles offline, 162-164
Real Audio, 213-214, 393-394
Real time, 162
Real-time communication, 517
Rec.antiques.marketplace (newsgroup), 450-451
Rec.arts.tv.soaps.misc (newsgroup), 404
Redbook's Best Beauty Buys, 485
Reference, sites for, 468-473
Reflectors, 110
Regional newsgroups, 143-144
Remote computer, 372
Replies to newsgroup articles, 156
Replying to e-mail messages, 89-90
Resources (Internet), twenty essential, 5
Responding to e-mail messages, 100
Responding to a newsgroup article, 159-162
Resrocket, 455-456
Restoring a window, 41
Retirement Calculator, 464
Retirement Zone, 467
Retrieving a file from a message, 83
Riddler, 387
Road Trips, 15-16
Rock and Roll Hall of Fame and Museum, 456
Roget's Thesaurus, 472
Rollingstone.com, 456-457
Rooms in Virtual Places
     attending an event, 360-361
     chatting in, 358-360
     entering, 357
     exiting, 361
     guiding a tour, 360
Root directories, 266
Rules of the Road (AOL), 361, 532

S

Safe transactions, 22
Safer Sex Page, 420

Salon magazine, 8, 387
Saving e-mail messages, 92-95
Saving and printing newsgroup articles, 169
Saving Web pages, 219-221
Schools Registry, International WWW, 3
Scientific American, 461
Scout Report (newsletter), 123
Screen names, 37, 64, 504, 511-512
Screen space, increasing, 59
Scripting language, 185
Scroll bar, 40
Scrolling, 40
Scrolling Mystery Theater, 405
ScubaWorld Online, 451
Search engines
     choosing, 208
     linking to multiple, 336
     people finders in, 331
Search FTP service (AOL), 269-270, 274-282
Search services, Web, 301
Search terms, Web, 303-304
Search tools, best Web, 304-321
Searching. *See also* Finding
     for AOL forums, 53-55
     with Archie on the Web, 270-274
     15-second Web search, 207-208
     good, 299-300
     for mailing lists, 322-324
     megasites, 332-334, 336-337
     for newsgroups, 144-147
     in newsgroups, 146, 324-326
     saved e-mail messages, 94
     for sounds, 316
Seattle P-I Plus, 399
Security
     AOL, 19-20, 22
     in Netscape Navigator, 352
Sending an e-mail message, 70
Server software, 19
Servers, 19, 174, 537
Settings, modifying, 511
Seussville, 439
Shakespeare, Complete Works of, 9
Shareware, 294-295, 525
Shareware.com, 394
Sharing your Web page, 256
Shockwave, 215
Shopping, 6, 183

Shortcut (link), 190. *See also* Links (Web page)
Shouting, in e-mail messages, 96
Sierra On-line, 420-421
Signatures (newsgroup article), 156, 159-161
Signing off, 37-38
Signing on, 34, 505-507
    as a guest, 509-510
    while travelling, 510
Sites. *See* Web page; Web site of your own; Web sites
SLIP, 537
Slow Web page, managing, 204-205
Smileys, 99, 537
Smithsonian Institute, The, 444
SnowLink, 478
Social network, 27-32
Social Security Online, 467
Software
    downloading, 261-295
    getting Net, 58-59
    Net, 26-27
    sites, 389-394
    table of AOL, 286
Software Search, 291-293
Software sites, 389-394
Softworld's Sewing Resource Guide, 451
Sound, adding to your Web page, 252
Sound files, hearing, 287
Sound plug-in (Real Audio), 213-214, 393-394
Sounds, searching for, 316
Spam, 80, 88, 537
Special Education Resources on the Internet, 416
Speed (AOL), 19
Spinner (AOL), 189, 537
Sports-related sites, 473-479
Squat, The, 405
SSL, 537
Standard Usenet newsgroup hierarchies, 139-141
Status bar, 537
Stock quotes, 463
Streaming sound, 213
Style and fashion sites, 480-485
Subhierarchies, Usenet newsgroup, 139-140
Subject line (e-mail), 67
Subjects (AOL News), 140
Subscribing to a mailing list, 110-113
Sundance Film Festival, 444-445
Surf, 537
Surflink.com, 421

Swank-O-Rama Cocktail Revolution Page, 421-422
Switchboard, 328-330, 387
Swoon, 462
System, recommended, 503

T

Tables (Web page), 181-182
TAXI, 457
Taxing Times, 467-468
TCP/IP, 26, 538
TCP/IP network connection, 502, 507-509
Technical support, numbers to call, 514
Teen Movie Critic, 439-440
Telnet, 372-377, 538
    basics of, 375
    CommNet, 373-374
    Hytelnet, 374-375
    links, 219
    Netscape Navigator support for, 352-353
    resources, 375
Templates (PP2), 235-236
Tennis Server Home Page, The, 478
Terms, indispensable, 515-540
Text box, 43, 538
Text document, 79
Text files, 165, 263
Text (Web page), 178-179
Theodore Tugboat, 440
Thermometer, 79
Threads, 129, 140, 157, 161-162, 538
Time magazine online, 462
Title bar (browser), 187-188
Title bar (window), 40
Tonga Page, The, 426-427
Tool bar (AOL), 50-52
Top Tips, 120
Topics (AOL News), 140
TotalNY, 400
Tour Bus (newsletter), 123
Tracking e-mail messages, 98
Tracking newsgroups, 147-149
Transactions, safe, 22
Travel & Entertainment Network, 493
Travel Health Online, 493
Travelling, and signing on, 510
Travelocity, 493-494

Travel-related sites, 490-496
TravelWeb, 494
Trip.com: Flight Tracking, 495
Tripod: Tools for life, 388
TUCOWS (Winsock Software), 432-433
Turkey, 424-425
Twenty essential Internet resources, 5
21st Century Adventures E-zine, 495
25 essential keywords for using the Net, 47-48

U

Ukraine FAQ Plus, 427
UltraSeek, 311-313
Unmoderated mailing lists, 106-107
Unofficial Netscape FAQ, 433
Unread vs. read newsgroup articles, 155
Unsending a message, 70, 72
Unsolicited e-mail, 80, 88, 537
Unzipping files, 288-289
Unix Listserv, 110
Upgrading AOL, 512-514
Upload, 538
Uploading files, 230
    with FTP, 267
    to My Place, 231-232
URLs, 139, 175-176, 538
    jumping to, 203-204
    sharing, 245
U.S. Census Bureau, 472
U.S. News and World Report Online, 489
U.S. Newspapers on the Net, 489
U.S. Soccer, 478-479
USA CityLink, 495
Usenet, 136, 539
Usenet news, 136
Usenet newsgroup hierarchies, 139-144
User name, 63, 64

V

Vacation planning, 4
Vacation.com, 496
VDO, 214-215
VeloNews Interactive, 479
Veronica, 539

Vertical scrolling, 40
Victoria and Albert Museum, 445
Video files, watching, 287-288
Video Game Yellow Pages, 411-412
Video plug-in (VDO), 214-215
Virtual Hospital, 7
Virtual Places, 15, 17, 353-361, 539
    attending an event, 360-361
    chatting in, 358-360
    entering rooms in, 357
    exiting, 361
    guiding a tour, 360
Virtual Tour of Israel, 427
Virus, 539
Virus alert, 284
Visitor counter, adding to your Web page, 249-250

W

WAIS, 540
Wall Street Journal Interactive Edition, 489-490
Wallpapers, 179
Warner Brothers Online, 388
WashingtonPost.com, 490
WAV files, 287
Weather Channel Web site, 4
Web
    best search tools for, 304-321
    clip art and art images on, 242
    defined, 540
    exploring, 171-223
    finding information on, 300-303
    how it works, 174
    as part of Net, 6
    retrieving files via, 267
    search terms, 303-304
    searching with Archie, 270-274
    where it is on AOL, 173
Web Developer's Virtual Library, 433
Web Diner, 433-434
Web directories, 303, 320-321
Web indexes, 303
Web page, 174. *See also* Web sites
    content, 176-177
    elements of, 177-186
    forms on, 180-181
    frames, 182-184

going back and forward between, 205
going to, 56-57
graphics, 179
location, 175-176
managing slow, 204-205
moving around in, 204
notable AOL home pages, 257-259
tables, 181-182
text, 178-179
turning off graphics, 180
Web search, 15-second, 207-208
Web search engines, people finders in, 331
Web search services, 301
Web session (browser), 188, 204-207
Web site (AOL's), 56, 58, 188, 196-197
Web site of your own, 57
　adding animation, 252-253
　adding background sound, 252
　adding a guestbook, 255
　adding HTML, 248
　adding multimedia files, 251-252
　adding a visitor counter, 249-250
　creating in one minute, 239-244
　editing, 246-248
　editing with an HTML Editor, 253-255
　help with design, 256-257
　listing, 255
　publishing, 225-259
　refining, 249-255
　sharing, 256
　printing, 221
　saving, 219-221
　three ways to make, 227-228
Web sites
　essential, 5
　featured, 379-496
　indispensable, 3-11
　integrated into AOL channels, 203
　keeping up with new, 199
　visiting, 198-199
WebCrawler, 317-318
Welcome to Mexico!, 427
Welcome screen, 37
Whispering, in e-mail messages, 97

Window
　cycling, 59
　elements of, 42-44
　maximizing, 40
　minimizing, 41
　restoring, 41
　using, 39-44
Window clutter, avoiding, 277
Window controls, 39, 41
Window panes, 15
Windows applications, using AOL with, 60
Windows Magazine, 394
Windows 95 version of AOL, 191-194
Windows preferences, 50
Winsock, 340-343, 540
Womanist is to Feminist... (site), 259
Women's Health Resources, 416
Work Style, 485
World Travel Guide, 496
World Wide Quilting Page, 451
World Wide Web. *See* Web
Worldwide Internet Live Music Archive (WILMA),
　405
World's Online Newspapers, 487
WWW Bible Gateway, 472
WWW help, 22
WWW Preferences window, 195
WWWebster Dictionary, 473

Y

Yahoo, 318-320
Yahooligans, 440
Yahoo's Picks of the Week, 123
Yellow pages on the Net, 327
Your Business, 121-122

Z

Zipcode lookup, 473
Zipped files, 263, 288-289, 540
Zipper: Gain a Voice in Washington, 422